ALSO BY RICHARD NIXON:

SIX CRISES (1962)
RN: THE MEMOIRS OF RICHARD NIXON (1978)
THE REAL WAR (1980)
LEADERS (1982)
REAL PEACE: A STRATEGY FOR THE WEST (1983)
NO MORE VIETNAMS (1985)
1999: VICTORY WITHOUT WAR (1988)

IN THE ARENA

A MEMOIR OF VICTORY, DEFEAT, AND RENEWAL

RICHARD NIXON

SIMON AND SCHUSTER

**NEW YORK LONDON TORONTO
SYDNEY TOKYO SINGAPORE**

SIMON AND SCHUSTER
Simon & Schuster Building
Rockefeller Center
1230 Avenue of the Americas
New York, New York 10020

Designed by Eve Metz
Manufactured in the United States of America

1   3   5   7   9   10   8   6   4   2

Library of Congress Cataloging in Publication Data
Nixon, Richard M. (Richard Milhous), 1913–
In the arena: a memoir of victory, defeat, and renewal/Richard Nixon.
p.   cm.
1. Nixon, Richard M. (Richard Milhous), 1913–   .   2. Presidents—United
States—Biography.   3. United States—Politics and government—
1945–   I. Title.
E856.A3N59   1990
973.924'092—dc20   LETP472C   90-30013
CIP

ISBN 0-671-70096-0

ISBN 0-671-72318-9 LTD. ED.

FOR
MY FAMILY

CONTENTS

FOUR

FIVE

SIX

It is not the critic who counts; not the man who points out how the strong man stumbles, or where the doer of deeds could have done them better. The credit belongs to the man who is actually in the arena, whose face is marred by dust and sweat and blood; who strives valiantly; who errs, and comes short again and again; because there is not effort without error and shortcoming; but who does actually strive to do the deeds; who knows the great enthusiasms, the great devotions; who spends himself in a worthy cause, who at the best knows in the end the triumphs of high achievement and who at the worst, if he fails, at least fails while daring greatly, so that his place shall never be with those cold and timid souls who know neither victory nor defeat.

—THEODORE ROOSEVELT

ONE

1

PEAKS
AND VALLEYS

It was an eerie ride from the airport to the government guest house in Beijing. In my years as Vice President and President, I had made official visits to the Vatican, the Kremlin, the Imperial Palace in Tokyo, Versailles, and Westminster, but nothing could prepare me for this—the first visit of a President of the United States to the People's Republic of China. President Ayub Khan of Pakistan had urged me to go to China when I saw him in Karachi in 1964. He had just returned from Beijing. I asked him what impressed him most. He replied, "People, millions of people in the street clapping, cheering, waving Pakistani and Chinese flags." The curtains on the Chinese government limousine were drawn. But as I looked through the tiny openings, I could see that except for a lonely sentry stationed every few hundred yards, the streets were totally deserted.

The airport ceremony had met all of the requisites of protocol—very proper and very cool. Chou En-lai, wearing a top coat but no hat in the freezing cold, started to clap as Mrs. Nixon and I came down the ramp. We clapped in return, since we knew from our visit to Moscow in 1959 that it was the custom in Communist countries. I reached out to shake his hand. I did not realize until later how much that meant to him. The honor guard was spectacular. I also found out later that Chou had picked the men personally. They were all tall, ramrod straight, and immaculately groomed. The Red Army Band played "The Star Spangled Banner." In my visits to other countries I had learned that the tune,

11

an old English drinking song, is difficult to play, and in fact it was hardly recognizable in some places. But the Chinese performed it superbly.

I did not know what to expect from our host. Henry Kissinger, whose standards for excellence in leaders are extraordinarily high, ranked him with de Gaulle as the most impressive foreign statesman he had ever met. At the same time, he likened him to a cobra that sits quietly, ready to strike at the opportune moment. Eisenhower's assistant secretary of state, Walter Robinson, had told me that Chou, charming as he was, had killed people with his own hands and then departed, calmly smoking a cigarette. A high-ranking foreign diplomat once said, "There was not a grain of truth in him . . . It's all acting. He is the greatest actor I have ever seen. He'd laugh one moment and cry the next and make his audience laugh and cry with him. But it is all acting."

Skilled diplomat that he was, he put me at ease immediately. As we left the airport, he said, "Your handshake came over the vastest ocean in the world—twenty-five years of no communication." I was surprised when he told me that he felt he knew me through my book *Six Crises,* which he had had translated into Chinese. He made an observation that he was to repeat several times during the visit—that my career had been marked by great defeats as well as great victories but that I had demonstrated the ability to come back. For example, on one of our plane flights in China, he observed that adversity is a great teacher and that men who travel on a smooth road all their lives do not develop strength. From one who had endured the Long March, I considered that to be an unusually high compliment.

The visits to the Great Wall, the Forbidden City, and other points of interest gave us an idea of how much there was left to see in this nation of a billion people and four thousand years of history. To paraphrase Lord Curzon, China is a university from which the scholar never gets a degree.

The state dinners in the Great Hall of the People, with the Red Army Band playing "America the Beautiful" and other favorites, left an indelible impression. Chou was the perfect host, serving us with his chopsticks and then joining me in toasting each of the over fifty people at the head tables with our one-ounce glasses of *mao-tai,* a fiery 106-proof Chinese brandy Chou assured me would "cure anything."

Most memorable were my meetings with Chou and Mao. We

12

learned later that Mao had already suffered a mild stroke, although the Chinese people did not know it. He was still treated with enormous respect by his aides and attendants and was sharp in his repartee. I had gotten an idea of what to expect from André Malraux when I gave a dinner for him at the White House shortly before our trip. He warned me, "You will be meeting with a colossus, but a colossus facing death. Do you know what Mao will think when he sees you for the first time? He will think, He is so much younger than I. You will meet a man who has had a fantastic destiny and who believes that he is acting out the last act of his lifetime. You may think that he is talking to you, but he will in truth be addressing Death." He turned to me and said fervently, "Mr. President, you operate within a rational framework but Mao does not. There is something of the sorcerer in him. He is a man inhabited by a vision, possessed by it."

Like Stalin, Mao was a voracious reader. His office was cluttered with books—not for show, but for reading. Like Chou En-lai, he said that he had read *Six Crises* and found that it was "not a bad book." Also like Chou En-lai, he showed his political acumen when he said, "I voted for you during your last election." When I responded, "When the Chairman says he voted for me, he voted for the lesser of two evils," he came right back and said, "I like rightists. . . . I am comparatively happy when these people on the right come into power." I responded, "I think the most important thing to note is that in America, at least at this time, those on the right can do what those on the left can only talk about."

The only sour note during the visit was sounded by Mao's wife, our hostess for a theatrical extravaganza called *The Red Detachment of Women.* I noted the perspiration on her forehead and thought at first that she might be ill. It was probably just tension. She obviously did not approve of the visit. She said to me sharply, "Why did you not come to China before now?"

The most substantive and by far the most fascinating meetings were the long negotiating sessions with Chou himself. He followed my practice of speaking without notes and without calling on his aides to provide information. His understanding of not just Chinese-American issues but international affairs generally was all-encompassing. We discussed our profound differences at great length. We supported South Vietnam; they supported North Vietnam. We supported South Korea; they supported North Korea. We had a military security alliance with Japan; they opposed it.

13

We supported non-Communist governments in the Third World; they opposed them. They demanded that we discontinue our sales of arms to Taiwan; we refused to do so.

In view of such irreconcilable differences, what brought us together? One China expert in the United States predicted that the first question Mao would put to me would be: "What is the richest country in the world prepared to do to help the most populous country in the world?" He was wrong. Not once during many hours of discussion did economic issues come up. Our common economic interests are the primary factors that keep us together today. They played no part whatever in bringing us together in 1972.

The real reason was our common strategic interest in opposing Soviet domination in Asia. Like the Soviet Union, China was a Communist country. The United States was a capitalist nation. But we did not threaten them, while the Soviet Union did. It was a classic case of a nation's security interest overriding ideology.

Kissinger and Chou worked out a brilliant formula for the Shanghai Communiqué, which was issued at the conclusion of the visit. Instead of trying to paper over differences with mushy, meaningless, diplomatic gobbledygook, each side expressed its position on the issues where we disagreed. On the neuralgic issue of Taiwan, we stated the obvious fact that the Chinese on the mainland and on Taiwan agreed that there was one China. We expressed our position that the differences between the two should be settled peacefully. And on the great issue which made this historic rapprochement possible, the communiqué stated that neither nation "should seek hegemony in the Asia-Pacific region and each is opposed to efforts by any other country or group of countries to establish such hegemony." This document has stood the test of time. The principles it set forth are still adhered to by both sides.

With the grueling work of hammering out the details of the communiqué completed, Chou spoke movingly of what we had achieved. He quoted from a poem by Mao, "The beauty lies at the top of the mountain," and from another Chinese poem that read, "On perilous peaks dwells beauty in its infinite variety." I remarked that we were at the top of the mountain now.

He then referred to a third poem, "Ode to a Plum Blossom." Chou said the poem meant that "by the time the blossoms are full-blown, that is the time they are about to disappear." He went on, "You are the one who made the initiative. You may not be there to see its success, but of course we would welcome your return."

On February 27, in my toast at the concluding banquet, I said that our communiqué was "not nearly as important as what we will do in the years ahead to build a bridge across 16,000 miles and twenty-two years of hostility which have divided us in the past." I raised my glass and said, "We have been here a week. This was the week that changed the world."

Some might say this was an overstatement. But Chou En-lai and I savored the moment because we both had been in the deepest valleys. We knew that we were now on the mountaintop. What we did not know was that in just four years, when I would return to China, I would have resigned from office and he would be dying of cancer. As de Gaulle once observed, victory had "folded its wings almost as soon as they were spread for flight."

THE WHITE HOUSE, AUGUST 9, 1974

I did not sleep well my last night in the White House. This was not unusual; after a major speech or press conference I get so keyed up I always find it difficult to get to sleep. That evening, in a nationwide address, I had announced my decision to resign the Presidency. It was 2:00 a.m. before I dozed off.

I woke up with a start. I looked at my watch; it was only 4:00 a.m. I went across the West Hall to the kitchen to get a glass of milk. I was startled to see Johnny Johnson, one of the stewards, making coffee.

I said, "Johnny, what are you doing here so early?"

He replied, "It isn't early, Mr. President. It's almost six o'clock."

My watch had stopped. After three years the battery had run down.

I asked Johnny to make me some corned beef hash with a poached egg rather than my usual spartan breakfast of wheat germ, orange juice, and a glass of milk. I showered and shaved and walked down to the Lincoln Sitting Room. It is the smallest room in the White House and my favorite. It is next to the Lincoln Bedroom, which used to be Lincoln's office. It once was shared by his two young secretaries, John Nicolay and John Hay. I sat down in my favorite chair and put my feet up on the ottoman. Pat had given the chair to me as a birthday present when we were living in California in 1962. We had taken it with us first to our apartment in New York and then to the White House. It is the chair in which I am sitting as I dictate this recollection.

I tried to make some notes for what would be my last speech as President. I had spoken to tens of millions the night before on television. Now I had to think of something personal to say to a few dozen members of my White House staff—dedicated men and women who had served so loyally during the tumultuous days of the Vietnam War and the even more difficult days of Watergate.

I couldn't concentrate. I put my head back and closed my eyes. I thought of some of the great events that had occurred in this room.

It was here on June 2, 1971, that I received what Henry Kissinger described as the most important communication to an American President since the end of World War II. I had been sitting in this same chair catching up on some of my reading material after a state dinner that evening. It was almost eleven o'clock. Henry burst into the room. He was breathless. He must have run all the way over to the residence from his West Wing office. He handed me a message. It was Chou En-lai's invitation to visit China, which he had sent through President Yahya of Pakistan. As Chou put it later, it was a message from a head, through a head, to a head. Neither Henry nor I generally had a drink after dinner, but on this occasion we toasted this historic event with a very old brandy a friend had given Pat and me for Christmas.

As I tried again to concentrate on preparing my farewell remarks, the thought that raced through my mind over and over was—how was it possible to have been so high and now to be so low?

There was a discreet knock at the door. Al Haig came in, holding a single page in his hand. I thought I had completed all of the signing the day before, including the veto of an agricultural appropriations bill that had exceeded my budget. His face was drawn as he handed me the last document I was to sign as President. It was a one-sentence letter to Henry Kissinger, Secretary of State: "I hereby resign the Office of President of the United States."

The first time I saw President Eisenhower in the Oval Office in 1953, he was signing some letters and other documents. He looked up at me with a twinkle in his eye and said, "Dammit, Dick, I wish my name weren't so long!" Mercifully, my name is short. I signed the letter.

After Haig left, I had only an hour left to get my thoughts together for my farewell to the staff. The day before I had found it difficult to control my emotions in a meeting in the Cabinet Room with my closest friends and supporters in Congress. I concluded by blurting out what I knew was true: "I just hope that I haven't let you down." Today, I had to find a way to lift up the loyal members of my staff. I knew I should not talk about Pat, Tricia, Julie, Ed Cox, and David Eisenhower, who would all be standing by my side on the platform. It would be too painful for them and for me. They had been magnificent in standing up against the merciless pounding in the media, which began after the 1972 election and, except for a brief period around my inauguration and the Vietnam peace agreement in January 1973, had gone on without any letup for over twenty months. Day after day it was the lead story in the newspapers. Night after night it led every television news show. The family had unanimously opposed my decision to resign. Tricia, whose quiet strength reminded me of my mother, fiercely insisted to the very last that I not even consider resigning. Two days before, I had worked on my resignation speech until 2:00 a.m. in the Lincoln Sitting Room. When I went to my bedroom to catch a couple hours' sleep, I found a note from Julie on my pillow:

Dear Daddy,
    I love you. Whatever you do I will support. I am very proud of you.
    Please wait a week or even ten days before you make this decision. Go through the fire just a little bit longer. You are so strong! I love you.

                                                        Julie

Millions support you.

If anything could have changed my mind, Julie's note would have done it. But I was too worn out to reconsider. It was not because I had given up the fight but because I knew that the decision I had made was best for the country. Two years of Watergate was enough. The nation could not stand the trauma of a President on trial before the Senate for months. The international situation required a full-time President.

Once my family knew that the decision was final, they backed it. Pat took on the superhuman task of supervising the packing of all the belongings we had acquired during the past five and a half years in the White House. She had not slept for forty-eight hours.

I don't know how she did it. The way she stood on the platform by my side, erect and proud though her heart was breaking, demonstrated what I have always said—that she is the strongest member of my family, personal or official.

Finally, I decided to talk to the staff about my roots. I remembered that when a superb group of black musicians had performed in the White House after one of our state dinners, the leader expressed his appreciation for the invitation and concluded his remarks by saying, "You know, Mr. President, it's a long way from Watts to the White House." I responded by thanking him and saying, "It's a long way from Whittier to the White House."

I spoke of my father and my mother. I read the moving tribute Theodore Roosevelt had written when his first wife died: "She was beautiful in face and form and lovelier still in spirit. When she had just become a mother, when her life seemed to be just begun and the years seemed so bright before her, then by a strange and terrible fate death came to her. And when my heart's dearest died, the light went from my life forever." TR had written those words when he was in his twenties. He thought the light had gone out of his life forever. But he went on to become President of the United States.

I went on, "We think sometimes when things don't go the right way, when we suffer a defeat, that all has ended. Not true. It is only a beginning, always. Greatness comes not when things always go good for you, but the greatness comes when you are really tested, when you take some knocks, some disappointments, when sadness comes. Because only if you have been in the deepest valley can you ever know how magnificent it is to be on the highest mountain.

"Always give your best. Never get discouraged, never be petty. Always remember, others may hate you, but those that hate you don't win unless you hate them, and then you destroy yourself."

The critics panned my remarks, not surprisingly, as being too emotional. They overlooked the fact that it was an emotional moment.

Finally, it was all over. We said goodbye to the Fords and were on our way back home to California, where we thought, mistakenly, we would at long last find peace and quiet.

As our plane circled the El Toro Marine Air Base on the afternoon of August 9, I could see hundreds of cars lined up trying to get into the already overflowing parking area. I had not thought I could find the energy to make another speech that day, but I managed to thank them for welcoming us home and I vowed to continue to fight at home and abroad for the great causes of peace, freedom, and opportunity that had been my motivating principles from the time I first ran for Congress in 1946.

As we walked toward the helicopter, I heard someone from the crowd shout out, "Whittier is still for you, Dick." My thoughts went back to a day I had spent in a Portland hotel room in September 1952. It was the middle of the Fund crisis, and it had seemed that everybody in the country, including most Republicans, were demanding that I get off the ticket. Tom Bewley and Johnny Reilly, two long-time friends, flew up to Portland to try to give me a lift. As they came into the room, Johnny said, "All the folks back in Whittier are behind you 100 percent." Just two days later, I was able to reverse public opinion in the country with one speech on television. This time, I knew it might never be possible to reverse it.

Thanks to Gavin Herbert and a group of volunteers from USC, La Casa Pacifica's grounds were beautiful almost beyond description. I said to Gavin, "It is good to be back in a house of peace."

But it was only a lull before a storm. The following day, the blows began to fall again. The special prosecutor, Leon Jaworski, had been delighted when Al Haig informed him of my decision to resign. He thought it would be in the best interests of the country. Haig reported to me that based on his conversation, he did not believe we would continue to suffer harassment by the special prosecutor. He had not reckoned with the young activists on Jaworski's staff. Far from being satisfied by the resignation, their appetites for finishing the injured victim were whetted. When Ed Cox urged me not to resign, he had warned me that this might happen. He had known several of Jaworski's staff at the Harvard Law School and had served with some in the U.S. Attorney's Office in New York. He said, "I know these people. They are smart and ruthless. They hate you. They will harass you and hound you in civil and criminal actions across the country for the rest of your life." He was right. They were following the dictum of the

19

nineteenth-century Russian revolutionary Sergey Nechayev: "It is not enough to kill an adversary. He must first be dishonored."

One after another, the blows rained down.

I resigned from the Supreme Court, California, and New York bars. The Supreme Court and California accepted my resignation. The New York Bar Association refused to do so and instituted disbarment proceedings.

Scores of lawsuits were filed against me by individuals who were seeking damages for assorted government actions. Few involved Presidential decisions. Most were dismissed, but all had to be defended.

The cost for attorneys' fees was staggering. In the fifteen years since I resigned the Presidency, I have spent over $1.8 million in attorneys' fees to defend myself against such suits and to protect my rights that were threatened by government action.

The Supreme Court ruled against me on my suit to gain possession of my papers and tapes, including those that were private.

A scandal magazine printed letters that I was supposed to have written to a countess in Spain whom I had never met. They were obvious forgeries, but the story was never retracted.

The pounding in the newspapers and on television continued unrelentingly. I was the favorite butt of jokes on the talk shows. Hundreds of columns attacked me. A number of anti-Nixon books were published. Those by critics I understood. Those by friends I found a bit hard to take.

For months we were followed and harassed by the media wherever we went. Manolo Sanchez, who proudly called himself my valet, was a hot-tempered Spaniard who was outraged by their behavior. He called them "the witches and the vultures." He thought the women were worse than the men.

One of the worst blows was the harassment of my friends. Bebe Rebozo was accused of being associated with the Mafia, gamblers, and drug barons. The special prosecutor's staff pursued him for over a year. He testified eighty-five times before the prosecutor's staff and the Ervin Committee. All of the charges were false. He had done nothing wrong, except to be my friend. In the end, he was cleared. His attorneys' fees were enormous.

Maurice Stans, a scrupulously honest man, paid fines for five technical non-intentional misdemeanor violations of the campaign laws—the moral equivalent of parking tickets. Similar violations by Democratic fundraisers were ignored.

The Rose Bowl game in 1975 was interrupted on television by an announcement of the conviction of John Mitchell and my other top aides. I could no longer even take refuge in my favorite avocation, watching sports on television.

By far the hardest blow was the pardon. My primary reason for resigning was to avoid having a President of the United States in the dock for alleged illegal activities. But the assaults had not stopped. As President, even after I had been crippled by Watergate, I could still set the agenda to an extent. My visits to the Soviet Union and the Mideast that summer had resulted in some significant diplomatic achievements. But now without the powers of the office, I was utterly defenseless. My public standing had been driven so low that I do not think there was any allegation about me, no matter how horrendous or base, that would not have been believed if it was aired or published. In fact many distortions and blatant lies about me, my family, and my friends were aired and published. It was not enough for my critics to say that I had made terrible mistakes. They seemed driven to prove that I represented the epitome of evil itself.

I will never forget the moment that Jack Miller, my attorney from Washington, came into my office in San Clemente on September 4 to inform me of President Ford's decision to stop the hemorrhaging by issuing a Presidential pardon. Now I had to decide whether or not to accept it.

We discussed it at great length. I told Miller I was worried the pardon would hurt Ford politically. He said that in the short run, it would. But he added that if the country continued to be obsessed by Watergate, President Ford and others in government would suffer even more from being unable to devote their attention to urgent problems at home and abroad.

Miller also knew my desperate financial situation. He pointed out that the attorneys' fees and the other costs of defending actions against me would bankrupt me. In view of what happened soon thereafter, he was remarkably perceptive when he added that he thought that I had taken as much physically, mentally, and emotionally as I could and that I should accept the pardon for my own well-being and my family's as well. His strongest argument was that because of the unprecedented publicity over the past year and a half, there was no way I could get a fair trial in Washington.

Next to the resignation, accepting the pardon was the most painful decision of my political career. The statement I issued at the time accurately describes my feelings then and now:

"I was wrong in not acting more decisively and more forthrightly in dealing with Watergate, particularly when it reached the stage of judicial proceedings and grew from a political scandal into a national tragedy.

"No words can describe the depths of my regret and pain at the anguish my mistakes over Watergate have caused the nation and the Presidency—a nation I so deeply love and an institution I so greatly respect."

The pardon was granted on September 8. The predictable occurred. Ford went down in the polls, and I was subjected to a whole new round of attacks in the media.

I have always believed that there is a direct relationship between mental and physical health. Events in the aftermath of the pardon proved it, as far as I am concerned. Twenty years had passed since I had last suffered from phlebitis, blood clots which usually occur in the legs. Just before my trip to the Mideast in June, my left leg began to swell. I have a rather high pain threshold and consequently did not report it to the doctor for several days. When I did, he did not advise me, as was later reported in the press, to cancel the trip to the Mideast. Hot and cold compresses reduced the swelling, but it increased alarmingly again when I had to stand too long at the various ceremonies. It became even more aggravated when I went to the Soviet Union in July and visited a war memorial in Minsk. I had to walk for almost a mile and a half over cobblestone paths, and the pain was excruciating.

When I returned to Washington, the pain subsided, and I was so busy in those final weeks before the resignation that I forgot about it completely. A few days after the pardon the swelling recurred, and I consulted my family doctor, Dr. John Lungren. He urged me to go to the hospital for treatment with heparin and coumadin, saying that if a clot should break loose and go to the lungs, it would be fatal. That got my attention. I went to the hospital.

I was there for almost two weeks, sleeping very little because the nurse had to come in every hour to refill the intravenous heparin medication. It was a miserable experience. When I returned home, I told Pat that I would never go to a hospital again. Within three weeks, I was back. Lungren had warned me that sharp pains in the abdomen would be a danger signal. After X-rays, the doctors decided that an operation should be performed immediately. I remember the pinprick of the needle administered by the anesthetist

22

and being wheeled down to the operating room, but for six days thereafter I was in and out of consciousness.

My first recollection was of a nurse slapping my face and calling me. "Richard, wake up," she said. "Richard, wake up." I knew it was not Pat or Lungren. In fact, only my mother called me Richard. When I woke up again, Lungren was taking my pulse. I noticed I was hooked up to intravenous feeding and other contraptions. I told him that I was anxious to go home. He said, "Listen, Dick, we almost lost you last night. You are not going to go home for quite a while."

He told me I had gone into shock after the operation. My blood pressure had gone down to 60 over zero before inching up to 70 over 55. Only after four transfusions over a period of three hours were the doctors able to push it back to normal. I learned later that Pat, Tricia, and Julie had been standing by me in the room for most of the night. When I woke up again, I asked Pat to come in. I now knew that I was in pretty desperate shape. Throughout the time we have known each other, Pat and I have seldom revealed our physical disabilities to each other. This time, I couldn't help it. I said that I didn't think I was going to make it.

She gripped my hand and said almost fiercely, "Don't talk that way. You have got to make it. You must not give up." As she spoke, my thoughts went back again to the Fund crisis in 1952. Just before we went on stage for the broadcast, when I was trying to get all of my thoughts together for the most important speech of my life, I told her, "I just don't think I can go through with this one." She grasped me firmly by the hand and said, "Of course you can." The words were the same but now there was a difference. Then I had something larger than myself to fight for. Now it seemed that I had nothing left to fight for except my own life.

Except for my family and Bebe, and Bob Abplanalp, who flew in from their homes in Miami and New York, no visitors were allowed. The first outsider was Jerry Ford, who was in California campaigning for congressional candidates. I must have looked like hell, because he blurted out, "Oh, Mr. President!", despite the fact that since my resignation we had been on a first-name basis. He did his best to give me a lift, but I knew that the pardon had hurt him and that the campaign was not going well.

Shortly afterwards, a nurse came in and wheeled me into another room with a window. She pointed to a small plane with a sign trailing behind that read: "God loves you and so do we." I learned later that Ruth Graham and some of her friends had arranged it. I am convinced now that had it not been for the support of my family and the thoughts and prayers of countless numbers of people I have never met and that I would never have a chance to thank, I would not have made it.

There was still bad news to come. A few days later someone brought the results of the 1974 off-year elections to my hospital room. The Republican Party was in even worse shape than I was. Some commentators pointed out that the energy crisis and the sharp recession that followed were partly responsible. But most pundits and politicians blamed Watergate. I knew that from that time on, the Democrats who won would be called Watergate Democrats and the Republicans who lost would be called Watergate Republicans. After the millions of miles I had logged and the thousands of speeches I had made for Republican candidates over the years, I knew that this was my final legacy to the party. It would be a heavy burden for the rest of my life.

When I left the hospital and returned home to La Casa Pacifica, I thought that now, at least, I might get a little relief from the merciless attacks of the critics. It was not to be. Judge Sirica wanted me in his courtroom to testify against John Mitchell and the other defendants. He ordered three doctors to come to San Clemente to examine me to see if the reports on the seriousness of my illness were true. In retrospect, he had some cause to do so. Doctors and so-called medical experts from all over the country who had never met or examined me had deluged the press and the airwaves with opinions on my condition. Some said the operation was not necessary. Others said that the operation was conducted negligently. Most said that it was really not all that serious. Lungren was infuriated that his fellow doctors would lend themselves to such political diagnoses. To his credit, one doctor who did not join his politicized colleagues in these attacks was Dr. Lawrence Altman, the medical writer for *The New York Times,* whose reports on my condition were accurate and fair. And yet even now, so-called biographers and journalists blithely inform their readers that I cynically arranged my near-fatal illness in order to quell public opposition to the pardon.

So Sirica's three doctors came to San Clemente. Each took turns poking and pinching and pulling and doing the other things that doctors do during an examination. One was obviously a little embarrassed by the whole exercise, but the other two seemed to enjoy their work. They were at least professional enough to report to Sirica that I could under no circumstances travel to Washington and testify.

I did not get the lift that I should have when I received the news that I would not have to go to Washington. For the first time in my life, I was a physical wreck; I was emotionally drained; I was mentally burned out. This time, as compared with the other crises I had endured, I could see no reason to live, no cause to fight for. Unless a person has a reason to live for other than himself, he will die—first mentally, then emotionally, then physically.

At some of the low points in the past, I have been sustained by recalling a note Clare Boothe Luce handed to me right after Watergate first broke, when she was sitting next to me at a meeting of the Foreign Intelligence Advisory Board. It was St. Barton's Ode: "I am hurt but I am not slain! I will lie me down and bleed awhile —then I'll rise and fight again." This time, it did not work. I did not have anything to fight for.

2

WILDERNESS

In his *Study of History,* Arnold Toynbee describes what he calls the phenomenon of withdrawal and return as a "disengagement and temporary withdrawal of the creative personality from his social milieu and his subsequent return to the same milieu transfigured in a newer capacity with new powers." His list of historical figures who illustrate this phenomenon is fascinating in its diversity. It includes among others Thucydides, Mohammed, Confucius, Peter the Great, Garibaldi, and Lenin. If he were writing today, he no doubt would have included Winston Churchill and Charles de Gaulle. In lesser ways, what I would describe as the wilderness syndrome is experienced by anyone who suffers a major defeat in life.

In 1932, most of his contemporaries dismissed Churchill, who was 57 years old, as a picturesque failure after he was forced to resign his post as chancellor of the exchequer in the Conservative government of Stanley Baldwin. Some, like Lord Beaverbrook, who later became one of Churchill's staunchest allies, dismissed him as a common scold because his Cassandra-like warnings about the rise of Hitler were so at odds with the conventional wisdom that downplayed the danger of war and with the intense desire of most of his countrymen to have peace whatever the price. While Churchill had been in the wilderness before, after the military disaster at the Dardanelles during World War I, there now seemed to be no chance that he might return to power. Like Lincoln, he suffered what he called Black Dog—weeks of depression in which his mental capacities were totally immobilized. He wrote, "Here I am discarded, cast away, marooned, rejected, and disliked." But he had a mission. He wrote books, he delivered speeches, and he

26

made sense. After eight years of wandering in the wilderness—at the age of sixty-five, when most men were contemplating retirement—he was called back into office to lead Britain in its darkest hour. His brilliant leadership in World War II prompted Isaiah Berlin to acclaim him "a mythical hero who belongs to legend as much as to reality, the largest human being of our time."

In 1946, Charles de Gaulle, after playing an indispensable role in restoring France to its rightful place in the family of free nations, became totally disillusioned by the French government system which provided for a strong Parliament and a weak President. He became convinced that he should resign from government and "withdraw from events before they withdrew from me." He called a meeting of his Cabinet, announced his decision to resign his office as President, and strode abruptly out of the room and into retirement. He had a sense of destiny and did not want to be the President of France simply for the sake of being President. He wanted to be President only when he thought he was the only man who could give France the leadership the nation needed. He was convinced that the time would come when he would be called back to lead, but on his own terms. In spite of his efforts to hasten that time, the call did not come. For thirteen years, he was in the wilderness, living on his farm in Colombey. At times he was profoundly discouraged by what he saw as the hopeless indecision and drift of the weak parliamentary government. But he never abandoned the conviction that only he was the one who could provide the strong leadership France needed to return to greatness.

In 1958, the government faced anarchy because of its inability to deal with the crisis in Algeria. De Gaulle again was the indispensable man. He returned to power on his own terms and gave France his greatest legacy—a new constitution providing for a strong Presidency which produced the stability France was to continue to enjoy even after de Gaulle again resigned in 1969.

I was aware of these examples of the withdrawal-return syndrome after I returned to San Clemente in 1974. I also had my own experience to learn from. In 1960, I had suffered a shattering defeat in the Presidential campaign. It was no comfort that it was the closest election in history and that a shift of a total of 11,085 votes in Illinois, Missouri, Delaware, and Hawaii out of 69 million cast nationwide would have changed the results. Of the thousands of letters I received after that defeat, one particularly made an indelible impression on me. Bob Reynolds, the All-American football player who headed the campaign's sports committee, passed on some advice he had received from one of his professors after Stanford's crushing loss to Alabama in the Rose Bowl. "Defeats are poison to some men," he wrote. "Great men have become mediocre because of inability to accept a defeat. Many men have become great because they were able to rise above defeat. If you should achieve any kind of success and develop superior qualities as a man, the chances are it will be because of the manner in which you meet the defeats that will come to you as they come to all men."

Two years later, I suffered another defeat that was even more shattering because the election was for a lesser office, governor of California. After the results came in, I had told the press off. And not surprisingly, the press proceeded to tell me off. ABC even dug up Alger Hiss to proclaim my political obituary. Not even my closest friends thought I had a political future. I agreed. I thought I was finished as a practicing politician. I decided to make a complete break with the past, both physically and politically. I moved my base from California to New York, which was the base of my major opponent, Nelson Rockefeller. In effect, I was withdrawing from politics, in my view permanently.

The move provided some significant benefits. My new law practice provided financial security. While Washington is the political capital of the United States, New York is the financial capital. I therefore had an opportunity to expand significantly my understanding of the world of finance and business. Practicing law in New York meant competing in the fastest legal track in the world. On two occasions I was to argue a major case in the Supreme Court of the United States.

Great as these benefits were, the most important advantage was that with my political commitments behind me, I had more time to reflect, to read, to recharge my mental and emotional batteries. It provided an opportunity to travel extensively abroad, particularly to Europe and to Asia, including several trips to Vietnam, which enabled me to keep up to date on the increasingly dangerous situation developing there. I wrote magazine and newspaper articles and made major speeches before high-powered non-partisan audiences on foreign policy.

As the 1964 election approached, some of my friends privately urged me to become a candidate again. But I believed that this was not going to be a Republican year, and I knew it was not my year. However, I spent two months campaigning all over the country for the ticket and particularly for candidates for the House, the Senate, and state governorships who were desperately concerned that they would become casualties in the Johnson landslide. Most of them lost. But I gained. An iron rule exists in politics: A winning candidate believes that he won it on his own; a losing candidate will always feel a debt of gratitude for anyone who tries to help him when he is almost certain to lose.

In 1966, I was the major campaigner for the Republican ticket and by a stroke of good luck predicted almost exactly the spectacular Republican gains of forty-seven congressmen, three senators, and eight governors. For the first time the heavyweights in the national media began to speculate seriously that I might have a chance to win the nomination in 1968. But there was a down side. The winners for whom I had campaigned were now my strongest competitors in the event I decided to seek the nomination.

It was then that I made what proved to be the best political decision of my career. One of my interrogators on a national talk show pressed me about when I would start campaigning for 1968. I answered that I was going to take a moratorium from politics for six months and would make no decision about the future until the end of that period. My friends were dismayed. My opponents were delighted. Most of the political experts were just mystified. They did not understand why I would give other candidates a chance to get a head start. My decision was a calculated one. While they were spending their time campaigning to be President, I would be devoting my time to learning more how I could best serve as President if I were elected.

Over the next six months I traveled to most of the major countries of Europe and Asia. I visited Vietnam again. I went to the Mideast. I visited the Soviet Union. I went to a number of countries in Latin America and in Africa. At the end of the six months, I felt better prepared to run for President in 1968 than I had been in 1960, after having served eight years as Vice President.

The moratorium was a risk, but it paid off. It should be noted that I would not have taken this risk had I not lost in 1960 and 1962 and therefore had to spend six years in the wilderness. This time also provided me an opportunity to reassess my views about the People's Republic of China. In 1967, I wrote an article for *Foreign Affairs,* "Asia After Vietnam," in which sophisticated observers were able to see that I was raising the curtain for the China initiative that became the centerpiece of my administration's foreign policy.

I learned a great deal in those years in the wilderness between 1963 and 1968. Three lessons stood out:

Defeat is never fatal unless you give up.

When you go through defeat, you are able to put your weaknesses in perspective and to develop an immune system to deal with them in the future.

You never know how strong you are when things go smoothly. You tap strength you didn't know you had when you have to cope with adversity.

My six years in the wilderness in the 1960s helped me survive the crisis I confronted in 1974. But residing in the deepest valley is far different from passing through the wilderness. Historical precedents existed for what I went through in the 1960s. Others lost major elections, yet came back to win later. But there was no precedent for what faced me in the 1970s. No one had ever been so high and fallen so low. No one before had ever resigned the Presidency.

Moreover, I had nothing to come back to. Even if I had wanted to, I could not run for President again because the Twenty-Second Amendment, for which I had voted as a freshman congressman, barred anyone from being elected President more than twice. Occasionally, some would suggest that I should run for senator or governor or accept a major ambassadorship. But no one who has held the greatest office in the free world can resign himself to squabbling over water projects or patronage appointments or to writing diplomatic cables to some State Department desk officer.

I was down but not out. My enemies wanted to make sure I did not rise again in view of my past record of comebacks. They tried to discredit everything I had done, to blame me for my administration's failures and to credit others for its successes. All the newspaper articles invariably referred to me as the "disgraced former President." I was hated by some, ignored by others. It became unfashionable for even my friends to say anything positive about the Nixon era. While in the wilderness, de Gaulle once sardonically remarked, "Insults would have been more tolerable than indifference." I didn't have that problem—I was never short on insults, and many of my friends maintained a discreet distance.

I could not, however, let myself become preoccupied with such matters. My immediate priority was to recover my health. I needed to do this to have the energy to engage again in creative activities. To my great surprise, golf became my lifesaver. I had played golf only two or three times a year during my five and a half years in the White House. There just wasn't time during the Vietnam War days to spend afternoons at the golf course. I was fortunate to have Colonel Jack Brennan as my administrative assistant in San Clemente. He had been my top military aide during my last two years in the White House. He was an excellent golfer, but even more important in the light of my physical condition, he was a patient and understanding partner.

Four months after the operation, I was strong enough to swing a club again. We soon began to play golf virtually every day. It was tortuous for me and must have been even more so for him. I had attained a 12 handicap in 1958, before giving up the game for my first run for the Presidency. Out of practice and physically weak, I shot 125 the first time we played after leaving the hospital. I almost quit on the spot. But the challenge intrigued me. When after several months I broke 100 and then 90, I kept the score cards. Combined with occasional swims in the cold water of the Pacific and a few laps in a heated pool, the golf routine did the trick. Within a year, I was shooting a few pars on the golf course and was back to par physically.

There was only one down side to my renewed interest in golf. We often played at the splendid Marine golf course at Camp Pendleton. In May 1975, as we were driving to the course, I looked out the car window and saw the camp housing thousands of Vietnamese who had been evacuated to the United States after the fall of Saigon. Every time we drove by their camp, I was saddened by the thought that had I survived in office, they might not have suffered this tragic fate.

I also had to recover my financial health. All of my assets were invested in real estate. My Presidential and congressional pensions took care of ordinary expenses. But I had to find a way to pay my attorneys' fees. In addition, the government allowance for office expenses was inadequate to cover the staff I needed to answer my huge volume of mail. I needed extra income. I ruled out one potentially lucrative source, honoraria for speeches. It was not the right time for me to begin to speak out. But even more important, I had had a policy of not accepting honoraria for speeches ever since I had been elected Vice President in 1952. What concerned me most was that I knew that most of the organizations that offered honoraria were really interested not in what I had to say but only in procuring a speaker who would draw a crowd solely because he once held a high government office. Also, given the fact that Presidents Hoover, Truman, Eisenhower, and Johnson all refused honoraria, I did not want to be the first former President to start the practice. I therefore decided to find some other source of income.

My physical recovery, while important, was not enough. A healthy vegetable is still a vegetable. As I recovered physically, I was able to tackle the more important but more difficult challenge of spiritual recovery. I could not have accomplished it without help. To recover physically involves regaining the ability to get up in the morning; to recover spiritually requires restoring the will and desire to do so.

No one can recover spiritually from a major loss without the help of others. Politics is not a team sport. While a political figure depends on others in many ways, he ultimately rises and falls as a result of his own decisions and actions. A personal defeat therefore is an isolating experience. In an unsuccessful campaign, staff members share in the loss, but only the candidate suffers a personal defeat. Spiritual recovery is hastened by overcoming the sense of isolation, by recognizing the fact that your family, friends, and supporters still stand with you, and by putting the defeat in perspective.

My first line of support was my family. No man has ever had a stronger family than I have had. They were by my side during my illness and during my stay in the hospital. In the weeks, months, and years of slow recovery, a day never passed without their offering an encouraging word of support. Never once did they moan about the disastrous impact of my shattering defeat on their lives. In many ways, it was worse for them than for me. They had to suffer in silence. They could not fight back. When they read or saw the latest negative column, news story, TV program, book, or movie, their instinct was to refute the distortions and falsehoods. But circumstances dictated stoic resignation in response to my detractors.

I also relied on support from my friends. When you win in politics, you hear from everyone. When you lose, you hear from your friends. After Watergate, it was a miracle that I had as many as I did. Some came to see me, some called me on the telephone, others wrote encouraging letters. As good friends, they did not dwell on the tragedy of the past. Thankfully, they did not express sympathy, for the only thing worse than self-pity is to be the object of pity from others. They talked only about the good times we had shared in the past and the even better times we could hope to share in the future. And finally, the mail—the letters from tens of thousands of people from all over the country and the world, most of whom I had never met—played an indispensable role in bucking up my spirits during a difficult time. I was, of course, unable to read and answer them all. But it was heartwarming to know that while there was no longer a silent majority, at least the minority which was left was not silent.

With the wounds of body and spirit healed, I was now prepared to deal with my greatest challenge—mental recovery. This was the decisive factor in my decision to write my memoirs. When I finished *Six Crises* after losing in 1960, I observed that writing the book was my seventh crisis, and I vowed that I would never write another one. But my memoirs served several purposes. It provided part of the income that I needed for my legal and other extraordinary expenses. It was an enormous mental challenge requiring the full use of all my creative abilities. Writing a book is the most intensive exercise anyone can give to his brain. Most important, it provided the therapy that was needed for a full spiritual recovery by enabling me to put Watergate behind me.

Reliving those days in cold print was not easy. But once I had done so, I tried to close the book on that episode. In the three years I spent writing my memoirs, I addressed every facet of the crisis my excellent editorial staff, Frank Gannon, Ken Khachigian, and Diane Sawyer, could uncover. I learned a number of things I had not known at the time as the events of Watergate unfolded. I was able to put all the events of that time in perspective—to learn not only what happened but why it happened, and to provide some guidance so that others could avoid a repetition of those problems.

As I wrote my memoirs, I was able to look back at Watergate and separate myth from fact. At the core of the scandal was the fact that individuals associated with my reelection campaign were caught breaking into and installing telephone wiretaps at the headquarters of the Democratic National Committee in the Watergate Hotel. After their arrest, others in my campaign and in my administration attempted to cover up this connection in order to minimize the political damage. I failed to take matters firmly into my own hands and discover the facts and to fire any and all people involved or implicated in the break-in. I was also accused of taking part in the cover-up by trying to obstruct the FBI's criminal investigation.

Alone, that would probably not have been enough to bring down my administration. But the term "Watergate" has come to include a wide range of other charges that my adversaries used to try to paint my administration as, in their words, "the most corrupt in American history." Together, these accusations represented the myths of Watergate, the smoke screen of false charges that ultimately undercut my administration's ability to govern effectively.

The most blatantly false myth was that I ordered the break-in at the Democratic headquarters. Millions of dollars were spent by the executive branch, the Congress, and the office of the special prosecutor to investigate Watergate. Not one piece of evidence was discovered indicating that I ordered the break-in, knew about the plans for the wiretapping, or received any information from it.

The most politically damaging myth was that I personally ordered the payment of money to Howard Hunt and the other original Watergate defendants to keep them silent. I did discuss this possibility during a meeting with John Dean and Bob Haldeman on March 21, 1973. In the tape recording of this meeting, it is clear that I considered paying the money. I should not have even considered this option, but the key facts were that I rejected offering clemency to the defendants as "wrong" and at the end of the conversation ruled out any White House payment of money to the defendants. Moreover, those who made this accusation ignored the even more crucial fact that no payments were made as a result of that conversation.

The most serious myth—and the one that ultimately forced me to resign—was that, on my specific orders, the CIA obstructed the FBI from pursuing its criminal investigation of the Watergate break-in. I discussed this possible course of action with Bob Haldeman in the famous "smoking gun" tape of June 23, 1972. At that time, I thought that in view of the fact that some former CIA operatives had participated in the Watergate break-in, the CIA would be concerned that their exposure would, in turn, reveal other legitimate operations and operatives, and that the agency would therefore welcome a chance to avoid that outcome. I thought that would also serve our political interests because it would prevent the FBI from going into areas that would be politically embarrassing to us. In my conversation with Haldeman, I made the inexcusable error of following the recommendation from some members of my staff—some of whom, I later learned, had a personal stake in covering up the facts—and requesting that the CIA intervene. But that mistake was mitigated by two facts. First, because of the good judgment of the Director of Central Intelligence, Richard Helms, and his deputy, Vernon Walters, they ignored the White House request and refused to intervene with the FBI, despite the pressure from members of my staff. Second, when FBI Director Pat Gray complained to me in a telephone call three weeks later on July 12 about attempts to suppress his investigation, I told him emphatically to go forward with it, and I instructed Haldeman and John Ehrlichman to make sure the campaign and the administration cooperated with the investigation "all the way down the line." No obstruction of justice took place as a result of the June 23 conversation.

The most preposterous myth was that I or members of the White House staff erased eighteen and one-half minutes of incriminating conversation from one of the White House tapes. My adversaries went to great lengths to try to make this accusation stick. They ignored the perfectly plausible explanation that, given the design of the tape recorder used by my secretary, Rose Mary Woods, it was possible to erase a tape accidentally. They overlooked the fact that Haldeman's complete notes of the meeting, which were turned over to the courts, contained nothing out of the ordinary. Moreover, it begs credulity to believe that I or my staff would erase this one segment of tape and yet leave untouched dozens of hours of other frank and earthy conversations that I clearly would have preferred not to see made public.

The most one-sided myth was that I used government agencies *illegally* by asking Secretary of the Treasury George Shultz to order Internal Revenue Service audits of a political adversary, Larry O'Brien. I have no regrets for that action. In the 1960s, when the Democrats controlled the White House, I was routinely subject to politically instigated IRS audits. Moreover, the IRS bureaucracy —long dominated by Democratic appointees and civil servants— was engaged in wide-ranging field audits of many of my close personal and political friends, including Billy Graham. I was simply trying to level the playing field, and everything I did was totally legal. In any case, I see nothing wrong with getting wealthy people to pay their taxes.

The most hypocritical myth was that the Nixon administration "sold" ambassadorships to major political contributors. It has been a standard, and continuing, practice to appoint a handful of principal contributors to choice embassies. Given the financial requirements of the social circuit in Paris and London, only a wealthy person could afford to serve as ambassador. That is one of the reasons why FDR appointed Joseph Kennedy ambassador to Britain. In the Nixon administration, some qualified contributors received such appointments, though others did not. In fact, while campaign laws in 1972 placed no restrictions on the size of individual donations, we consciously limited, or even refused, money from wealthy supporters whom we wanted to appoint as ambassadors simply to avoid the appearance of impropriety. Walter Annenberg, who made no campaign contribution, was chosen for London, and no one who donated over a million dollars was ever appointed to any ambassadorship.

The most personally disturbing myth was that I deliberately lied throughout the Watergate period in my press conferences and in my speeches. While I did some stupid things during the Watergate period, I was not that stupid. Given the multiple investigations of the scandal, both by the government and the media, I knew the facts ultimately would come out. It would therefore have been suicidal to lie. The problem was that as the events were unfolding I was never able to get the whole truth. I would hear one set of facts from one staff member and another set of facts from others, partly because many knew only bits and pieces of the whole and partly because many were simply looking after themselves. I made no statements that I did not think were true at the time I made them. As far as the June 23 conversation was concerned, it was an error of recollection, not a deliberate falsehood. I recalled telling Gray on July 12 to go ahead with his investigation. In fact, it is in the diary notes I dictated right after the telephone call. My fatal mistake was that I simply did not recall the details of the earlier conversation on June 23.

The most widely believed myth was that I ordered massive illegal wiretapping and surveillance of political opponents, members of the House and Senate, and news media reporters. Among the more bizarre accusations that appeared in newspapers and on the networks were that the White House:

· put Senators Muskie, Percy, Proxmire, and Javits under surveillance;
· wiretapped the telephones of Democratic Presidential candidates;
· conspired with the Justice Department to wiretap Senator McGovern's telephones to gather information for my reelection campaign;
· wiretapped the telephones of friends of Mary Jo Kopechne, who had drowned in Senator Ted Kennedy's car after he drove it off a bridge at Chappaquiddick, Martha's Vineyard;

- placed electronic listening devices in the offices of Senators Mansfield and Fulbright;
- obtained copies of Senator Eagleton's medical records before they appeared in the press;
- orchestrated undercover political activities conducted by so-called FBI suicide squads against opponents of the administration;
- operated a secret police force to conduct illegal wiretaps and burglaries against left-wing radicals.

All of these charges were false, and no evidence was presented to substantiate them. None was ever retracted by those who made them.

My administration did have a carefully limited and totally legal policy of conducting wiretapping for reasons of national security. I do not at all regret having that policy. We were at war in Vietnam. We were conducting a broad array of sensitive secret initiatives with the Soviet Union and China and were involved in secret negotiations to achieve peace with honor in Indochina. At the same time, we were subject to a series of catastrophic leaks of top-secret information to the press, which led, in one case, to the publication of our fallback position in the Strategic Arms Limitation Talks with the Soviet Union. We were concerned that leaks might abort our secret China initiative and our Vietnam peace negotiations. I believed then, and continue to believe now, that some wiretapping was necessary, proper, and justifiable to discover the source of the leaks and thereby prevent further damage to our national security initiatives. Moreover these wiretaps, which were conducted without a court order, were not illegal at the time I ordered them. Only after a Supreme Court ruling in June 1972 did such wiretaps require warrants. My administration discontinued this policy after the decision.

I was particularly outraged by the double standard my adversaries used in accusing me of conducting a massive wiretapping campaign. In fact, it was during the tenure of Attorney General Robert Kennedy that the greatest number of wiretaps without warrants were ordered. In addition, those taps were not restricted to cases involving leaks of national security information. In one case, the Kennedy administration placed a wiretap on the telephone of a newspaper reporter who was writing a book on Marilyn Monroe. In another case, it wiretapped the telephones and bugged the rooms of the Reverend Martin Luther King, Jr. Yet, during the

Watergate period, my administration's justifiable legal national security wiretaps were treated as unprecedented transgressions of the law.

A related accusation was that I ordered members of the White House staff to arrange the break-in to the office of Daniel Ellsberg's psychiatrist in September 1971. In fact, I did not know anything about the plan or approve it. I received no information from the break-in. No evidence has ever been presented to the contrary. Moreover, on the White House tapes, I clearly expressed shock and condemned the break-in when my aides finally informed me about it in March 1973.

The most ridiculous myth was that I was the first President to tape some of my conversations. In fact, FDR was the first to do so. Scores of tapes are kept in the Eisenhower Library. Several thousand hours of tapes are stored in the Johnson Library, none of which will even be examined until the year 2022—fifty years after his death. Of the several hundred hours of tapes in the Kennedy Library, only 12 percent have so far been made public. The rest, according to the Kennedy Library officials, will be kept secret indefinitely.

The most unfair myth—and the one that most angered me—was that I profited from my service as President. After the 1968 election, I voluntarily declined to accept $176,000 owed me as severance pay from my law firm. It would have been perfectly proper to take such payment, as other lawyers who joined the administration did, because this was compensation for services rendered before we joined the government. But because a President has jurisdiction over the whole range of government activities, I wanted to be absolutely sure that no question would be raised on a possible conflict of interest, no matter how remote. For the same reason, I owned no stocks or bonds while I served as President. My entire net worth was in real estate and government certificates of deposit. Today, I am the only living former President who has never taken honoraria for speeches. I am also the only one who has voluntarily given up my Secret Service protection, an action I took in 1985 that has already saved the taxpayers over $12 million.

The most damaging charge in this respect was that the government spent $17 million on my homes in San Clemente and Key Biscayne for my benefit. In fact, all of those expenditures were for security and for staff. When a President maintains a private residence outside Washington—which has been a standard practice throughout this century—the Secret Service, understandably, must build facilities for their agents and install surveillance and other equipment to secure the premises. The government must also install the facilities for secure communications with Washington. I neither requested nor supervised any of these alterations to my homes. All of the facilities were removed upon my resignation. As it turned out, the work done on my home in San Clemente actually reduced its value because grounds that had been torn up to install secure telephone cables could not be restored to their former pristine condition. In addition, I was accused in the media of using $1 million in campaign funds to buy my San Clemente home, of maintaining $1 million in corporate campaign contributions siphoned off into a secret investment portfolio, and of stashing away piles of cash in Swiss bank accounts. All of these charges were false, and no evidence was presented to substantiate them. None was retracted by those who made it.

The most vicious myth was that I tried to cheat on my income taxes. After I returned to San Clemente in 1974, I looked into my tax situation personally for the first time. I was shocked. I found that I had paid over $300,000 more in taxes than the law required. When the controversy over my taxes arose while I was in office, I said I would abide by the findings of the joint congressional committee looking into the matter. Given the fact that the committee was dominated by Democrats, my naive belief in its willingness to be fair and objective turned out to be expensive indeed.

The critical issue involved a gift of some of my Vice-Presidential papers to the National Archives. Lyndon Johnson had urged me to donate those papers and to take the tax deduction, just as he, Hubert Humphrey, and other Democratic officeholders had done previously. On March 27, 1969, my papers—600,000 documents appraised at $576,000—were delivered to the archives. Congress later passed and I signed a law that would disallow deductions for such gifts after July 25, 1969. After the law became effective, a member of my staff signed a deed of gift for the papers and pre-dated his signature before the law was to take effect. In 1974, the congressional committee ruled against the deduction. After I resigned, Dean Butler, an expert California tax attorney, urged me to reopen the case. The key point, he vigorously argued, was that the deed was irrelevant because I had delivered the papers four months before the deadline and therefore the gift had been consummated for tax purposes. I told Butler that I could not reopen the issue, given my promise to the committee. Ironically, while the joint committee held that I had not made a legal gift, the archives held that I had done so and refused to return the papers. I therefore lost both the deduction and the papers.

Where the joint congressional committee left off, the IRS picked up in auditing my past tax returns. In one case, I had deducted the cost of six hundred fifty corsages I had personally bought for the wives and mothers of the returning Vietnam POWs when we gave a state dinner for them in May 1973. My tax accountant, properly, deducted this expense as a cost incurred as part of my official conduct. But the IRS disallowed the deduction on the ridiculous grounds that the government could have paid for the corsages. Ironically, if it had done so, it would have cost the government twice as much as the deduction would have. Some of the nitpicking was ludicrous. When I heard that some of my critics were demanding that I should pay for taking my dog on the airplane with me when I went to San Clemente or Key Biscayne, I recalled an incident that occurred when I visited President Johnson after the 1968 election at his home in Texas. As he escorted me to the helicopter that brought me to his ranch, his dog raced ahead, went up the steps, and got into the helicopter. Johnson carried him out and then jokingly scolded me, "Look here, you've got my job, you've got my house, you've got my helicopter, and now you are going to take my dog!" When Roosevelt's dog Fala supposedly rode on a destroyer, it was a good laugh. When Johnson's dog rode on a plane, it was what everyone—the dog included—expected. When Nixon's dog rode on a plane, it was a crime for not reporting the airfare as income, even though the animal did not take up a seat.

What, then, was Watergate? When the break-in first hit the news, my press secretary, Ron Ziegler, aptly called it a third-rate burglary. To compare Watergate with Teapot Dome, the Truman five-percenter scandals, and the Grant whiskey scandals misses the point totally. No one in the Nixon administration profited from Watergate. No one ripped off the government, as was the case in previous scandals. Wrongdoing took place, but not for personal gain. All administrations have sought to protect themselves from the political fallout of scandals. I detailed my mistakes in this respect at length in my memoirs, a third of which dwelled on Watergate. In retrospect, I would say that Watergate was one part wrongdoing, one part blundering, and one part political vendetta.

The Watergate break-in and cover-up greatly damaged the American political process. While not unusual in political campaigns, these actions were clearly illegal. Over the years, I had been the victim of political dirty tricks and other kinds of vicious tactics in the cut-and-thrust of political warfare. What happened in Watergate—the facts, not the myths—was wrong. In retrospect, while I was not involved in the decision to conduct the break-in, I should have set a higher standard for the conduct of the people who participated in my campaign and administration. I should have established a moral tone that would have made such actions unthinkable. I did not. I played by the rules of politics as I found them. Not taking a higher road than my predecessors and my adversaries was my central mistake. For that reason, I long ago accepted overall responsibility for the Watergate affair. What's more, I have paid, and am still paying, the price for it.

Apart from its illegality, Watergate was a tragedy of errors. Whoever ordered the break-in evidently knew little about politics. If the purpose was to gather political intelligence, the Democratic National Committee was a pathetic target. Strategy and tactics are set by the candidate and his staff, not the party bureaucracy. Moreover, in view of the 30 percent lead I had in the polls, it made no sense to take such a risk because the likely Democratic nominee, Senator George McGovern, stood virtually no chance of winning. I also contributed to the errors. As a student of history, I should have known that leaders who do big things well must be on guard against stumbling on the little things. To paraphrase Talleyrand, Watergate was worse than a crime—it was a blunder.

When I was first informed about the break-in, I did not give it sufficient attention, partly because I was preoccupied with my China and Soviet initiatives and with my efforts to end the war in Vietnam and partly because I feared that some of my close political colleagues might be somehow involved. Some have said that my major mistake was to protect my subordinates. They may be partly right. I believe that in any organization loyalty must run down, as well as up. I knew those who were involved acted not out of desire for personal gain but out of their deep belief in our cause. That knowledge may have contributed to my hesitation in tackling the question. In retrospect, it is clear that I should have focused on the issue immediately, dug out the truth on a top-priority basis, fired everyone involved, and taken the political heat.

But what we remember as the Watergate period was also a concerted political vendetta by my opponents. Anyone who knows the workings of hardball politics knows that the smoke screen of false accusations—the myths of Watergate—were not at all accidental. In this respect, Watergate was not a morality play—a battle between good guys in white and bad guys in black—but rather a political struggle. The baseless and highly sensationalistic charges, the blatant double standards, the party-line votes in congressional investigating committees, and the unwillingness of my adversaries and the media to look into parallel wrongdoing within Democratic campaigns, all should tip off even the casual observer that the opposition was pursuing not only justice but also political advantage.

Only in 1982 was it revealed how a small group of liberal Democrats tried to exploit this advantage during Watergate. For a brief period in 1973, after Vice President Agnew resigned in a personal scandal unrelated to Watergate and before Gerald Ford was confirmed by the Senate, Democrat Carl Albert, then Speaker of the House, stood next in line to the Presidency. Ted Sorensen, a former speechwriter for President Kennedy and a highly partisan critic of my policies, asked Albert for permission to write a secret "comprehensive contingency plan" so that the Democrats could take over the White House swiftly if I were to leave office. Albert agreed. The plan even included suggestions for the tone of the new President's inaugural address and an agenda for his first week in office. Albert is a fine American who would not have been involved in anything improper. But the prospect of winning through Watergate what they had failed to win at the polls was evidently too much for some Democrats to resist. Albert himself quoted Bella Abzug, then a left-wing congresswoman from New York, as saying to him, "Get off your goddamned ass, and we can take this Presidency." So it was without irony that in my memoirs I referred to the final struggle over Watergate as my final political campaign.

When a balanced historical appraisal emerges, the partisan political dimension of the investigation and prosecution will stand out as a prominent feature of the period. Honorable men like Maury Stans suffered far more than they would have had even-handed justice been at play. The smoke screen of false accusations magnified tenfold the public's perception and outrage over the wrongdoing that actually occurred. In writing my memoirs, I came to accept Watergate and the resignation simply as one major defeat in a career that involved both victories and losses, both peaks and valleys.

What I found most frustrating—and most outrageous—about this vendetta was the brutal harassment of my friends. Bebe Rebozo was mercilessly investigated for eighteen months by the General Accounting Office, the Senate Watergate Committee, the IRS, and the special prosecutor. Among the charges that were leaked out of these investigations and publicized by major newspapers and television network commentators were that he had illegally laundered millions of dollars of gambling money in his bank in Key Biscayne; that he managed a million-dollar fund from unreported political contributions that might have been diverted to my personal use; and that he had converted part of a $100,000 contribution from Howard Hughes for his own use, despite the fact that the money was returned intact to the donor just as he had received it. Over $2 million of government money was spent on investigating him. In January 1975, the special prosecutor, Leon Jaworski, finally issued a statement that there was no evidence against Rebozo on any of the charges that had been made. But Jaworski's statement was not carried at all by *The New York Times* or by any of the three networks, all of whom had given broad coverage to the false charges.

After I completed my memoirs, the only time I addressed Watergate at any length was in the televised interviews conducted by David Frost. I agreed to make the broadcasts not by choice but by necessity. I faced a major financial crunch because of attorneys' fees. The entire amount I received from the broadcasts of $540,000 went to my lawyers. The weeks of preparing for and the twenty-six hours of taping the broadcasts proved to be the major ordeal of my stay in San Clemente. Writing my memoirs required me to engage in detached analysis and intense concentration. The Frost interviews required me to gird for intellectual combat. I did not expect the telecasts to be positive or even balanced, and I was not surprised when they turned out to be highly negative. It was a commercial enterprise, and these do not pay off by producing enlightening discussion but by producing clashes between personalities. I vividly recall my first meeting with the British media magnate, Sir James Goldsmith, who visited me while I was taping one of the programs. He was a strong supporter and was shocked by what he considered to be the vicious anti-Nixon bias of Frost's top researchers, James Reston, Jr., and Bob Zelnick, now Pentagon correspondent for ABC News. I knew he was right, and the choice of topics, the slant in the questions, and the editing of the final broadcasts reflected the bias. At the time, however, I had no choice in such matters.

Those first four years in San Clemente were profoundly difficult and painful. I succeeded in recovering physically, spiritually, and mentally from the cataclysmic defeat I suffered in 1974. As I look back over those years in the wilderness, I would say that I was sustained by always bearing in mind three principles:

· Put the past behind you. Analyze and understand the reasons for your defeat, but do not become obsessed with what was lost. Think instead about what is left to do.
· Do not let your critics get to you. Remember that they win only if they divert you into fighting them rather than driving toward your goals.
· Devote your time to a goal larger than yourself. Avoid the temptation of living simply for pleasure or striving only to leave a larger estate.

While few people will experience a loss as devastating as resigning the Presidency, these principles remain valid for the great defeats we all suffer, whether in business, in sports, or in personal life. The key is to live for something more important than your life. As Einstein said, "Only a life lived for others is worth living."

On my sixty-fifth birthday, January 9, 1978, I made a major decision. I had completed my memoirs, and fortunately the book turned out to be a bestseller. I was in excellent condition physically and thought that I was now in a condition to tackle other projects. I had to decide what to do with the rest of my life. In a sense, this was a life-or-death decision. If a person quits after a defeat, he dies spiritually and will soon die physically.

While I profoundly believe this to be true, I had a difficult problem: What goal could I now set for myself? I could not seek office again. In any case, seeking office by itself is not a worthwhile goal. What separates the men from the boys in politics is that the boys seek office to *be* somebody and the men seek office to *do* something. Yet, so much still remained to be done in achieving the goals that led me to run for office in the first place. I reread a passage of a letter from Whittaker Chambers to me after my defeat in 1960: "I do not believe for a moment that because you have been cruelly checked in the employment of what is best in you, what is most yourself, that the check is final. It cannot be." He went on to say that he recognized that the executive office had passed to the other party for a long time to come. Even so, he wrote, "That changes your routing and precise destination. It does not change the nature

44

of your journey. You have years in which to serve. Service is your life. You must serve.''

After my resignation, my routing again changed, but my destination remained the same. Throughout my political life, I had dedicated myself to furthering the causes of peace, freedom, opportunity, and justice, not only for the people of the United States but also for all the people in the world. These causes are lofty and certainly unattainable by the efforts of any individual or even any single nation. I was fortunate to have had the opportunity to work for those causes while holding the greatest office in the free world and was therefore capable of achieving more than I would have otherwise. But meaning in life does not derive from the station in life you attain, and the depth of personal satisfaction you feel does not depend on the height to which you rise. Fulfillment comes from dedication and service to a worthy cause, whether as a foot soldier or as the commander-in-chief.

In 1978, I rededicated myself to the causes that had always inspired my actions. As I analyzed the world scene, I was profoundly troubled by the geopolitical momentum behind Moscow's expansionism and by the paralysis of political will in the Western world. I therefore chose to devote myself to advocating a more energetic and assertive American role in leading the free world, a stronger and more skillful strategy for the continuing East-West conflict, and a more far-sighted geopolitical approach to managing global affairs in a world with new emerging power centers in Europe and East Asia.

I began writing my first book on foreign policy, *The Real War,* published in the spring of 1980. I knew that only a limited number of people read books or listen to speeches by a former President, but I wanted to set forth my ideas for those who were interested. *The Real War* turned out to be the right book at the right time. It not only became a worldwide bestseller but also made a difference in the foreign-policy debate at a crucial turning point both in American politics and in the East-West struggle. When I completed the book in January 1980, I knew the time had come to leave San Clemente and to return to the arenas in which I could more effectively serve the causes to which I had committed my life.

3

RENEWAL

On November 30, 1978, as I walked into the hall where I was to address the Oxford Union, the crowd greeted me with a standing ovation. I had received a very different reception outside. Several hundred demonstrators, many of them American students attending Oxford, surrounded my car as we entered the grounds. It was an ugly crowd. Some pounded on the car doors. Others jumped on the hood and had to be forcibly removed by the university security officers. For a moment, my mind flashed back to the brutal attack on my motorcade by an anti-American mob in Caracas, Venezuela, twenty years before.

We could hear the crowd outside chanting—"Nixon go home!" —as the president of the Union introduced me. I could see that he was somewhat embarrassed, but I put him at ease when I opened my remarks by observing that the demonstrators made me feel very much at home.

This was my first appearance before a university audience since leaving office. I chose Oxford because I had been impressed with the intellectual caliber of the students when I had spoken there in 1958. At that time, the first questioner after my speech had set the tone for the meeting. Obviously making a wry reference to the Fund crisis in 1952, he called out, "What are you here for, a loan?" The questions were tough and some were irreverent. But unlike many university audiences in the United States today, they did not try to shout the speaker down. They wanted to hear what he had to say.

I found the same kind of audience when I returned to Oxford twenty years later. A contingent of American reporters who were covering the event were surprised by the extremely favorable reception I received on a university campus. In retrospect, I believe there were three reasons for the good reception. The students liked the fact that I spoke without notes; they thought that I was giving my own views rather than reading a canned speech that others had written for me. They particularly liked the question-and-answer period, which was filled with tough questions and equally tough rejoinders. Above all, they were serious students of world affairs. While they did not necessarily agree with me, they were interested in my analysis of the forces that moved the world, which could affect their lives and the future of the world for years to come.

It was no cakewalk. The questioners were respectful but they pulled no punches. The high point of the event for me was when one of them asked whether I had any regrets for ordering the "invasion" of Cambodia in 1970. I answered that my only regret was that I had not done it sooner. I am sure that most did not agree with the answer, but the unexpected sharpness of the rejoinder brought a burst of applause. I added that to accuse the United States of "invading" North Vietnamese–occupied areas of Cambodia in 1970 would be like accusing the Allies of "invading" German-occupied France in 1944.

The most intriguing question came toward the end. Someone asked what my plans were for a future role in American politics or in foreign affairs. I responded that my political career was over but that while I had retired from politics, I had not retired from life. I concluded my answer by saying, "So long as I have a breath in my body, I am going to talk about the great issues that affect the world. I am not going to keep my mouth shut. I am going to speak out for peace and freedom." The question was unexpected, but the off-the-cuff answer set forth exactly the guidelines I was to follow in my appearances in the United States and abroad in the years ahead.

After my reception in Oxford and an extraordinarily positive reaction to a three-hour question-and-answer session on primetime television in France, some American pundits speculated that I was launching a campaign for a comeback. They were right in one respect but wrong in another. I was indeed launching a campaign, but not for a personal comeback, which would have been both unrealistic and, even more important, contrary to my real goal. I had spent thirty years of my life studying and acting in the area of foreign policy. I had some unique experience and had developed some strong views about the mistakes that had been made in the past and the need for new policies in the future. I wanted to share those experiences and those views with others who had responsibilities for making or affecting the decisions that would make a difference in the world scene.

From an intellectual standpoint, the decade between 1978 and 1988 was the most creative period of my life. As a congressman, senator, Vice President, and President, I was so busy with day-to-day decisions and actions that I had little time left to think and reflect about what ought to be done. I had to depend more than I would have liked on others to do some of the conceptual thinking. While they may have done it better, I was still uncomfortable with that reliance because, after all, people had voted for me, not for those I chose as my advisers. I felt this way even though I set the general course, retained the responsibility of making the final decision, and insisted that as options were developed I would be present at their creation and not just at their implementation.

Some years before he was elected President, Woodrow Wilson made a profoundly perceptive distinction between men of thought and men of action. There is a place for both. Thinking alone with no contact with the real world leads to theoretical treatises that gather dust in the archives. Acting alone without thinking is dangerous. As an active student of history, with a particular interest in political biography, I had the opportunity to do a lot of thinking while out of office in the 1960s and had developed my own perspective and views on foreign policy. More recently, I had also had a course in action at the highest levels. Now I wanted to focus on integrating the lessons I learned from history and those I learned while making history.

First of all, it was necessary to keep up to date. Oral and written briefings from government officials helped, and I read scores of columns, articles, and books on developments around the world. I also had the benefit of the counsel of former government officials who served in my administration, including Frank Carlucci, Bob Ellsworth, Al Haig, William Hyland, Henry Kissinger, John Lehman, Bud McFarlane, James Schlesinger, Brent Scowcroft, and William Van Cleave. I found particularly helpful conversations on foreign and economic issues I had with a number of experts from both government and the private sector, including Howard Baker, Leo Cherne, Brian Crozier, Alton Frye, Maurice Greenberg, Mike Oksenberg, Felix Rohatyn, Dimitri Simes, Joe Sisco, Strobe Talbott, Robert Tucker, and Stephen Young. I did not limit my search for new ideas to those who stood on the same side of the political fence. I also discussed the world situation with Zbigniew Brzezinski, Ed Muskie, George McGovern, Christopher Dodd, Tony Coelho, Sam Nunn, and Les Aspin. Some shared many of my views, while others had sharp differences with my analyses. But I knew from past experience that policies that lacked broad-based bipartisan support could not be sustained if adopted.

Still, there was no substitute for seeing the world for yourself. The world had changed a great deal since I had left office, and the pace of historical change seemed to be accelerating. My travels during those ten years were extensive. They included visits to China, the Soviet Union, England, France, Germany, Spain, Austria, Switzerland, Turkey, Egypt, Saudi Arabia, Jordan, the Ivory Coast, Morocco, Tunisia, Japan, Korea, Singapore, Malaysia, Thailand, Pakistan, Burma, Bulgaria, Hungary, Romania, and Czechoslovakia. In most of these countries I met with heads of government.

From an intellectual standpoint, these trips were by far the best I had ever taken. Since I was no longer in office, I was able to keep social events to a minimum and avoid sightseeing. Where possible, I ruled out speeches and press conferences. When I met the major leaders, they did not dwell on parochial bilateral issues between their country and the United States. They welcomed the chance to express their views on developments in other parts of the world, and a number of them were first-class strategic thinkers. We need to remember that simply because the United States is the major military power in the free world, that does not mean that we have a monopoly on intellectual power.

In my meetings, I represented neither the U.S. government nor any business clients. I personally paid for my travel expenses. Where possible, I had one-on-one conversations. I brought no aides into the meetings, and since I was not in office our ambassador did not need to attend. I have found the more people that participate in a meeting, the less candid the conversation becomes. This is particularly true when somebody from the American Embassy is present. In that case, your host simply dishes out the same tired rhetoric he has already served up to visiting American government officials.

As a result, I found the discussions I had with foreign leaders after leaving office to be far more informative than those I attended as a government official. And my counterparts were even more candid than they had been in meetings from 1962 and 1968, apparently because at that time I was considered to be a potential candidate for President, which to an extent inhibited the candor of the conversations.

I had visited all of these countries before, and the trips I took in this period gave me the opportunity to see first hand the changes that had occurred and to talk with new leaders as well as with old friends. My decision to forgo voluntarily my Secret Service protection also improved the quality of my trips. In addition to saving the government over $3 million annually, I now had the freedom I wanted to go anywhere in the world without the very efficient but nonetheless very intrusive presence of the Secret Service. In thousands of miles of travel since then, both at home and abroad, I have not had an unpleasant incident and have never been concerned about my personal safety. In fact, when you travel in the Communist world, the reverse is the problem—you are too safe.

In a speech I made in Kansas City in 1971, I said that I foresaw the emergence in coming decades of a new world order in which the interaction of five major power centers—the United States, Western Europe, Japan, the Soviet Union, and China—became the principal axis of history. As I traveled abroad since leaving office, I have found that this continues to be a useful conceptual framework through which to view the world. In 1971, I spoke of "power centers" defined in terms of potential economic power; today, I would broaden the concept to mean global political clout. While economic power represents a key ingredient of such power, military forces, ideological appeal, domestic political cohesion, skill in statecraft, and commonality of interests with other major powers also must be factored into the equation.

While many analysts dismiss the countries of Western Europe as geopolitical has-beens, we would be making a fatal mistake to accept their assessment. It is true that the European powers in NATO, exhausted by the two world wars, have turned inward and have become more parochial in their outlook. It is true that alone no European power possesses the capabilities of a superpower. But it is also true that for the United States—and for the Soviet Union—the countries of Western Europe, taken together, continue to be the most strategic piece of territory in the world. They contain over a quarter of the world's economic power and represent our forward line of defense against the Soviet Union.

Moreover, Western Europe has come a long way since 1945. Britain and France are no longer rivals, and France and Germany are no longer enemies. Our allies have made great strides in unifying their economies and have taken the first halting steps toward political unity. On two visits to Turkey, I saw that despite major problems a nation that had for decades been known as the "sick man of Europe" was firmly on the road to economic progress. And Spain, once so isolated, had now become a respected economic and military partner in the European Community.

Since leaving office, I have been impressed by the gradual psychological and spiritual recovery of the peoples of Western Europe and by the caliber of many of their top leaders. I did not expect that Western Europe would so quickly adopt and move forward with the plan for economic unification starting in 1992. I now expect that in the decade ahead we will see movement toward coordinated European foreign policies that might enable the fragmented giant of Europe finally to begin to emerge as a powerful geopolitical player.

When I met with President Mitterrand in June 1982, he recalled that we had met in 1957, when he had been representing France and I had been representing the United States at a diplomatic event in Tunisia. I was impressed by the depth of his understanding of international issues and by his typically French logical analysis of those issues. He began our meeting with a well-organized monologue that marched like a lawyer's opening statement. As we surveyed the world scene, he repeatedly emphasized his stern anti-Soviet position. He said that he concurred with the views I had expressed in *The Real War* and that a strong deterrent was a prerequisite for effective negotiations with Moscow. At the same time, he argued against economic sanctions because they had not worked "since the time of Napoleon."

Mitterrand took issue with positions I had taken on Third World conflicts. On these points, he candidly said, "We differ." He argued that left-wing movements in the Third World were not at the outset explicitly Communist or creations of the Soviet Union. Instead, they adopted the Marxist philosophy and aligned themselves with the Kremlin only because the West opposed them. "I know El Salvador's leftist leaders," he exclaimed, "and they are not Communists!" I could not help noting to myself that, whatever their true philosophical roots, the guerrillas in El Salvador were certainly not democrats. Communist nations provided their arms, and their leaders refused to take part in elections and promised to continue their war against any democratically elected government.

Mitterrand also said that, in checking the records, he found that de Gaulle had always seen me on my trips to France during my years out of office in the 1960s and that he wished to follow the same practice. In part of my response, I mentioned to him that I thought de Gaulle's greatest legacy was the constitution of the Fifth Republic, which provided for a strong presidency. He answered, "We didn't like it when he was in, but we like it much better now that we are in!"

I was very impressed with Prime Minister Thatcher. She is a leader who has made a profound difference for the better in the life of her nation. I first met her in 1978, while she was leader of the opposition and Britain was still in the economic doldrums. When I saw her next, in 1982, she had become prime minister and had through her strong leadership produced what many now call the British economic miracle. In our meetings, she took a reasoned hard-line position on East-West issues and forcefully argued the British point of view on other questions, such as the Middle East. Unlike some women leaders, who acted like men but expected to be treated like women, she gave no quarter and asked for none simply because she was a woman.

Madame Kazuko Aso, the daughter of Japan's legendary postwar prime minister, Shigeru Yoshida, described Thatcher to me this way: "Her mouth smiles, but not her eyes. She is a very tough, strong, and highly intelligent leader. I respect her, but I would not want to be married to her. But I *do* like the way she treats her husband!"

Eisenhower used to say that the British could be very difficult allies in peacetime but that there was nobody he would rather have on his side when the going was tough in wartime. I would agree but would add that there is no one I would rather have on my side in a fight than Margaret Thatcher.

She deserves the major share of credit for Britain's economic recovery. It is easy to forget how far the country had traveled down the socialist road—and how much damage this had caused to the British economy—before she came into office. Nationalized industries, socialized housing and medicine, burdensome government regulations, immensely powerful trade unions, irresponsible monetary policies, and an enormous welfare state had all brought economic progress to a virtual standstill. Layer by layer, she removed the obstacles to economic growth, despite strong opposition even within her own party. While President Reagan rightly receives great credit for slowing down the growth of government in the United States, we should recognize that Margaret Thatcher's repeal of socialism in Britain represented a true revolution. We can only hope the Europe of 1992 will be modeled on Thatcher's Britain rather than on some of the bloated welfare states on the continent.

Economic unity alone, even as far advanced as it will be after 1992, will not make Western Europe a major geopolitical player. It also needs to face up to the steps needed to assure its own long-term security and to chart out some positive joint political initiatives. To achieve the former, Western Europe must come to terms with the need for maintaining an American nuclear deterrent in Europe and for concentrating arms control talks on reducing the Soviet superiority in conventional forces. To achieve the latter, Western Europe should play the leading role in assisting the Eastern European countries seeking to make the transition to capitalist economic systems and democratic political systems.

In the aftermath of the Intermediate Nuclear Forces Treaty of 1987, which eliminated all theater-range, ground-based nuclear weapons in Europe, Moscow's key objective has become the removal of all tactical nuclear weapons, which, if achieved, would leave Western Europe vulnerable to conventional aggression and political intimidation. Former German Chancellor Helmut Schmidt accurately observed to me that Mikhail Gorbachev's main objective was now to neutralize Germany by denuclearizing Europe before the West could achieve a balance in conventional weapons.

Unfortunately, the INF Treaty has compounded the pressures on West European leaders, particularly in West Germany, to give in to Soviet demands. This, in turn, has created sharp tensions within NATO. As Turkey's foreign minister told me in commenting on the treaty, "Gorbachev has killed three birds with one stone. He divided Europe from the United States, divided Europe against itself, and divided the German coalition."

In my meetings, leaders both in Britain and France understood the risks inherent in the INF formula. When I saw him again in 1987, Mitterrand spoke critically of the emerging agreement, though he felt he could not publicly oppose the formula given the German and American positions on the issue. Although many French leaders from both sides of the political spectrum argued that France would use its nuclear weapons to defend West Germany, it is difficult to believe that Moscow would take that threat seriously, not only because France has historically recoiled from taking any actions in World War I or World War II that might risk the destruction of Paris, but also because a Soviet first strike—by French estimates—would leave France with sufficient long-range weapons to target only 5 percent of the Soviet population and economy. It is therefore indispensable to keep a credible U.S. nuclear deterrent in Europe that inextricably links our strategic deterrent to NATO's defense posture, and to focus arms control talks on the real threat to European peace and stability, Soviet conventional superiority.

In my travels and meetings, I also concluded that the first major political initiative of a more united Western Europe should focus on Eastern Europe. In 1982, I visited every country in Eastern Europe except Poland, which I had visited in 1959 and 1972, and East Germany. In Hungary, where the government had permitted some freedom for market forces in the economy, I could see that even modest departures from doctrinaire Marxist policies sparked economic progress. Despite iron control from the top, I could sense in all these countries that just below the surface there was a kind of seething discontentment and total disenchantment with the Soviet-imposed political and economic systems. In walking the streets of each Communist capital, I was overwhelmed by a general sense of drabness and of a depressed people, cowed and beaten down. While we associate communism with the color red, the real color of communism is gray.

Ironically, former Romanian President Nicolai Ceausescu—who even then ran one of the most repressive regimes in Eastern Europe—saw the need for change in the Communist world. He said that after Brezhnev a new generation of leaders would take power in Moscow and that the Soviet Union desperately needed an infusion of new ideas. He spoke approvingly of Khrushchev's efforts to initiate change and to break new ground. He also said that Brezhnev had erred in invading Czechoslovakia in 1968, arguing that the then Czechoslovak Communist Party leader, Alexandr Dubcek, simply wanted to take a different road to socialism and that the imposition of martial law in Poland had been a tragedy made necessary by Solidarity's excessive demands. He adamantly insisted that the Soviet Union should allow its allies to pursue their own paths to progress. Unfortunately for the Romanian people, Ceausescu failed to see that his own country needed reform even more than its neighbors did.

For the West, the dramatic developments in Poland, Hungary, East Germany, Czechoslovakia, Bulgaria, and Romania present an historical opportunity to overcome the division of Europe. We must not allow these bold efforts at fundamental economic and political reform to fail.

In my trips to Japan, the contrasts with what I saw during my visit as Vice President in 1953 were stunning. A shattered nation had risen to the status of an economic giant. Shigeru Yoshida, along with General Douglas MacArthur, must be credited with laying the foundation for the Japanese economic miracle. He not only adopted shrewd economic and political policies but also prepared younger leaders who would follow him in office and carry forward his vision. Japan's phenomenal success resulted not just from the extraordinary abilities of the Japanese people but also from the smooth succession of responsible and moderate governments that has provided the continuity and stability indispensable for progress.

Yet Japan remains a timid giant, uncertain of its role in the world and reluctant to take on tasks commensurate with its vast economic power. But this is beginning to change. As Singapore's Prime Minister Lee Kwan Yew aptly observed to me over twenty years ago, "The Japanese are a great people. They cannot and should not be satisfied with a world role that limits them to making better transistor radios and sewing machines and teaching other Asians how to grow rice."

I noted a subtle but definite change in the attitudes of Japan's political leaders on the several visits I made there in the 1980s. At the beginning of the decade, they continued to take what the Japanese call a "low posture" in foreign policy, always pointing out the constitutional restrictions on their military power and, consequently, their political role. Over time, however, their attitudes shifted. As Japan became the dominant regional economic power and a global economic superpower, its leaders became more confident and more assertive, not only in bilateral issues with the United States but also in presenting their points of view on distant regional disputes, such as the conflict in the Persian Gulf.

Prime Minister Yasuhiro Nakasone exemplified this trend. When I met with him in 1985, we discussed the need to reverse the trend toward protectionism in the United States and to reduce the non-tariff barriers discriminating against foreign goods in Japan. Unlike most previous Japanese prime ministers, Nakasone was looking beyond bilateral issues to Japan's role on the world stage. He conceded that Japan needed to spend more on defense, though he stressed this would have to be done in ways that would not alarm neighboring countries. We both agreed that Japan should explore non-military means for strengthening the security of the West, such as increasing foreign aid to key countries in Central and South

America and taking on the issue of Latin American debt. I added that these points were interrelated, noting that, while Japan was so strong economically that it could survive a rise in American protectionism, such a policy would have a devastating effect on other countries such as Brazil, where it would make the debt problem insoluble.

Throughout East Asia, the issue of Japanese rearmament remains sensitive. In a 1985 meeting, Lee Kwan Yew argued that it would be a mistake to press the Japanese toward full-scale rearmament because hatreds from World War II still burned too hot. Moreover, he said that if the United States were to withdraw or reduce its presence in the Pacific, the smaller nations in the region would have the unenviable choice of Japan or China as the principal counterweight against the Soviet Union. We agreed that stability in the Pacific required an active U.S. role in managing security issues with the Japanese and Chinese and in checking Soviet ambitions.

While Japan has begun to take on a wider global role, its ultimate shape remains undetermined. Although Japan's and America's interests would be best served by a collaborative relationship, the prevalence of Japan-bashing in the United States and America-bashing in Japan casts a dark cloud on the future of our relationship. With the rise of a new generation of Japanese leaders—many of whom have no personal memories of the U.S. postwar reconstruction of Japan—the danger exists that our trans-Pacific ties will fray or even snap. We therefore need to elevate our relations from the constant arbitration of individual trade disputes—many of which though politically potent are economically petty—to the higher plane of shaping the international order in the Pacific, of taking on jointly challenges such as solving the debt crises in Mexico and other Latin American countries, and of helping ease Japan's entrance onto the world stage by linking our approaches to global economic and political issues. Spirited economic competition between the United States and Japan is one thing. But it must not be permitted to degenerate into economic warfare. Enhancing the shared responsibility of the United States and Japan to cooperate in protecting and extending peace, freedom, and prosperity in Asia and the developing world will go a long way toward reducing the nationalist recriminations that politicians in both the United States and Japan hurl across the Pacific from time to time.

In four visits to the People's Republic of China from 1976 to 1985, I saw the country evolve from one of the world's most reactionary, doctrinaire Communist nations into one of its most progressive in terms of breaking free from the dead hand of Marxist ideology. One hundred sixty years ago, Napoleon had called China the "sleeping giant." Today, China has become an awakened giant. It has left behind forever its policy of self-imposed isolation of the 1960s and will for the foreseeable future represent a major geopolitical power center in world affairs.

In the spring of 1989, two parallel events—the Sino-Soviet summit and the pro-democracy demonstrations in Tiananmen Square —cast into stark relief the key questions of China's future courses in foreign policy and domestic reform. Where these dual events will take China will largely determine how the U.S.-Chinese relationship will develop in the remainder of this century.

While Moscow and Beijing normalized their relations in 1989, I do not believe the West need fear a restoration of the ideology-based Sino-Soviet bloc of the 1950s. In 1982, Ceausescu told me he believed the two principal Eurasian powers would reconcile their differences because they had the "same ideology." I would disagree. In reality, they restored full relations not because of shared ideology but because they shared the same border for thousands of miles and because Gorbachev had moved to satisfy China's three conditions for normalization, a Soviet withdrawal from Afghanistan, a reduction of Soviet forces on the Chinese border, and a Vietnamese withdrawal from Cambodia.

The bottom line is that Moscow has very little to offer China. As Lee Kwan Yew told me, "The greatest Chinese need is economic progress, and in that respect the Soviet Union offers a very poor second choice compared to the West." Gorbachev cannot offer foreign investment, advanced technology, and expertise, let alone a viable economic model. The choice between East and West is simply no contest. But that does not close the question. As Prime Minister Nakasone observed to me, "Gorbachev is romancing China, but he will succeed only if the Chinese give up on the West. The United States, Japan, and Europe must give the Chinese an economic stake in good relations with the West."

Many have wrongly concluded that a night of brutal repression in Tiananmen Square wiped away a decade of progressive reforms in China. Deng Xiaoping's economic reforms and opening to the West have irreversibly changed his country. Reactionary hard-line leaders cannot fully turn back the clock. When China's leaders have looked at the rest of the world, especially the rimland of Asia, they have been astonished and shamed by the backwardness of their country. What was particularly disturbing was the stark contrast between the poverty of the Chinese on the Communist mainland and the high living standards of Chinese living and working in capitalist Taiwan, Singapore, and Hong Kong. When the Chinese people watched televised reports on Deng's visit to the United States in 1979, the backdrops of modern cities, advanced factories, and technological wonders fundamentally altered their world view. Accustomed to thinking of China as the Middle Kingdom—the center of civilization—the Chinese suffered a needed rude awakening. While this alone could not change anything overnight, it did condition them against wanting to turn back to their old ways and stimulated a genuine revolution in their thinking.

In my meetings with the top Chinese leaders, I candidly discussed with them the process of reform, both the need for change and problems it produced. In 1982, Party Secretary Hu Yaobang broached these issues by asking me whether Americans believed China was a stable country. I answered that there was some concern on this point, given the dramatic swings in China's policies in the past and the presence of conservatives in the party bureaucracy and military. Hu responded that opponents of reform existed, though they numbered no more than 200,000 people and were scattered across the country. With respect to the army, he smiled and said that the military had always been locked into the political leadership and did not represent "an independent force." While Deng was very old, Hu continued, there were "hundreds and even thousands" prepared to carry on his progressive policies.

Three years later, when I met with Hu in the same compound in which I had conferred with Mao in 1972 and 1976, our discussion focused on the Sino-Soviet relationship. Hu remained wary of Moscow, arguing, "Gorbachev's words are different, but the policy remains the same." I noted that in 1972 the Soviet threat in Asia brought the United States and China together, and that many believed a less threatening posture from the Kremlin might lead to closer Sino-Soviet ties. As Hu responded, he became very animated, gesturing to his colleagues, and like Brezhnev, often standing up to stress a point. "For China to move toward the Soviet Union would be a repudiation of China's whole independent policy over the past thirty years," he said. "China's 'honor' would be questioned all over the world. China will never again be a puppet! If we submit to Moscow, we would give up all that we have gained over the past thirty years."

There was an odd, melancholy atmosphere to our meeting. At the conclusion of a diary note I made at the time, I wrote, "I sensed that he felt this would be his last hurrah." Whatever the cause for this impression, it was not long before events landed Hu in political hot water. In early 1987, he was accused of failing to act forcefully enough in suppressing pro-democracy student demonstrations and was removed from his top leadership post.

In 1985, I met with Prime Minister Zhao Ziyang in the same room in which my formal meetings with Chou En-lai were held in 1972. He said that China's economic changes were irreversible, that there could be no turning back, and that no major opposition to the reforms existed. He argued that the economic difficulties brought on by reform had been exaggerated and, in any case, would be remedied through controls on excessive growth. He repeatedly stressed that China needed to place highest priority on the "intelligence" of the people and that the government needed to devote more resources to education and training.

Ironically, China's present prime minister, Li Peng, who by all accounts became Zhao's bitter rival for power in the aftermath of the Tiananmen massacre, also attended our meeting. As we left the room, I mentioned the fact that he had studied in Moscow. He laughed and retorted that he wanted me to understand that he was not a Soviet "mole." Zhao chimed in that although many Chinese leaders had studied in Moscow, China would never again be closely allied with the Soviet Union. With a smile, he added, "What possible advantage could there be in such an alliance for us?"

In my meetings with Deng Xiaoping in 1985, I noted that he looked less nervous and more fit than in our previous encounters in 1979 and 1982. I had been told by the foreign minister that the eighty-two-year-old Deng swam an hour every day, as well as walking two miles. It reminded me of the famous 1971 photograph of seventy-eight-year-old Mao purportedly swimming the Yangtze.

In our wide-ranging conversation, Deng touched both on China's international position and its domestic reforms. He opened the meeting with a pro forma recitation of the official line that the Soviet Union and the United States represented equal threats to China, though everything he subsequently said contradicted that position. I could not help thinking how strange it was that, if Deng's remarks reflected reality, China had failed to impose "three conditions" for normal relations with the United States. In any case, Deng continued to take a skeptical line on Gorbachev, whose policies he dismissed as "loud thunder and little raindrops." He also stressed that the United States need never fear that technology transferred to China would end up in Soviet hands. "We have far more differences with the Soviet Union than with the United States," he said, "but we don't want to tie ourselves to one chariot."

Deng was far less categorical than Hu or Zhao regarding China's economic reforms. He said that China would try them out and, as long as they worked, would continue with them. "But if they fail," he continued, "we will drop them. In three to five years, we can decide our future course. The reforms are irreversible in their direction, but tactics could change." He said that opposition to the reforms existed—"China, after all, is a big country"—but that these groups would remain insignificant as long as the reforms worked. Given the fact that the initial agricultural reforms had improved the lives of 90 percent of China's farmers, Deng believed the reforms had gained the support of a majority of the people.

As our meeting drew to a close, I observed that given their success China's reforms could perhaps serve as a model for many Third World countries, particularly because the Soviet model had been discredited and the American model might be too advanced for undeveloped countries. In a very animated response, Deng said that he did not believe in exporting economic models and that the Soviets would never concede the superiority of China's approach. "They," he stressed, "try to have all follow *their* model."

In the aftermath of the Tiananmen Square massacre, some observers called for the United States to punish China's leaders by breaking off all relations, by imposing wide-ranging sanctions, and by isolating the Chinese until the repressive policies were reversed. No one would dispute that the use of lethal force to suppress the demonstrators was shockingly cruel and incredibly stupid. The wiser course clearly would have been to accommodate the legitimate demands of the students, as many top Chinese leaders urged, or at least to clear Tiananmen Square with non-lethal riot-control methods. But to destroy the U.S.-Chinese relationship would be a tragic error that would serve neither our interests nor those of the Chinese people.

My sixth visit to China in October 1989 was potentially the most sensitive and controversial since my first trip seventeen years before. This time virtually all of my close friends urged me not to go. They predicted that my critics would hammer me unmercifully for appearing to try to salvage the China initiative by tipping glasses with those who had ordered the Tiananmen crackdown less than five months before. I agreed with them. But I believed that doing what I could to restore momentum to one of the most important bilateral relationships in the world was more than worth the risk to my own image.

At the time I was unaware of the secret delegation President Bush had sent to Beijing in early July. But even if I had known . about the mission, I would have gone ahead with my own plans. The tragedy at Tiananmen had dealt a devastating blow to Sino-American relations in large part because it had occurred on live television. Private expressions of regret, while important, were not enough. I knew the American people were realistic enough to understand that we had to continue to have constructive relations with the most populous nation in the world. But they deserved to have their sympathies for the student demonstrators expressed both publicly and directly to the Chinese leaders. I in turn was realistic enough to know that my role in the rapprochement between our two countries gave me privileged status as an "old friend" of China. I knew that even if I said things the leaders did not want to hear, they would listen. To underscore the importance of my visit in their eyes and also to give it a bipartisan character, I asked Dr. Michel Oksenberg, a leading China specialist and formerly the Carter administration's top China expert, to accompany me. I also consulted with a bipartisan group of senators and congressmen before leaving.

My four days in Beijing were the most arduous I have spent in a foreign country since leaving office. I had over twenty hours of one-on-one meetings with China's top leaders—including Deng, Li Peng, and Deng's designated successor, General Secretary Jiang Zemin—and also several highly impressive younger leaders, as well as Deng Yingchao, the widow of Chou En-lai, who is a top Communist Party leader in her own right. My purposes in these meetings were threefold: to show the leaders that even China's friends in the United States were outraged at the events of June 2–4 and that China would have to take steps to address our concerns; to draw the leaders back into a discussion of geopolitics after months of preoccupation with their domestic problems; and to establish a dialogue about the future of Sino-American relations.

On October 31, I had what will probably be my last meeting with Deng Xiaoping. It was also his last meeting with a Western figure before announcing his retirement. In the American media he had been transformed virtually overnight from bold visionary—he was *Time*'s Man of the Year in 1978 and 1985—to bloodthirsty villain because of his role in the crackdown. I expected to find him distracted and defensive. His physical condition had deteriorated noticeably in the four years since I had last seen him. He was less steady on his feet, and his hearing was so poor that he had two translators: one to make a record of our conversation and another to shout my comments into his left ear. But his mind was still sharp and his energy level remarkable.

I began by telling Deng, "I have watched Sino-U.S. relations closely for seventeen years. There has never been a worse crisis than now in those relations, because this time the concerns come not from those who are enemies of China but from those who are friends. In our talks we must examine those differences and repair the damage to the respect among China's friends in the United States for some of the leaders of China."

During my earlier meetings on this trip, Deng's colleagues in the leadership had repeatedly taken what was clearly the current party line. Quoting a Chinese proverb, "He who ties the knot must untie it," they had asserted that the chill in our relations was the fault of the United States, which had overreacted to the purely internal matter of some troublesome "counterrevolutionary" students. Deng was far more subtle. "In putting an end to this recent past between us," he said, "the United States should take the initiative. China is weak and small, while the United States is large and strong. I am not just concerned with trying to preserve face. Rather, if I and my colleagues do not maintain respect for China, we should step down. This is a universal principle." Deng was playing an old revolutionary's tune, appealing for sympathy as leader of a nation that had been the victim of generations of foreign domination and exploitation. While it is true that China has good cause to resent foreign interference in its internal affairs, it is also true that as a nation which now seeks to benefit from relations with foreign countries, it must learn to be sensitive to their concerns about human rights and other issues.

Still, at the end of my three-hour, no-holds-barred exchange with China's paramount leader, I was more convinced than ever that despite our disagreements over the tragedy that had darkened his last months in power, Deng Xiaoping—the first major Communist leader to sense the failure of communism as an economic doctrine and to take dramatic steps to reform it—was one of the most important leaders of our era.

To drive home my message about Tiananmen Square, I used my formal public toasts at two of the banquets the Chinese leaders held in my honor.

I told Li Peng, the hard-line premier, that our differences over the massacre were "huge and unbridgeable." I asked him whether China would "turn away from greatness and consign itself to the backwater of oppression and stagnation? Or will it continue to venture forth on the open seas on a journey which may at times be rough but which leads to progress and peace and justice for its people?"

In responding to the toast of China's president, Yang Shangkun, who was also closely linked to the crackdown, I warned that "many in the United States, including many friends of China, believe the crackdown was excessive and unjustified" and that it had "damaged the respect and confidence which most Americans previously had for the leaders of China." I asked him a series of tough questions that I knew he and his colleagues did not expect to hear, especially from one they considered an old friend. Would martial law and political repression be permanent features of life in China? Would the courageous and bold economic reforms Deng had initiated ten years before be abandoned to the stagnation that had nearly strangled China previously? In rooting out corruption and inflation, would China also root out the delicate new growth of individual enterprise that had doubled the per capita income of its people?

It was uncomfortable for me as a guest to ask these questions, and I am sure the Chinese were surprised by my blunt criticism. But I felt it was essential that they understand the depth of the outrage in the United States over the events of June 2–4. I knew it would have more impact coming from a friend rather than one of their hostile American critics. They could also see that my intention was to show that the crackdown blocked the road to a goal we both wanted to reach eventually: a return to better relations between our two countries. I concluded my toast by observing that while the death of innocent people in June had been a great tragedy, "another tragedy would be the death of a relationship and of policies that have served so well." My message was clear: While what they had done in June was tragic and inexcusable, it was in the interests of both the United States and China for our relationship to continue in spite of it.

I left China guardedly optimistic about the future. While I was still in the country its leaders had already taken two small but telling steps. They had modified the enforcement of martial law in the capital by replacing People's Liberation Army soldiers with less-threatening Beijing police officers. Also, Li Peng had complied with my blunt demand that the soldiers who were guarding the entrance to the American Embassy be ordered to put away the AK-47 automatic rifles they had been brandishing at American diplomats.

But I was not naive enough to believe that these two small gestures meant anything in the long term. The true source of my optimism was a renewed sense that after some necessary retrenchment Deng's economic reforms would continue and that with them would inevitably come renewed pressure for political reforms. Each leader I had met had expressed strong support for the fundamentals of Deng's reforms. Particularly impressive in this regard were younger leaders such as the able education minister Li Tieying, the brilliant propaganda minister Li Ruihuan, and the extraordinarily competent mayor of Shanghai, Zhu Rongji. They all know that the road back to doctrinaire Marxism-Leninism is a dead end. The only thing that could drive China back down that road would be a renewed effort by the West to isolate China because of the June crackdown.

When I met with President Bush upon my return, I predicted that in the wake of Deng's retirement there would be a major battle for power between the reformers and the reactionaries who want to return China to the policies that existed before 1972. If the United States adopts a policy of isolating China, it will only be grist for the mill of the reactionaries. Contact and cooperation with all the major Western countries are essential if those who support Deng's reforms and his opening to the West are to prevail in the inevitable struggle for power.

America must take the long view in charting its course. China is a nuclear power. It is one of the world's five major geopolitical power centers. It continues to be a key player in the crucial regional conflicts in Afghanistan, Cambodia, Korea, and the Middle East and the Persian Gulf. In addition, Taiwan's security interests and the interests of the people of Hong Kong are best served by close ties between its friends and Beijing. The United States and China also promote common interests on bilateral issues, such as intelligence cooperation, trade, and cultural exchange. And with the environment now becoming a major concern in the industrialized countries, how is it going to be possible to deal with global environmental problems without the cooperation of those who rule over one fifth of all the people in the world?

As much as we might not like it, we must accept that fact that our relations to other countries should be determined primarily by what they do outside, not inside, their borders. But apart from our strategic concerns, a policy of sanctions and isolation would run contrary to the interests of the Chinese people. In our efforts to punish the leaders of China, we would punish the people of China even more. Such a policy would tend to enhance the position of leadership factions that would turn toward Moscow. It would also undercut those in the Chinese leadership who seek to put their country's progressive reforms back on track. Contact with the West has been a major impetus for peaceful change in China. In fact, without our rapprochement in 1972 and Deng's policy of opening to the West, the ideas of inalienable rights and democratic government which fueled the democracy movement would have remained largely unknown in China. If we wish to encourage future political and economic reform, we must not isolate China and thereby remove one of the principal forces propelling peaceful change. The Great Wall of China is very thick. It is difficult enough to be heard when you are inside the wall. It is impossible to be heard when you are outside the wall.

Restoring the close working relationship between our two countries will not occur, however, until the Chinese leaders respond to President Bush's conciliatory actions and put China once again on the path to economic and political reforms. The crisis in our relations that I described to Deng persists in spite of the failure of the Congress in January 1990 to override President Bush's veto of the bill to protect Chinese students studying in the United States. The bill was not needed, since the administration had already promised that no student would be sent back to China against his will. If the veto had been overridden, the door that we opened in 1972 might have slammed shut. In making a purely symbolic, redundant gesture to 40,000 students in the United States, Congress would have risked destroying whatever opportunity 40 million students in China might have had to study in the United States. But as I warned the Chinese ambassador a few days after the vote, the failure of the override effort would not necessarily mark the end of the efforts by some in Congress to impose further sanctions.

During my meeting in Beijing with General Secretary Jiang, Deng's designated successor, I presented a list of sixteen steps

China could take to show the world it was not deaf to calls for progress on human rights. Some of the steps have now been taken, including the lifting of martial law, the release of some student demonstrators, the reinstatement of a Peace Corps program in China, and the lifting of sanctions against the Voice of America. Other issues I discussed with the Chinese, including the release of dissidents Fang Lizhj and his wife and the suspension of the crackdown on dissidents, had not been resolved as of early February. The Chinese leaders must understand that these issues stand in the way of improved Sino-American relations.

Especially in view of the ouster of hard-line regimes in Eastern Europe, it is not easy for those in Beijing to make concessions to forces they may feel seek to bring about the same result in their country. But the political realities faced by President Bush and other supporters of good relations with China make it essential that China's leaders deal with these issues forthrightly. In mediating between two fundamental interests—maintaining stability in China and constructive relations with the West—the Communist government in Beijing faces the greatest test since the revolution that brought it to power forty-one years ago.

In 1985, I asked Hu Yaobang if he thought the new Soviet general-secretary, Mikhail Gorbachev, would follow China's lead in reforming and opening up his country's economy. He smiled and answered, "If he does not, the Soviet Union will disappear as a great power by the middle of the twenty-first century." When I met Gorbachev for the first time in the Kremlin in 1986, I was impressed by his charisma, his intellect, and his decisiveness. But what impressed me most was his absolute self-confidence. Unlike other Soviet leaders I had known, Gorbachev was so sure of himself and his purpose that he could openly accept the validity of Hu's dark prophesy.

As I stood in his splendidly decorated office, I thought back to the time that I had met Khrushchev and Brezhnev on my visits to the Soviet Union and on their visits to the United States. While Khrushchev knew the Soviet strategic arsenal was inferior to ours, he tried to cover up that shortcoming by bragging shamelessly about Soviet capabilities. By 1972, while Brezhnev knew the Soviet Union had nearly caught up with the United States in the strategic balance, he felt it was necessary to insist at every opportunity that the Soviet Union *was* equal and no longer inferior.

Gorbachev knew that the Soviet Union was now superior in the most powerful and accurate strategic weapons, land-based intercontinental missiles. Unlike Khrushchev and Brezhnev, Gorbachev was so confident of his strengths that he did not fear talking about his weaknesses.

I found him to be just as tough as Brezhnev but better educated, more skillful, more subtle, and not as obvious while making the same points. Brezhnev used a meat ax in his negotiations. Gorbachev uses a stiletto. But beneath the velvet glove he always wears, there is a steel fist.

He observed that the United States and the Soviet Union have in common the fact that we are both very big continental countries. Consequently, we both have a world view rather than a parochial view. Then he went on to say that while we were the two strongest nations in the world, we were essentially "islands in an ocean of other countries."

He had a very fast reaction time. I referred to one of his recent speeches, in which he had said that the security of one nation cannot be based on the insecurity of another. I pointed out that the historical record clearly demonstrated that neither the United States nor the Soviet Union could or would allow the other to have superiority and that the concept of attempting to gain security by achieving and maintaining nuclear superiority over the other was a myth. When I finished this analysis, I remarked that by making these points to him it was like a preacher preaching to the choir. He got the point instantly, laughed uproariously, and responded in effect that what we needed in the world in this respect was more preachers and bigger choirs.

Our most spirited discussion involved the Strategic Defense Initiative. He said that the Soviet Union was a strong country with enormous resources and was prepared to do anything necessary to defend its interests. He said it was a myth that the Soviet Union opposed SDI because it feared the huge cost to the economy or because it could not keep up technologically. He went on to say that the Soviets had their own SDI program and that their research was making progress in different ways than ours. He was emphatic in declaring that the Soviet Union would be able to evade and overcome any SDI system that the United States might eventually deploy.

His major objection to SDI, he insisted, stemmed not from economic or military concerns but his belief that if SDI went forward, there would be a massive spiral in the arms race that would inevitably lead to increased tensions between the Soviet Union and the United States and destroy any chance for a new, less confrontational relationship. He declared that only if we could reach an agreement on controlling the arms race could we expect to make significant progress on regional conflicts, trade, and other issues where we have a common interest. He made these points vigorously and persuasively, but there is no doubt whatever in my mind that his major concern was and remains that the huge cost of competing with the United States in developing SDI would bankrupt the already strapped Soviet economy.

I found Gorbachev to be a very cool customer in our conversation. Whenever I made a statement to which he objected, he would come back strongly and forcefully. At times he seemed to find it difficult to control his emotions. I wondered at the time whether it was anger or acting. It was probably a little of both. Cold calculation generally dominated his demeanor. At the conclusion of our conversation, I asked him if I could speak to him personally, and he nodded. I said, "You are a fortunate man—you are the same age I was when I was elected President. I made a small difference in terms of my initiatives toward the Soviet Union and China. You have many more years ahead of you in office, and you can make a much bigger difference by establishing a better relationship between the Soviet Union and the United States, not only with President Reagan but also with his successors." While I was simply trying to plant a positive idea and wrap up the meeting on a positive note, he reacted impassively. Such idealistic.rhetoric had very little effect on him. Like his predecessors, Gorbachev was always coldly calculating in major substantive discussions.

As I traveled around Moscow in 1986, I detected little change in the conditions of everyday life since my first visit in 1959. The people were reasonably well dressed, the cars slightly more numerous, the roads still atrocious, and the vodka lines profoundly depressing. In spite of this, I came away with the same favorable impression of the Russian people that I always had from my visits. They are a strong and proud people, patriotic to the motherland but not the party-state apparatus, and desperately wishing for friendly relations with America. It again reinforced my belief that the Soviet state, not the Soviet peoples, represents our adversary in the U.S.-Soviet conflict. We should always remember that Russians and Americans can be friends. Because of our irreconcilable differences, the governments of the Soviet Union and the United States cannot be friends but cannot afford to be enemies.

When I saw him in London in 1985, Christopher Soames, Churchill's son-in-law, recounted a telling incident from a trip to the Soviet Union. He was touring the farmlands of the Ukraine with the then Soviet prime minister, Aleksei Kosygin. At the time, Soviet agriculture was in one of its characteristic slides from bad to worse. In a moment of candor, Kosygin remarked, ''Both of our countries will change, but we will move more toward you than you toward us.'' Gorbachev's reforms—which in rhetoric, if not reality, stress the need to introduce market forces—have borne out Kosygin's prediction.

Whether Gorbachev's reforms will go far enough or fast enough to rescue the Soviet economy from its apparently almost terminal illness remains to be seen. But he has one advantage over his predecessors. He knows his weaknesses, faces up to them squarely, and possesses the will to consider and even possibly implement drastic reforms.

I saw another side of Gorbachev when I met in 1987 and 1989 with General Abdul Rahim Wardak, one of the top military leaders and field commanders of the Afghan resistance. He provided a stark contrast to the popular American image of the Afghan freedom fighter as a primitive, poorly educated Islamic warrior. A former officer in the Afghan government army before the Communist takeover in 1978, Wardak had been the top graduate in his class in the U.S. allied military exchange program. In our conversation, he not only demonstrated an acute understanding of military science in explaining his tactics in ''Operation Avalanche,'' a resistance attack in which hundreds of Soviet troops were killed, but also displayed an impressive grasp of geopolitics.

Gorbachev's benign image in the West was belied by his actions in Afghanistan. When he came into power in 1985, he drastically escalated the war against the resistance and the KGB-sponsored terrorist bombing campaign in Pakistan. In 1987, I asked Wardak whether Gorbachev's apparent new interest in UN-sponsored peace talks on Afghanistan indicated that he was simply trying to ''get rid of a loser.'' Wardak answered that he thought Gorbachev had a more subtle strategy. Given Russia's longstanding desire to control Afghanistan and the Soviet Union's proven determination not to allow the toppling of a Communist regime, he argued, Gorbachev's likely motivation was to lull the West into a sense of false security and to win the war through diplomacy. I agreed, and his analysis turned out to be right.

Unfortunately, U.S. policymakers naively assumed that Gorbachev would simply roll over and play dead in Afghanistan after the 1988 Geneva agreement. In 1989, when I met with Wardak again, Soviet forces had withdrawn from Afghanistan, and he had just returned from leading his forces in the battle for the eastern city of Jalalabad. His efforts to take the city had been derailed by the United States' failure to adequately equip and supply the resistance to fight in the new conventional phase of the war. While the resistance had to call off all offensive operations because of an acute shortage of ammunition, Gorbachev poured in hundreds of millions of dollars' worth of weapons each month for the Kabul regime. Though frustrated, Wardak stressed that the resistance could still win militarily but that further progress would be impossible without additional supplies. What Wardak knew, and what the West must learn from Afghanistan, was that while Gorbachev might have changed tactics, the Kremlin's geopolitical goals remain the same.

In addition to visiting the major powers, I also toured many parts of the Third World since leaving office. In 1985, I went back to many of the countries I had visited on my first trip abroad as Vice President in 1953. The contrasts I witnessed were mind-boggling, particularly in Korea, Hong Kong, Singapore, Malaysia, and Thailand. It is astounding how they have been transformed by the free-market policies that have fueled their economic takeoffs.

But the most profound change I noticed was on the ideological front. In every country I visited in 1953, I met a number of non-Communist educators, labor leaders, and even political officials who were debating among themselves whether the Communist model, despite its flaws, might be the best path for rapid economic development. Some thoughtful people were still enamored with the vision of Lincoln Steffens, an American newspaper reporter, who after returning from a visit to the Soviet Union shortly after the Bolshevik Revolution wrote, "I have been over into the future and it works." Today, leaders throughout the Third World have seen that future and know that it does not work. They have also seen that free-market policies *do* work, not only in the West but also in East Asia.

My saddest experience in traveling abroad was the funeral of the Shah of Iran in Cairo, in July 1980. No one was sent from Washington to represent the United States at a funeral for a leader who had been one of our staunchest and most loyal friends. I was reminded of a haunting remark President Ayub Khan of Pakistan made to me in 1964. In commenting on U.S. complicity in the assassination of President Diem of South Vietnam, he said that event proved "that it is dangerous to be a friend of the United States; that it pays to be neutral; and that sometimes it helps to be an enemy." It was an observation that again came to mind when I was informed of the mysterious death, in an airplane crash apparently caused by sabotage, of another staunch friend of the United States, President Zia ul-Haq of Pakistan.

Since I first spoke of the five emerging major power centers in 1971, global change has accelerated and transformed the geopolitical landscape. Western Europe has rapidly advanced toward becoming an economic superpower, though it remains politically fragmented and could well lose the cohesion provided by NATO if Gorbachev's diplomatic offensive continues to meet little resistance. Japan has achieved the status of an economic superpower, but has advanced only haltingly toward establishing a commensurate political role. China has exceeded all expectations by doubling its GNP and per capita income from 1979 to 1989 and has become the number-three political player on the world scene, despite the setback caused by the tragic events at Tiananmen Square. It is the Soviet Union that has fared the worst. Its geopolitical offensive in the 1970s yielded a collection of economic basket cases, and its huge military machine has placed a crushing weight on its sagging economy.

In academic circles, it has been fashionable to argue that in the late twentieth century the United States has become a declining power. That view is profoundly mistaken. We do have difficult problems, such as the federal deficit, rampant drug abuse, high crime, and too many mediocre schools. But we must keep in mind that the U.S. economy ranks number one in terms of overall productivity, that access to the U.S. market remains indispensable to our allies and friends, that the dollar continues to be the central currency of the international system, and that our people have kept our country in the forefront of technological and scientific innovation.

In geopolitical terms, the United States continues to be the world's only military, economic, political, and ideological superpower. Moscow has military might. Western Europe and Japan have economic clout. China, because of its size, enjoys political influence. But the United States alone is a major player in all dimensions of world power. It is a distinction that implies a profound responsibility for shaping the course of world events.

These tens of thousands of miles of travel abroad were indispensable in keeping me abreast of the changes sweeping the world and in helping me shape my ideas about the opportunities for the United States to develop new policies to advance its interests and values.

I chose five different ways to disseminate my views to those who made decisions—books, speeches, columns, television, and backgrounders.

My books illustrate the progression over the years of my thinking on foreign policy, particularly regarding the U.S.-Soviet relationship. At the core of my view was the idea that American policy must involve a balance among three elements — deterrence, competition, and negotiation. In *The Real War*, I put the emphasis on the need to strengthen our deterrent, both on the strategic level and in the geopolitical competition around the world. Published in 1980, the book was a *cri de coeur* in which I stressed the need to counter Moscow's aggressive probes. Despite his unquestionably good intentions, I believed that President Carter had failed to assess accurately the expansionist impulse behind Moscow's foreign policy and that in trying to preserve detente at almost any cost had sent the wrong signals. It was critically important, in my view, to restore American strength and leadership.

In *Real Peace: A Strategy for the West*, which I published in a private edition in 1983, I shifted the emphasis toward the need to develop a new diplomatic relationship with Moscow. I believed the Reagan administration understood the need for deterrence and competition but lagged in developing the necessary superpower diplomacy.

In *1999: Victory Without War*, published in 1988, I addressed the new situation we faced with Gorbachev in power in the Soviet Union and with the old bipolar distribution of power beginning to give way as new power centers emerged in Europe, Japan, and China. I believed that the United States lacked a coherent long-term strategy of deterrence, competition, and negotiation. I tried to chart out such a course, not only for coping with challenges presented by the new leadership in Moscow but also for orchestrating common policies with the new three other emerging power centers.

In between my foreign-policy books, I wrote two other works, *Leaders* in 1982 and *No More Vietnams* in 1985. *Leaders* was a treatise on leadership. It was a series of monographs on some of the major world leaders whom I had met—such as Churchill, de Gaulle, Adenauer, Yoshida, Chou En-lai, and Khrushchev—who had made a difference in history. In *No More Vietnams,* I pointed out that the tragedy of the Vietnamese boat people and the human catastrophe of the Cambodian holocaust could have been avoided if we had only enforced the Paris Peace Agreement in 1973 and provided Saigon and Phnom Penh with as much support as the Soviets gave Hanoi. In Vietnam, we tried and failed in a just cause. I wrote that the slogan "No More Vietnams" could mean we would not try again but should mean we would not fail again.

I personally find writing to be a major effort. It does not come easily to me. Fortunately, I had excellent editorial assistance from Ray Price on *The Real War* and *Leaders* and from Marin Strmecki and John Taylor on *No More Vietnams, Real Peace,* and *1999.* It took me months to develop the first outlines and to dictate the first drafts. In editing later drafts, I would sometimes take a full day to craft a sentence to convey a precise thought or to formulate a memorable line. After each book, I have vowed that it would be the last. But apart from the benefit of publicizing my views, writing books had another invaluable fallout. The process forced me to think through all aspects of the problem. It is only when you totally concentrate on a problem that new ideas come to you.

In retrospect, I sometimes wondered whether devoting the time and effort to write books was justifiable. While *Six Crises, RN: The Memoirs of Richard Nixon, The Real War, No More Vietnams,* and *1999* were all international bestsellers, a serious non-fiction bestseller at best reaches only about a hundred thousand people. The books, therefore, had to be supplemented by other activities. First of all, I decided to follow up with speeches. My problem at the outset was to choose which audiences to address. In the eight years after I returned to New York in 1980, I received over 6,400 speaking invitations from all over the United States and over 1,200 from abroad. Since I had a policy of not accepting honoraria, I was able to select the best forums for serious foreign-policy discussion without regard to any financial consideration. I accepted invitations to address a few audiences where I knew that heavyweight opinion makers would be in attendance. These included the American Society of Newspaper Editors, the American Newspaper Publishers Association, economic clubs in New York, Detroit, and Chicago, and foreign affairs councils in Texas and in California. While the speeches were well received and the question-and-answer periods always stimulating, the lasting impact of a speech was less than that of a book. The same was true of columns and op-ed pieces which I wrote for *Time, Newsweek, The New York Times, The Wall Street Journal,* the London *Sunday Times,* the *Washington Times,* and the *Los Angeles Times* syndicate.

One of my favorite forums was off-the-record backgrounders for the editorial boards of *The New York Times, The Wall Street Journal,* the *Washington Times,* the *Los Angeles Times,* the Hearst Corporation, the news magazines, and the television networks. Some of my friends wondered why I spent the time required to give such backgrounders since none of them gave me any publicity. They missed the point. My purpose was not to get publicity for myself, but if possible to provide insights that might be useful to the boards as they prepared their editorials, columns, and news reports.

I turned down scores of requests to do television interviews. They would have provided publicity, but most of those who made the requests were interested in the man and not his ideas. I was fortunate, however, in finding several commentators who were interested in my views and who asked probing, serious questions and allowed me to give responsive answers. They included Patrick Buchanan, Jerry Dunphy, Bryant Gumbel, Peter Jennings, Morton Kondracke, Ted Koppel, Bernard Shaw, Barbara Walters, Theodore White, and the panel of Tom Brokaw, John Chancellor, and Chris Wallace on a special hour-long edition of NBC's "Meet the Press." On reflection, I am still not sure it was worth appearing on these programs because television is essentially an entertainment and not an educational medium.

What positive effect if any all this activity has had, I do not know. I do know that it had one negative fallout. Despite my statement at Oxford, my critics saw what they considered to be a sinister purpose—that I was "orchestrating yet another comeback." If this is so, my "orchestra" is really a one-man band, because I do not have any control over what anyone else thinks, says, or writes.

Besides, as I told the "Meet the Press" panel in 1988, if I am trying to make a comeback, "What am I going to come back to? We already have a very good mayor in Saddle River, and we have a very good governor in the state of New Jersey. It isn't a comeback. It isn't to be well thought of. The purpose is to get a message across, and then let history judge." When Chancellor asked me how history would remember me, I predicted, "History will treat me fairly. Historians probably won't, because most historians are on the left."

The more successful an appearance, the greater the counterreaction. The owner of *The Washington Post,* Kay Graham, was so impressed by the enthusiastic applause I received after addressing her fellow publishers at their convention in San Francisco that she ordered her editor to put a smiling picture of me on the cover of *Newsweek* with the title "He's Back." My friends were pleased and my opponents were livid. The *Columbia Journalism Review* even went so far as to urge the national press not to report my future activities, except presumably my obituary. Most of its readers, I am sure, shared that view. But the same pattern that had plagued or benefited me all of my public life repeated itself: While they liked me even less than before, I was news. Like moths to a flame, reporters cannot resist reporting a good news story.

In any case, their views were irrelevant as far as I was concerned. As I said at Oxford, I shall continue to speak up for the policies that will lead to peace and freedom as long as I live. If people are interested in what I have to say, they can tune in. If they aren't, they do not have to. I intend to continue to speak out on the important issues for those who do want to hear my views.

But to continue to be even marginally effective, I can accept only a fraction of the invitations that come in. The quicker road to "rehabilitation" would be to exploit the inevitable public sympathy that comes to even the most controversial public figure with the onset of old age. It would be easy to play the kindly, omnipresent elder statesman, attending Rotary conventions and Boy Scout jamborees by the score, offering the same warmed-over platitudes to audience after audience, and appearing before the TV cameras whenever I was asked to offer free, unsolicited advice to the President on the latest international or domestic crisis.

In short, to stop being a villain in some people's eyes, I would have to become a deadly bore in everybody's eyes. I could be less controversial but also less relevant, or I could remain controversial but retain a certain amount of influence. I chose the latter, more difficult path. I am not saying that as a result I am always right and others always wrong. But the person who thinks before he speaks and speaks only when he has something meaningful to say, instead of answering spasmodically every time someone asks him for his opinion, is far more likely to make a real contribution to solving the many problems we face as a nation.

As I look back on the dark days after my resignation, my most vivid memory is of a conversation I had with Ambassador Walter Annenberg shortly after I returned to San Clemente in 1974. He knew I was discouraged. He tried to buck up my spirits. He said, "Whether you have been knocked down or are on the ropes, always remember that life is ninety-nine rounds." Today, the battle I started to wage forty-three years ago when I first ran for Congress is not over. I still have a few rounds to go.

TWO

4

FAMILY

I always find it amusing when psycho-historians I have never met conclude that I have what they consider to be a warped personality. Usually they trace it to my poor, lower-middle-class family. In fact, these pseudo-biographers are telling you more about themselves than about me, because it is obvious that in their books, *lower* class equals a *lack* of class.

When Lou Gehrig was honored at Yankee Stadium after it became known that he was suffering from a fatal illness, he responded to the fans' emotional ovation by saying, "Today I consider myself the luckiest man on the face of the earth." I am sure my younger brother, Ed, and the other three who have passed away, Harold, Don, and Arthur, would have agreed with me that the five Nixon brothers were the luckiest boys in the world precisely because of our family heritage.

In speaking of his early life during the first speech he gave in the 1952 Presidential campaign, General Eisenhower said, "We were very poor, but the glory of America is that we didn't know it then." I suppose it could be said that we too were poor. But our parents left us a legacy far richer than anything money could buy.

I would not recognize my father from the grotesque caricatures that have appeared in some of the media. They picture him as a crude, uneducated oaf who did not have the respect of his sons and was disliked by most who knew him. If they had been privileged to know him as I did, they would have painted a very different picture.

I have never known anyone who worked harder and longer than he did. His mother died of tuberculosis when he was eight years old, and he had to quit school and go to work full time after he finished the sixth grade. He worked as a streetcar motorman and on a farm in Ohio, as a sheep shearer in Colorado, as an oil field roustabout in California, and as a carpenter. He built the house where I was born in Yorba Linda, California—and he built it well, because it is still standing. He was self-educated but well educated. School for him was not the end but the beginning of his education.

He was a gifted, natural speaker. My cousin, Jessamyn West, told me that he was the best Sunday School teacher she ever had, just as her father, Eldo West, was the best Sunday School teacher I ever had. He had driving ambition, not for himself but for his sons. Above all, he wanted them to have the education he had been unable to have.

He was a fighter, but always verbally, never physically. He argued with people because he believed things deeply. But the one with whom he probably argued the most, Bill Ross, a liberal Democrat who sold Hygrade bacon and ham to our market, was one of his best friends and a pallbearer at his funeral. He also fought for his rights. I recall the time he received a speeding ticket when he was on his way to hear the great evangelist, Paul Rader, speak in Los Angeles. Rather than pay the $15 fine, he contested it in court. When the traffic judge ruled in his favor, he wrote out a check for $15 and sent it to Paul Rader. I have always assumed, incidentally, that the judge must have liked Rader as well as my father did.

He wanted me to become the best orator and debater in the country. I vividly recall my first debate. I was in the sixth grade, and our teacher pitted the girls against the boys. The subject was "Resolved: That it is more desirable to own a home than to rent one." The girls were assigned the affirmative, and the boys were stuck with the negative, which I thought was a sure loser. My father advised me to concentrate on the financial aspects of owning and renting. He pointed out that it might make you feel better to own a home, but it cost less to rent one because you left the burdens of repairs and utilities to the landlord. He helped me add up the numbers in a sample case. That argument in hand, the boys won the debate.

The next year, the debate subject was "Resolved: That insects are more harmful than beneficial." Again the boys were assigned the negative, and again I thought we were stuck with a loser. How could anyone defend flies, mosquitos, gnats, and all the irritating insects that made it necessary to spray our lemon trees with foul-smelling chemicals each year? Again, though, my father took matters in hand. Advising me to consult an expert, he drove me to

Riverside where I talked to my uncle, Philip Timberlake, who was married to my mother's oldest sister, Aunt Edith. He was an entymologist for the State Inspectors Service who prided himself on having one of the finest butterfly collections in the state. He was the only one in our large extended family who smoked. While my father didn't approve of smoking, every year at the family Christmas reunion he gave Uncle Tim a can of Prince Albert tobacco, the most popular brand in our store. I can see Uncle Tim now, after our noontime Christmas dinner, lighting his pipe and taking off for the woods with his butterfly net. Some people thought he was a bit strange, but my father knew he was just smart. When I told him my problem, he pointed out that without bees and other insects that carry pollen from tree to tree and bush to bush, all foliage would die. With that argument, we trumped the girls and won the debate.

Thanks to my father, I learned an invaluable lesson in those first two debating experiences—that the best tactic in a debate is always to concentrate on one fundamentally strong argument rather than to scatter your fire over a broad area. When I was in college, my father accompanied me whenever he could to debates. On the way home, he would dissect the arguments of our opponents and take a few shots at the judges who had voted against us. His encouragement and advice were the primary factors that led me to develop any talents I may later have had as a debater.

In those days before radio and television, conversation was much more in vogue than today, and politics was one of our favorite subjects. One of the few times my mother and father disagreed politically was in 1916, when she voted for Woodrow Wilson because he had pledged to keep us out of war, and he stuck with Charles Evans Hughes. For years thereafter he did not let her forget that Wilson got us into war. He was definitely not a stand-pat Republican, however. He was for Bob LaFollette in 1924 because he thought LaFollette was more for the little man than Calvin Coolidge. He was always taking the side of the underdog. Because ours was a small independent grocery store, he was an all-out opponent of chain stores and favored legislation like the Robinson-Patman Act that would have controlled them. Years later when we served together in Congress, Wright Patman and I seldom agreed on anything, but I recall how delighted he was when he learned that what he had done as a young congressman from Texas had made an impact way out in California on the proprietor of a little country grocery store. My father was even a supporter of the

Townsend Plan, which would have given everybody over sixty $200 a month, because during the Depression, he was so concerned about the effects of unemployment that he felt something radical had to be done about it. He felt that if older people could afford to retire, younger unemployed people would get their jobs.

While he sometimes sounded gruff, he was really a soft touch when somebody needed help. The tramps who used to trudge along Highway 101 often stopped at the store for a handout. He never turned them down, but he always insisted that they do some work for what he gave them. The work did not amount to much, but he said that no one should get something for nothing.

He was a man of many talents. During the years my mother was in Arizona caring for my brother Harold, he took on the responsibility of baking pies and cakes for the store as she had. They were not as good as hers in the beginning, but within a few months he became an excellent pastry cook. And for our Sunday dinner he always prepared a delicious pot roast garnished with potatoes, carrots, and onions.

What I remember most vividly about him was his passionate belief in self-reliance. Harold suffered with tuberculosis on and off for ten years. The medical costs were a great burden on the family budget. When his condition became so bad that he had to go to a sanitarium, my father sold half the property on which our store was located so he could send him to a private sanitarium rather than the county hospital.

He believed in charity for others but never for himself. When I won the Constitutional Oratorical Championship at Whittier High School, I had worn my only suit, which happened to be brown. Some well-intentioned ladies in the parent-teacher association thought that it would be better if I had a blue suit for the regional finals competition. They offered to buy one for me as a gift. My father was outraged. "We don't need to accept any charity," he said. "We can afford the new suit." He bought it—and incidentally, I have never worn a brown suit since!

One of the disadvantages of living in a rich society is that we sometimes become obsessed with such superficialities of fashion and culture. Do we read, or at least pretend to read, the right books, go to the hottest shows, attend the right parties, and wear only white shirts after five? Worrying about such things is a luxury you can afford only when you have stopped worrying about affording the basics—shelter, food, decent clothes, a good education. One of the tragedies of our prosperity comes when people who have gotten ahead as a result of the sacrifices of others either forget those who have made their success possible—or, even worse, judge them for failing to match our newfound level of sophistication.

One of my best friends was a Greek restaurant owner in Miami. He was very proud of his nephew, whom he was helping to get the college education he had not been able to afford for himself. One day, while I was serving as Vice President, we had lunch together. The nephew spent most of the time correcting his uncle's poor grammar. I could see from the strained look in his eyes that he was embarrassed to be with his uncle. He obviously thought his uncle lacked class. He had it wrong. If he wanted to see someone without class, all he had to do was to look in the mirror.

The incident reminded me of the time my father's Uncle Lyle traveled by bus from his home in Ohio to visit us. My father felt particularly close to him because he had been so kind to him after the death of his mother. Uncle Lyle had never seen the ocean before, and more than anything else he wanted to take a dip in the Pacific. He did not have a swimsuit, and so we had to rent one from a concession stand at Seal Beach. The only one we could get that fit him was an old-fashioned, grotesque-looking knee-length model. He looked like one of those characters in a Mack Sennett comedy. I was somewhat embarrassed when other people on the beach laughed at him. But as he splashed around in the waves, I could see that he was having one of the best times of his whole life. Afterwards, I was ashamed of myself for feeling embarrassed and vowed that never again would I think of myself on such an occasion if some slight embarrassment for me made someone else happy.

As for those who say that my father lacked class, I would simply say that there was never a day I was not proud of him.

I shall always remember the last time I saw him, shortly after I had been nominated for Vice President at the Republican Convention in 1956. He had been desperately ill and asked me to shave him, because he was too weak to do it by himself. When I had finished, he said he felt better.

I told him, "I will see you in the morning."

"I don't think I'll be here in the morning," he replied.

"Dad, you've got to keep fighting," I said.

His last words to me were, "Dick, *you* keep fighting." The next day, he died at the age of seventy-five.

My mother came from a long line of Irish Quakers. My great-grandmother, Elizabeth Price Milhous, died in 1923 at the age of ninety-six, when I was ten years old. I vividly remember how alert she was until the very end. Her great-granddaughter, my cousin Jessamyn West, used her and one of her forebears as the models for Eliza Cope Birdwell in her novel *The Friendly Persuasion,* which later was made into what became Mamie Eisenhower's favorite motion picture and was also selected by Nancy Reagan to show to the Gorbachevs when they visited Washington in 1988. Elizabeth had a reputation as a spell-binding speaker in our branch of the Quaker church, which allowed ministers and choirs like other Protestant denominations. One of our favorite stories at family reunions was of the time she was traveling from her home in Iowa to speak at a Quaker meeting in another part of the state. Since there was no dining car on the train, she made some sardine sandwiches and stuffed them in the pockets of the Quaker cape she always wore. She got so busy preparing her remarks that she forgot to take them out before she spoke. She had chosen one of the Bible's most famous parables as her text. When she took her hands out of her pocket to make an expressive gesture, the sardine sandwiches landed in the laps of those sitting in the front row. It was without question the most realistic sermon on the loaves and the fishes ever delivered.

My grandmother, Almira Milhous, raised nine children and had scores of grandchildren and great-grandchildren. She loved us all equally, but she seemed to take a special interest in me. She wrote poems for me on my birthday and other special occasions. Once she gave me a picture of Lincoln with Longfellow's Psalm of Life in her own handwriting beneath it: "Lives of great men oft remind us/We can make our lives sublime. And, departing, leave behind us/Footprints on the sands of time." The picture hung over my bed until I left home to go to law school in 1934. When I graduated from high school, she gave me a biography of Gandhi, whose concepts of peaceful change and passive resistance appealed to her and to me as well. When she was eighty-eight years of age, she traveled across the country with my family to attend my graduation from law school and brought as a graduation gift a beautifully bound copy of Farrar's *Life of Christ*. She always used the plain speech—Is thee going? Is this thine? My mother used the plain speech in speaking to her sisters and to her mother, but not to her children. What I particularly remember about my grandmother was that her deep passion for peace only increased her concern for the victims of war. She regularly had one of her children or grandchildren drive her to the veterans hospital in Sawtelle to spend a Sunday afternoon visiting with the patients, reading to them, and writing letters for them.

In my farewell remarks to the White House staff on August 9, 1974, I spoke of my mother as a saint. Jessamyn, who loved her as I did, wrote to me afterwards, "I don't think of Hannah as a 'saint.' Saints, I feel, have a special pipeline to God which provides them a fortitude not given ordinary mortals. Hannah was not ordinary; but she did what she did and was what she was through a strength and lovingness which welled up out of her good heart and because of her own indomitable character." She studied for two years at Whittier College before she was married. She was particularly proficient in languages—Greek, German, and Latin. Her assistance and encouragement were probably why Latin was my best subject in the four years I took it in high school. She taught me to read before I went to grammar school and to play Christmas carols on the piano before I had a lesson. While I was still in grade school, I was an avid newspaper reader. I once told my mother I did not think a newspaper should take sides on controversial issues. She pointed out the difference between two kinds of articles, saying an editorial should take sides, but news stories should be objective without editorializing. Too often that distinction is not made today.

She would get up at four o'clock in the morning to bake the pies and cakes we sold in the store to help defray the costs of Harold's illness. She taught us many things, not the least of which was a strong sense of equality and opposition to racial prejudice. Those who came to work on occasion in the store—an Indian girl, a black man, a Mexican boy—always had dinner and supper with the family. There was never a second table in our home. She seldom talked about her religion, but she always lived it. I remember the time we learned that one of our best customers, who attended our church, was a shoplifter. An officer from the sheriff's office recommended arrest and prosecution. My mother objected. She did not want to hurt her. She said, "Let me talk to her." She followed the woman to her car one day and asked her if she wanted to pay for the two items she had slipped into her shopping bag. The woman broke down and cried. She said her husband would divorce her if he found out. My mother asked her to estimate how much she had stolen over a period of several months. She said about $100—a lot of money in those days. She agreed to pay it back at $5 a month. She never came to the store again, but she kept her word, and

85

thanks to my mother, no one in the community ever heard of what she had done.

My mother sacrificed everything for her children. She was like Bebe Rebozo's mother in that respect. Bebe, the youngest of nine children, often tells how his mother would prepare a chicken for the family's dinner and insist on taking the neck for herself. She said she preferred it, but Bebe knew it was because she wanted her children to have the choice pieces. He laughingly recalls that he was fourteen years old before he learned that the neck was not the best part of the chicken.

I shall never forget the three years my mother spent in Prescott, Arizona, where she had taken Harold in the hope that the dry climate would help him recover from tuberculosis. To help make ends meet, she rented a big house and took in three other patients —Larry, Leslie, and a man we called "the Major," a Canadian who had been gassed in World War I. She cooked and cleaned, gave them bed baths and alcohol rubs—everything a nurse does for a patient. As each of them died, she felt their deaths as deeply as if they had been her own sons.

When I joined Eisenhower at the rally in Wheeling, West Virginia, after my "Fund" broadcast in 1952, my mother's wire to him, which she had prepared by herself without my knowledge, was the one he chose to read from among the thousands he had received. It read, "Dear General: I am trusting that the absolute truth may come out concerning this attack on Richard, and when it does I am sure you will be guided right in your decision, to place implicit faith in his integrity and honesty. Best wishes from one who has known Richard longer than anyone else. His mother."

The last time I talked to her, she was in the hospital recovering from a very painful operation. She was not as political as my father, but she always knew exactly what was going on. She had read a column in the *Los Angeles Times* which concluded that because of my defeat in 1962 and my attack on the press thereafter, I had no political future. I could sense that she was depressed about something, and as I was about to leave, I said, "Mother, don't give up."

She pulled herself up and said almost sternly, "Richard, don't *you* give up. Don't let anybody tell you you are through."

For my mother, religion and love were sacred, and she never spoke of either in a familiar way. Whenever I had a major speech to make, she always wrote a note of encouragement, but it was never, "I will be praying for you." It was always, "I will be thinking of you." In her whole life, I never heard her say to me or to anyone else, "I love you." She did not need to. Her eyes expressed the love and warmth no words could possibly convey.

5

RELIGION

Before the 1960 campaign, President Eisenhower suggested that it would be very effective if I were to refer to God more in my speeches. After all, he pointed out, America is a Christian nation, so voters will relate to someone who quotes the Bible and shows in other ways that he shares their faith.

It should have been easy for me to follow his advice. No one could have had a more intensely religious upbringing. My mother was a devout Quaker. My father was a devout Methodist. After they were married, they compromised, and he became a Quaker, too. We regularly went to church four times on Sunday—Sunday School and a worship service in the morning, a young people's meeting called Christian Endeavor, and another worship service in the evening. I played the piano for Sunday School and taught a Sunday School class. We never had a meal without grace. Usually it was silent. Sometimes each of us would recite a verse of scripture. On a few special occasions my mother or father might say a prayer. I read the Bible regularly and still do.

While I was a student at Whittier College, which had a strong religious tradition, my belief in the literal accuracy of the scriptures was shaken, though my faith remained as firm as ever. In an essay I wrote for Dr. Herschel Coffin's class in the Philosophy of Christian Reconstruction, I summarized my belief after three years of college. "The greatness of the universe is too much for man to explain," I wrote.

I still believe that God is the creator, the first cause of all that exists. . . . How can I reconcile this idea with my scientific method? . . . For the time being I shall accept the solution offered by Kant: That man can go only so far in his research and explanations; from that point on we must accept God. What is unknown to man, God knows. The resurrection symbolically teaches the great lesson that men who achieve the highest values in their lives may gain immortality. Orthodox teachers have always insisted that the physical resurrection of Jesus is the most important cornerstone in the Christian religion. I believe that the modern world will find a real resurrection in the life and teachings of Jesus.

I adhere to those same beliefs to this day.

At Duke, I attended worship services every Sunday at the magnificent Duke chapel, where two great ministers, Dr. Elbert Russell, a Quaker, and Dr. Frank Hickman, a Methodist, alternated in preaching the sermon. They had obviously reached a more even division of spiritual labor than had my parents.

With this background, why has it been so difficult for me to follow Eisenhower's advice? Because mine is a different kind of religious faith, intensely personal and intensely private. My mother prayed regularly but always privately, even following the biblical admonition of going into her closet when other people were about. To her, religion was sacred, and she did not believe in speaking familiarly about sacred things. I can never recall her saying, "God bless you." She never questioned the customs of others to be more public in their professions of faith. But she insisted on doing it her way, and I followed her example.

My reticence about public displays of religious faith flows both from the style of my family's religious observances and from a belief that God's will is expressed by men through their actions toward and on behalf of others. In living a Christian life, faith is the first step. Acknowledging your faith is the second. But the most important step is using the energy and creativity faith gives you to make the world a better place.

It would have been out of character, even demagogic, for me to inject my personal religious faith into my speeches. On the few occasions I tried to do so, it was uncomfortable and unnatural. But I understand that it is easier for others. One of my closest friends is former Congressman Joe Waggonner of Louisiana. We talk on the phone regularly. He always concludes a conversation by saying, "God bless you." It sounds natural coming from him. It would sound unnatural coming from me. I have no problem saying, "God bless America." But to say, "God bless you" is too personal and contrary to the way I was brought up.

One reason my asking Henry Kissinger to kneel with me in silent prayer in the Lincoln Bedroom the day before I resigned the Presidency got so much attention was that it was uncharacteristic. It was a very difficult moment, however, and people sometimes do uncharacteristic things at such times. It was not the only unlikely revelation that got attention in those dark days. One of the most unfortunate was the disclosure that I had used profanity. As a matter of fact, most people do, at one time or another—especially in Washington. But since neither I nor most other Presidents had ever used profanity in public, millions were shocked. I have heard other Presidents use very earthy language in the Oval Office, but none of them had the bad judgment to have it on tape. If they did, the tapes are still tucked snugly away—as they should be.

I was the target of considerable criticism when I initiated the custom of Sunday worship services in the White House, despite the fact that those who attended had the opportunity at various times to hear outstanding messages from Protestant preachers, Catholic priests, and Jewish rabbis. Some suggested I should have gone out to church instead of attending a service in the White House. I respect every President's right to determine how he wants to worship on Sunday. But in my case, I much preferred a private service to descending on a church with hordes of pistol-packing Secret Service men and pencil-packing reporters who have to get up early on Sunday and then get down on their knees just because the President has. I had also been repelled by reports of publicity-hungry ministers lecturing Lyndon Johnson about his conduct of the war in Vietnam. Finally, I would not tolerate the spectacle of draft dodgers defiling a church by demonstrating outside because a President was in attendance.

While I did meet with religious leaders in the White House on a number of occasions, I have strong feelings about mixing religion and government. I treasure the friendship and wise counsel Billy Graham has extended to me over the years. On a few occasions, however, I have been in the position of advising him. In 1960, 1968, and 1972 I advised him not to endorse me, or for that matter any other candidate for office. I also urged him not to join the Moral Majority, not because I do not support most of the candidates they do, but because I believe a minister cannot carry out his major mission in life as effectively if he dabbles in politics.

A minister's mission is to change the lives of men and women, not to change governments. The great need in the United States and throughout the world is not just to change governments but to change the people who run and who live under those governments. With all of the talk about the power of the Presidency as a bully pulpit, we must remember that government cannot reach into people's hearts and change them for the better. Only religion can. As I told Billy Graham, he would weaken his ability to change people if he moved over the line and engaged in activities designed to change government.

It is significant that the sharp 35 percent decline in membership of mainline Protestant denominations associated with the National Council of Churches has occurred during the period when social and political crusading has increasingly taken the place of religious messages from the pulpits. As one critic has observed, too many churches seem to have a "political agenda masked with the veneer of spirituality." In the long term, whether a church is on the right or the left, the more political it becomes, the less appeal it has religiously. In a pathetic attempt to be "relevant" on current political issues, many churches have become irrelevant to their major mission of giving people inspiration and guidance on timeless moral and spiritual issues.

Pope John Paul II no doubt approves of some governments and disapproves of others. But one of the major reasons for his enormous influence in the world is that he directs his powerful message of faith directly to people. Those who criticize him and others like Billy Graham for trying to bring their message to people ruled by atheistic Communists are off base. On the contrary, there can be no greater mission than to provide the vision of faith in God to people whose leaders have faith only in themselves.

I believe children should be allowed to have a moment of silence in schools. But I do not believe an amendment allowing school prayer belongs in the Constitution. America has become a great nation in large part because we are conceived and nurtured in strong religious faith. But the real test of faith is whether it is strong enough to tolerate other faiths.

While the majority should not impose its religious views on the minority, the minority should respect the views of the majority. Reverse bigotry by the minority is just as reprehensible as bigotry by the majority. For instance, to oppose the display of Christian religious symbols in public places at Christmas time in the name of separation of church and state is both petty and silly. Christmas is not just another excuse for retailers to rake in profits. It is the celebration of Christ's birthday. Martin Luther King, Jr.'s picture is displayed in public places on the day we celebrate his birthday, and it should be. I am sure he would have agreed that public displays commemorating the birth of Jesus are equally appropriate.

Another equally acrimonious debate has raged from time to time over whether religious training belongs in public schools. My view is that it does—especially since our schools already teach students about the pseudo-religion of Marxism-Leninism. I do not share the views of some well-intentioned anti-Communists that students should not be exposed to courses on Marxism. Being indoctrinated in Marxism is one thing. Learning about a philosophy which in effect still governs one quarter of the world's people is something else. Every educated person should have the opportunity to do so. By the same token, while Marxists are atheists, Marxism is a religion. Students in a free society should be encouraged to learn about their own religious heritage without being prohibited from doing so because of the doctrine of separation of church from state. It is ludicrous to teach young people about the atheistic philosophy adhered to by our major adversaries in the world and yet be denied the opportunity to learn more about the spiritual precepts on which our own nation was founded.

Many of the Europeans who came to the New World were fleeing repressive religious authority, so it is no surprise that the Founders called for a strict separation of church and state. It was not that they were irreligious but rather that memories of a tyrannical church made them see the wisdom of a separate civil authority. Hundreds of years later, many in our intellectual elite mistakenly interpret the Constitution as requiring our society to be totally secular. Whatever their religious backgrounds, they recoil instinctually from symbols as inherently peaceful and non-threatening as a manger on the firehouse lawn at Christmastime or an angel on a postage stamp. Their position is that people who do not share the Christian faith should not have to have such things imposed upon them. Others openly ridicule religious leaders or criticize them for having the gall to state their heartfelt opinions on issues such as abortion or adultery.

Such critics forget how the very spiritual precepts they reject helped make it possible for our society to take root and thrive for as long as it has. This does not mean that every American must be Christian. But it does mean that every American should recognize that the society in which he lives is firmly and inalterably rooted in Judeo-Christian beliefs.

Some say the basic teachings of religion, especially those that have to do with people's relationships with one another, can easily be translated into secular terms. You don't have to believe in God to honor your parents, or to be honest in your business dealings, or to treat others as you would have them treat you. But to separate the teachings of any religion from its mysteries, to demand adherence to its rules without faith in the higher authority from which they flow, is to cut man off from a source of spiritual power that over the centuries has inspired, strengthened, and comforted millions. At a time when the challenges of life are greater than ever, why deprive ourselves of that power? At a time when it is so fashionable to talk about the terrible mess man has made of the world, why do so many intellectuals assume that man alone, without the guidance of God, is capable of fixing it? The miracle of America is that it is "one nation under God." Without God as part of the equation, what makes us special? Many of our opinion leaders are satisfied to think of the United States as just "one nation" among one hundred sixty moral, if not necessarily military or economic, equals. I am not. Perhaps I am being old-fashioned, but I still want America to be something more.

I share with Whittaker Chambers the belief that skeptics are organically unhappy because, as he wrote, "Believing in nothing includes an inability to believe in themselves. Every civilization embodies a certain truth to which it gives reality. When that truth, which is in turn embodied in a faith held religiously whether or not it is wholly religious—when that faith loses its power to inspire men its downfall is at hand. The success of communism . . . is never greater than the failure of all other faiths." If the choice is godless capitalism, which rewards greed, or godless communism, which insists on rigorous egalitarianism, we are in deep trouble.

In the end, it all comes down to whether the individual believes in something greater than himself. As Stepan Trofimovich observed in Dostoyevski's *The Possessed*, "The one essential condition of human existence is that man should always be able to bow down before something infinitely great. If men are deprived of the infinitely great, they will not go on living and will die of despair."

6

TEACHERS

Like most five-year-olds, my youngest granddaughter, Melanie Eisenhower, sometimes likes to stay home rather than go to nursery school. Once, when I asked her why, she said, "I hate school." I told her that I thought she liked her teacher, whom I had met recently on a visit to her school. She thought a moment and said, "I hate school, but I love my teacher."

She comes by her affection for teachers quite naturally. Her grandmother, Pat, was one of Whittier High School's most popular teachers when we first met in 1938. During the eighteen years I attended public grade and high schools, Whittier College, and Duke University Law School, I can recall no poor teachers. I can remember a number of very good ones. I was fortunate to have attended school before the wave of "progressive" reforms in the 1960s radically changed the curriculum and seriously weakened the quality of teaching.

My mother was my first teacher. She spent countless hours encouraging me, helping me with homework, and challenging me to learn. My first-grade teacher was outstanding. My first report card had all E's on it except for writing, in which I got a U, the only time I ever failed a course. Handwriting and drawing never appealed to me. I often wonder if some of the good grades I got in later years were due to the fact that my teachers couldn't read my writing. My fifth-grade teacher, Miss Burum, launched me on a life-long love affair with geography; *National Geographic* became my favorite magazine. My seventh-grade teacher, Lewis Cox, who was also our part-time coach, sparked the interest that led me to become a history major in college.

I found math difficult. But Mr. Miano in algebra and Miss Erns-

94

berger in geometry challenged me to make math one of my best subjects. I vividly recall the time in my sophomore year at Fullerton High School when Miss Ernsberger gave our geometry class a difficult problem and told us that anyone who solved it would get an A in the course. I started to work on it at nine o'clock at night at the table in the kitchen. It was a bitterly cold night, and I kept warm by lighting the fire in the gas oven and leaving the door open. Right after my mother came down to bake pies for the store at four in the morning, I got the answer. After that I never thought there was a problem I couldn't solve if I worked hard and long enough.

Mr. Swartling made chemistry and physics fascinating even for those of us who were more interested in what are now called the "language arts" and "social studies." In his course in oral English, H. Lyn Sheller taught us that a speaker will be more effective when he uses a conversational style rather than flamboyant oratory. Long before television made that approach mandatory, he drilled it into me, and I have followed it throughout my career. Miss Fink loved the English language, and her insistence on strict compliance with the rules of grammar made an indelible impression on me.

Jenny Levin, my American history teacher at Whittier High School, was the toughest grader I ever had. I was not alone in the assessment. Several years later I learned that so many parents complained about the low grades she gave their children that she was relieved of her teaching duties and assigned to be a study hall supervisor. What a loss to her profession that was. In teaching a subject that was easy for me, she was pushing me to reach the level of excellence of which I was capable rather than just being satisfied with being better than average. I have always found that the best teachers were those who graded the hardest, just as the best dentists are those who aren't afraid to hurt you in order to clean out the cavities.

At Whittier College, my first-year French teacher had just completed two years of graduate work in Paris. Long before Professor Higgins made the point in *My Fair Lady,* she insisted that we not only learn how to write the language well but also to pronounce it correctly. Dr. Paul Smith was an inspirational lecturer on American history and the Constitution. I remember him most for his love of books. His mouth would literally water as he read aloud from some newly published book to our class. It was a standing joke among his students that as great as our affection for him was, we avoided sitting in the front seat for fear that some of his moist enthusiasm would reach our desks.

Dr. Albert Upton taught a revolutionary new course called Basic English. I learned from him that the most effective way to write and speak was not with big words but with sparse, lean prose. It was at his suggestion—in fact, insistence—that I read everything that Tolstoy had written in the summer before my senior year.

In his course on the Philosophy of Christian Reconstruction, Dr. Herschel Coffin taught us not just to read the Bible but to understand its profound lessons for our daily lives.

Something else about my teachers at Whittier College continues to amaze me. During the Depression years from 1930 to 1934, the four people I have mentioned, all of whom were full professors with PhDs, took voluntary 25 percent cuts in their $2,500 annual salaries to keep the college from going under. The fact that it did survive and today is rated as one of the better small colleges in the nation is a tribute to their sacrifice and dedication to education.

The Duke Law School did not have such financial problems. Dean Justin Miller was able to recruit a teaching staff of brilliant young professors from throughout the country. Douglas Maggs in Constitutional Law, Charles Lowndes in Taxation, Malcolm McDermott in Criminal Law, Bryan Bolich in Property, and Claude Horack in Equity, were all outstanding scholars in their fields.

David Cavers, who had been first in his class at Harvard Law School, taught Conflict of Laws and was the faculty adviser for our law review, which was then called *Law and Contemporary Problems*. Some people can do two things at the same time. He is the only man I know who could do three. He could grade papers, help me edit a law review article I was writing, and blow absolutely perfect smoke rings. Since smoking anywhere on campus was prohibited at Whittier, I was surprised when professors and students even smoked in the classrooms at Duke. Cavers once told me that Duke also had a no-smoking rule—except when products were made by the American Tobacco Company, which was then the major source of Duke's huge endowment.

Cavers gave me some excellent advice about writing. When I told him how hard it was for me to find exactly the right words to express my thoughts, he said, "You have an affliction common to most writers—intellectual constipation." He said it was sometimes better to write more freely in the first instance rather than trying to write a first draft that would measure up to the standards

UPI/Bettmann Newsphotos

When I arrived in Beijing in 1972, Chou En-lai told me, "Your handshake came over the vastest ocean in the world—25 years of no communication."

My 1985 decision to forgo Secret Service protection improved the quality of my foreign trips. In thousands of miles of travel since then, there has never been an incident. (Meeting people of Beijing during his 1989 visit)

Wide World Photos

When Churchill visited Washington in 1954, he told me an American friend had given him one of those "machines"—a Dictaphone—but that he preferred to dictate to a pretty secretary.

My conversations with de Gaulle were among the most valuable ones I had during my public career. (In Paris in 1969)

A friendly reporter told me, "The worst thing you can do to a member of the press corps is to prove that he has been wrong on a major issue." That is precisely what I did on the Hiss case, and it would not be the last time.

Most of the Peruvian students wanted to shake hands. But soon I felt something glance off my shoulder, and Vernon Walters (in cap behind RN) whispered in my ear, "They are throwing stones." (In Lima in 1958)

Paul Schutzer, *Life* magazine © Time Inc.

My first debate with Kennedy was actually over the Taft-Hartley Act in 1947, when we were both first-term congressmen. On the sleeper train back to Washington, we drew straws to see who would get the lower berth. That time, *I* won. (With Kennedy after the first televised Presidential debate in 1960)

If I had not taken a six-month moratorium from politics in 1967, I would have been chewed up in the early skirmishing for the nomination. Instead, the pieces fell into place. (With Julie, Tricia, and Pat on election night in 1968)

NIXON'S THE ONE!

Claus Meyer/Black Star

Al Fenn, *Life* magazine © Time Inc.

At the urging of Eisenhower's doctor, I asked the President to cancel his plans to add an event to his schedule in Illinois, a key toss-up state in the 1960 campaign. (Campaigning with Eisenhower in 1960)

A campaign teaches a candidate what the voters want, and voters learn what kind of leader the candidate will be. (Campaigning in 1972)

Today Secret Service agents protect candidates from maniacs, and pollsters protect them from voters. (Campaigning with Pat in 1960)

A politician should not assume that the more press conferences he has, the better. It is important not to cheapen the currency by becoming too available. (Meeting the White House press corps in October 1973)

Russians and Americans can be friends. The governments of the Soviet Union and the United States cannot be—but they cannot afford to be enemies. (RN in Minsk, July 1, 1974)

Elliott Erwitt/
Magnum

In 1959 Khrushchev jokingly tried to convince me he was being reasonable by calling one of his colleagues "a hopeless Communist." Gorbachev also still believes in the fatally flawed tenets of Marxism-Leninism. His goal is not to replace the Communist system but to strengthen it. (ABOVE: During the Kitchen debate with Khrushchev in 1959. BELOW: Meeting Gorbachev in 1986)

Tass

of an article for a law review. He must have taught me well, because he sent the article to Supreme Court Justice Robert Jackson, who thought well enough of it to write back a letter of commendation. I was also indebted to Cavers for recommending me for a position on the legal staff of the Office of Price Administration, my first Washington experience. Nothing gave me greater pleasure as Vice President than when I was able to debunk some ludicrous charges that were made against Cavers of pro-Communist sympathies.

I learned one unforgettable lesson in law school from a student rather than a teacher. Over half of the members of my first-year class were Phi Beta Kappas, and I worried whether I could keep my scholarship against such formidable competition. When I confided in Bill Adelson, a third-year student with a brilliant record, he reassured me. "You don't have to worry," he said. "I've noticed how long you study in the law library. You have all that it takes to learn the law—an iron butt." I also learned a lot from working my way through school. I was an assistant to the librarian, Miss Covington; did research for the dean, Claude Horack; and spent a summer mimeographing a new case book on constitutional law for Douglas Maggs. Sometimes the work was boring, but I never resented having to do it.

The professor who influenced me the most at Duke was Dr. Lon L. Fuller, who finished his teaching career at Harvard. He taught the basic course in Contracts as well as it could possibly be taught. But I was particularly fortunate to be one of three third-year students selected to take his course Readings in Jurisprudence. It was a mountaintop experience to have one of the top legal philosophers in the nation share his wisdom with us on our legal heritage from the Greeks, the Romans, the Germans, the French, and the British. His book *The Morality of Law,* based on the Storrs Lectures he delivered at Yale in 1965, should be required reading for anyone interested in law or philosophy. He was also a man of great courage. For a Harvard Law School professor to head the national Scholars for Nixon Committee in 1960 took guts.

Some may be surprised that I have not mentioned a political science professor. The reason is that I never had a course in political science and in fact would not advise anyone who plans a political career to take one. Why? Because politics is an art, not a science. It is the art of getting along with people, and you can learn more about people clerking in a store than sitting in a political science course.

97

Others might contend that four years of Latin in high school was a waste of time, and that four years of French in college could have been compressed to a six-week Berlitz course. I would agree that studying Latin, though useful, is not necessary as a preparation for courses in the modern Romance languages. But I would still recommend Latin for two reasons. First, it is the most disciplined and orderly of all languages. The hours I spent studying Latin taught me to think in a more logical, disciplined way. A second advantage is that English translations do not adequately capture classics of our Roman heritage such as Caesar, Cicero, and Virgil. This is even more true of French. French is a very subtle language. Literal translations sometimes can't convey the real meaning of a French text. Only by reading Rousseau, Voltaire, Montesquieu, and other classics in French can you get their true flavor.

Critics of the kind of education I received might point out that, except for the law, it did not provide useful information about the practical problems a person faces in life. But that is not the point of education. School should discipline and strengthen the mind, teach young people how to think about and solve problems, and make them realize that the world did not begin the moment they were born.

In the sixties, schools became a social and cultural wasteland. In college, curricular decisions were held hostage to student demonstrators who thought they knew better than teachers and administrators what and how young people should learn. In high school, educators and students seemed to spend more time arguing about smoking areas, hair length, and hemlines than they did teaching and learning. In elementary school, students became guinea pigs for the latest theoretical crazes imported from Washington.

In the confusion, the fundamental mission of education was lost. Before the sixties, the job of education was to help students become productive members of society. Good schooling prepared them for the responsibilities of having jobs and families. But during the sixties, the very idea of "having jobs and families" was judged to be hopelessly banal, even corrupt. It became the job of education to mold students into culturally and politically correct citizens of some ideal world that existed only in the brain of the ideologue or theoretician.

It became "racist" to teach Shakespeare to Hispanic children, "racist" to teach traditional English to inner-city black children, "racist" *not* to teach white children Latin American literature or *not* to teach non-English-speaking children in their own language.

Competition was ruled to be dangerous, so grades were tossed out at many colleges—to be replaced by "Pass" or "Fail"—and competitive sports were frowned upon. Standard tests were judged to be racist, sexist, or both. Only last year a women's group complained that a test that asked women about stock dividends was inherently anti-women. In fact, what was anti-women was the group's implicit, condescending suggestion that women couldn't understand dividends as well as men.

Some of the education reforms were probably well meaning. Many, thankfully, have been modified or eliminated completely. But while many of their authors were either naive or ignorant, they were so powerful in the way they controlled the educational system that they risked crippling an entire generation of young people.

When they ruled traditional English "racist," they forgot to tell employers to stop hiring people on the basis of how well they could speak or write.

When they pampered students with non-competitive sports and classes, they left them ill-prepared to deal with law school, medical school, job hunting, and life itself—all of which are ruthlessly competitive.

When they provided places on campus for children to smoke cigarettes, they lost the moral standing to tell them that it is deadly and also wrong to become addicted to cigarettes, alcohol, or drugs.

When schools and colleges were transformed from molders of youth to temples of youth, educators abrogated the responsibility to share the wisdom that can only come from having read more, studied more, suffered more, and triumphed more than young people. In the sixties and seventies teachers did not want to hurt young people by lecturing them, or making them pray, or punishing them, or being too authoritarian. Instead, they struggled to *understand* their students, to be their friends. But the students did not need friends. They needed teachers. By becoming ashamed of American society and uncertain about whether it really had anything of value to offer young people, many educators betrayed the youth of America. They left them alone, bereft, to learn about the world from heavy-metal rock records and slasher movies.

What should they learn instead? My views may not be the conventional wisdom, but because I feel so fortunate to have had a good education, I want to share them with others.

Each student should leave twelfth grade reading English at a twelfth-grade level or better. He should have read great English writers such as Shakespeare, Dickens, the Brontës, and, in translation, great Russian writers such as Tolstoy, Spanish writers such as Cervantes, Latin American writers such as Borges. Black students should know something about Hobbes, Locke, and Rousseau, and white students should know about Gandhi and Martin Luther King, Jr. In short, every student should know a little bit about everything, so he can make an intelligent decision about what he wants to study in greater depth in college.

He should know algebra, geometry, and pre-calculus and the fundamentals of biology, chemistry, and physics. Our students' persistent weakness in these subjects is our educational system's greatest failure. Ever since the Soviets launched Sputnik in 1957, educators have been pushed to emphasize science and math. Today the United States spends more per student on education than Japan, France, Britain, Italy, or Canada. And yet students in all these countries test higher in either science or math than students in the United States. Special interest groups that insist calls for better education should be matched with more government spending on education miss the point. Renewed educational excellence will be found not in dollars alone but also in the deportment of educators rededicated to the traditional methods and values of teaching that helped push the United States to the forefront of the industrialized world.

A student should know the rudiments of a foreign language, be able to recognize at least a few of the great works of Western music, and understand the tenets of Christianity, Judaism, Islam, Buddhism, and the world's other great religion, Marxism-Leninism.

He should have spent some time playing a competitive sport.

He should know the history of his country, and something about the history of the world. This should include contributions of women and minorities that were left out of the curriculum in earlier eras. But these new elements can be added without ejecting the classics of the past. He should know that black soldiers volunteered and fought as free men in the Civil War, and that women have made great scientific discoveries and have composed symphonies, painted masterpieces, and written some of the greatest works of literature.

When he is finished, and he is standing on the stage receiving his diploma from his principal, he should look out over the audience, and his mind and heart should fill to overflowing, not with uncertainty or guilt or confusion, but with pride in what he has accomplished and anticipation about what is to come. He should feel that there is nowhere he cannot go, nothing he cannot accomplish. Making every high school graduate feel these things should be the goal of every elementary and high school teacher.

To keep things in perspective, let me emphasize that when my other grandchildren, Jennie, Alex, and Christopher, bring their friends to visit us in Saddle River, I am amazed by their knowledge of the world and by how bright they are in fields we were not even aware of in our time. They know all about pulsars, black holes, and computers. Young college graduates I meet invariably impress me with how much they know. What concerns me is not the breadth of their education, but the depth. What they must guard against is becoming what Chambers described in *Cold Friday:* "The educated man who knew all about the time-space concept but did not know how to tell what time it was."

We have a magnificent heritage and can never learn too much about it if we are to be able to defend it and to pass it on to our children. It is not fashionable to teach values these days. It is said that we must be flexible enough to meet the challenges of a changing world. But it is even more important that in a changing world we always hold firmly to certain unchangeable values.

In the final analysis, it always comes back to teachers.

In too many communities today, teaching is the most underpaid, unappreciated profession. The physical facilities of the schools I attended would be considered hopelessly inadequate today. But sixty years ago no profession had a higher standard or was more respected than teaching. When we were living in Yorba Linda, our teachers used to come to our home for a family dinner at the end of the school year. It must have been a chore for them, but for my brothers and me these were very special occasions. I particularly remember the time my mother served homemade ice cream topped with maraschino cherries for dessert. I had never had them before. My third-grade teacher ate the ice cream but left the cherries on her plate. People did not count calories in those days, and I always assumed that she left the cherries for me since she could not have helped but notice how much I had enjoyed my first exposure to that delicacy.

Any program of educational reform should put the primary emphasis on the quality of teaching. While we cannot expect our children to love all of their teachers, it is vital that they respect them, and that their teachers be worthy of that respect.

Teachers will earn more respect if they begin to focus more on teaching and less on theory and politics. Teacher unions pass resolutions against funding for the contras, investigate the political and cultural content of books and television programming, and lobby tirelessly for higher salaries and benefits. The National Education Association recently wasted union money by distributing illustrated ''congressional trading cards'' with pictures of each member of Congress, prompting congressmen to waste taxpayers' money by writing one another to request autographed copies of their colleagues' cards so they could complete their sets. As was the case even back when I attended Whittier College fifty-five years ago, the excruciatingly boring courses offered to education majors still emphasize *how* to teach rather than *what* to teach. Many teachers still worry more about their students' feelings and cultural awareness than whether they can read, write, add, or think.

Someday there may be time for all of these elective subjects, but for now teachers have to get back to the basics—a tougher curriculum, more time in the classroom for each student, and raises for teachers based on performance as well as seniority. Without these and other measures, such as parental choice, our young people will fall so far behind that we will run the risk of entering the next century as a nation of semi-literates in a world of PhDs.

7

STRUGGLE

In his eloquent keynote speech at the 1952 Republican Convention, Congressman Walter Judd told a charming story about helping his daughter with her homework. "I can get the right answer almost every time, and she would like to have me do it for her," he said. "I'll help, suggest, advise, counsel, nudge, maybe pray, but I don't work them for her, not because I don't love her, but because I do, and I want her to succeed, and that is the way for her to grow and to learn how to solve problems." One of the hardest things for parents is to resist the temptation to make life too easy for their children. It is contrary to human nature, but nonetheless true, that not giving children something they want is often an indication not of how little you love them, but how much.

My father's life-long ambition was that his five sons would have what he was unable to get: a college education. He never went into the dreary routine that we had life so much better than he had it, since he had to quit school when he was eleven to go to work full time to help the family make ends meet. Instead, he held up as an example to us his younger brother Ernest, who had worked his way through college, earned a PhD, and was teaching at Penn State. He did not know it, but he gave us something we could never learn in college—the knowledge that life is not easy and that the time to develop the strength to meet its challenges is during your younger years. I do not mean to suggest that it is good to make life hard for children. But if you make it too easy, their inevitable realization as adults that life is a continuing struggle may find them unprepared for it.

In our private talks in Beijing, Chou En-lai often came back to the theme that those who travel smooth roads do not develop strength. Certainly anyone who had survived the Long March could speak with authority on that subject. But Mao Tse-tung carried the concept too far. For him, struggle was the end, not a means to an end. He could lead a struggle, but he could not build a nation. Because he felt that life in the 1960s had become too easy for young people, he put China through the horrors of the Cultural Revolution. Teachers were forced to work in factories; scientists were made to work as peasants in the rice fields; and China's quest for progress was set back at least a generation.

In the United States in the sixties there was a swing to the other extreme. The era of permissiveness and the ridiculous concept that "the kids are always right," that children knew more than parents and students knew more than teachers, led to ugly consequences for the young and for the nation. We are still living with them today. George Bush is right in focusing our concern on children growing up in ghettos without hope or love or without guidance or support from their parents. If we do not act now, their personalities will be permanently twisted and their lives destroyed. But we must not let our compassion push us to the other extreme of assuming that hard work and struggle in early life stunt a personality and that those who endure it cannot compete with those who had it easy.

Next to my father, the man who influenced me most was my coach. I was not a good athlete. I went out for football, basketball, baseball, and track, and never made a letter. But I learned more about life from sitting on the bench with Chief Newman than I did getting As in philosophy courses.

He taught us how to win. You don't win by playing as well as you think you can. You win by playing better than you think you can.

He taught us how to lose. He never repeated that tired refrain, "It is not whether you win or lose, but how you play the game." We must always play to win but accept that sometimes we lose. When we lose, we should get mad—not at the other team but at ourselves, for not playing better.

He taught us how to come back. We must never accept defeat. No matter how many times you get knocked down, get up, and don't let it happen again.

He drove us to over-achieve. I can never remember a time when the Chief congratulated a great player for playing a good game, since the player was only doing what he was capable of doing. But he was always hard on those who did not play up to their capabilities.

In a sense, he taught me a lot about humility. Because I worked hard, I was better than average in academic subjects. The fact that I was lower than average in sports reminded me that no one should get a swelled head because of what he has achieved in his field, since there are always others who are far better than he is in their fields.

In his first years of coaching, the Chief developed a notorious reputation for losing his temper. I remember a game against San Diego State in my sophomore year. We were behind after three quarters but made a sensational comeback for an upset win. During the final quarter, with Whittier ahead, San Diego was driving for what would have been the winning touchdown. Like Tom Landry, Chief always wore a hat. When the San Diego fullback drove for a first down through the center of our line, Chief jumped off the bench and threw his hat on the ground. The San Diego fans booed. Chief called over Byron Netzley, a linebacker, and gave him instructions for changing the defense. All the time Chief was talking, Netzley was running in place in front of him to warm up. He went into the game and made the play that made the difference. Chief was delighted—but then he looked down. Netzley had warmed up on his new hat. Chief was a very serious man, but he broke out in a huge laugh. From that time on, he never lost his temper in a game.

It did not occur to me at the time, but Chief also taught us a lot about civil rights forty years before that movement became popular on college campuses. He never asked for respect because he was an American Indian. The fact that he was one of the best players of his time at USC earned our respect. He treated the two fine black players on our squad exactly the same as the white ones. If they didn't perform up to what he thought their capabilities were, he told them so, just as he would a white player. Under Chief, no one was entitled to better treatment because he happened to be black. There was never a hint of racism on that team. This was perhaps in part because Whittier, though non-sectarian, had a Quaker background. But it was also because we knew that if any of us got out of line by failing to keep our grades up, by not playing up to par, or by mistreating someone else because he happened to be black, we would be kicked off the squad.

He not only talked a good civil rights game, he lived it. In 1921, when he was a star at USC playing tackle on defense and fullback on offense, Chief went into his favorite restaurant near the campus with Bryce Taylor, one of the first black players ever to play on a Trojan team. The counterman said he couldn't eat there. Chief exploded, "You serve him or you don't serve me." Forty-three years before the Civil Rights Act outlawed discrimination in public facilities, it ended at that restaurant.

In my senior year at college I did not make the traveling squad, so I drove down to Tucson to see the final game of the season against the University of Arizona. When I arrived, Chief took me aside and told me that he had learned that the hotel dining room did not serve blacks. He was livid, but did not want to create an incident before the game. He gave me three dollars and asked if I could discreetly invite Bill Brock, our black all-conference fullback, to join me for a steak dinner in one of the good restaurants in town. We must have handled the situation well, because when Bill came to see me in San Clemente in 1976, he told me that he remembered the dinner but had never been able to figure out why I had invited him.

The atmosphere of racial tolerance at Whittier left me completely unprepared for what I was to find at Duke. There were no blacks in the law school at that time, but there was also no overt racism. In fact, I don't recall race ever being discussed, in or out of class. I saw the magnitude of the problem only when Fred Albrink and I went downtown in Durham one afternoon just at the time that the tobacco plants were having a change of shift. Pouring out of the factory doors like smoke from a furnace came thousands of blacks on their way home after work. They walked down one side of the street and we walked down the other. No one really seemed to think of them as individuals. They were just a mass of people who were doing their work, earning their money, and living their life as a race completely apart from the rest of us. Disraeli saw two nations, the rich and the poor, in nineteenth-century England. That day in Durham, North Carolina, I for the first time saw two nations, black and white, in twentieth-century America.

Some of the Chief's players complained that he was too strict a disciplinarian. They thought that he should praise them more for doing well and not be so hard on them when they did poorly. But as was the case with Woody Hayes, everyone privileged to play under Chief Newman can look back on those years with appreciation for the lessons of life he taught us so well. One is that when you seek praise for its own sake, you are playing to the wrong audience. Chief didn't want us to play well to satisfy him. He wanted us to play well to satisfy ourselves.

That is why I believe all young people should devote some time to competitive sports. The lessons you learn in sports—how to win, how to lose, how to come back—are invaluable in life. The joy of winning and the disappointments of losing prepare you for what you will find in any profession you may choose.

In 1956, President Eisenhower gave me the assignment of setting up the President's Council on Youth Fitness. He told me he was concerned about studies showing that European youth were more physically fit than Americans. I do not think, however, that his goal was just to get Americans to do more situps or go out for football in greater numbers. He knew the point of physical health was to enhance mental and emotional health. Eisenhower himself was a fierce competitor. In war, politics, golf, or bridge, he always played to win. If his football career at West Point had not been cut short by an injury to his knee, I am confident that he would have been a great running back in the tradition of Mr. Inside and Mr. Outside, Doc Blanchard and Glenn Davis.

With all of this talk about struggle, aren't we taking the fun out of life? We should not go overboard and make life so grim, so tough, that we take all of the joy out of living. But we should recognize that having fun in the popular sense is not enough. In earlier eras, most people's energy was devoted simply to survival. Today, fun is the boom industry. Newspapers are full of fat sections about travel, entertainment, and enhancing domestic life. Many have sections called "Life" or "Living," which makes me wonder what the rest of the paper is supposed to be about. Some sociologists have even decided that we are about to become a "leisure society" and that the most important decision modern man will make in the future is how to "allocate" his leisure time.

But life is not cooking and computer games and Club Med. Life is a process of recognizing and trying to overcome challenges, of sometimes succeeding and sometimes failing. Nothing of any value, in business, in culture, in politics, in sports, or in any other field, was created without struggle. Struggle is what makes us human instead of animals. Einstein observed, "Well-being and happiness never appeared to me as absolute aims. I am even inclined to compare such moral aims to the ambitions of a pig."

Struggle is a fact of life, but not necessarily an unpleasant fact. We can get more fulfillment from struggling for a good cause beyond ourselves than living a life of strictly fun for ourselves. Struggle is not fun. But it is better than fun. Those who welcome and enjoy it will get something out of life far more rewarding than those who do not. In rethinking our educational priorities, we must not forget this simple truth. Without the fires of challenge and competition, children will grow up untempered by struggle and soft in character, and later in life they will be ill-equipped to deal with its inevitable and often frightening trials.

8

WEALTH

In 1965, I was the luncheon guest of Paul Getty in his magnificent home at Sutton Place near London. His other guests and I were served gourmet delicacies on gold plates with a superb vintage Bordeaux. He had graham crackers and milk. He could afford anything. But either by choice or medical necessity, the richest man in the world had the simplest and least expensive food imaginable.

Most people seek wealth for their personal financial security. Some seek it for the status it provides. Others seek it for what it allows them to do. Getty left a priceless art collection. Some, like Walter Annenberg, endow colleges and foundations. Others use their wealth to acquire influence and power through control of the media or of major financial and business enterprises.

In the 1960s, it became fashionable among young people to deride wealth as an evil in itself. In the 1980s, there has been a tendency to swing to the other extreme, with "Go for it" becoming the slogan that inspired our young people. To paraphrase Vince Lombardi, some people these days say that money isn't everything; it's the only thing.

In my third year at Duke Law School, Bill Perdue, Lyman Brownfield, Fred Albrink, and I shared two double beds in one bedroom in a farmhouse in the middle of the Duke forest. We called it Whippoorwill Manor. We had no indoor plumbing, running water, or central heating. But it only cost five dollars a month, and as a result we were able to afford to go to law school. It was rugged, but we all graduated with honors and never once complained about how tough things were. We didn't think of ourselves as poor, we did not envy others who had more than we did, and we all look back on those days as among the best times of our lives.

I am delighted that young law students these days don't have to go through what we did. I like the good life and feel fortunate that I can afford it. But I would gently remind young people that wealth can make life easier but not necessarily better. When the material goods of life are harder to get, you appreciate them more when you have them. And the fact that we had to live a hard life to get our education made us appreciate that education more when we got it. We learned a lot about law in those Depression days at Duke, but we learned even more about life. We all sought wealth, but never as an end in itself. We knew wealth was important, but we never considered it to be the only thing.

Wealth is the means by which an individual can afford food, housing, clothing, and leisure, which are among the essentials for a good life. It is the means to produce economic progress, opportunities, and jobs for people. It is the means by which an individual can gain power to choose the direction he believes is best for the nation. It is the means by which one can help others who are less fortunate.

While I have never had the urge to accumulate wealth, I have great respect for those who do, because I can see the worthwhile things many rich people do with their money. When I left Washington in 1961, after fourteen years as congressman, senator, and Vice President, all Mrs. Nixon and I had managed to accumulate was $48,000 of equity in our home. This was not just because I believed politicians should not profit from public service. It was also because I never wanted more wealth than I needed to provide a comfortable life for myself and my family.

Both as a former Vice President and former President, I turned down a variety of schemes for making a lot of money by expending very little effort, such as by "consulting" or accepting huge fees for speeches. Even today, some of my friends cannot understand why I turn down $700,000 a year in honorarium offers. One reason is that I do not believe it would be appropriate for me to accept them. But another is that I do not need the money. In the past twenty years, except for the series of TV interviews I agreed to do in order to pay my legal expenses, I have made money only from my writing and the profits from the sale of our various homes. It has proved to be more than enough. The closest I ever get to the stock market is listening to experts like Bill Simon tell me about their own risky but highly profitable exploits on Wall Street.

Fortunately, others feel differently than I do. The building of great fortunes helps drive the world's most productive economy. And yet many Americans have an instinctual dislike for corporate wealth. This is in part a result of our political system, which does not permit too much power to gather in too few hands. Such sentiments cut across ideological and party lines. TR, the Republican Roosevelt, was the greatest trustbuster in history, while the breakup of the telephone monopoly was begun under Jimmy Carter but vigorously executed by Ronald Reagan's Justice Department.

But another reason for the anti-corporate urge is the powerful but often unseen lure of the failed religion of Marxist-Leninist socialism. Marx believed that those who have capital exploit those who don't and that the solution was to give all capital to the state. The capitalist democracies chose to control the excesses of the robber barons by regulating business to protect workers' fundamental rights and interests. Almost everywhere the Communist model has been adopted, leaders are now desperately groping for ways to reintroduce capitalist principles to get their countries moving again.

In practice, the Communist model is completely bankrupt, but intellectually its rhetoric still has great appeal. The evil, greedy corporate boss remains a favorite target for the spinners of morality tales in Hollywood and the nation's newsrooms. It is not that these people are Communists. It is just that they have consciously or subconsciously subscribed to communism's guiding tenet, which is that great wealth is the root of all injustice.

Undeniably, the salaries and bonuses some overrated CEOs receive are obscene. This is a function not so much of greed but of starry-eyed boards of directors who think their publicity-conscious management superstars can walk on water. But if a $1 million executive has just one $2 million idea a year, he has more than earned his keep. A profitable corporation, earning big dividends for its shareholders, adding jobs each year, paying taxes to the federal government and its community, and creating and testing new technologies, is an essential institution of a modern democracy.

When people are out of work, corporate executives earning six or seven figures a year make easy targets. But in better times, they make decisions that put people back to work. As long as politicians and editorial writers resort to politically popular attacks on wealthy interests, the United States runs the risk that corporations will someday find themselves overtaxed, over-regulated, and eventually even swallowed up by the state. It happened in Great Britain after World War II, and it has taken ten years of Margaret Thatcher's privatization policies for Britain to recover.

Greed is not good. But wealth is, if it is used to good purpose. While capitalism may be driven by greed, it produces wealth, and democratic institutions help a society decide how its wealth should be used. Communism punishes greed by seizing wealth, and then totalitarian institutions are needed to manage the grinding poverty that is produced instead.

In recent years, as their societies suffered under the weight of the Communist system, leaders in China, the Soviet Union, and even Vietnam have begun to sound like college economics students, issuing grave-sounding manifestos about supply and demand and price elasticity. During one of my recent visits to a major Communist country, I received a patient, half-hour lecture from a high-ranking agricultural official about the novel idea that the profit motive might increase a farmer's incentive to grow more.

As an economic system, capitalism has defeated communism. But the philosophical appeal of communism is still powerful enough to defeat capitalism. Capitalism, unlike communism, is not a religion; it is a morally neutral set of economic principles. It is a tool, not an end in itself, and it can be put to bad uses as well as good ones. It is up to business people to be constantly aware of their social responsibilities in good times so that in bad times their opportunistic critics will not be able to turn them into scapegoats for society's problems by saying they only cared about lining their own pockets.

The go-for-it ethos of the 1980s was a refreshing change from the gone-to-pot era of the 1960s. But the best society is one in which all those in power, whether because they hold high office or command great economic resources, recognize that great power should only be used for the greater good.

A nation's greatness should never be measured in terms of its material wealth alone. America was a great nation two hundred years ago, when it was poor in goods but rich in spirit. The ideas that brought the new nation into being and which it represented inspired free people, and those who wanted to be free, all over the world.

How do we want America to be remembered two hundred years from now? As a people who built the biggest houses, drove the fastest cars, and wore the finest clothes? As a society whose rock stars were more admired than great teachers; beautiful people more than interesting people; scandal more than good deeds? Or do we wish to be remembered as a people who created great music, art, literature, and philosophy and acted as a force for good in the world?

A hundred and fifty years ago, de Tocqueville wrote about two contrary tendencies in America—the relentless, selfish pursuit of material wealth, and the generosity with which people contributed their time and money to volunteer organizations serving unselfish purposes. At a time when "do it for yourself" appeals to young people more than "do it for others," there is a danger that materialism rather than idealism will be what America comes to represent to the rest of the world.

We should not rest our case on the now-obvious fact that our system is far superior to communism in producing wealth and material progress—as Chambers put it, "that suffocating materialism which, more than want or hunger, recruits the forces of revolution in the West." For the Communists, material progress is everything. They seek it as an end in itself. For us, it is only the beginning of the good life, not the end. We seek wealth and material progress as a means to an end—a richer and more meaningful life in ways that cannot be measured by money, what Edmund Burke called "the unbought grace of life."

Some pundits ridiculed George Bush's rhetoric about "a thousand points of light." Admittedly, volunteer efforts alone will not solve the stubborn problems of the homeless and other disadvantaged people. But the critics overlook the fact that a goal which inspires us to devote some of our efforts to helping others makes us a better people than if we were motivated solely by what Russell Kirk has described as cosmic selfishness.

The first time my picture appeared in the newspaper was in 1916, when I was three years old. My mother had taken my brother Don and me to Los Angeles to buy clothes for school. A collection was being taken to benefit war orphans in Europe. She gave each of us a nickel to put in the collection basket, and a photographer snapped our picture. It appeared on the front page of a Los Angeles daily. He probably picked us because we seemed to be a typical American family. We did not have much ourselves, but we were generous with what we had if it could help those who had even less.

That ten cents my mother found in her purse wasn't much, especially compared to the lives of the thousands of Americans who fell in Europe during World War I. But as individuals and as a nation, Americans have always been willing to give selflessly of themselves, even make the ultimate sacrifice, for a great cause. It is that characteristic which makes us worthy of the blessings of our great wealth.

THREE

9

PURPOSE

When young people ask me whether they should choose politics as a career, I always answer with another question: "What do you want to achieve?" A person chooses law or medicine because he wants to practice law or medicine. But if he goes into politics only because he wants to practice politics—if he doesn't have a larger purpose he wants to pursue in public life—then he has picked the wrong profession.

Far too many people make just that wrong choice. Some go into politics because they want a good income, others because they want social status. Still others are attracted by the sheer excitement of being a player in the greatest game in the world.

No one should choose politics if his primary goal is a good income. The average lawyer can make twice as much as a congressman with half the effort. As far as excitement is concerned, any candidate for Congress will tell you that while getting there can be exciting, being there, especially as a freshman, can be deadly dull.

If you want social status, you should think again. A successful lawyer or a middle-level executive in even a small company usually rates a nice office. A freshman congressman is lucky if he gets two musty rooms on the fifth floor of the Cannon House Office Building, and that's for his entire staff of as many as ten people. After a term or two he might rate a reception or dinner invitation every night of the week, not because his hosts necessarily enjoy his company but because they enjoy being seen with a congressman, *any* congressman. Lobbyists will send him on fancy vacations, not because they want him to get plenty of rest but because they want to get his vote for their pet programs. In short, social status in Washington is cheap, illusory, and demeaning.

117

As for popularity, polls show that those in many other professions, including building contractor and funeral director, are respected far more than politicians. When he returns to his district after a successful term, a congressman should not expect his grateful constituents to lace garlands through his blow-dried hair. They are far more likely to lace into him about the local toxic waste dump or the rise in the inflation rate.

Politics is the riskiest of professions. You risk losing when you run the first time. Even if you win, you never can be sure that you will win the next time. When someone tells me he will run for office only if he is sure to win, I advise him not to run. With that attitude, he will be a poor candidate.

All the great leaders I have known have had goals greater than themselves. They sought high office not to be great but to do great things. Britain owes its existence to Churchill, France to de Gaulle, West Germany to Adenauer, Italy to de Gasperi, Japan to Yoshida, Israel to Ben-Gurion, and India to Nehru. Some were driven from office by smaller men, but history will remember them as titans for what they achieved. Each could have been rich beyond his dreams if he had applied his talents to making money. But they dreamed not of making great fortunes but of building and sustaining great nations. The impact such leaders have on the world is incalculably great. They all accomplished their goals through the prosaic nuts and bolts of democratic politics. But none ever made the mistake of thinking of politics as an end rather than a means.

The principle of seeking office to do something rather than to be somebody is best exemplified by Dwight Eisenhower. At the conclusion of World War II, he was the most admired man in the world. He had never suffered a defeat. He was not rich by some standards, but he was comfortably well off. He had never been in politics. He knew that if he sought the Presidency, there was an even chance that he would not win the nomination and that if he was nominated, he would have no better than an even chance to win the election. He proved to be a successful politician, but he never liked the cut-and-thrust of partisan campaigning.

So why did he seek the Presidency? He was not an egotist, but as a realist he knew that the victory in World War II which had been won at such great cost might be lost unless the United States provided strong, enlightened leadership for the free world. He believed he was the best-qualified man to provide that leadership. The fact that he ended the war in Korea, firmly held the line against

Soviet aggression, and kept the United States at peace for the balance of his eight years in office demonstrated that he was right.

The cost of seeking and winning office is high—not just the financial sacrifice but the time spent away from your family, the abuse from political opponents and the media, the long hours of grinding hard work. You should not enter politics unless you are prepared to pay the price. The paradox is that you cannot imagine how high it may be until you are already in the maelstrom.

Without vision, a leader not only literally but also figuratively does not know where he is going. All purposeful action must begin with the definition of ends. Without fixed reference points and destinations, a life, even if it is filled with motion, will produce no progress and have no meaning. No person should live a life not rooted in a higher purpose.

De Gaulle made this point eloquently in *The Edge of the Sword:*

> All leaders of men, whether it is political figures, prophets, or soldiers, all of those who can get the best out of others have identified themselves with high ideals and this has given added scope and strength to their influence. Followed in their lifetime because they stand for greatness of mind rather than self-interest, they are later remembered less for the usefulness of what they have achieved than for the sake of their endeavors.

Today, many in the political establishment are repelled by politicians they consider to be overly motivated by purpose. Pundits celebrate candidates for their moderation, their realism, their willingness to compromise. While a candidate is expected to put forth some kind of vision, once he does, media analysts pick it to pieces and, especially if it is a conservative vision, confidently predict that after he is in office he either will learn to be more realistic or will have reality thrust upon him. We have become so worried that a leader will abuse his power that we have begun to restrict his latitude to use it legitimately but broadly. Politicians who make waves, who challenge the established order, are considered "obstructionists" and "loose cannons." And yet our nation could find itself becalmed if it runs out of leaders who are willing to risk their standing with the Washington and media establishments by doing or saying what they believe is right, whether or not it is popular.

As I look back to the time I made the decision to enter politics forty-three years ago, three goals motivated me: peace abroad, a

119

better life for people at home, and the victory of freedom over tyranny throughout the world. I have taken some great risks and have fought many battles in attempting to serve those goals. By exposing Alger Hiss, I earned the undying enmity of many powerful people who might otherwise have at worst taken a neutral view of me. I do not regret losing these people's support. But by going to China, I lost the support of many fellow conservatives who believed we should not have normal relations with any Communist power, even if it was unfriendly toward the Soviet Union. By refusing to accept any but the most honorable and equitable peace in Vietnam, I lost the support of many liberals, conservatives, and moderates who felt that supporting me was just too risky politically. These are examples of the perils of purpose. If you stay a difficult or dangerous course, even your most loyal friends may desert you, either because they do not share your vision or because they do not want to share the risks you are running in trying to make your vision a reality.

Still, as I look back, while it has been a rough game, it has been worth it. I might not want to do it again, but I would not have missed it. The reason is that I know I have lived for a purpose, and I have at least in part achieved it. You must live your life for something more important than your life alone. One who has never lost himself in a cause bigger than himself has missed one of life's mountaintop experiences. Only by losing yourself in this way can you really find yourself.

10

TIME

Time is a person's most important possession. How he makes use of it will determine whether he will fail or succeed in whatever he is undertaking. This is particularly true in politics, where one misplaced word or misspent day can mean defeat. Four dramatic examples show how the failure to use time properly may have affected the course of history. All involve candidates who did not schedule themselves so as to be at their best in crucial public forums or confrontations.

In 1912, Wisconsin's Progressive senator, Robert LaFollette, was a leading candidate for President. He was scheduled to appear before a major press audience in Philadelphia along with the Democratic frontrunner, Woodrow Wilson. LaFollette was a great orator, but he had developed a reputation for speaking too often and too long. On that occasion he was completely worn out after a long day of campaigning and worried because his daughter was undergoing a serious operation.

Wilson spoke briefly but brilliantly. LaFollette followed him to the podium and rambled on and on for over two and a half hours. As some in the audience began to leave, he became irritated and incoherent and repeated himself time and again. When he finally sat down, he was finished as a candidate in 1912, and despite his great gifts he never again became a serious contender for President.

Wendell Willkie was one of the most charismatic candidates ever nominated by either party. He was an excellent campaigner. He was smart and tough, and when he ran against FDR in 1940 he had what many thought was a surefire issue—the no-third-term tradition. His one fatal weakness was that he could not say no, and would not let someone else say no for him when it came to allocating his time.

He wowed audiences of thousands at whistle-stops throughout the day. At each one, he captivated the hundreds of individuals who would come up to shake his hand. By the end of the day, he was exhausted. By the end of the campaign, his voice was gone. When he was talking to millions on radio in the closing days of the campaign, he could only croak out the words.

Because he was President and because of his physical disability, Roosevelt limited his public appearances and was gangbusters when he went on radio. Willkie probably would have lost anyway. But if he had planned his time in order to be fully rested when he was talking to millions rather than just thousands or hundreds, it might have made a difference.

In the 1960 election, I made a similar mistake. I had lost two weeks of campaigning to a knee injury that kept me in the hospital, and so I felt I had to make up for lost time. On the day of the crucial first debate with Jack Kennedy, I agreed to an appearance before a carpenters' union convention. The appearance went well, but the audience was tough. Such a session always takes something out of you. In the debate that night, I apparently did well enough on substance, since polls of radio listeners gave me the edge. But five or six times as many people saw the debate on television, and polls of these viewers gave Kennedy the edge. I did not feel tired but I looked tired, and I had foolishly not put on makeup to compensate for the bags under my eyes and my five-o'clock shadow. Kennedy might have won the election anyway. But my failure to use time properly could have made a difference.

In 1988, Michael Dukakis lost the election the night of the second debate. A major reason was that he had been under the weather and was over-scheduled that morning. The contrast to George Bush, who came through as strong and relaxed, was devastating. Dukakis was burned out, and it showed. Bush might have won the election even if Dukakis had been at his best. But Dukakis's failure to use time correctly could have made the difference.

The opportunities and constraints presented by television have altered the way Presidential candidates use their time during the campaign. Today, they can have a greater impact through coverage of one event on the evening news programs than they used to have by attending a dozen jam-packed rallies. Theoretically, any Presidential candidate should seriously consider having only one event each day that is designed to combine national impact with local impact in states that are critically important to his strategy. He is also perfectly justified in limiting his access to the press, as both Dukakis and Bush did in 1988, since sound bites from his answers to press questions will frequently supplant coverage of his major speeches.

While a one-event, no-press strategy would arguably be the most rational way to use time in a campaign, any candidate who adopted it would be condemned as cynical and opportunistic. Besides, his staff would always be able to dream up ways to fill the empty spaces on the schedule. "Why sit around reading and thinking when we can fly over to Cedar Rapids for a quick rally?", the aides would say. "It can't hurt, and it's better if we look busy." And as far as the press is concerned, few candidates and campaign functionaries can stand up for very long to reporters' acidic complaints about lack of access.

But the fact remains that television has given candidates new ways to reach masses of people with far less physical effort than ever before. Campaigns still barnstorm frenetically around the countryside in large part because that is what campaigns are supposed to do. If the man has not been awake for nineteen hours, he is not thought to be doing his job. But television has turned this kind of campaigning into an anachronism.

In a way, it is more cynical to patronize people by wasting energy in an illusion of playing politics the old-fashioned way. Instead, it might be prudent to harken back to an even earlier era. A hundred years ago, it was considered unseemly for a candidate to go out on the stump and ask for votes. Many ran from their front porches. Today, they could run from their home television studios.

Personally, I would be sorry to see the death of traditional political campaigns. I hope candidates continue to knock themselves out by giving 110 percent on the stump, because that is what makes politics interesting and helps us see what the candidates are made of. Still, by clinging to an outmoded approach we miss out on a great potential benefit of the technological revolution.

It is frequently said that in the modern world people are in perpetual motion, never slowing down to think about what they are doing with their lives. Television has contributed to the process by destroying the art of conversation and replacing moments of introspection and social interaction with hours of video-induced catatonia. But if used in politics to its full potential, television could actually make politics *more* illuminating and intelligent. Candidates could spend less time traveling and more time thinking. They could give fewer vacuous fifteen-minute rally speeches in order to participate in more televised debates. There would not be as much aimless activity, as much transitory "news," or as many opportunities for the reporting of meaningless gaffes. But there would be more opportunities for voters to learn what the candidates would actually do as President of the United States.

Presidential candidates could use their time more efficiently if they chose to do so. But a President does not have a choice. His time is the most valuable in the world, and if he does not use it properly, the nation and even the world can suffer.

To a President, everything is important. He has to choose carefully among answering letters and memoranda, making telephone calls, having appointments, presiding over meetings of his Cabinet, National Security Council, and other groups, and recreation. More important than all of these is that he leave time in his schedule to adequately prepare for his public appearances. And most important, he must reserve time to think through his major policies and decisions. In politics as in sports, the greatest mistake you can make is to wear yourself out and leave your game on the practice field.

I once asked Eisenhower what the hardest thing was for him to learn after he became President. He answered, "To sign a bad letter." Eisenhower was an excellent writer who particularly enjoyed dictating letters to his friends. But as President, he found that the number of his friends had multiplied a thousand-fold. He did not mean that his staff was preparing truly bad letters for him. They were only bad because he would have written them differently.

The bad-letter principle can be applied far more broadly. It is often said that the mark of a good executive is that he can delegate to others things that they can do better than he can. Eisenhower's lesson was that a good executive, particularly if he is President, must learn to delegate to others even when he believes they cannot do it as well.

In allotting time for telephone calls and appointments, the executive must discipline himself and if possible those he talks to to keep it short. Senator Ed Muskie, a Calvin Coolidge buff, tells a revealing story about that underrated President. After Coolidge took office as Vice President, his successor as governor of Massachusetts asked him, "How did you manage to see so many visitors in a day and always leave the office at five? I find that I have to stay as late as nine. What is the difference?" Coolidge thought a

124

moment and answered, "You talk back." A President never wants to seem unresponsive to those he sees or talks to on the telephone. But whenever he is tempted to talk at length, he should remember that he is probably taking time from something that is far more important.

Meetings with the Cabinet, the NSC, legislative leaders, and other groups over which the President is expected to preside can actually be one of the poorest uses of his time unless both he and they are carefully prepared and unless the meeting has a lean, strong agenda. That is why I usually had the other participants submit their ideas in writing before the meeting began. This helped me be prepared and ensured that they would be as well. A President should never have to consider half-baked ideas. Food for thought does not need to be saucered and blown, but it must at least be ready to digest.

Sometimes a President is tempted to dispense with meetings altogether and make his decisions based on reading rather than listening, which after all takes much less time. But it just won't work. First, many executives retain information better when it is presented orally. Second, to be candid, the official with the idea needs to show and tell. That is why the suggestion that the Vice President relieve the President by presiding over routine Cabinet meetings will not work except in extraordinary circumstances such as when the President is physically incapacitated. Cabinet officers have big egos, and if the President is not presiding they tend to send their deputies to the meetings.

Another argument for meetings is that the give-and-take of free discussion on occasion is beneficial. Sometimes only the clash between two good ideas will produce a better one. Besides, it is vital to give everybody on the staff and in the Cabinet a sense of being on the team. It doesn't do any good for a quarterback to call a good play if his linemen don't know which way to block.

The President's chief-of-staff plays an indispensable role in assuring that meetings are not just time-wasters. He must insist on a disciplined agenda and on a presentation that will make maximum use of a President's time. No one should be allowed to take an hour to make a point that could be made in five minutes simply because he has not disciplined himself beforehand.

How a President disciplines himself to prepare for meetings varies. Some simply read, study, and think. Others prefer batting ideas around with members of their staff. While I have always enjoyed bull sessions, I have seldom found them productive and hardly ever the best use of time. A bull session generally produces precisely what you expect a bull to produce. Even a labor-intensive President has only about three hundred sixty working hours a month. When you consider the challenges and crises he faces at home and abroad, wasting even an hour of that time is an intolerable sacrifice of the world's scarcest resource.

11

TEMPERANCE

I first saw Winston Churchill in 1954, when I had the privilege of welcoming him at the airport on his visit to Washington. He was seventy-nine years old and had returned to power as prime minister after his shattering defeat in 1945. I had heard that age and the aftereffects of a stroke had taken their toll and that he was not the man he had been during the war. That may have been, but he was still quite a man. He was frail physically, and some said he was not as sharp as he once had been. But mentally Churchill at half speed was better than almost anyone else at full speed. For five days he held everyone he met in rapt attention with his incomparable repartee.

I saw him for the last time in November 1958. Then eighty-three, he was no longer in office and had suffered another stroke. He was slouched down in a reclining chair with a blanket pulled over his knees. He greeted me with a wan smile and a limp handshake. He looked like a zombie.

Then he ordered brandy. I sipped mine, but he emptied his glass in one gulp. It was like lighting a match to dry leaves. The conversation began to crackle. His humor warmed the room. Since I had visited Ghana the year before when it celebrated its independence from Britain, I asked him what he thought of the reports in the morning papers that negotiations were taking place which would have the effect of Ghana taking over Guinea. He growled, "I think Ghana has enough to digest without gobbling up Guinea." For almost an hour, he was as sharp as he had been in Washington four years before.

Doctors and moralists might cringe at the thought, but alcohol was just what Churchill had needed. It stimulated a metabolism

127

dulled by illness and age, giving him the opportunity to better enjoy our conversation and me a memory I shall never forget of the greatest leader of our time displaying his legendary effervescence and insight. Would I urge anyone else to take a belt to fortify himself for an important meeting? Never. But I wouldn't have kept that snifter from Churchill for the world.

Churchill's reputation as a drinker more than matched his skill as a politician and writer. Some suggest that much of it was a pose. After all, it was said that while he always had a cigar in his mouth, he seldom finished one. But even assuming that alcohol was like mother's milk to him, it is undoubtedly poison to others. The rest of us must know our limitations. Even Churchill recognized that he had some, as illustrated by a perhaps apocryphal story that my translator, Gyorgy Banlaki, now Hungary's counsul general in New York, told me when I visited Budapest in 1982.

At one of the World War II conferences, Stalin had invited Churchill to dinner at his quarters. The only other person present was Stalin's translator. Both men were night owls, and they ate and drank until three in the morning. Finally, Churchill went back to his quarters. He awoke with a start at eleven the next morning and thought, "My God, what did I say to that fellow last night?" He called in his secretary, and pacing the floor, dictated a three-page, single-spaced letter that began, "Dear Marshal Stalin: I enjoyed our dinner last night. It is my understanding that these are the matters that we discussed and we agreed upon."

He sent the letter to Stalin by special messenger. Within the hour, Stalin's reply arrived. It read, "Dear Mr. Prime Minister: Don't be concerned about what you said last night. I was drunk, too." A postscript read, "And the translator has been shot."

Everyone would agree that Churchill was not an ordinary man. After God made him, He must have broken the mold. Based on my experience, I would recommend that people in public life should bear in mind that alcohol will affect them in different ways under different circumstances. A drink on vacation or with family and friends may have little effect. A drink when you are tired or tense can have an explosive effect. When you hear someone say, "I need a drink," it is the precise time he should not have one.

Most people have less tolerance for alcohol as they get older. Chou En-lai was seventy-three when we toasted each other and his other guests at the first state dinner in Beijing in 1972. To show the potency of *mao-tai,* the 106-proof Chinese brandy, he poured a little into a saucer and lit a match to it. It flared up like a roman candle. Imagine what it does when it hits the stomach. He told me that when he was on the Long March he could drink as many as twenty-five cups, almost a quart, each day. He said that now he had to limit himself to two cups a day. Neither of us finished a cup during the dinner. I have followed the same practice during scores of *mao-tai* toasts at the banquets I have hosted and attended during my five visits to China since 1972. Many Chinese pride themselves on their ability to consume large quantities of *mao-tai* and are always willing to go head to head with a guest who believes his capacity rivals theirs. But they also respect a person's judgment that he has reached his personal limit.

While the fiery brew is served, along with Chinese wine, at every luncheon or dinner, not everyone joins in. When Deng invited me to luncheon in the Great Hall of the People during my 1985 visit, his staff played host to my two staff members in an adjoining room. Mike Endicott, a retired Secret Service agent who now serves as my private security coordinator, noticed that while the waiters kept everyone's *mao-tai* cups filled to the brim, three people at the table—two of Deng's bodyguards and the young woman who served as his personal physician—drank only water.

It is a truism that alcohol helps loosen up participants in a diplomatic negotiation. Whether or not it is true, it is vitally important that you carefully watch what your opposite number does. Khrushchev, for instance, had a reputation for drinking too much. In fact, in 1959, at a luncheon at the Kremlin where there was no serious talk, he let himself go and insisted that we all throw our fine crystal glasses into the fireplace after we had toasted each other. But when we met at his dacha for a four-and-a-half hour lunch where the discussion was much more intense and about far more complex issues than at the famous kitchen conference we had had the day before, I noted that Khrushchev barely sipped the vodka and wines that were served in such quantity. I followed his example.

Brezhnev handled the situation differently but with the same result. In 1972, he invited Kissinger and me for a working dinner with Nikolai Podgorny and Aleksei Kosygin. We met in a small room before going in to dinner. For three hours, they hammered me on Vietnam. None of us gave an inch. Not a drop of alcohol was served. At 11:00 p.m., we went in to a sumptuous dinner with vodka, Russian wine, and champagne—and no serious conversation.

Eisenhower was very disciplined in his eating and drinking. He always enjoyed two scotches before dinner, even when he had to make a major speech, but he never showed any effect from them. He probably enjoyed them even more when his doctors told him after his heart attack that a couple of mild drinks would be good for him. I noticed that while several of his friends were martini drinkers, he never ordered one. I asked him why he didn't like martinis. He answered, "Oh, that's the problem. I like them too much. That is why I never drink them."

Herbert Hoover handled the problem in a different way. For years, he had two martinis, extra dry and straight up, before dinner. After he turned eighty, his doctor limited him to one. He had no trouble following the doctor's orders. He just doubled the size of the glass.

My first experience of excessive alcohol consumption occurred when I was in law school. North Carolina was a dry state. Few students could afford the bootleg products that were available, except occasionally at football games when some would get smashed on a home brew called Carolina Corn. Most of us were too concerned about keeping our grades up to indulge ourselves in this way.

But twice a year, after examinations, we had a law school dance at which liquid refreshments were an inviolable tradition. We handled the situation legally by making up a kitty from our modest resources and turning it over to one of the students who owned an automobile. He drove to the nearest town in Virginia, ironically called South Boston, where a liquor package store could be operated legally.

These parties were real blasts. Most of us drank a lethal concoction of sloe gin and grapefruit juice. The next day we all awoke with terrible hangovers, vowing that we would never take a drink again—at least, not until the next law school dance. One morning after one of these parties, Bill Perdue said he felt as if he had "been drug through hell and beat over the head with a shit bag." Incidentally, Bill finished first in the class.

I had a more pleasant encounter with alcohol when I visited Baltimore in the summer of 1936. My classmate, Dick Keiffer, took me to a pub that featured five-cent beer and ten-cent crab cakes. The glasses were small, but the beer must have been outstanding. I have had crab cakes many times since in Washington, New York, and in Miller's great seafood restaurant in Baltimore. I have paid as much as twelve dollars a serving, but never have I tasted any that

130

were as good as those ten-cent crab cakes we had that summer—although I must admit that the nickel beer probably whetted our appetite and produced the right chemistry to fully appreciate this delicacy.

The greatest orator I ever heard on the House or Senate floor was Congressman Dewey Short of Missouri. When sober, he was the mildest of men. He never made a speech without having several drinks first. He had received a superb education at Oxford. Quoting freely from the Bible, Shakespeare, and the classics, he held the House spellbound every time he rose to speak, regardless of the subject. His excessive consumption of alcohol probably didn't shorten his life—he died at the age of eighty-one—and it gave him the rare ability to move the hearts of the most worldly and cynical audience in the country—the U.S. Congress. I am sure he died with a smile on his lips. The best storyteller I have ever known was his colleague and close friend from Maine, Frank Fellows. Without a drink, he was a perfectly sober down-Mainelander. But late in the day, when he opened a bar in his office, he regaled all who were privileged to be there with his stories. In the case of both Short and Fellows, the question is whether they would have been as eloquent without the stimulus of alcohol.

The liquor didn't create Short's eloquence or Fellows's high spirits; it freed them. For some reason, neither man was at his best, at least as a performer, unless he was under the influence. It worked for them. But there is no way to know whether it incapacitated them in other, unseen ways or whether some other remedy —a simple, naturally induced boost in self-confidence, perhaps— might have had the same effect without the inevitable side effects of drinking. Many people drink to dull the senses. That is a different problem. The people I am talking about drink to enhance their senses—to be smarter, or funnier, or more eloquent. All that is happening is that talents and qualities that were there all the time are being brought to the surface as inhibitions fade.

It is too easy to be moralistic and say that such people should find some other way to accomplish the same thing. In fact, many do become alcoholics, and eventually their drinking dulls their abilities rather than enhancing them. But not all do. The trick is to use alcohol rather than letting it use you. Serving a rare vintage wine at dinner can stimulate the appetite and also provide an interesting subject for conversation. For calming the nerves, for bringing out the orator or raconteur in you, or simply for the pleasure of it, alcohol, judiciously used, can enhance life. Recklessly used, it will inevitably destroy life.

In my own case, I have followed the practice of never eating or drinking before making a speech, having a press conference, or engaging in any serious discussion of major issues. Speaking as I do without notes requires intense concentration. I am not sure that I speak better because I don't eat or drink before speaking. I *am* sure that I would speak worse if I did.

The public man is always on parade. He must assume that even his friends will be intolerant of him if he drinks to excess. I have known Senator John Tower for thirty years. I have never seen him drunk. But the fact that even some of his friends said that they had proved fatal when he was being considered for Secretary of Defense. What was particularly unfair was that for many who opposed him, including some who were themselves pretty good drinkers, the allegations about his drinking were an excuse, not their real reason for opposing him. Some disliked his manner, others his hawkish foreign-policy views. But it is far easier to say you oppose a man on the grounds of personal misbehavior than because you disagree with policies that millions of Americans may support. Nobody likes a drunk, or even an alleged drunk.

But nobody likes a hypocrite, either. If Tower's opponents had applied the same rigorous standards to themselves and permitted only sober, chaste members to vote on his nomination, they might well have had difficulty mustering a quorum. Perhaps the public realized this. The Tower affair was the first of a series of crises that rocked Congress during 1989 and brought it to a new low in public respect.

Sadly, the crisis also showed that character assassination still works. Especially now, the safest course would be for public men to be teetotalers. If they believe an occasional social drink either relaxes or inspires them, they should bear in mind that the line between being amusing and being silly is a very fine one. When you do not know whether you have crossed it is the time to join Alcoholics Anonymous.

"Temperance" is defined as drinking in moderation or total abstinence. Many would favor expanding the definition to include drug use, with the implication that using drugs in moderation is acceptable. Despite the misery and death drugs have brought to our homes, neighborhoods, and schools, some still favor this permissive approach. They urge the government to go ahead and bomb the Colombian drug plantations and clean out the ghetto crackhouses, so long as the weekend cocaine and marijuana user is left in peace to unwind in whatever manner he pleases. This approach was proved wrong twenty years ago. It would compound the tragedy to let the elite, casual user off the hook again.

America's leadership class will be remembered for the role it played in helping lose two wars: the war in Vietnam and, at least so far, the war on drugs. The leadership class is made up of highly educated and influential people in the arts, the media, the academic community, the government bureaucracies, and even business. They are characterized by intellectual arrogance, an obsession with style, fashion, and class, and a permissive attitude on drugs. In Vietnam, they felt more comfortable criticizing the United States for trying to save South Vietnam than criticizing the Communists for trying to conquer it. In the drug war, they simply went over to the other side. For years, the enemy was them.

Now that polls show a majority of the American people fear drugs more than war, poverty, crime, or the deteriorating environment, being against drugs is as fashionable as being on drugs was two decades ago. Every young politician who admits taking a puff of dope in the sixties is talking tough on dope in the eighties. But for years the elite class accepted and even celebrated "recreational" drug use. Some still say that the casual user is not the problem. But when the casual user is a powerful movie director, a millionaire rock star, or an influential columnist, he is more dangerous than a hundred Brooklyn drug pushers. Drug users in the leadership class helped create a climate of social, cultural, and political acceptance that permitted the drug plague to take root. As it began to spread through our colleges and schools, attempts to contain it were condemned in leadership circles as paternalistic efforts by the older generation to suppress the creative urges of its children. Those who did not openly condone drug use coyly looked the other way.

When I rejected the recommendation of a Presidential commission that called for the decriminalization of marijuana in 1972, one liberal columnist scoffed at our hard line. "There is no real cause for panic about drug abuse and its effect on crime," he wrote in *The New York Times*. "There is no evidence that a crackdown will be the answer: quite the opposite." Under the leadership of Dr. Jerome Jaffe, we did adopt a tough, coordinated policy, ranging from diplomatic pressure on Turkey to stop exporting heroin to the first treatment program for inner-city addicts. But even more crackdown then and in the years that followed might well have meant less crack now.

Even today, when most of the prestige media have managed to crowd onto the anti-drug bandwagon, they could not help indulging in a revolting orgy of nostalgia during the twentieth anniversary of Woodstock last year. The smarmy retrospectives glossed over the fact that Woodstock's only significant legacy was the glorification of dangerous illegal drugs. At least the seven Woodstock performers who eventually died from drugs got obituaries in the newspapers. Thousands in the audience who also became victims of drug abuse weren't even that lucky.

To erase the grim legacy of Woodstock, we need a total war against drugs. Total war means war on all fronts against an enemy with many faces. Some, such as the South American drug barons, are easy and even appropriate targets. But making the drug war largely a foreign-policy issue is a convenient way to blame others for our own domestic problems. Some people do not want to admit that the enemy is also as near as the face they see in the mirror— the inner-city or suburban father who walks out on young children who need his influence to avoid drugs, the Wall Street broker buying a couple of grams of cocaine in the subway station, the columnist smoking marijuana or snorting coke on Saturday night and then going to the office Monday and writing that drugs are really just a problem for poor blacks. All are links in a steel chain of greed, proverty, neglect, and self-indulgence that is being drawn tighter and tighter around our throats. All must be fought and stopped before the chain can be broken and our country finally freed of its chemical, economic, and cultural addiction to illegal drugs. But nothing can be accomplished, no anti-drug initiative will be successful, if our society does not face the hard fact that *any* tolerance of *any* use of *any* illegal drug is wrong.

For this reason, calls for legalization of drugs are totally misguided. Police, parents, and teachers in the inner cities, the soldiers on the front lines in the drug war, know that if drugs were legalized, they would be cheaper and easier to get. As a result, there would be far more people on drugs. The way to win a war is not to give all the ammunition to the other side.

The war also cannot be won on the cheap. If Abraham Lincoln had been worried about the budget in 1861, George Bush would need a passport to visit Atlanta. Instead, Lincoln spent what he needed to win the Civil War and ran up a $500 million deficit.

The war on drugs is our second civil war. If winning it requires a tax increase, so be it. In that event the Bush administration should seriously consider proposing a new tax on cigarettes and alcohol, with the funds earmarked exclusively for drug interdiction, prosecution, treatment, and education. Timid advisers who warn the President that the political heat will be too great if he proposes such a tax are wrong. The American people expect him to do what is necessary to win the war no matter what the cost, so long as his measures are bold enough to have a chance to work. The war cannot be won without strong leadership from the top. Today, fifty-eight government agencies share responsibility for fighting drugs. Too often they end up spending more time fighting each other for turf than fighting the enemy. A drug czar who has little more than the symbolic power of a British king will not be able to knock heads together to end the civil war in the bureaucracy and make a victory possible in the civil war against drugs.

A tough policy can also be a compassionate one. When I visited the Daytop Village drug rehabilitation center in Swan Lake, New York, in 1988, I met scores of young people who had fallen into the drug trap. With guidance from Monsignor O'Brien and his dedicated colleagues, they were now on the road to productive, drug-free lives. Daytop offers twenty-four-hour-a-day supervision, stiff punishments for patients who stray, and regular follow-up testing after they go home. Because many such programs rely solely on private donations, only a fraction of those who need them can get in. No matter what else President Bush does, he should make it a national goal to ensure that no one who really wants to beat drugs is ever excluded from treatment. Any American who saw the hopeful faces of the young people at Daytop Village would gladly open his heart and his checkbook if it meant saving even one more child from oblivion.

12

READING

Some of my public statements have been interpreted to mean that I believe television is an unmitigated disaster. In fact, it can be a source of inexpensive, provocative, and occasionally even worthy entertainment. Anyone who has visited a hospital or retirement home knows how much it means to patients and old people. For parents and grandparents, it is an inexpensive baby-sitter that can teach children their numbers and the alphabet by age four. Politically, it saved my career in 1952, set it back in 1960, and helped me come back in 1968.

On the other hand, television puts emphasis on appearance over substance. It has been disastrous for the age-old art of conversation. But its most negative impact is its contribution to the decline of reading, both for pleasure and enlightenment. The most dramatic impact has been on the newspaper business. Some cities that once supported three or four papers now barely support one. Why would a frequent critic of the press mourn the death of newspapers? Because a diversity of journalistic viewpoints in a community helps keep the press honest. In the media as in other big businesses, monopoly breeds arrogance.

I must admit to a lifetime personal prejudice for reading. My mother taught me to read before I went to school. I was fortunate to have had outstanding teachers who inspired me to love books. Except when my favorite teams are playing, I always prefer reading to TV.

More pleasurable than TV, reading is also more efficient than talking. While a good conversation is stimulating, seeing something in writing is the best way for me to assimilate, analyze, and understand ideas. I found this particularly true during the White House

136

years. A decision maker must absorb massive amounts of information, and reading is the fastest and best means to do so. Requiring an adviser to submit his ideas in writing forces him to think them through more carefully. Bad ideas and superficial thinking are almost always exposed in the stark black and white of the typewritten word. Reading also negates the almost hypnotic impact of spoken eloquence. C. P. Snow observed that Trotsky sometimes swayed himself with his own eloquence. Orators who have that capability will have no difficulty swaying others.

Being briefed in writing rather than orally also takes less time. A person can read four or five times faster than he can listen. Most important is the mental discipline that reading enforces on both the reader and the writer. Those who say they are "thinking out loud" are not thinking very clearly. Most people think better when they put it on paper.

Presented with a pile of policy memoranda, I would organize them in order of least to most important. I would first skim the less important papers so that I could devote more time to the weightier ones—assessing them, taking them apart, analyzing their strong and weak points. The fact that I am not a speed reader was a liability in the sense that I could not get through as much material, but an asset in that it ensured I would thoroughly digest all of the issues on an important question before making a decision.

When Lyndon Johnson took me on a tour of the White House after the election in 1968, I noticed that he had three television sets in the Oval Office, three in the small private office next door, three in the office bathroom, and three in his bedroom in the residence. He also had a wire service ticker. While we were talking, I vividly remember him getting up and tearing the latest report off the ticker to see how some appearance or statement of his had been reported.

I had all this equipment removed, not because of a lack of interest but because of a lack of time. During my years in the White House, I hardly ever watched the evening news and never went through the ordeal of watching the Sunday talk shows. Instead, I read highlights of the programs. That way you save time and also avoid becoming obsessed with how the media is treating you. I always insisted on knowing what the critics were writing or saying. But reading it was far less disturbing than hearing them say it in my living room.

One of the best ideas I instituted in the White House was the daily news summary. A busy official with a multi-newspaper habit can waste an enormous amount of time reading essentially the same story as written by different reporters. It is also a mistake to read only the Washington and New York newspapers, which just reflect the consensus of Beltway thinking, or the news magazines with their mixture of sensationalistic but irrelevant cultural reporting and increasingly bland, homogeneous political and national coverage. A President should designate a competent staff member to summarize articles, columns, and TV reports on both sides of a question from all over the country, and for that matter from all over the world. Some of the best writing on the American political scene, for instance, appears in *The Economist* in London. What I considered most important was that the news summary present all points of view—from *National Review* to *The New Republic*. I might not have liked what my critics were writing, but I had to know what people were reading.

The summaries of the network news were most important. Sometimes one of a President's more intellectual aides will come in on Monday and effuse about a highly positive article that might have appeared on page four of *The Washington Post*'s Sunday opinion section. The problem is that only a few thousand people will have read such an article through. Far more important is what the network news programs say about the same issue to 23 million people. A President may think as I do that TV news is generally trivial, sensationalistic, or slanted, but it is also most Americans' principal news source. To know what people are thinking, he must know what they are seeing.

The dynamic of national news becomes even more complicated when you consider the extent to which television journalists take their cue from print journalists. A White House reporter like Fred Barnes of *The New Republic* reaches only 95,000 subscribers. But since he is widely respected among his colleagues for his accuracy and the quality of his secret sources in the White House, what he writes can be amplified three hundred-fold by TV reporters if they reflect it in their own reporting. A good news summary helps a President measure this effect.

I always resisted the temptation to read personal articles in their entirety, as distinguished from articles about issues in which I played a part. It didn't matter if a profile was positive or negative. Reading the negative ones cannot help but distract you from the really important issues. Reading the supportive ones cannot help but trigger overconfidence.

In reading news stories, columns, or policy memoranda prepared by staff members, you should always consider the source.

Every writer worth reading has a point of view. Whether he genuinely tries to be objective or not, his writing is bound to reflect his prejudices. That is why it is useful to have opposing points of view submitted along with the majority view so that you can make the decision rather than leaving that to a staff member, no matter how much confidence you have in him. Also, when a senior staffer submitted a policy memorandum, I insisted that he give me the names of those who worked on it. Nothing does more for a lower-level bureaucrat's morale than to get a note or a call from the President thanking him for his work.

A President must spend many hours a day reading for work. He should not forget to read for pleasure. Theodore Roosevelt, the most prolific reader of all American Presidents, once said he would never go anywhere, "not even to the jungles of Africa," without books to read. On safari he always had a book or two packed in his saddlebag or pocket so that no opportunity for reading would be lost. I did the same thing in the jungles of Washington.

When I visited Australia in 1965, Prime Minister Robert Menzies told me that he always set aside a half hour a day and an hour on Saturday and Sunday for reading for pleasure and urged me to do the same. I have never received better advice. A President should never be so burdened by what he has to read that he does not have some time for what he wants to read.

It might be argued that reading for pleasure is purely escapist and that leaders cannot afford to waste their time on it. But no one would disagree that a leader needs some relief from the heavy burdens of his office, and reading is one of the best ways to get it. Watching movies or television can also serve this purpose, but both are passive forms of entertainment. Reading is active. It engages, exercises, and expands the mind.

Reading can be particularly useful in times of crisis. It is then that a leader most needs perspective. If he is to keep his mind focused on his long-range goals, he must step back from the problems of the present. Reading helps him do that. He may not find an answer to his problem in what he reads, but new thoughts will refresh the mind and permit him to tackle his problems with renewed energy.

The purpose of a good college education is to expand the mind, widen the horizon, and provide perspective. A reading program should serve the same purpose. Most people stop that kind of reading when they finish college. They continue to read what they need to read to do the job. But otherwise their education comes to a halt. Their horizons become narrower. They lose their perspective. They end up knowing everything about some things and nothing about everything.

One of the most difficult questions to answer is to advise someone what to read. I happen to prefer history, biography, and philosophy. But I agree with columnist Murray Kempton, a prolific reader who recently told me that one should not rule out great novels. You can learn more about the revolutionary forces that convulsed Russia in the nineteenth century from Tolstoy and Dostoevski than from the turgid scholarly histories of the period. And some of the better current novels are a more accurate portrayal of real life than most of the narrow and biased tomes emanating from the ivory towers of academia.

Oliver Wendell Holmes and Louis Brandeis, two legendary Supreme Court Justices, were close friends. Court buffs have a favorite story about their reading preferences. Holmes liked mysteries. Brandeis felt his friend should improve his mind by reading more serious books. Once when Holmes went on vacation, Brandeis gave him some to take along. After a day, Holmes returned the books to Brandeis and went back to his mysteries. They clearly did him no harm. More than any other Justice he had the ability through his terse, clear opinions to dispel much of the mystery surrounding the complex cases argued before the Court.

13

CONVERSATION

Before I went to Moscow in 1959, I asked a number of people for advice about how I should handle Khrushchev. I particularly recall three of those conversations.

I saw John Foster Dulles at Walter Reed Hospital, where he was dying of cancer. I told him that most of the media pundits were writing that my major purpose should be to convince Khrushchev that the United States was for peace. Dulles disagreed. He said, "You don't have to convince him that we are for peace. He knows that. You have to convince him that he cannot win a war."

British Prime Minister Harold Macmillan had recently seen Khrushchev in Moscow. He observed that Khrushchev was a very proud man and that above all, it was important to treat him as an equal. He wants to be "admitted into the club," Macmillan said.

Probably the most significant advice I received came from an unexpected source, Walter Lippmann, one of the fairest of my many critics in the press. He said that above all I should be prepared. Otherwise, Khrushchev would snow me under with the usual Communist propaganda rhetoric. He urged that I be specific, that I should determine in advance what issues I wanted to talk about, and that I should divert attention from the issues that he wanted to talk about. This advice was a major factor in helping me to be prepared to counter Khrushchev's arguments in what became known as our Kitchen Debate in Moscow. It is the same advice I would give to anyone who has an appointment to meet with a major leader, whether in politics or in any other field.

These three incidents illustrate how conversation can play a role not only in private life but also in historical situations. Like politics, conversation is an art, not a science. But it is not as unstructured as modern art. There are a few rules of thumb I would suggest to prevent a conversation from degenerating into a self-indulgent and useless exercise in free association.

The Lippmann rule is indispensable. Not being prepared means that you will ramble, the conversation will be unfocused, and you will gain nothing from it except having met an important person.

A second rule is to keep it short. When someone boasts to me that he had three hours with a major official, I know that he struck out. During the 1960s, while I was out of office, President de Gaulle saw me every time I visited Paris. Except for a relaxed two-hour luncheon that he and Madame de Gaulle gave for Mrs. Nixon and me in 1963 at the Elysée, every one of my appointments was for exactly thirty minutes. Even if we were in the middle of a discussion, he would politely but firmly cut it off. If he did not, I would get up from my chair and take my leave. Since we both knew that we had a limited time to talk, neither of us indulged in the usual pleasantries. He covered the items that he wanted to cover and I covered the ones I wanted to cover. These conversations, brief as they were, were among the most valuable ones I had during my public career.

Keeping it too brief can be carried to an extreme. Former Senator Ed Muskie tells this story about a prominent Washington socialite who was seated next to Calvin Coolidge at a state dinner. She was aware of his well-deserved reputation for brevity. As the soup was being served, she gushed, "I wonder, Mr. President, if you would help me win a bet? My friend has wagered that I won't be able to get you to say more than two words during dinner." Coolidge responded, "You lose," and went on eating his soup.

A third rule for getting the most out of conversations is whenever possible to make them one-on-one. Every person you add to a meeting dilutes the quality of the conversation.

Another good rule is not to take notes during the conversation. It destroys spontaneity. Only when he is conducting detailed negotiations should a leader take notes. One of the reasons my conversations with foreign officials as President were not as useful as those I had out of office was that notetakers had to be present because of the necessity of keeping a precise record. When out of office I have always followed the general practice of never bringing an aide or even a translator with me when I meet with a foreign leader. That way, I avoid getting the same boilerplate a leader dishes out to the American ambassador.

Another rule is, don't violate a confidence if you want to be invited back. If the person you are talking to thinks he is talking for the record, he will talk to the record. If he thinks he is talking for history, he will talk to history. What you want him to do is to talk to you, with complete candor, confident that you are not going to violate the trust that he has put in you. This same rule applies when a President or other public official wants honest advice from his associates or members of his staff. One of my best advisers was Arthur Burns, who served as counsel to the President before I appointed him as chairman of the Federal Reserve. He had previously served as chairman of the Council of Economic Advisers during the Eisenhower administration. In one of our earliest conversations, he told me that most people tell a President what he *wants* to hear. He felt that as my counsel he should tell me what I *needed* to hear. That kind of adviser is as invaluable as he is rare.

Who should do most of the talking depends on who is participating in the meeting. Some of the most useful and fascinating meetings I had were with General MacArthur in New York City. When you had a conversation with MacArthur, he did the talking and you did the listening. It was always a stunning performance. He would pace the floor of his magnificent apartment in the Waldorf Towers declaiming on foreign policy, economic issues, and politics with incredible knowledge and almost hypnotic conviction. His thoughts were always tightly organized, and his rhetoric was brilliant. If a stenographer had taken down everything he said and transcribed it, it would have required no editing whatsoever. The only leader I have met who was his equal was Lee Kwan Yew of Singapore. If the two of them had ever met one-on-one, I would have given anything just to have been a fly on the wall.

Winston Churchill, without doubt the most fascinating leader of this century, had a similar tendency to dominate the dialogue. C. P. Snow describes the difference between Churchill and Lloyd George in this way. If the subject of balloons came up, Churchill would hold you spellbound for one hour as he tells you all about balloons. Lloyd George, on the other hand, would ask what *you* know about balloons and then listen for an hour. Churchill, however, had a profound understanding of the art of conversation. In his glowing assessment of Balfour in *Great Contemporaries*, he wrote, "Everyone who met him came away feeling that he had been at his very best." The best way to make someone else feel he has been at his best is to ask for his opinion and then listen to him. On the other hand, if you want him to think that you have been at your best, you must make sure that you say something worthwhile.

But if you are the guest, you should allow your host to pick the subject. The first time I met Woody Hayes was at a party celebrating Ohio State's victory over Iowa in 1957, which gave them the Big Ten championship. I wanted to talk about football, but he wanted to talk about foreign policy. We talked about foreign policy.

One of the most intriguing questions I have been asked is who was the best conversationalist I ever met. After forty-two years, during which I met some of the most fascinating men and women of the age, it is difficult to choose one. Certainly the most interesting was Alice Roosevelt Longworth. She had an incredible ability to draw out her guests, but she contributed as much as she received from them. She could talk with equal authority on history, politics, foreign policy, and social issues. But above all, she was an expert on people. Many VIPs were guests at the dinners at her Washington townhouse. But she was always the star. No one, no matter how famous, could ever outshine her. She was never afraid to express her opinions on controversial issues. She loved gossip. She once told me, "I like to be naughty." She was not always right, but she was never dull. If he had known Alice Longworth, Cardinal Richelieu would never have advised Louis XIII, "Intellect in a woman is unbecoming." The only man I have met who was in her league was Robert Menzies of Australia. Had he been born in England rather than in Australia, he would without question have been a great British prime minister in the mold of Winston Churchill.

Eisenhower was also an excellent conversationalist. I first realized this when I met him in Paris in 1951. I was a junior senator from California and not yet committed to a candidate for 1952. He was not yet a candidate, but everyone assumed he would become one. Throughout his life he always insisted that he was not a politician, but no one could have been the leader of the Allied Forces in Europe in World War II without being not only a politician but a great one. During our meeting he immediately put me at ease. Rather than sitting behind the desk as de Gaulle did, he invited me to sit on a couch beside him. He had studied my background and spoke warmly of my work on the Hiss case, remarking that what particularly impressed him was that I had conducted the investigation fairly. Most would expect one of the world's great military leaders to have addressed military issues. But rather than concentrating on the need for adequate military strength in Europe to

144

meet the Communist threat, he put the primary emphasis on the need for Europe's economic recovery. Never once during an hour's conversation did he mention the upcoming election. He knew that the best way to get an office was to appear not to be seeking it. In my case, he made a sale.

Among the literally thousands of conversations I had before and after serving as President, several others left an indelible impression. I still marvel at the coincidence of views expressed independently by de Gaulle, Adenauer, and the great Philippine foreign minister, Carlos Romulo, in 1963 and 1964. Without having consulted with the others, all three urged me to explore the possibility of developing a new relationship between the United States and China. Three years later, I reflected their view in an article in *Foreign Affairs,* which became the first step toward the accommodation with the People's Republic of China that came to fruition when I visited Beijing in 1972.

Another leader who impressed me one-on-one was Manlio Brosio, who had served as Italy's ambassador in Moscow and in Washington and was shortly to become NATO general secretary. In the mid-1960s, when most Europeans were urging detente with the Soviet Union, he expressed reservations. He said, "I know the Russians. They are the greatest actors in the world. They are great liars. They do not consider it wrong to lie. They consider it their duty to do so if it serves their cause."

I suppose in part because we speak the same language, I found that every British leader I met was a superb conversationalist. In addition to Churchill and Macmillan, I benefited from conversations with Jonathan Aitken, Julian Amery, Ted Heath, Alex Home, Christopher Soames, Margaret Thatcher, and Harold Wilson.

There is no doubt that Gorbachev is a big-league conversationalist as well. Having heard of his legendary charm, I was not surprised when he hit all of the right grace notes when he received me in the Kremlin in 1986. But what impressed me even more was that for an hour and a half, without ever consulting a note or an aide, he discussed U.S.-Soviet relations, particularly the complexities of arms control, with a unique combination of subtlety, knowledge, and firmness. He had also done his homework. When I mentioned Churchill's "Iron Curtain" speech, he interrupted me by saying, "Yes, at Fulton, Missouri. That was the speech that started the Cold War"—deftly setting aside the fact that it was

Stalin who started the Cold War by his ruthless occupation of Eastern Europe. Whoever talks to Gorbachev should always be prepared. No one does a better job of selling a bad case.

Conversation can be one of the most powerful weapons in a statesman's diplomatic arsenal provided he follows these guidelines:

Be prepared to make the other party feel he has done well.

Try to leave the other party with the impression you have done well.

Keep it short.

Keep it confidential.

What about the custom of having the other party in for drinks in order to make a conversation flow more freely? I know this is a common practice among diplomats, but I don't recommend it. If you want to enjoy a conversation, that is one thing. If you want to learn something, that is something else. I have found that the most productive conversations take place during business hours rather than at social events. One should always remember Samuel Johnson's wise counsel: "Alcohol does not improve conversation. It only alters the mind so that you are pleased with any conversation."

14

MEMORY

There are probably more myths about memory than any other human faculty. Among the most persistent are these: Those whose memories are poor can never improve. Most great politicians have a phenomenal memory for names. If you have a good memory in one field, you will have a good memory in other fields as well. In old age, memory is always one of the first casualties.

Memory is a mystery. Even the experts don't really understand it. But based on personal experience, I would question some of the conventional wisdom. A few people may have photographic memories, but for most a good memory is an acquired rather than an inherited trait. My good friend Elmer Bobst had an excellent memory even when he was ninety. I once asked him how he did it. He replied, "I punish my memory. I use no crutches; I force myself to remember." He never made notes during a conversation, yet the next day he could reconstruct the discussion almost verbatim. Few people have his extraordinary discipline. But everyone should remember that if you don't use your memory, you will lose it. Making notes during a conversation is sometimes necessary to be sure that you have the words exactly right. But where possible, it is useful to force yourself to remember what you have heard independent of the notes you have taken.

To see the legendary Jim Farley work a room at a big reception or dinner was always an eye-opening experience. He remembered not only names and faces but, even more impressive, usually people's background, family, the places they lived, and jobs. How did he do it? The answer is simple. He worked at it. Why? He liked people. People were his business.

While not in Farley's league, I am reputed to have a pretty good memory for people's names. In fact, when I was in the House and even in the Senate, I could almost unerringly remember the names of hundreds of county chairmen, city chairmen, precinct chairmen, volunteer workers, newspaper reporters and publishers, and prominent business people. As President, I was not as efficient, not because I was older but because there were just so many more to remember. But whenever I knew I was going to meet people at a reception, a dinner, or other function, I thought that the least I could do was to remember guests' names, occupations, family backgrounds, and hometowns. I always made it a practice, when time permitted, to study the guest list for at least a half hour before each event. My secret, if it could be called that, was that after this brief moment of study, whenever I heard a name, a place, or a position, it immediately triggered my thinking processes and I would be able to put them together. When someone came through the line, the usher would give me the name and I would say, "I'm glad to see you again. I remember when we met at a rally in Cedar Rapids in 1952." Most people were naturally pleased and surprised and no doubt wondered how I did it. It was not because of any natural gift. Like Farley, I worked at it. People were my business.

We generally remember what we want to remember. My ten-year-old grandson, Christopher Cox, is an ardent baseball fan. He has an incredible memory for statistics. He can recite the batting averages not only for the Mets and Yankees but also for opposing teams. He also happens to be an excellent student in school. But he finds it far more difficult to remember the date of the Triple Entente than the number of triples Dave Winfield hit his last year with the Padres.

Because I like music, as a very young boy I developed an excellent faculty for playing classical numbers from memory on the piano. I often marvel at how some great conductors can lead an orchestra through a two-hour performance without ever looking at the music on the podium. Yet when that same conductor is accepting an award at a banquet, he has to read every word of his two-minute response. Even actors who can commit a long part to memory often find it difficult to make a speech without notes or cue-cards. Why? Not because of lack of intelligence. An individual has to have high intelligence to be a great actor. But acting is his business. Making speeches is not. When you don't have to remember, you find it difficult to remember.

In fact, speaking without notes is not all that difficult. But once you rely on a TelePrompTer, a written text, or notes, you will find that your capability for memory and speaking extemporaneously is severely reduced. When I first ran for Congress forty-three years ago, I experimented. I sometimes wrote out a speech entirely and read it. Other times I used extensive notes. I got by, but the audiences pretty much sat on their hands. One evening, at a critically important meeting, I threw away the text and spoke without notes. The audience responded enthusiastically. That doesn't mean that you should just speak off the top of your head, and it doesn't mean that you memorize the text word for word. If you do, you will sound stilted and risk losing your train of thought. Instead, train yourself to remember ideas. Think the speech through, preferably in writing. When you deliver it, once you have the ideas thoroughly in your mind, the words will come out spontaneously.

Like any other activity, what is most indispensable is practice. Only with experience will you be confident that when you get up to speak you will not forget what you have to say. But delivering a speech without notes is impossible unless you have thought through your ideas and written them out in your own words. Remembering what you have written yourself is far easier than remembering what someone else has written for you.

I follow the same practice of speaking without notes now that I am out of office. Because my writing takes so much time, I only give two or three major addresses a year, so I have the luxury of plenty of preparation time. Still, it astonishes me how surprised people are that a political figure can stand before them for thirty or forty minutes and speak without notes. Afterwards, they come up and congratulate me as if I had just announced a cure for some major disease. With each speech it seems to intrigue them more. It may be because I am seventy-seven years old and they are surprised I am still ambulatory. But it also may be because in this era of sound bites and quick quips, politicians are becoming lazier, not because they don't want to do a good job of speaking but because so little is expected of them when they do speak and so little attention is paid by the media to any serious or thoughtful comments they make.

Today a President can make a wide-ranging foreign-policy speech and get on the evening news only if he gets a date wrong or happens to pick his nose. It should therefore come as no surprise that frequently when you pick up the paper to read about the evolution of a major Presidential address, what you see instead is a profile of the speechwriter, complete with mug shot. Why should any leader think an issue through, prepare a speech, and then commit it or an outline to memory if no one is going to pay any attention? So he hands the task over to his eager young writers, and a vicious circle soon develops. If policy statements become less important, a leader will spend less time on them. But thinking a speech through helps a leader think his policy through, so when a speech ceases to be his own, so does the policy. In the end, the public suffers, and so does the leader, because he has no reason to force himself to use his imagination and memory to the hilt.

If you do adopt the practice of not making notes during a conversation, as soon thereafter as possible and certainly before the day is out you should either dictate or write out your recollections of the conversation. Once you start this practice, you will find it relatively easy to do. Since I never make notes during my meetings with foreign leaders, I had to develop that faculty. I could recall conversations almost verbatim, again not because I was born with a good memory but because circumstances required me to use a faculty everybody has—the capability of remembering what you have heard and what you have said.

In the years I served in Washington as congressman, senator, and Vice President from 1947 to 1961, I was always enormously impressed by the top political reporters who interviewed me. The best ones did not have tape recorders and never made notes. But when I read their columns or news stories the next day, I found that almost without exception they reflected almost exactly what I had said. These were classic examples of good memory at work.

Today, tape recorders are required equipment for most reporters. It is the easiest way to conduct an interview. It is also the laziest way. But it is not the best way. The advantage is that the reporter is able to get it right, word for word, and he can protect himself from any legal action. But when they write their stories or columns, they sometimes miss the larger idea in their zeal to capture every dangling participle. Also, when the reporter is using a tape recorder or making notes, an official is far more inhibited in what he says than when it is a free-flowing conversation.

Writing based on the transcripts of a tape recording lacks the synthesis of a top-flight reporter and an official thinking through a difficult, controversial issue. The writing may be accurate, but it is also usually dull. The deterioration in good political writing is similar to that which has taken place in sports writing, which was infinitely better in the days before television. A reporter then had to let the reader see the game through his eyes. I can still remember the classic descriptions of football games by great writers like

Braven Dyer, Bill Henry, and Paul Zimmerman. To read today's drab, statistics-laden sports stories after watching a good game on television is like eating warmed-over hash.

When I am asked to name the best orator, the best TV performer, or the best conversationalist I have ever met, it is always a close call. As far as best memory is concerned, there is no contest. I first met Vernon Walters in 1958. That year I made a thirty-minute speech in English before the Uruguayan Congress. Since I knew that many in the audience were bilingual, I spoke at my normal clip without pauses. Walters, who had not made a note while I was speaking, proceeded to translate the entire speech into Spanish. One of the bilingual Uruguayans who heard it told me Walters had been letter-perfect.

Walters has an international reputation for being fluent in seven languages. He is also a top-drawer strategic thinker, in contrast to another UN diplomat described by Paul Johnson as being the only man alive "who could be totally incomprehensible with complete fluency in four different languages." I have met others who have great language skills, but no one who approached Walters in his memory capability. He has deservedly received many compliments for his extraordinary skill. The greatest came from General de Gaulle. De Gaulle never spoke English but understood it well. He proved it to me during a state visit to Washington in 1960 by dismissing a consul general who botched the translation of a toast he proposed at a dinner I gave in his honor. When I had one-on-one conversations with him in Versailles on my state visit to France in 1969, he asked that Walters do the translating for both of us. Again, Walters made no notes, no matter how long our statements were. I asked Walters how he did it. Just like my old friend Elmer Bobst, he quipped, "I punished my memory." His refusal to use the crutch of notes, combined with his high intelligence, produced an incomparable memory.

It is generally assumed that memory declines in old age, since older people often repeat themselves and forget names and dates. But recent research indicates that that does not have to be the case. Many younger people also lose their capacity for memory at early ages simply because of their failure to use it. When older people no longer have any interests or other reason to remember, their memory capability naturally declines. But if they remain interested in the world around them, they can be as sharp as people half their age. I last talked to Chou En-lai and Charles de Gaulle when they were in their seventies, Herbert Hoover and Winston

Churchill when they were in their eighties, and Adenauer when he was ninety-one. All were not as physically well as they had been in earlier years. But they were still vitally interested in the world around them and preferred to talk about the present and the future rather than the past. Their memories might not have been as good as when they were younger, but they were far sharper than most people I have met of any age. Some memory loss in old age has specific physiological causes. But it is becoming increasingly clear that when we indulge old people, and they indulge themselves, with vague talk about creeping senility, they are being consigned to the human junkheap when they still have the capacity to enjoy life and make real contributions to their communities.

15

THINKING

On a flight from Los Angeles to New York in 1965, my seatmate was Broadway lyricist and producer Alan Jay Lerner. My most vivid recollection of our wide-ranging conversation was his answer to a question about why he thought so many of his shows were great hits. He said that the brain was like a muscle. If you don't use it enough, it becomes soft and weak. If you use it properly, it becomes firm and strong. But if you overuse it and it becomes muscle-bound, you should relax it so that you can continue to think creatively. I could see how a man with such a disciplined, sensitive mind could create the sure hit he had just finished, which was appropriately titled *On a Clear Day, You Can See Forever*.

Thinking is the most important and least exercised of man's faculties. Because it is the hardest of his activities, a person will go to the greatest lengths to avoid it.

The language abounds with sayings about thinking. You think on your feet, you think things through, you talk without thinking, you think out loud, you are too busy to think, you put on your thinking cap. Like the weather, everybody talks about thinking, but too few do anything about it, especially these days.

One of the culprits is television. It has enriched life for millions, particularly shut-ins whose only world is what they see on television. But watching television does not exercise the brain. A heart specialist will tell you that walking downstairs is passive exercise, while walking upstairs gives the heart the exercise it needs. For the brain, reading or conversation is like walking upstairs, because they engage and exercise the brain. Watching TV is like taking the elevator.

But to criticize television as a passive medium does not begin to

153

describe the active harm it is doing to our society. Computer specialists have a saying—"Garbage in, garbage out"—which they use when they want to make the point that a computer is only a mechanism for processing information, not creating it. The same principle applies to television. Young people used to learn their lessons from McGuffey's Readers; the baby-boomers learned them from the Beaver and Gilligan. As the postwar generation came of age, it spawned a new generation of TV programmers, who in turn have put more triviality, sex, violence, and bad manners on the air than anyone ever thought possible. Trash TV could only have been created by people who were raised on the tube. Garbage in, garbage out.

I know I am in a minority even in my own family when I say that computers themselves are another culprit in the decline of thinking. I am too old to understand the things, but my grandchildren can't spend the day without them. When I took math in school, we used slide rules for the same calculations today's students solve with electronic calculators. In learning to use the slide rule, we learned something about the interaction of numbers that calculators cannot teach. The way things are going, computers will soon be doing so much for us that the only thinking that will be required will be by those who build and program them. I know the standard reply is that the computer only does routine tasks, freeing the mind for more creative thinking. It is certainly much better for a secretary who has to change a couple of words on a page to put it through a word processor in a few seconds than to have to type over the whole page. What we should bear in mind, however, is that we should always use a computer as an aid to thinking rather than a substitute for it.

Thinking is particularly vital for politicians, whose statements, whether thought through or not, can have enormous consequences both for themselves and their people. As de Gaulle observed, "Great men of action have always been of the meditative type. They have without exception possessed to a very high degree the power of withdrawing to themselves." Too often in politics, the man of thought cannot act, and the man of action does not think. The ideal is one such as Woodrow Wilson, who was a creative thinker and, when still at his best, a decisive man of action. Politicians should follow the advice of Henri Bergson: "Act as men of thought. Think as men of action."

Because thinking is such an individualistic faculty, there are no general rules for how, where, when, or what a person should think.

Churchill apparently did some of his best thinking while dictating his great speeches. When he visited Washington in 1954, I asked him if he had ever considered using a Dictaphone. He replied that an American friend had given him one of those "machines," but that he preferred to dictate to a pretty secretary. I asked Brezhnev that same question when I saw him in the Kremlin in 1974 and got exactly the same answer—with an earthy postscript. "When you wake up in the middle of the night and want to make a note," he said, "it is very convenient to have someone in the room with you to take it down."

When I visited Paul Getty at his home near London in 1965, his secretary told me that every afternoon he had a custom of sitting in his library alone for a solid hour during which he read nothing, made no telephone calls, and made no notes. Instead, he just thought. Then he would get up and place a phone call or two which might add several hundred million dollars to his estate. I don't know if that is a sure way to become a billionaire, but it would be worth a try.

While some people need solitude for creative thought, others' minds seem to thrive in the midst of chaos. I marvel at how newspaper reporters can think with their fingers on a typewriter or computer on a crowded campaign bus or in a noisy city newsroom. I'm told the wire service rewrite man is a dying breed. These highly specialized journalists, who hook a phone over their ears and type out a final draft of a hot news story from raw data called in by a reporter, have to be the most highly qualified, underpaid people in the business.

The great leaders I have known always used every opportunity to think before commenting on a question. Although neither de Gaulle nor Chou En-lai ever spoke English in their talks with me, I know they understood a great deal of it. But neither ever interrupted when the interpreter was translating what I was saying into French or Chinese. Even though they knew what I had said or had a pretty good idea, by letting the interpreter repeat it, they bought time to think.

Some think better at night, others in the early morning. Some prefer a large room, others a small one. Some think on a typewriter or word processor; others prefer a pencil or pen. The critical element is not *how* but *when*. The irony of life in the fast lane—in politics, business, or in any other field—is that brilliant, powerful people who could benefit the most from creative thought are the ones who have the least time for it.

Recognizing that what works for one person may not for another, these are some of the procedures that work best for me.

I prefer a small office to a large one, and particularly one that provides no temptation for diversion. If there is a window with a good view, I sit with my back to it.

I have always insisted, even in the White House years, that my staff provide time in the schedule for thinking. For a major speech or press conference, I insisted on two or three days. And even after a speech had been prepared, I set aside at least an hour of free time before the appearance to get my thoughts together and get up for the delivery. It was especially hard to do this in the White House and on campaigns, when aides saw every blank space on the schedule as a potential stroking session with a state party chairman or interview with a local anchorman.

Even when there was no speech or other appearance to prepare for, I always tried to reserve an hour or two a day for thinking. Some of the best ideas come when you are not focusing on a specific subject. In my case, I find that reading is the best use of that time. I am not a speed reader. For me, reading is like eating. To digest it, you have to chew it well. My reading may not provide specific ideas for whatever I am working on at the time. In fact, it is sometimes better to read in an area that is different from the subject of your current preoccupation. Later, when you are working on something specific, an idea will pop into your head from your reading. Reading also is indispensable for providing perspective, so that when you tackle a specific problem you will think broadly and not narrowly, deeply and not superficially. Most of the great leaders I have met—Churchill, de Gaulle, de Gasperi, Menzies, Yoshida, Mao Tse-tung, Chou En-lai—were prolific readers. Each of these men was a far-sighted strategic thinker not because he inherited that trait but as the result of his habits of reading and contemplation.

There are many sources of information for a leader, including books, articles, briefing papers, and conversations. The way he ingests his food for thought depends on the subject and his own tastes. Some like to bat ideas around with aides over lunch. But I generally preferred to get analysis from others in writing, not because I disliked the fellowship but because I tried not to mix fellowship with work. Besides, most smart people express themselves better in writing than orally. You also tend to be more precise and less glib in your analysis if you are forced to commit it to paper.

On those occasions when I do decide to absorb other people's thoughts in conversation, I find that conversations with a group are not as useful as a dialogue with one person for stimulating creative thinking. And such a conversation is useful only in the research phase of decision making. When it comes time to decide, there is no substitute for sitting alone and thinking the problem through. What works best for me is to list all of the ideas that relate to the subject I must act on and then organize the material in an orderly way. If you have not put your own thoughts in order, you will be unable to convince others to do so. I make at least four outlines for every major speech or question-and-answer session. A single critical sentence can require two or three hours of concentrated thought to frame and hone.

When you run into a roadblock in trying to put your thoughts in order, think around it rather than through it. Or this may be the time for a break—a cup of coffee, a short walk, a look out the window, a bit of reading from a good book. But you must be careful to use these breaks to improve your thinking rather than as an excuse to avoid it.

It is important not to become brain-tired, or as Lerner put it, muscle-bound. Ironically, however, sometimes you do your best thinking when you are the most tired. I had my first and only White House press conference as Vice President after Eisenhower suffered his stroke. It was a difficult period, and I was so tired that I was worried I had not been up to par. Frank Stanton, the president of CBS, called me later that day and told me he was sending me a recording of the conference, because he thought it was the best I had ever had.

When I told him of my concern, he said that a person was at his best on radio or television when he was physically tired. Because of the awareness of fatigue, we raise the level of concentration to compensate. It is something like a sinker-ball pitcher in baseball. If he is too fresh, he puts too much on the ball, and it doesn't sink.

Worrying is not thinking. This does not mean that you should be blithely optimistic and unaware of the seriousness of your problem. But worrying about things you can't do anything about is a waste of time. After I ordered the attacks on the Communist-occupied sanctuaries in Cambodia in 1970, there were violent demonstrations against my action across the nation. Some of my staff members wondered aloud whether we had made the right decision. I always put a stop to that kind of Monday morning quarterbacking by saying, "Remember Lot's wife. Don't look back." In that case,

I was confident I had made the right decision. But whether you are right or wrong, when you worry about the past, you cannot think about the problems you face in the present and future.

There is nothing more exhausting than thinking. I have been more physically tired after two hours of concentrated study than after shaking a thousand people's hands in two hours or making fifteen whistle-stop speeches in a day of campaigning. Because thinking is so tiring, we rebel at it and look for excuses not to do it. But the rewards are worth it.

There is no greater exhilaration than the sense of accomplishment you feel after making a decision based on careful, intense thought. In the end, thinking provides the inner peace and serenity necessary for decisive and effective action.

16

RECREATION

In 1977, President Carter was trying to set an example for economy and modesty in government by cutting back on Presidential perks. He decommissioned the Presidential yacht, grounded some of the Presidential aircraft, dispensed with the fancy matchbooks on Air Force One, and cut back on the use of limousines by staff members. He had to modify some of these decisions later, but the public generally approved of his efforts. I learned that he was also planning to decommission the Presidential retreat at Camp David. I sent a message to him urging that before making that decision, he visit Camp David, because I was sure he and his wife, coming as they did from the rustic surroundings of Plains, Georgia, would be captivated by it. They were. They kept Camp David, and it was the site of the most important achievement of his Presidency—the 1979 Camp David Accords between Israel and Egypt. Perhaps more important, it was a welcome refuge for the Carters throughout their time in Washington.

Why should one who has a reputation for playing political hardball be so solicitous about a President from the other party? Because while recreation is useful for all people, I believe it is absolutely indispensable for whoever holds the toughest job in the world.

When I visited Moscow in 1972, Brezhnev told me that all top Communist Party officials were expected to take off a month each year for vacation. This was not because the party cared whether Brezhnev bagged his annual quota of wild boar, but because it believed time off would enable the top officials to do a better job.

We can't require our Presidents to take time off for recreation, but we should applaud them, not criticize them, when they do.

159

Only someone who has served as President knows how much it takes out of a person.

Woodrow Wilson, a mental giant with a great capacity for work, used to suffer from blinding headaches. He could get relief only by going to Bermuda or some other vacation spot. Herbert Hoover went to Florida and to a fishing camp in the mountains near Washington. Franklin Roosevelt went to Warm Springs, Georgia. Harry Truman went to Key West. Lyndon Johnson went to his Texas ranch. Kennedy went to Hyannisport and Palm Beach. Occasionally some eager-beaver investigative reporter will count up the number of days the President is away and compare it to the time spent in Washington. But while a President may leave the White House, the office always goes with him. The measure of a President's leadership is not how many hours he spends at his desk or where the desk is, but how well he makes the great decisions. If getting away from the Oval Office helps him make better decisions, he should get away.

While a President should not be defensive about his need for recreation, he should avoid giving the impression that he has not devoted enough time to his job. Theodore Roosevelt, whose most severe critics would never accuse him of being shy about publicity, drew the line on publicizing his recreational activities. In a letter to William Howard Taft, who was campaigning to succeed him in 1908, he urged Taft to keep mention of his fishing and golf out of the press. The American people, he wrote, regard politics as "a very serious business and we want to be careful that your opponents do not get the chance to misrepresent you as not taking it with sufficient seriousness."

Dr. Robert Hutchins, the University of Chicago's highly regarded chancellor in the late 1940s, once said, "When I feel the urge to exercise, I lie down until the feeling passes." I doubt if that rule should apply to college presidents. I know it should not apply to Presidents.

I saw first hand how much Eisenhower needed exercise to give him relief from the tensions of the job. Without it, he would pace the floor of the Oval Office like a caged lion. When he did finally have a chance to get away, his temperament would change completely. One day he presided over a National Security Council meeting where there was a very heated discussion of some controversial foreign-policy issues. Afterwards, he invited me to ride to Burning Tree golf course with him. For the first five or ten minutes

160

of the drive, he continued to talk about the issues. Then he shifted gears suddenly and started to talk about the upcoming golf game.

One of his most difficult decisions was asking for the resignation of his chief-of-staff, Sherman Adams. He had asked Meade Alcorn, the Republican national chairman, and me to try to convince Adams that he should resign. When I told Adams that I believed that was Eisenhower's wish, he did not want to take my word for it. He said that he would have to go in and talk to "the boss." He went directly to the Oval Office. The meeting did not last long, but it must have been a terrible ordeal for both men. A little later, as I was leaving the White House to go back to my office in the Capitol, I saw Eisenhower by himself, hitting five irons on the White House lawn. That was his way of breaking the tension that might have devastated someone else.

When I took office in 1969, I noticed that the wood floor near a door that leads to the Rose Garden was pitted with small puncture marks. I could see immediately that they had been left by Eisenhower's golf cleats. I asked my staff to replace that portion of the floor and carve up the old piece to distribute to some of Eisenhower's old friends as souvenirs.

While I am now a firm believer in plenty of recreation and exercise for anyone in public life, I must admit that I did not set a good example during my years in Washington. I took no regular exercise from the time I graduated from college in 1934 until after I was elected to the Senate in 1950. I did not hit a golf ball until I was thirty-eight. Eisenhower was the one who shamed me into taking up the game seriously. He invited me to play with him at Burning Tree in the spring of 1953. Unfortunately for him, he took me as a partner, gambling that I had to be better than my 20 handicap. Eisenhower was a very competitive man. He played to win and hated to lose. If his partner played the wrong cards in bridge or blew a hole in golf, he did not hesitate to show his displeasure. We lost the match and the bet. He talked to me like a Dutch uncle. "Look here," he said. "You're young, you're strong, and you can do a lot better than that."

I had learned in the Navy that when your superior officer makes a suggestion, you should take it as a command. For the first time, I took some lessons and began to play regularly. Four years later, I had a 12 handicap. In 1959 I had to drop golf because the upcoming Presidential campaign required all of my time. During my White House years, I played only two or three times a year. I did not feel that the demands of those extraordinarily busy war years permitted any more, either practically or symbolically. Bud Wilkinson, my fitness adviser, urged me to exercise regularly. I promised I would, but I never got around to it. I did bowl occasionally and went swimming whenever I visited Camp David, San Clemente, or Key Biscayne. I could have gone swimming at the White House as well, but shortly after the inauguration in 1969 I decided that the press corps should be moved out of their crowded quarters in the West Wing, near the President's office, into more adequate surroundings. So we drained the indoor pool and filled it up again with reporters and TV producers. Some of the old-timers complained about being "pushed in the pool," but I believe most of them would now agree that it was a better use of space to make it available to the working press rather than for the enjoyment of the President and members of his staff.

Some medical experts believed my lack of exercise contributed to the phlebitis that caused me such difficulty in 1974 after I left the White House. But far more important than physical health, although directly related to it, is mental health. When you feel better, you think better. The major purpose of exercise and recreation is to change the pace, to rest the mental muscles used for work and exercise others. Recreation plays an indispensable role in recharging your emotional batteries and refreshing your attitude. No matter how mentally or physically tired I was, after a day or two at Camp David I came back the next week with a totally new perspective and renewed energy—ready, as Chief Newman used to say, "to hunt bear with a switch."

What kind of recreation is preferable depends on each individual. For example, I hate calisthenics. I get tired just watching Jane Fonda promote her workout tapes on television. But I can't deny that they get results. President Reagan looks ten years younger than he is in part because he thoroughly enjoys his morning workouts.

There is far more to recreation than just exercise. Roosevelt got relief from the enormous pressures of World War II by turning to his stamp collection or enjoying a game of poker with close friends. Hoover, like Carter, was an excellent fisherman. Both wrote books on the pastime. Like Harry Truman, I occasionally relaxed by playing the piano. One of my most pleasant memories is how pleased he was when I flew out to Independence, Missouri, in the spring of 1969 and presented to him, for display in the Truman Library, the piano he and his daughter Margaret had played in the

White House. If I had followed my daughter Tricia's advice, I might have chosen music as my profession. In 1956, when she was ten years old, she was taking piano lessons and I was trying not too successfully to convince her how important it was to practice. She finally turned to me and said, "Daddy, *you* should have practiced more when you were a little boy. If you had, you might have become famous and gone to Hollywood and they would have buried you in a special place."

In a delightful article, "Painting as a Pastime," Winston Churchill observed that worry is an emotional spasm which occurs when the "mind catches hold of something and will not let it go." The only way to deal with this condition, he went on, is to "gently insinuate something else into the mind's convulsive grasp. If this something else is rightly chosen—the old undue grip releases and the process of recuperation and repair begins. The cultivation of a hobby and new forms of interest is therefore a policy of first importance to a public man." For Churchill most of the time and Eisenhower part of the time, that elusive "something else" was painting.

While not as physically dangerous as his heart attack two years before, Eisenhower's stroke in 1957 was a much more emotionally painful ordeal. I remember going to the White House residence as soon as he was able to see visitors. He received me in a small room that had been converted to a painting studio. He told me a little about his ordeal. There was nothing wrong with his thinking processes; he just could not find the words to match his thoughts. What was fascinating was that throughout our talk he was busily engaged in painting a portrait of Prince Charles that he gave Queen Elizabeth when it was completed. Painting, like golf, was a lifesaver for him.

People sometimes ask what a seventy-seven-year-old former President does for exercise and recreation. Again, I do not set a very good example. I have never gone hunting, and fishing just isn't my bag. I tried deep-sea fishing once as a teenager and gave it up because I used to get seasick. When I told Churchill in 1954 of my problem, he said, "Don't worry, young man, as you get older, you will outgrow it." I was forty-one years old at the time. Incidentally, he proved to be right. I did outgrow it but too late to become a good fisherman. After the Republican Convention in 1952, Eisenhower tried to teach me how to cast for trout. It was a disaster. After hooking a limb the first three times, I caught his shirt on my fourth try. The lesson ended abruptly. I could see that he was disappointed because he loved fishing and could not understand why others did not like it as well as he did.

I don't ski or play tennis. Perhaps because of the chess analogies that are frequently used to describe relations between nations, people often ask me whether I play the game. I don't, but my grandson Christopher plays well enough already to give his father a run for his money. While I don't play bridge, it isn't because I don't like it. I played a number of times in the summer between my first and second years at Duke. But I enjoyed it so much that I knew I could become addicted, so I have never played it since. The one and only time I played gin rummy was in 1944, on a twelve-hour flight from Guadalcanal to Hawaii in the belly of a C-54 transport. The learning process was so expensive that I decided to stick to poker, which I still play once a year with Walter Annenberg and other members of the Benevolent Marching and Philosophical Society of Philadelphia.

I go to an occasional baseball, football, or basketball game. My most vivid memory of a sports event was seeing my first major league baseball game on July 4, 1936. The Yankees crushed the Senators in a doubleheader. A rookie outfielder for New York, Joe DiMaggio, hit a home run into the sun bleachers at Griffith Stadium where I was sitting. The next time I saw the Yankees play on the Fourth of July was on a blisteringly hot Monday afternoon in New York forty-seven years later. Dave Righetti threw a no-hitter against the Boston Red Sox—his first, and mine as well. I shall never forget the high drama of the moment when he struck out Wade Boggs, the best hitter in baseball, with a high inside fastball for the final out.

I quit golf ten years ago. It was a hard decision, because I enjoyed the game. It combines physical exercise, stimulating competition, and warm companionship. And it has another advantage that the non-player cannot possibly appreciate. George Smathers, with whom I served in the House and Senate, once told me that golf courses are on the most beautiful real estate in the world. I hadn't thought about it that way before, but he was right. No one could help but get a lift out of playing such spectacular golf courses as Cyprus Point, Augusta, Oak Hill, Baltusral, Bel Air, or the Valley Club near Santa Barbara.

Playing abroad is also an interesting experience. The girl caddies on Japan's immaculately groomed courses may not understand much English, but they are all great diplomats. Whenever you hit a ball, whether it goes into the bunker or out of bounds, they always say, "Good shot, good shot." There is no better balm for a bruised ego.

So why did I give it up? There were two reasons. From the time Eisenhower gave me that lecture about improving my game, I tried to follow his advice. One day in late 1978, I broke 80. I must admit it was on a relatively easy course in San Clemente, but for me it was like climbing Mt. Everest. I knew I could never get better, and so the competitive challenge was gone. Breaking 80 was an even greater thrill than getting a hole-in-one. Incidentally, I did get a hole-in-one once, but I don't remember much about it, except that it was on the third hole at Bel Air on Labor Day, 1961, I used a MacGregor six iron and a Spaulding Dot ball, and my partner Randolph Scott birdied the hole.

The other reason I quit golf was the decisive one. I had to meet a deadline for my third book, *The Real War*. I simply could not do it and also find four hours a day to play golf. This time, however, I found a substitute. In 1969, I asked President de Gaulle what he did for exercise. He told me that he believed that walking was the best thing a leader could do for his mental, physical, and emotional health. I now follow his advice and walk four miles a day. While I miss the competition and fellowship, I get three times as much exercise as I would playing a round of golf and riding between holes in a cart.

I find that when I am writing a speech, article, or book and run into a mental block, it is best to put the work aside. An idea or phrase will come to me on a quiet walk alone at five-thirty the next morning. Walking, combined with swimming when the season allows it, has proved to be exactly the right combination for me.

But I hasten to add that what works for me may not work for others. What is important is that everyone should find time from his busy life for recreation and exercise. Leaders in all fields should insist on it, not only for themselves but for their employees. Especially in high-powered professions such as politics, business, and the law, net performance is sometimes confused with gross hours. To impress partners, ambitious young associates at top law firms make sure their office lights are on all night and arrange to have themselves paged on Saturdays even if they're not around. Young executives or political aides vie to be the last one out at night and the first one in the next morning. But I would rather have a well-rested subordinate in by nine with a good idea or two instead of one who is in by six-thirty and asleep at his desk with his tie in his coffee by seven.

No one should feel guilty for interrupting his work with a little fun, so long as he does not take it a step further and assume that having fun is the sole purpose of work.

Sometimes I am asked, "Was it fun being President?" This trivializes a very profound question. Any leader welcomes the responsibility and exercise of power. Otherwise he would not pay the price of getting and keeping it. Being in power enables him to realize his life's ambition of making a difference for the better for his nation and the world. Being President is hard work. A President can enjoy great victories or suffer disappointing defeats. Successful Presidents are those who can take each in stride, recognizing that both are inevitable parts of the job.

Recreation is a means to an end, not the end itself. You don't want to be President so that you can have fun. You want to have fun so that you can be a better President. The same is true in many other fields. Writing is not much fun, either. But when you create a book, an article, or a speech, it gives you far more enjoyment than making a birdie in golf.

17

ILLNESS

Do great men make history, as Carlyle insisted, or does history make great men, which both Tolstoy's novels and Toynbee's massive *Study of History* suggest? While we cannot be sure, I believe a strong case can be made that in at least three cases illnesses of great men may have changed the course of history.

At Waterloo, Napoleon was suffering from hemorrhoids and gallstones. Military experts agree that he made several uncharacteristic errors in conducting the battle. Wellington, the victor, admitted that "It was a close run thing." If Napoleon had been at his best, the course of history might have been dramatically changed.

Woodrow Wilson's massive stroke cut short a coast-to-coast campaign to build support for ratification of the Treaty of Versailles. Had he been able to complete the tour and rally the nation behind his inspiring vision of a more peaceful world, there is a chance that the United States would have joined the League of Nations and that the course of events leading to World War II would have been different.

Even Roosevelt's friendliest biographers agree that he was not up to par in the closing phase of the war. He was weak physically and lacked the mental vigor that had always served him so well. Had he been at his best at Yalta, he might have joined Churchill in resisting Stalin's ruthless diplomatic conquest of Poland and the other countries of Eastern Europe.

Serious illness decisively affected my own career twice. In 1960, I had pledged in my acceptance speech to campaign in all fifty states. As the campaign began in September, I had to spend two weeks in the hospital for treatment of an infected knee. I compounded this misfortune by making the mistake of not following my advisers' recommendation that I reduce my schedule and concentrate only on the major states. Finally, while I was mentally up to par in the first debate, I was weak physically and appeared that way on television, in contrast to Jack Kennedy, who looked tan, rested, and in vigorous good health. Since I lost the election by fewer than 119,000 votes out of 69 million cast, it is hard not to conclude that my bum knee was one of the factors that could have made the difference.

In 1973, illness put me out of action for the first time as President. While I was recovering from a debilitating case of viral pneumonia, the existence of the White House taping system was made public. I was faced with a difficult decision. Some of my advisers urged me to destroy the tapes, while others urged me to keep them, because they felt the courts would support our contention that confidential conversations should not be made public. Most of my friends and even some of my critics agree that I made the wrong decision. If I had been up to par physically, there is certainly a chance that I would have stepped up to the issue and ordered the tapes destroyed.

No one can be absolutely sure what might have happened in these cases had illness not intervened. But I do know that my exposure to illness in my early life played a decisive role in affecting my approach to public policy.

In 1947, a number of politicians and pundits wondered why a conservative Republican from California had joined Jacob Javits and other Republican liberals in urging support for an increased federal role in health care. The program we advocated was modest by present standards, but at the time it was considered to be a bold, even reckless departure from conservative principles. While I oppose compulsory national health insurance, I have always supported federal assistance for catastrophic health care. My strong feelings in this respect are a direct result of losing two brothers to tuberculosis. My youngest brother, Arthur, contracted tubercular meningitis. Mercifully, his illness was brief. But for ten years, my oldest brother, Harold, fought a courageous battle against tuberculosis of the lungs before his death in 1933 when I was a junior in college. It was a terrible ordeal for him and the family. We all had to work to pay the astronomical cost of hospitals, doctors, and nurses. My father had to sell a valuable piece of real estate at half price to meet one of the hospital bills.

Because of the miracles of modern medicine, both my brothers would have recovered today. But the experience made an indelible impression on me. From the time I went to Congress in 1947, I was determined to support any proposal to help other families meet such extraordinary expenses without breaking the family budget.

In 1971, some observers were surprised when I included in my State of the Union message a request for the Congress to appropriate $100 million to launch a war on cancer. Why cancer? Why not some other worthwhile program? Again, the reason can be found in my background.

When Pat was thirteen years old, her mother Kate Ryan died of cancer. She had to assume much of the responsibility for keeping house for her two older brothers and her father.

I had great affection for each of my mother's five sisters, but I was closest to my Aunt Beth. She loved a good time. She liked to dance, a pastime in which the other ladies in our rather conservative Quaker family did not indulge. What appealed to me most was that she would take me to the Whittier College football games while I was still in high school. I shall never forget the ordeal she went through when she contracted breast cancer. Her husband, Uncle Russell, borrowed money to take her to some quack in the Midwest who claimed to have a cancer cure. They tried everything, but finally honest doctors told them that the cancer was inoperable. When she died at thirty-three, it was almost as if my own mother had died. And yet few people would openly mention the cause of her death. Cancer was little understood and even less discussed, especially when it struck one so young.

It is generally conceded that Douglas MacArthur was one of the handsomest men ever to wear the uniform. Hoyt Vandenberg, the Air Force chief-of-staff, could certainly have competed with him for that accolade. I vividly remember a National Security Council meeting I attended in 1953. Vandenberg sat on President Eisenhower's right. His mind was alert, but it was obvious from the frailty of his body that he was not well. That June, cancer of the prostate forced him to resign, and he died ten months later. We were all grief-stricken. But his closest friend, General Jerry Persons, Eisenhower's military aide, was particularly affected. He kept saying that Vandenberg's death was so unnecessary. If only he had had the same annual physical examinations that he insisted upon for the men serving under him, the doctors would have discovered the cancer, and an operation would have saved his life. Even as treatment progressed, people's awareness of the disease was so stunted by myth and fear that they resisted taking routine steps such as regular exams that might have saved their lives.

169

In the spring of 1953, I addressed the annual meeting of the Business Advisory Council at the Homestead Hotel in Hot Springs, Virginia. Senator Robert Taft preceded me on the program. Virtually all of the CEOs in attendance were his friends; many had supported him for the 1952 Presidential nomination. And yet he made what many considered to be an ill-tempered and unfair attack on Eisenhower's budget proposals. The audience was shocked. There was only a smattering of applause. Then, in what appeared to be an affront to me as well as to Eisenhower, he left the room before I spoke. I can see him now, limping painfully as he pushed his wife Martha, who had suffered a stroke, in a wheelchair. When some of the council members criticized him in talking privately to me afterwards, I told them that I sensed there was something wrong with him, that everyone should withhold judgment. Within three months, he had died of cancer. As was so often the case with cancer sufferers only a generation ago, he had withheld the news even from close friends who could have given him tremendous emotional support.

While I was presiding over the Senate in the summer of 1957, a young minister who had given the invocation that day asked me to sign an autograph for his nine-year-old daughter, who was being treated for leukemia at the National Institutes of Health. A few days before, Sophia Loren had come to my office and given me two beautiful Italian walking dolls for Tricia and Julie. I learned that the minister's daughter was sharing a room with another nine-year-old girl who also had leukemia. Tricia and Julie enthusiastically agreed that I should take the dolls to them. My half-hour visit with them was one of the most memorable experiences of my eight years as Vice President. I shall never forget the delight in their eyes as they played with their new dolls. If they had looked closely, they might have seen the tears in mine as I thought of the tragic fact that these two beautiful children had only a little time left to live.

These and similar instances were the major factors behind my decision to launch the war against cancer under the leadership of Benno Schmidt. I consider it my most important domestic initiative.

The greatest need was for dramatic increases in funding for research. But our initiative was also a way to help bring a disease that afflicted millions each year into the open. Today, we not only talk more about cancer but do more about it. Preventive and early detection measures we now practice routinely might well have

170

saved or at least lengthened the lives of sufferers like Kate Ryan, Aunt Beth, Hoyt Vandenberg, and Bob Taft. The most dramatic progress has been made in combating leukemia in children, a disease which was previously considered to be incurable. Had we known just three decades ago what we know now, the little girls I saw at the National Institutes of Health might be alive today. The war on cancer has not yet been won. But hundreds of thousands of individual battles against the disease are being won each day, both by patients and by medical researchers seeking a cure.

Even though I am a strong advocate of government leadership in helping people bear health-care costs and helping scientists fight dread diseases, I have seen so many times that the ability to prevail over disease must ultimately come from deep within its victims. Even for leaders who have led great armies into battle, the greatest enemies are the pain, weakness, and discouragement that come with illness.

When Eisenhower had his heart attack, he went through a long period of deep depression. He talked like a man who felt his public career was finished. He did not even want to discuss the possibility of running the following year. The Republican national chairman, Len Hall, was naturally terrified. When reporters asked him about the election, his stock reply was that the ticket would be Ike and Dick. Finally, one reporter asked the dreaded question: "What happens if Eisenhower decides not to run?" Hall blurted out, "We will jump off that bridge when we come to it." Fortunately, he did not have to make that fatal decision. Eisenhower finally recovered his health and his will to live and to win. He was reelected by a landslide in 1956.

In 1957, I received a telephone call from Sherman Adams. He was, without question, the most unflappable man ever to serve as chief-of-staff. But when he tersely asked me, without even saying hello, "Dick, can you come down to the White House right away?", I could tell from his voice that something very serious had happened. When I arrived in his office, he went right to the point. Eisenhower had had a stroke.

I asked him how serious his condition was.

He answered, "We will know more in the morning. This is a terribly, terribly difficult thing to handle. You may be President in the next twenty-four hours." I am sure he said that because he remembered how depressed Eisenhower had been after his heart attack. But the stroke had exactly the opposite effect on him. He fought back. He was as infuriated as I was when some newspaper editorials questioned whether he could or should continue in office. His mind and reasoning powers had not been impaired. But he often could not get his words to match his thoughts. When he wanted to say, "tomorrow," he might say, "yesterday." When he wanted to say, "window," he might say, "mirror." When he wanted to say, "ceiling," he might say, "floor." Usually, he spoke rapidly; now he had to measure and pace his words. It was an enormously frustrating experience for him. But he was determined to recover and serve out his term as President. By iron discipline, that is exactly what he did. In war and peace, Eisenhower won many battles. His recovery from the stroke was his greatest victory.

Foster Dulles waged an epic battle against cancer. At a time when he could not digest solid food and had to subsist on a diet of raw eggs, he flew to Europe for a major NATO meeting. Others who attended observed that they had never seen him sharper or more effective mentally. I called on him a number of times at Walter Reed Hospital during the last weeks of his life. I could see that he was in excruciating pain. He sucked on ice cubes while we were talking to reduce the pain in his throat. But I found him to be even more alert mentally than during all the time we had spent together in the years before his illness. What apparently happens is that when they are sick, some people actually improve their performance because they are trying to compensate for it.

In 1983, I contracted shingles. My high pain threshold did not help this time. My doctor, Harvey Klein, said it was one of the worst cases he had ever seen. It was aggravated by the fact that I was taking coumadin, a blood thinner, to avoid another attack of phlebitis. The sores bled so heavily my sheets and pajamas had to be changed several times a day. I received a lot of sympathetic mail during that period, but one letter that gave me a real lift was from my old friend Norris Cotton. He, too, had had shingles, and he wrote that no one who had not experienced the disease knew how painful it was. He added, "Thank God you don't die from them—just wish you could." Despite the physical suffering, however, it was in this period that I did some of the most intensive and effective creative work I have ever done in completing the manuscript for my book *No More Vietnams*. Like Dulles, I apparently was over-achieving to compensate for what I knew was a serious physical weakness. I am obviously not suggesting that people should welcome illness as a productivity enhancer. But even those with lingering or chronic ailments should realize that periods of physical weakness due to illness can by an act of will become periods of mental strength and creative activity.

Expressions of sympathy to people who are ill are always deeply appreciated. Because of my position, I have received letters, cards, telephone calls, and bouquets of flowers by the thousands while I have been sick. But the next time you visit a sick friend or relative, don't just commiserate and say how sorry you are. Talk about anything except hospitals, doctors, and illness. Dulles and I never once discussed his symptoms, pain, or prognosis. We talked about what was happening in the United States and the world and how we might better deal with the trouble spots and other problems that had arisen. These conversations are among the most memorable I have ever had in my public life. It was good for me. More important, I believe it was good for him.

18

TENSION

When I visited Monsignor O'Brien's Daytop Village drug rehabilitation center, an attractive teenage black girl, who had recovered from a drug dependency she had acquired in a New York City ghetto, stumbled over a word or two as she was making a presentation to me before an overflow audience in the main meeting room. As she completed her remarks, she blurted out, "I am so nervous!" When I got up to speak, I told her that she shouldn't be embarrassed, because while I had made thousands of speeches in my career, I always experienced nervousness before a major appearance.

Even those who lead relatively uneventful lives must at times deal with tension. A job interview, college entrance examination, bar examination, big game, play opening, major speech, critical presentation, or board meeting can all lead to tension. You must be up for such events without being uptight. That way, tension will be a creative rather than destructive force.

In our fast-paced world, some experts claim to have established a direct relationship between bad nerves and poor health. Doctors routinely advise their patients to cut back on tension-producing activities as well as on smoking, cholesterol, and gin. Some corporations urge their executives to meditate instead of taking coffee breaks. The bestseller lists proliferate with books full of advice about "feeling good about yourself."

It is probably true that a life filled with tension simply for tension's sake will not be a productive or healthful one. But it is not true that all tension is inherently bad. Look at the way the definition of the word "nervous" has evolved. In the eighteenth century, it meant "strong or vigorous." Today, it means "worried or

174

jittery." We often hear that someone worries too much. But in some fields, politics included, you *can't* worry too much, if worrying means recognizing that things may go wrong and planning how to deal with these inevitable setbacks. Those blissful souls who speed so self-confidently along life's straight, smooth highways are often the ones who end up in the ditch when the road suddenly veers into a sharp curve.

A certain healthy measure of tension can help a person anticipate a crisis. It can also help him to deal with it when it comes. In 1962, I published my first book, *Six Crises*. I have written seven books since then; I have stopped counting the crises. In each of them, I have found that tension plays a critical role in three ways:

Tension is necessary for any creative action.

Tension is a natural reaction when you face a crisis.

Tension is harmful only when you are more concerned about it than the crisis you have to deal with.

Two examples, one involving political survival and the other physical survival, illustrate these points.

After General Eisenhower selected me as his running mate in 1952, Joe Martin, the convention chairman, asked Pat and me to come to the podium so that he could introduce us to the delegates. I felt that the cheering and demonstrations were going on a bit too long, and I suggested that he call the convention to order. He smiled and said, "Let them cheer a while longer. You have to get in the hay while the sun is shining."

The sun shone brightly until our campaign train pulled out of Pomona, California, for the first leg of our West Coast swing. Then it went into total eclipse. A liberal opposition newspaper in New York had reported that a $16,000 fund, which had been raised by some of my supporters to cover office expenses not covered by the government appropriation, was actually for my personal use. The charge was false, but it hit like a bombshell on our train and a nuclear explosion on Eisenhower's. He had campaigned to clean up the Truman scandals; now his running mate for Vice President was involved in one of his own.

Everybody hit the panic button. The *New York Herald Tribune*, Eisenhower's leading supporter for the nomination, called for me to resign or for Eisenhower to dump me. Eisenhower told the reporters on his train, virtually all of whom wanted me off the ticket, that I would have to come through "clean as a hound's tooth." Governor Tom Dewey was my contact with the Eisenhower campaign staff. He recommended that I go on national television and defend myself. Eisenhower agreed. We left the campaign trail in Portland and flew back to Los Angeles. I had just forty-eight hours to prepare the speech that would either end or save my political career.

I worked non-stop with very little sleep during those two days. Many times I have found that my best ideas come when I thought I could not work for another minute and had to drive myself to finish the task before a deadline. I broke the tension only once, when I took a long walk with Bill Rogers the night before the speech and tested some of my ideas on him. Sometimes such a change of pace can recharge a mind that has become sluggish from overwork. But while it may be necessary and helpful to take the machine out of gear once in a while, it is never wise to turn the engine off and let the motor get completely cold.

Two hours before broadcast time, everything seemed to be in order. There was only one question left. Dewey had recommended that at the conclusion of the speech I ask the listeners to call, write, or telegraph their opinions about whether I should stay on the ticket. I had to decide whether to ask them to send the message to Eisenhower or to me. I was still mulling this over when I got an urgent call from Dewey. He told me that while he did not agree, a majority of Eisenhower's advisers had just met and wanted me to submit my resignation to Eisenhower at the end of the broadcast. He thought that I should say that while I felt I had done no wrong, I did not want my presence on the ticket to be a liability to the Eisenhower campaign. When he asked me what he should tell them I was going to do, I exploded and said I didn't have the slightest idea and they should listen to the broadcast. "And tell them I know something about politics, too!" I said.

I decided to reject their advice and to submit my fate to the television audience. Rather than having them write or wire me or Eisenhower, I decided it was best to ask that they contact the Republican National Committee. If the broadcast did not persuade the listeners, the politicians rather than Eisenhower could take responsibility for removing me from the ticket. If the broadcast was a success, Eisenhower would need and welcome the backing of the National Committee for keeping me.

I completed my notes, and Pat and I rode together to the studio. I rode in the front seat of the car so I could look over my notes again. We arrived at the El Capitan Theater just twenty-five minutes before broadcast time. There was no rehearsal. There was no advance text. There was no TelePrompTer. They used a salesman who resembled me as a camera stand-in. Ten minutes before air time, we went on stage to check the set and have the lights adjusted. The director asked what movements I would make and I told him, "I don't have the slightest idea. Just keep the camera on me."

Then we went back to the dressing room. Three minutes before air time, my television producer, Ted Rogers, knocked on the door. I turned to Pat and said, "I just don't think I can go through with this one." I was uptight.

"Of course you can," she said, with the firmness and confidence in her voice I desperately needed. We walked back on stage. I sat and watched the second hand go around and around, and then the director brought his hand down and pointed to me. This was it. The moment I began to speak, the enormous tension that had built up for the past week and seemed almost unbearable suddenly went out of me. I felt in complete control of myself and my material. I was calm and confident. I knew what I wanted to say, and I said it from the heart. I learned a lesson then that served me well for the rest of my political career. In a moment of great crisis, a man calls on resources of physical, mental, and emotional power he never realized he had.

The speech was an enormous success. Hundreds of thousands of wires and letters and telephone calls poured in to the National Committee. The vote was virtually unanimous that I should stay on the ticket, and Eisenhower followed their recommendation. The press reaction, however, was mixed. The reporters traveling with me were for me. The reporters on the Eisenhower train were against me. As Jim Bassett, my press aide, put it cryptically: "They are here so as to have front-row seats for the hanging."

What particularly irritated them was an idea that occurred to me on the plane flight from Portland to Los Angeles and that I had written down on an airline postcard. I remembered that Roosevelt had come under attack in 1944 supposedly for sending a destroyer to pick up his dog Fala when it had been left in the Aleutian Islands. Roosevelt had destroyed his critics by saying, "I don't resent attacks on my family or on me, but Fala does resent them." In my own speech, after rebutting all of the false charges about receiving illegal gifts, I said that there was one gift I *had* received. Someone in Texas had sent us a little black-and-white cocker spaniel puppy. My daughters had named it Checkers. They liked the dog, and I said that regardless of what anyone said about it, I was going to keep it. That reference is what gave the speech its name.

177

The reporters thought the Fala story was cute. They thought the Checkers story was corny. But the television viewers liked it, and that was all that mattered. The crisis was over, but there were still dangers ahead. An inaccurate news report from Cleveland, where Eisenhower was speaking that night, said he wasn't satisfied with the speech and had to get more information from me before he made a final decision. I blew my stack. I sat down and wrote a resignation from the ticket. My campaign manager, Murray Chotiner, tore it up. Ironically, a telephone call from Bert Andrews of the *Herald Tribune* made me see things in perspective. There was no question that Eisenhower was going to keep me on the ticket, he said. The broadcast had decided that. But this man had been the general of all of the Allied armies in Europe, and I had to let him make the final decision in his own way. The storm blew over. The campaign ended in a landslide victory for Eisenhower, and the Republicans won majorities in both the House and Senate, something that had not happened since 1928 and was not to happen again even in the Presidential campaign landslide victories of 1972, 1980, 1984, and 1988.

The Fund crisis taught me a lesson which may be of value to others. Being under great tension before a do-or-die speech or some other pivotal event should not concern you if you are well prepared. If you have made a final decision after thorough consideration of all the options, you will find within yourself the calm, confidence, and strength to perform far beyond your expectations. When you feel *no* tension, you will probably do poorly.

The events culminating in the violent, Communist-led demonstrations that engulfed Pat and me in Caracas in 1958 began a few days earlier in Montevideo. The reception on our arrival in the Uruguayan capital had been enthusiastic. But I noted as we drove past the university that a few students—from their appearance, I would guess that they had been students for a long time—held up signs reading *"¡Fuera Nixon!"* ("Nixon, go home!") After consulting with our ambassador, Bob Woodward, I decided to make an unscheduled stop at the university. I happened to walk right into an election that was being held for student officers in the law school. I answered questions, some of them hostile, for over an hour. The signs disappeared, and the students cheered. The left-wing agitators had suffered a humiliating defeat.

In Lima, Peru, the demonstrators were out in full force. I was scheduled to speak at San Marcos, the oldest university in the Western Hemisphere. Its director took me aside at a reception the night before and recommended that I cancel the visit because of threatened student demonstrations. I told him I would be glad to cancel if he would withdraw the invitation, but he would not take that responsibility. The chief of police also urged me not to go but declined to make his recommendation public, because he did not want to leave an impression that the police were incapable of protecting me. That left it up to me. No one else was willing to take the heat. Most of my own advisers, concerned for my physical safety, recommended that I cancel the visit.

Fortunately, our ambassador in Peru was an experienced and wise foreign service officer, Ted Achilles. He was mild-mannered on the outside but steel on the inside. He said that from a personal standpoint, it would be safer not to go. But he pointed out that if I made that decision, the Communists would boast throughout Latin America that the students of one of the oldest and greatest universities in the Western Hemisphere had scared away the Vice President of the United States.

It was past 2:00 a.m. when I went to bed. I had only eight hours to decide whether to fight or run away. Outside my window the mob was chanting *"¡Fuera Nixon!"* over and over again. I did not get much sleep that night because of the noise and the almost unbearable tension.

It is in a difficult period of indecision that the tension is the greatest. I remembered Eisenhower telling me in 1953 on an automobile ride from Quantico to Washington that he had gone through hours and days of mental and physical tension before making the final decision to go forward with the Normandy landing. Once the decision was made, his mind and body relaxed, he slept restfully, and he was in prime shape for the subsequent decisions essential to the success of D-Day. So I knew that in this case, while I faced a decision that was far less important than Eisenhower's, the same thing would happen to me. Once I decided, the tension would disappear.

The following morning, I made the decision to go, and directed that only Jack Sherwood, a Secret Service agent, and Colonel Walters, my official translator, accompany me. We reached San Marcos and walked directly into a mob of two thousand chanting students. It took them by surprise. Most of them wanted to shake hands, but the leaders in the rear would not tolerate another propaganda defeat like Montevideo. I felt something glance off my shoulder and Walters whispered in my ear, "They are throwing stones." We moved back toward our car while continuing to face the mob and talking to those nearest to us, as though we were taking our leave but not retreating. I stood on the back of the car as we moved away and shouted out, with Walters translating in rapid-fire Spanish: "You are cowards, you are afraid of the truth, you are the worst kind of cowards!"

We drove to Catholic University and got an emotional, hand-clapping, foot-stomping reception from friendly students who had heard what had happened at San Marcos. We were pummeled and spit upon by another mob that was waiting for us when we returned to our hotel. But we had won the day. From that day on, everywhere we went in Peru the crowds were shouting, "¡Viva United States, viva Nixon!"

In Caracas, the Communist agitators took their last shot, and it was a good one. At the airport, they were no longer shouting, "¡Fuera Nixon!"; it was now, "¡Muera Nixon!"—"Death to Nixon!" We had gone ahead with the visit after the Venezuelan government assured us it could control the demonstrations. But a junta had just overthrown a dictator and tossed out his police force with him. The new recruits were unable to handle the situation. From the time our car entered the city's main thoroughfare, the rocks rained down on us. It was like being on the inside of a drum with somebody pounding on it.

In the middle of the city, our motorcade was brought to a halt by a roadblock of buses and automobiles backed up behind a huge dump truck that had been deliberately parked in the center of the street. Crowds of demonstrators swarmed around us and ripped the Venezuelan and American flags from the front of our car. Six Secret Service men who had flown in from Washington for the stop in Caracas jumped out of the car behind us and tried to fend off demonstrators who were kicking the fenders and doors of the car. The Venezuelan police officers refused to get off their motorcycles. Some of them took off like scared rabbits. We finally broke through this blockade and a second one only to run into a third one, where banks of buses, trucks, and automobiles had been parked directly in the path of the motorcade.

Out of the alleys and side streets poured a screaming mob throwing rocks and brandishing sticks and pieces of steel pipe. For twelve minutes we sat there with the crowd milling about, shouting, and attacking. Our Secret Service agents were superb. But just as one pushed someone away, another would slip behind and attack again. One of the "student" ringleaders—I would guess that he was about forty years old—started to bash in the window next to me with a big iron pipe. The glass splattered into the car. Walters got a mouthful, and I thought for an instant: "There goes my translator." Some of it nicked me in the face.

Then we heard the ringleader shout a command and our car began to rock. I knew what that meant. It is a common tactic for mobs to rock a car, turn it over, and set it afire. Sherwood pulled his revolver and said, "Let's get some of these sons of bitches." He told me later, "I figured we were goners and I was determined to get some of those bastards before they got us." At that point, I made a quick decision. I reached forward, put my hand on his arm, and told him to hold fire. I don't know why I did this except I knew intuitively that firing a gun would be the excuse for the mob to get completely out of hand. They rocked the car more and more, and then suddenly we were off. The driver of the news photographers' truck in front of us had edged his way into the oncoming traffic lane, clearing a path for us like a blocker for a running back. In a few minutes, we were safe at the American Embassy.

It was a close brush with death. But I was absolutely calm throughout. Those who have experienced the tension of a crisis before are better able to handle another one. Some said I had been brave. That is nonsense. Anyone who says he has never felt fear is a liar. It was not so much a question of courage as of experience.

There are a number of lessons that can be learned from these two examples of tension—one involving danger to my political career, the other to my life.

Tension in such situations is normal and can actually be healthy in preparing you to be at your best in dealing with a problem.

Tension disappears once a decision is made and action begins.

The easiest period in a crisis situation is the battle itself. The most difficult is the period of indecision before the battle—whether to fight or run away. The most dangerous period is the aftermath. It is then, with all resources spent and his guard down, that an individual must watch out for dulled reactions and faulty judgment.

The bigger the problem, the broader its consequences, the less an individual thinks of himself. "Selflessness" is the greatest asset an individual can have at a time of crisis. "Selfishness," in its literal rather than its lay sense, is the greatest liability. The very fact that the crisis is bigger than the man himself takes his mind off his own problems.

I do not believe that some people are naturally more cool, courageous, and decisive than others in handling crisis situations. Some may be stronger, less emotional, quicker, smarter, or bolder than others. But these attributes are for the most part acquired, not inherited, and many times acquired suddenly under tension. Dealing with such intense levels of tension is like climbing a mountain—once you do it, you can be confident of being able to do it again.

FOUR

19

RISKS

In his Pulitzer Prize-winning biography of Huey Long, Harry T. Williams recounts a classic anecdote about Long's first statewide campaign in Louisiana. When he began his tour of southern Louisiana, the local political leader told Long that he should bear in mind that there would be a lot of Catholic voters in his audience. Long, a Protestant, said, "I know." In his speech, he handled the religion issue this way. "When I was a boy," he said, "I would get up at six in the morning on Sunday, hitch our old horse up to the buggy and would take my Catholic grandparents to mass. Then at 11:00 a.m. I'd hitch the old horse up again and take my Baptist grandparents to church." The line went over like gangbusters.

That night, the local leader said, "Huey, you have been holding out on us. I didn't know you had Catholic grandparents." "Don't be a damn fool," replied Huey. "We didn't even have a horse."

In retrospect, if I had considered the risks, I would never have run for Congress in 1946. Long didn't own a horse; we didn't own a house. We didn't own a car. I didn't even own a civilian suit. Our net worth was $10,000, a combination of what I had saved from my Navy pay, my poker winnings in the South Pacific, and Pat's job with OPA in San Francisco while I was overseas. I had never run for office before. I had never met a congressman, and except for a couple of speeches for Wendell Willkie before small audiences in 1940, I had no experience whatever in partisan politics. In addition to all of this, we were expecting our first child in February 1946.

How did it happen and why? Politics is the most prolific mother of myths. Harry Wismer, the Washington Redskins' announcer, once introduced me at a sports banquet as a great football player

185

who had been named to the little All-American football team. He was surprised when I told him that I had never even made a letter at Whittier College. The myth about how I became a congressional candidate is that I answered an ad in a newspaper. If there was such an ad, I never saw it. The fact is that in September 1945, while I was stationed at Middle River, Maryland, terminating Navy war contracts with the Martin Corporation, I received a letter from a long-time family friend, Herman Perry, the manager of the Whittier branch of the Bank of America. The letter was short and to the point. Would I consider becoming a candidate for Congress in the 12th Congressional District? He was a member of a "committee of one hundred" that had been set up to find someone who would have a chance to unseat Jerry Voorhis, a ten-year veteran who appeared to be unbeatable. Perry wrote, "The Republicans are gaining." That did not impress me too much, because I recalled that he had predicted in 1936 that Alf Landon was going to beat FDR. He had good company. The *Literary Digest* poll also predicted a Landon victory that year; I've never completely trusted a poll since.

Pat and I talked far into the night and decided that we should take the chance. It would mean that we would bet everything we had on the outcome. All of the $10,000 had to be spent to cover our living expenses and some of our campaign costs as well. It was not a rash, impulsive decision. We both had worked our way through school and looked forward to a life of some financial security. We liked Whittier. But we also liked adventure. In 1941, the year after we were married, we saved enough to take the last cruise of the United Food Company banana boat, *Ulua,* to Central America. Our accommodations were the cheapest available, but we treasure the memories of that trip as much or even more than those of the grand tours we made in the Vice-Presidential and Presidential years. The *Ulua,* incidentally, was sunk by German submarines a few months after that cruise.

But what primarily motivated me was that I was part of the World War II generation. We had strong feelings about war and peace and the kind of nation we had been fighting for. We respected the leadership that had led us to victory in war, but we felt that the challenges of peace required new, younger leaders. My campaign slogan would be: "America needs new leadership now." When I wrote back to Perry, I emphasized that I would campaign as a progressive Republican looking for solutions to postwar problems.

It was not easy. We rented a house from my barber. It was adequate but atrociously furnished. The main difficulty was that our neighbors raised minks for a living. Minks make beautiful coats, but as animals they are repulsive because they eat their young. I can still remember working on speeches late at night and hearing the screaming of the baby minks next door.

I began the campaign with an ostensibly non-political speech before the Whittier Rotary Club on January 14, 1946, five days after my thirty-third birthday. I told the story of how nine extraordinary ordinary men did a superhuman job one day on Bougainville unloading heavy equipment from our SCAT transport planes and helping the Army nurses take care of men who had been wounded in a Japanese air raid the night before. These enlisted men were a cross section of America, including an American Indian, an Italian, a Pole, and a red-headed Irish boy from New Jersey who was later to travel with me to Green Island on a PBY seaplane. They would receive no medals for bravery, but they all deserved a medal for doing routine, tough, hard work without complaining.

Typical of the group was my master sergeant, Tex Massengale. One morning his left arm was swollen almost twice its size because he had been bitten the night before by one of the huge Bougainville centipedes. When I asked him if he wanted to go to sick bay, he said, "Oh hell, Lieutenant, don't worry about me. They grow twice that big down in Texas."

I spoke also of my admiration for another group of unsung heroes of the Pacific War, the Seabees. I knew them well because they ran the best mess on the islands where I was stationed. I could have eaten with the Marines, but I chose the Seabees because while the Marines can fight, they never learned to cook. I shall never forget one night when the Seabees ignored an air-raid alert and continued to run their bulldozers at top speed so that they could meet the deadline for finishing an air strip on Green Island. I developed a life-long respect for these hard-driving construction workers. They wore hard hats, but they had good heads and warm hearts and were among the closest friends I had during my service overseas.

Finally, I told how impressed I had been by the bravery of the Army nurses who ignored an air-raid alert and insisted on staying on our SCAT transport plane with seriously wounded men who were being evacuated.

The audience listened with rapt attention as I spoke of my experiences with those men I had been privileged to know during my

187

wartime service. I learned then a lesson that every politician should bear in mind. The best way to make a political speech is to make it truly non-political.

The greatest risk I took during the campaign was to participate in debates with my far more experienced opponent. I did well in the first debate, but most people agreed that it was a stand-off. Murray Chotiner, who was managing Bill Knowland's campaign for the Senate and advising me part time, urged that I challenge Voorhis to more debates. He was blunt. "Dick, you're running behind, and when you're behind you don't play it safe," he said. "You must run a high-risk campaign. You may not win the debate, but if you don't debate you won't win the election." It was one of the best pieces of advice I ever got.

The debates were not about communism, as some "historians" have struggled to demonstrate, but about the economy. I could speak persuasively on the issues because I spoke from personal experience. People were fed up with wartime wage and price controls, and I knew why. When we were living in New York in the summer of 1945, in a rented apartment on West 93rd Street, Pat had told me that it was impossible to buy meat with our ration cards. In desperation, I went in to a shop and told the butcher that having worked in a store, I knew how frustrating it was not to be able to give customers what they wanted. Whether it was my pitch or my service uniform, he took pity on me and sold me a couple of lamb chops at a reasonable price.

I remember how excited Pat was when I brought them home. We hadn't had fresh meat for weeks. I could not bring myself to tell her that I hated lamb because I had eaten so much rank-tasting, over-ripe Australian mutton in the South Pacific.

The Republican national slogan, which we adopted for our own campaign, was: "Had enough?" Since Voorhis was a liberal with a socialist background, he defended rationing and the wage and price controls. I opposed them and became one of the winners in the Republican landslide of 1946. There were many other winners, but because I had taken the risk of running against a New Deal liberal who seemed to be unbeatable, I was called a giant killer. By risking all, I had earned a national reputation even before I cast my first vote in Congress.

In the summer of 1948, Pat and I thought we were sitting on top of the world. Julie had been born on July 5 to join two-year-old Tricia, whose baby picture had appeared on our first piece of campaign literature. Nineteen forty-seven had been a great year for us. A liberal freshman congressman from Massachusetts, Jack Kennedy, and I had drawn straws with other new members to determine our rank on the House Labor Committee. He drew the short straw on the Democratic side and I drew the short straw on the Republican side. We were both hard workers and developed a reputation for being good questioners of committee witnesses. We had our first debate at McKeesport, Pennsylvania, on the Taft-Hartley Act. I was for it. Coming from a labor district in Massachusetts, he was against it. On the sleeper train back to Washington we drew straws to see who would get the lower berth. This time I won. We talked most of the night, not about labor and other domestic issues but about foreign policy, where we found we were generally in agreement. Both of us had voted for President Truman's Greek-Turkish aid program. It was a relatively easy vote for him as a Democrat. It had been another substantial political risk for me, as a Republican representing a district where most voters tended to be isolationists.

In September 1947, as a member of the prestigious Herter Committee, I traveled throughout Europe. Our mission was to make recommendations to Congress about authorizing funds for the Marshall Plan. Europe had been devastated by the war. Its people were hungry and desperate, its leaders virtually powerless to begin the task of rebuilding their shattered economies. Meanwhile Communist parties and movements were filling the breach with their empty but insidiously appealing promises of a better world.

I returned to the United States convinced that only a massive infusion of American aid could prevent Western Europe from going the way of Soviet-dominated Eastern Europe. But when I took a mail poll in my district, I found 75 percent of my constituents were opposed to foreign aid. It was foolhardy for a first-term congressman to risk his seat by going against such massive odds. It was a dilemma faced by every elected official at one time or another. Edmund Burke described it eloquently in a speech to his constituents in Bristol in 1774. "Your representative owes you, not his industry only," he said, "but his judgment; and he betrays instead of serving you if he sacrifices it to your opinion." I returned to California for an intense round of speeches throughout the district, arguing that only the generosity of the American people could save our allies from starvation and communism. The voters of the 12th District eventually came around to my position, and when the Marshall Plan passed the House the following spring by a vote of 318 to 75, I had voted yes—without risking that my vote could be used against me when I ran for reelection the following year.

This incident illustrates a lesson every elected official should always bear in mind. He is tempted to play it safe—to take the path of least resistance right down the middle of a graph of polling data, choosing his positions based on the lowest common denominator of his constituents' positions. But the essense of leadership is being willing to go against people's uninformed wishes and eventually even bring them along. Leadership requires both risk taking and also a higher regard for the good judgment of informed voters than is currently fashionable. A leader is not required to sacrifice himself in the face of immutable political opposition. But neither should he sacrifice his principles when a little creativity and hard work would permit him to turn that opposition into support.

I was also appointed to the Committee on Un-American Activities, on which Jerry Voorhis had served. This gave me the opportunity to understand the insidious threat to American interests posed by domestic communism. Because of the time required by the Labor Committee, which was considering the landmark Taft-Hartley Act, I did not play a major role in the most publicized hearings of 1947, when the committee investigated allegations of Communist infiltration into the movie industry. One of the sessions marked the first time I saw Ronald Reagan in person, when he testified before the committee as president of the Screen Actors Guild. Pat and I had seen him in the movies and liked him because we preferred movies where the good guys won, and he always played a good guy. I don't recall asking him any questions, but he made a good impression in his testimony.

My press was excellent that first year in Congress. Along with Kennedy, I was generally considered by Washington's political experts to be a comer with a good future. On August 7, 1948, all of this changed virtually overnight.

Alger Hiss, a highly respected former diplomat, had appeared before the committee that day and denied categorically charges made two days before by Whittaker Chambers that he had been a Communist while holding high positions in the State Department. He not only denied the charges but went further. In what proved to be his fatal mistake, he denied ever having known a man by the name of Whittaker Chambers.

The roof fell in on us. Most in the press were harsh critics of the committee anyway, because of its sloppy procedures and the un-substantiated charges that were routinely made by its witnesses. Now those covering the hearing were virtually unanimous in believing Hiss and condemning the committee for putting Chambers on as a witness before checking out his story.

In our executive session after the hearing, almost everyone believed that we had been had by Chambers and that the best thing to do was to turn the matter over to the Justice Department for investigation and prosecution. Only Bob Stripling, our chief investigator, and I held out. We knew that is was virtually impossible to determine whether or not Hiss was a Communist. On the other hand, we thought we should be able to find out by thorough investigation whether Hiss and Chambers had known each other. I was named as a member of the subcommittee to investigate that issue. With our tiny staff of six up against the combined forces of the White House, a Democratic administration's Justice Department, and the Hiss defense team, the odds seemed impossible. But we had one thing going for us: we were right. Chambers had told the truth, and Hiss had lied. Two years later, he was convicted of perjury.

If taking on a highly unpopular cause is the greatest risk you can take in politics, then continuing the investigation was a risky, even reckless decision. Hiss was popular, the committee was unpopular, and the administration and the media were lined up against us. By going along with the other members of the committee and dropping the investigation, I would have risked nothing. By going forward with the investigation, I risked everything. Failing would deal a severe setback to a promising political career. In the Hiss case, my risk paid off. But there was a down side. From that time on my press, except for the work of a few objective reporters, turned sour. As Bert Andrews, who covered the case for the *New York Herald Tribune,* warned me, "The worst thing you can do to a member of the press corps is to prove that he has been wrong on a major issue." That is precisely what I did on the Hiss case, and it would not be the last time.

After I lost the 1960 election, a good friend was commenting on how close it was. He noted that my press had not been nearly as positive as Kennedy's and expressed the opinion that if it had not been for the Hiss case, I would have won. On the other hand, had it not been for the Hiss case, I would not have had the chance to run for President in 1960. You must only run a risk of this magnitude if you have great goals to achieve by doing so. I was sustained throughout the Hiss case by the firm belief that Chambers was telling the truth and that exposing Hiss was in the vital interest of the nation.

In 1948, I was reelected to the House after winning both the Republican and Democratic nominations under California's cross-filing system. The Hiss case had made me a major national figure and assured me a safe seat in the House as long as I chose to stay in Congress. Many believed I could reach a top leadership position, possibly even Speaker.

Sheridan Downey, a popular, non-controversial establishment Democrat, was the senior senator from California, and it was widely assumed that he would run for reelection in 1950 and win. Risking a safe seat in the House for a longshot chance for a seat in the Senate seemed to be both rash and stupid. Yet I decided to take that risk, for several reasons. Continuing to serve in the House was not an exciting prospect, since there was little I could do that could match what I had done in the Hiss case. Another factor was intuition—a useful but at times dangerous faculty which politicians tend to possess in greater degrees than others. While Truman had upset Dewey in 1948, he was still not popular, and I felt that 1950 might be a good Republican year. Downey had fairly broad support, but his support was thin, and I knew that the left wing of the California Democratic Party had become increasingly disenchanted with him because of his refusal to support some of their extreme positions. In short, while the polls told me not to run, my intuition told me I should consider it. It was not a case of coolly calculating the odds but of a gut feeling that I might be able to beat them.

Late in 1949, I began to survey my close friends and political supporters. Those who had supported me for Congress in 1946 were unanimously against my running. Why risk the certainty of having a good representative in Congress for the uncertainty of a run for the Senate? Their reasoning made sense, and I was leaning against running until a critical conversation led me to change my mind.

The three major Republican newspapers in California were then the *Los Angeles Times, San Francisco Chronicle,* and *Oakland Tribune.* They always acted together in endorsing candidates. Since Bill Knowland, the junior senator, was from the north, the consensus was that the other senator should be from the south. Hence I knew that the two northern papers would follow the lead of the *Times.* Kyle Palmer, a close friend who was the *Times's*

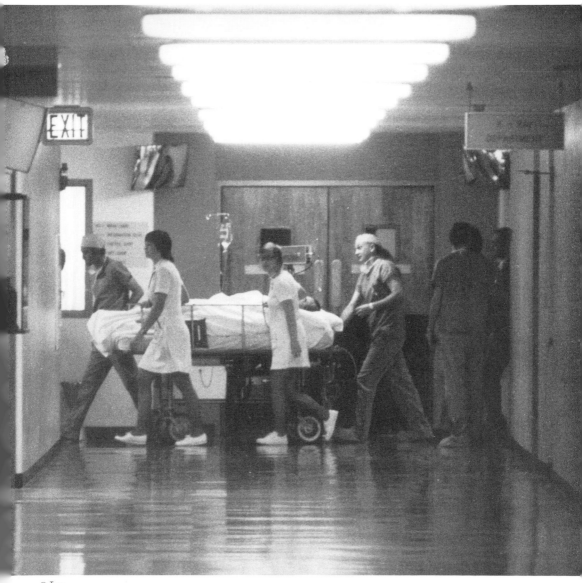

Had it not been for the support of my family and the thoughts and prayers of countless people I have never met, I would not have pulled through. (Leaving operating room in 1974)

My father had driving ambition—not for himself, but for his sons. My mother, my cousin wrote, "did what she did and was what she was through a strength and lovingness which welled up out of her good heart . . ." (With Harold, Donald, and Richard, 1917)

Los Angeles Herald

Children
Help
Germanic
Relief

Left to Right, Miss Mabel Wingert and Donald Nixon, Richard Nixon and
Evelyn Williams

The first time my picture appeared in the newspaper was in 1916. My mother gave us a nickel each to put in a collection basket for war orphans, and a photographer snapped our picture. (RN is second from right)

At Duke a friend told me I shouldn't worry about keeping my scholarship. He said, "I've noticed how long you study in the law library. You have all that it takes to learn the law—an iron butt." (RN, in back row, with his third-year class)

My press was excellent my first year in Congress. Along with Jack Kennedy, I was considered to be a comer with a good future. (With Pat and Tricia in Washington, Spring 1947)

When Tricia was ten and I urged her to practice the piano more, she told me, "Daddy, *you* should have practiced more. If you had, you might have become famous and gone to Hollywood and they would have buried you in a special place."

Julie had a toy bunny she carried everywhere. When we were making a campaign commercial in 1950 and she came to the key line, "Vote for Nixon!" she sang "Vote for bunny!" instead. I won anyway. (With Julie, bunny, Pat, and Tricia)

I began my first campaign by telling the story of how a group of men did a superhuman job on Bougainville after a Japanese air raid the night before. (RN in South Pacific, wearing helmet, at far left)

Senator Frank Carlson once expressed his unbounded appreciation for Pat's campaigning ability. He said, "Dick, you're controversial, but *everybody* likes Pat." (In Los Angeles in 1955)

The Secret Service's code name for Pat was ''Starlight.'' She fitted it to a T.
(At the White House in 1972)

When Tricia and Julie were growing
up, Pat found time to compensate
for my own lack of attention. Now
we both enjoy our grandchildren.
(ABOVE: Mrs. Nixon with Jennie
Eisenhower and Christopher Cox on
a visit to the "Sesame Street" set in
1981. RIGHT: RN at the circus in
1989 with Alex Richard, Jennie, and
Melanie Eisenhower, and
Christopher Cox)

political editor, invited me to lunch at the Biltmore Hotel. He had a fruit salad, and I ordered one of my favorites, a hot tamale with beans on the side. He came to the point in his usual blunt way. "I think you would be a damn fool to run against Downey," he said, "but if you decide to run, I am authorized to tell you that the *Times* will support you and that the *Chronicle* and *Tribune* will probably follow suit." When I returned to Washington, Bill Knowland dropped by my office and told me that the *Tribune* would support me. The publisher of the *Chronicle* called the next day and pledged his support. I knew that this kind of backing meant a sure nomination, because in those days newspaper endorsements had far more influence than they do today. Ironically, today some great newspapers have abrogated the responsibility to endorse at all in Presidential elections. They will still advise voters who to pick for county water commissioner but not for the most powerful office in the world.

Pat was not overwhelmed by the idea of going through another tough race. But, like me, she was intrigued by the long odds. She was even more persuaded by the fact that if I were to win, we would not have to campaign for reelection every two years.

When I announced in November 1949, the polls were overwhelmingly against me. I did fairly well in southern California, but I needed to be better known in the Central Valley and in northern California. A friendly automobile dealer, Henry Kearns, lent me a second-hand Mercury woody station wagon. We attached loudspeakers on the top and put "NIXON FOR SENATE" signs on the sides. On the first trip, only one man, Ace Anderson, came along. He was a fifty-year-old veteran campaign worker whose major qualification was that he was a good driver. He drove the station wagon and ran the public address system.

Our campaign plan looked good on paper. We were to pull into the center of the small towns, stop at a busy intersection, and play a popular song on the loudspeaker to attract a crowd. Then I was supposed to stand on the back of the station wagon and make a speech. Our first stop was in Taft, a small town near Bakersfield. It was a disaster. Only a half-dozen people bothered to listen, which was probably best since I did not have much to say. Murray Chotiner had found that Downey had not delivered on some local federal project in that area, and I proceeded to charge him with "not bringing home the bacon." That might have been the case, but the speech laid an egg. The voters did not seem to care much about the issue; even more discouraging, neither did I.

I was running like a dry creek when we got a break. Downey decided to withdraw from the race for health reasons, but not before doing serious damage to Helen Gahagan Douglas, a favorite of the California Democratic Party's left wing who was challenging him for the Democratic nomination. Manchester Boddy, a Los Angeles newspaper publisher who was in the more conservative wing of the party, immediately announced that he would oppose her for the nomination. Now I had an issue I wanted to talk about —foreign policy. She had joined other left-wing Democrats in voting against the Greek-Turkish aid program, which Kennedy and I had supported. Boddy, Downey, and the other leading conservative Democrats called her "the pink lady" and criticized her for her membership in and support of a number of Communist front organizations. I followed their lead. I did not question her loyalty, but like her fellow Democrats, I criticized her judgment.

Boddy lost the nomination, but his efforts helped make it possible for me to win the election. I could never have won with Republican votes alone. Conservative Democrats joined in to give me a 680,000-vote margin in November, the biggest in any Senate race in the nation in 1950.

The campaign had its lighter moments. At most of my major appearances, left-wing activists heckled me. That helped, of course, because it increased the size of the crowds. When I spoke at the final campaign rally in Long Beach, several hundred people demonstrated outside the hall while I was talking to an overflow crowd inside. Ace Anderson pulled the station wagon near the demonstrators and turned up the volume on one of his favorite records: "If I Knew You Were Coming I'd Have Baked a Cake." The hecklers dispersed.

There was only one debate, before the San Francisco Press Club. Both Douglas and I spoke behind a black cat, a symbol meaning that anything said behind it would be off the record. In her remarks, she had complained bitterly about the monied interests which she claimed opposed her and were supporting me. When I spoke, I said that while in fact we were having trouble raising adequate campaign funds, I had just received a big lift from a letter. I pulled it out of my pocket and read it to the audience. "Dear Congressman Nixon," it said. "I am delighted that you are running against Mrs. Douglas and only wish that my contribution could be greater." A check for $500 was enclosed. I then said that the letter was signed by Eleanor Roosevelt. Mrs. Douglas almost jumped out of her chair. Then I read the address—Oyster Bay,

New York. It was not FDR's widow. It was TR's daughter-in-law, who was always described by Alice Longworth as "Eleanor the Good." The audience, which had generally leaned to Mrs. Douglas, broke up with laughter. She did not agree to any more debates.

Liberal historians contend that she lost because I attacked her record unfairly. But she had made the record; all I had done was to tell the voters what it was. She lost because she was not a mainstream Democrat. One of those most pleased by my victory was Jack Kennedy, who had delivered a cash contribution of $1,000 to me in my office during the primaries. He said that it was a campaign gift from his father.

Another risk had paid off. If I had followed the polls and the advice of my friends, I would not have run. I must admit that I was lucky. But it is only when you take big risks that you are around to cash in on luck.

My campaign for governor in 1962 was a classic example of taking a poor risk and making a bad decision. But ironically, in the long run it produced a good result.

After I lost in 1960, Tom Dewey, who had suffered two consecutive defeats in Presidential elections, urged me to take a long time off before making any decisions about my future. It was excellent advice. Today, I pass it along myself whenever I call or write to losing candidates. Unfortunately, I did not follow it in 1961. It was one of the busiest years of my life. I was counsel to an excellent law firm in Los Angeles. I made speeches for Republican organizations all over the country. I agreed to write *Six Crises,* which turned out to be ten months of the hardest work I had ever done. By October 1, my mind totally worn out from all this activity, I had to decide whether to run for governor.

As usual, I received conflicting advice. President Hoover and General MacArthur strongly urged that I not run for governor and recommended that I run for Congress instead, as John Quincy Adams had after he left the Presidency. MacArthur put it bluntly: "Because of your experience in foreign policy, you should be in Washington, not in Sacramento." Jimmy Byrnes, who had served with great distinction both in Washington and as governor of South Carolina, told me that he thought I would enjoy being governor. The California Republican chairman, Cap Weinberger, wanted me to run because he felt that no one else could win. President Eisenhower urged me to run for the powerful reason that a person who does not answer the call of his party when it needs him may lose the support of his party when he needs it.

The most persuasive argument for running was made by Whittaker Chambers in the last letter he wrote to me before his death on July 9, 1961. "Some tell me that there are reasons why you should not presently run for Governor of California," he wrote. "Others tell me that you would almost certainly carry the state. I simply do not know the fact. But if it is at all feasible, I, for what it is worth, strongly urge you to consider this. There would be a sense and an impression of political come down? Great character always precludes a sense of come down, greatly yielding to match the altered circumstances."

Pat made the most persuasive arguments against running. She believed it was the wrong office at the wrong time and the wrong place. The wrong office, because she did not think I would like being governor. The wrong time, because it was too soon after an exhausting national campaign. The wrong place, because we had been away from California for fourteen years, and she knew how difficult it would be to build a political organization, particularly at the county, city, and precinct levels. She was right on all three counts.

In not following her advice, I ignored two axioms every politician should bear in mind. You should never make a major political decision in the euphoria of victory or the despondency of defeat. And you should never be a reluctant candidate, because a reluctant candidate is always a lousy candidate.

Our loss in 1962 was not for want of trying. We both gave it everything we had. Pat campaigned with me up and down the state, just as she had in 1950. After falling behind the incumbent, Pat Brown, in early 1962, we closed the gap, and three weeks before the election we thought we had a good shot. Then came the Cuban missile crisis. This galvanizing drama brought our momentum to a halt. California's voters were far more interested in what was happening in Washington than in deciding whether to replace their governor. Some attributed my loss to bad luck. But you will generally find that bad luck comes when you have made a bad decision.

I had the satisfaction of taking on the press afterwards for what I considered to be biased coverage. The pundits unanimously agreed that such blunt talk about the press would finish me politically. I felt that I had been finished already by losing two elections in a row. Everyone wrote me off; I wrote myself off.

We all tend to rationalize our defeats, but I believe that there is some merit in my own 1962 postmortem. Had I been elected, I would have undoubtedly been drafted as a candidate in 1964 and lost to Lyndon Johnson, since no one had a chance to beat him after Kennedy's assassination. Had I not run for governor at all, I probably would have run for President in 1964. If that had happened, I would probably have lost the nomination to Barry Goldwater and would certainly have lost to Johnson in the general election. I would then have been in the position of Tom Dewey, who despite his great abilities was finished after two straight losses in campaigns for the White House.

There is no question that running for governor was a bad risk. But the road to victory is sometimes paved with defeat. By running and losing, I stayed on the sidelines in 1964 and was able to regroup and run again for the Presidency in 1968.

Because I won in 1968, you might assume that it was the year I took the smallest risk. In fact, it could well have been the greatest. After the Republican victories in the races for House, Senate, and governor in 1966, the field of potential candidates for President expanded explosively almost overnight. Had I not played my hunch of going against the advice of my supporters and taken a moratorium from politics for six months in 1967, it is likely that I would have been chewed up in the early skirmishing for the nomination. In that case, either Nelson Rockefeller or Ronald Reagan might have been nominated. Instead, the pieces fell into place, and this time both luck and the vote count were on my side.

In politics more than in any other profession, the risks worth taking are those where the odds are great. The more you risk if you lose, the more you stand to gain if you win. Nothing great can be accomplished without taking great risks. You should consult a lawyer only if you want to know what risks *not* to take. Lawyers are experts on how not to do something. They play it safe. They seldom will advise you to take a risk. In determining what risks to take, you must never be obsessed by what you might lose. You must always keep front and center what you might gain.

Those who choose politics as a career are embarking on a perilous voyage. But they should always remember the words of St. Thomas Aquinas seven centuries ago: "If the highest aim of a captain were to preserve his ship, he would keep it in port forever."

20
POLITICS

In the forty-three years since I first ran for Congress, we have seen a revolution in politics. Forty-one years ago marked the last Presidential campaign without television. Since I had won both the Republican and Democratic nominations in the June 1948 primaries for reelection to Congress, I campaigned around the country for Tom Dewey. I found that the content of speeches mattered, newspaper endorsements were influential, the writing press had great impact, issues were more important than personalities, substance was more important than style, the political parties were strong. None of these statements is true any longer. Politics is a more simplistic, less subtle, less thoughtful pursuit today. The reason for the change is television.

Ironically, one event that year presaged the coming dominance of the electronic media: a radio debate between Dewey and Harold Stassen. It led to Dewey's nomination for President and the end of Stassen's political career. Broadcast nationwide from Portland, Oregon, the debate was over a bill I had authored with Karl Mundt requiring Communist organizations to register with the government. Stassen favored the bill but inaccurately insisted that it would outlaw the Communist Party—the same position taken by our left-wing critics. Dewey correctly argued that our purpose was not to make it illegal to join Communist organizations, but only to enable the government to identify and publicize Soviet bloc support for such groups.

Dewey carried the day with his moderate, persuasive arguments, picking up momentum that would take him all the way to victory at the Philadelphia convention. While this was the first decisive electronic confrontation in American political history, it was uncharacteristic of today's politics in that it involved a relatively sophisticated discussion of an actual issue. In the 1980s, the results of TV debates are tallied not by the political writers but by the networks' instant quip counters and gaff-o-meters. A candidate who would dare discuss the pros and cons of a vital piece of legislation instead of doling out one-liners and applause lines prepared by his media consultants is destined for oblivion.

In the television age, style not only takes precedence over substance but threatens to completely eclipse it. Thirty-second sound bites are more influential than carefully thought-out thirty-minute speeches, campaign joke writers are often treated better than White House speechwriters, and makeup artists are more important than researchers. In one of life's great ironies, media commentators blame the candidates for these developments, when in fact candidates are only adapting to the limitations of the medium that has come to hold their fate in its hands. You can blame politicians for a lot of things, but inventing television is not one of them.

Next to TV, but in part because of the cost of using TV, the astronomical increase in what it costs to finance a campaign has inalterably changed politics. In 1946, the total cost of my campaign against an incumbent in a marginal district was $37,500. In 1950, it cost $750,000 to run for the Senate in a hotly contested race. Today, the average cost of a congressional race is $223,000, and some have spent over $1 million. The campaign for the Senate seat in California in 1988 cost $15 million. Even taking inflation into account, it can cost on an average over five times as much to finance a campaign for the House and Senate today as it did forty years ago.

Another profound change is the increasing weakness and even irrelevance of political parties. The endorsement of the Right to Life lobby or the National Rifle Association can be more decisive in a close contest than the support of a political party. No one should be surprised that special interests dominate the agendas of congressmen, because it is special interests that get them there.

Another new factor is the obsession with polls. Every well-financed campaign has a private pollster to advise the candidate not on what his position ought to be after studying the issue but on what position will please a majority of voters, even though they may be uninformed on the issues. Candidates used to try to educate the voters. Now they find it safer to placate them.

I strongly believe that candidates should resist the advice to slavishly follow the polls. Taking uninformed voters where they want to go is easy. Taking them where they *should* go is the role of a leader. To make what is unpopular popular is the supreme test of leadership.

One of the greatest strengths of American politics is that members of the press have always felt free to ask tough questions on the major issues of the day. One of the negative fallouts of Watergate is that a new breed of reporters, seeking money, fame, and Pulitzer Prizes, has elevated Peeping Tom journalism and character assassination to a new level of respectability. Editorials in the nation's great newspapers pontificate that no public institution or company can investigate itself. But when members of the media engage in questionable practices, the same editorial writers piously insist that the media is perfectly capable of investigating themselves and correcting such abuses. It is interesting to speculate how the Founders, with their concern about letting too much power gather in any of the three branches of government, would have reacted to the rise of this fourth power center.

The incumbency lock is another highly negative characteristic of today's politics. Congress has become an incumbent's protective association. In 1988, despite a decisive Republican victory for President, 98 percent of the incumbents who ran for the heavily Democratic House were reelected. Forty-two years ago, one hundred five new congressmen were elected to the much-maligned 80th Congress. Fifty-two of them defeated incumbents. Two of them went on to become President. Ten became senators. Five became governors. Most of those who defeated incumbents would have no chance to be elected today. Unless the incumbency lock is broken by eliminating gerrymandering and allowing challengers to compete with incumbents on a more level playing field, we will have completely vitiated the Founders' goal of a Congress that renews itself constantly to reflect the changing views of the voters.

After eight years of a popular President in the White House and three Republican Presidential landslides, the number of Republican congressmen is seventeen less than when Ronald Reagan was inaugurated as President in 1981. This development has profound implications for the future. For the balance of the century, we will probably have Republicans in the White House with Democrats holding a majority in the House and possibly in the Senate as well. Because of the incumbency lock, Republican candidates for President, no matter how great their victories are, can no longer bring along majorities in both the House and Senate.

It is a sign of the intellectual sterility of political science that there is actually a theory among some academics that the American people, in their infinite wisdom, purposely elect Republicans to the White House and Democrats to Congress in order to create a "balance." This is like saying that the American people enjoy watching political gridlock. The theory probably tells us more about the political inclinations of academics than it does about politics. To most pundits, when the President was Democratic and the Congress Republican, as in 1948, Congress was a reactionary restraint on enlightened Presidential leadership. When the President is Republican and the Congress Democratic, as during my administration and much of Reagan's, Congress is the people's safeguard against excessive Presidential power. Historically, however, the Congress and White House accomplish more when they are working together than when they are at odds. The incumbency lock ensures that for the foreseeable future, such a partnership will never recur.

What advice would I give someone considering running for Congress for the first time? First, be prepared to spend an inordinate amount of time raising money rather than campaigning for votes. In 1980, a young conservative Republican, John Hiler, was elected to Congress in a closely contested race in Indiana. He has won reelection four times by relatively small margins. He came to Washington full of high ideals, hoping to make a difference on major issues. To his dismay, he found that because of the need to attend fundraising events, he could not spend as much time as he wanted working for his program.

Except for the first six months of his two-year term, a congressman from a close district today must spend over half his time raising money for his reelection. The results of the non-stop campaign hustle are inevitable. Idealistic young congressmen are disenchanted by the grind. Some who would have sought higher office in earlier eras recoil from doing so, since they would have to raise ten times more money. Scandals such as the one that engulfed Jim Wright become inevitable as members work the angles instead of working for the people. Opportunities to establish policy expertise are lost. Even if given the opportunity, an able young congressman like John Hiler could not afford to risk stepping off the fundraising treadmill long enough to devote the kind of attention I did to the Hiss case. As a result, shots at national exposure are missed as members forsake committee work and even floor speeches in favor of schmoozing with their PACs and fat cats at private cocktail parties.

In sum, my advice to a talented young person considering a run for the House might be "just say no." But while I might give that advice to others, I must admit I probably would not follow it if I were a potential candidate.

The House's decline is not irreversible. The most-talked-about proposed amendments to the Constitution—prohibiting abortion, establishing the line-item veto, setting one six-year term for Presidents—all are non-starters. But there is one change that all those interested in better government should support. The terms of members of the House should be extended to four years, with one half being elected in the Presidential year and the other half in the off-year. This would mean that for at least two years of his four-year term, a congressman could be a congressman rather than a perpetual candidate spending 75 percent of his time raising campaign funds and campaigning for reelection.

No matter how long his term of office will be, any candidate, unless he comes from a rural district, must learn to use television. He will be dismayed to find that whether he has had his hair blown dry may be more important than what he has between his ears. He may insist that he wants to be a legislator, not an actor. But unless he learns to be an actor, he will never have a chance to be a legislator. I often wonder whether the two acknowledged giants of the Senate in the post–World War II era, Bob Taft and Dick Russell, could have been elected if they had entered politics in the age of television rather than at a time when the writing press and radio were dominant. I remember seeing a sound bite in the New Hampshire primary in 1952 in which a painfully candid Taft was trying to explain to a little girl why he couldn't sign autographs because it took more time than shaking hands. He was right, but it was devastating on TV.

No one should enter politics today unless he is prepared for brutal media exposure. To an extent, this has always been the case. But the influence of television and the glorification of investigative reporters have led to increased emphasis on the trivial, the lurid, even the irrelevant at the expense of discussion of major issues.

The candidate must be prepared to put his fate in the hands of professional campaign managers, pollsters, and TV advisers. If he wishes, they will write his speeches, train him for television, pick the color of his ties, tell him where and how to campaign, and advise him on what to say. It is here that he must draw the line. He should accept the expert's advice on how to campaign. He must reserve to himself the decision about what to say. Even now, when there is so much emphasis on style, the message remains all-important. No one should seek public office unless he has a message. And only he can determine what it should be.

No one should consider becoming a candidate unless he recognizes at the outset that politics is the most hazardous profession. A businessman who fails to make a sale earns less profit. An athlete who loses a championship tries again. But a politician who loses an election must usually look for another line of work. He must be determined to win, but he must not be afraid to lose. Those who will not enter a contest unless they are guaranteed in advance that they will be adequately financed and are relatively sure of winning make poor candidates. Those who are willing to risk all to gain all make the best candidates.

While taking into account all of the hazards, a potential candidate should dismiss out of hand the fatuous nonsense that politics is a less than honorable profession. I have known business leaders who are more ruthless than any politician and church and academic leaders who schemed as deviously as any politician to promote their careers. In politics, the competitive aspects simply get more attention than they do in business, education, or the media. In these other fields, competition is just as keen but better concealed. And when the stakes are large questions of public policy or even the nation's survival, the competition is nobler than when it involves the market share of a particular brand of deodorant or a point or two in the Nielsen ratings.

The bottom line is the goal. A candidate's primary purpose in getting into politics should never be self-interest. He can make far more money, suffer far less abuse, and exert far less effort if he chooses some other field of endeavor. But if he has a purpose larger than himself and his personal ambitions that he wants to pursue, he must not hesitate. Win or lose, he will have the ultimate satisfaction of knowing that he did not stand on the sidelines when others were making decisions affecting his fate and that of his country.

21

POWER

When we met with Mao Tse-tung in Beijing in 1972, Henry Kissinger remarked that he had assigned Mao's writings to his classes at Harvard. With typical self-deprecation, Mao said, "These writings of mine aren't anything. There is nothing instructive in what I wrote."

I said, "The chairman's writings moved a nation and changed the world."

He replied, "I haven't been able to change it. I've only been able to change a few places in the vicinity of Peking."

I could have responded that this was far more than I had been able to do in the vicinity of the White House.

One of the first orders I issued as President in 1969 was to tear down the World War I–era "temporary" buildings on the Mall, which were an eyesore in the very heart of the nation's capital. Even though they now had the world's largest office building, the Pentagon, to house all their services and agencies, officials at the Navy Department dragged their feet. No bureaucrat ever voluntarily gives up office space, no matter how ugly. Nevertheless, I followed up with oral and written orders to the White House staff and other agencies. Virtually every time I flew in to the White House by helicopter and saw the buildings still standing, I would mention my interest in getting them removed, each time with no results.

I soon found that even an order to the military from the commander-in-chief would not be carried out if military bureaucrats could find a way to avoid doing so. Several years passed before the buildings were finally torn down and the Mall restored to its pristine, pre–World War I beauty. So far as I have been able to determine, our military readiness did not suffer.

Not even White House aides are immune from letting self-interest get in the way of following orders. I do not play tennis, and besides, I felt that the tennis court on the White House grounds marred the original simplicity and elegance of the South Lawn. I ordered it removed, thus sparking a crisis among my aides, many of whom did play tennis and enjoyed using the White House court. Each time I would mention tearing it up, they would resolve to study the matter for a few months and then see whether I mentioned it again. When I did, there would be yet another study. Eventually, I realized that the only way to get rid of the White House tennis court would be if I rented a bulldozer one night and did it myself. President Bush, who enjoys playing tennis, can thank my staff for not carrying out my order!

These examples may seem picayune compared to the big issues a President deals with. But they illustrate a point many self-proclaimed experts on the Presidency overlook. The President of the United States is said to be the most powerful man in the world. This is true only in the sense that he leads the most powerful nation in the world. In fact, the President's power is far more circumscribed than that of most other world leaders. The point is often made that because the National Security Council is much more efficient than the cumbersome Soviet bureaucracy, President Bush can respond more quickly to a crisis than can President Gorbachev. This analysis misses the point. Because of his dictatorial power, Gorbachev can always get his way in the end if he insists. Bush can do so only if he can persuade others that his decision is the right one. Those who oppose Gorbachev will no longer lose their heads, but they risk losing their jobs. Those who oppose Bush can usually live to fight another day. If they leak their views, they might even become media heroes.

The President's power was wisely limited by the Founders in the Constitution. Congress decides what money can be spent, and the courts decide what is legal. The President's power has been further limited by Congress in ways the Founders would not have approved. One of the more unfortunate fallouts from the Vietnam War was the War Powers Act, which was passed over my veto in 1973. Along with most Presidents who have succeeded me, I believe it is clearly unconstitutional and contrary to the intent of the Founders, but until the Supreme Court decides that it is, it will severely limit a President's power to act in a timely fashion in a crisis, assuming the Congress ever musters the courage to insist on strict compliance with its terms.

The Founders would also probably have opposed the Budget Control Impoundment Act. Year after year, Congress passes budgets that are testaments to its inability to say no to special interests. Beginning with Jefferson, Presidents impounded funds the Congress appropriated which would have busted the budget. I used impoundment to restrain some of the willy-nilly spending of the massive, and now largely discredited, Great Society programs I inherited. This sent the Democratic majorities in Congress right up the wall, but there was nothing they could do about it until the congressional power grabs that followed Vietnam and Watergate. In 1974 Congress took the impoundment power away, thus reserving to itself the right to spend irresponsibly without constraint.

There is plenty of blame to go around for today's massive budget deficit, but one obvious villain is that bill. Many believe that an answer to the problem is to give the President a line-item veto so he can surgically remove excessive spending from the budget. This is a surefire cheer line before conservative audiences, but politically it will never happen. Congress will jump at the chance to curb the power of the executive but it will never limit its own power. The only way the President will ever be able to restrain the spendthrift Congress again would be to force a court test of the anti-impoundment provision and hope that the Supreme Court goes along with him.

The Founders could also not have imagined how the power of the bureaucracy and the power of the media would restrain the President. There were fewer than five thousand civilian government employees when Madison was President. Taking into account the increase in population since then, this would amount to five-hundred thousand today. In fact, there are 3.1 million. Of those, the President appoints fewer than twelve hundred to substantive policymaking positions, many of whom are made political eunuchs by rough Senate confirmation hearings. While the media do not directly inhibit the President's power, they have enormous influence on the voters, without whose support he cannot govern effectively.

In view of all these restraints, the periodic talk about the "imperial Presidency" is ludicrous. In fact, most such complaints should be dismissed out of hand, since many who make them spoke lyrically of the need for a strong Presidency when individuals who shared their liberal political views occupied the White House and became concerned about excessive Presidential power only when a conservative President who disagreed with their political views came into office.

We need a strong President to deal on an equal footing with the strong leaders of other powerful countries. The alternative to strong Presidential government is government by Congress, which is no government at all.

Before the United States became a world power, we could afford the luxury of a weak Presidency. But great initiatives both abroad and at home have always been undertaken when we have had strong Presidents in the White House. Some take the view that in times of peace and prosperity, the less leadership there is from the White House, the better. I do not agree. Times of peace and prosperity are precisely when a great nation should use its resources to help make the world safer and freer. Great initiatives conceived and carried out in a quiet period of peace and prosperity are sounder and more lasting than those rushed through in a period of crisis.

Peace and prosperity never last forever, and when the inevitable crisis comes, the President must have the will, the stature, the vision, and the power to lead the country through it. But if he has declined to lead when times are good, the nation may not turn to him when times turn bad. At such moments, the idea of congressional leadership is little more than a bad joke. As de Gaulle once observed, "Members of Parliament can paralyze action. They cannot initiate it."

When I saw an embittered Lyndon Johnson after he left the White House, he told me, "People don't support you because they like you. You can count on a person's support only when you can do something for him or something to him." Even he would probably have agreed that this was an overstatement, since all Presidents have friends who will support them regardless of the political costs. But he was right that in general charm and good personal relations do not affect people when their interests are at stake. This is equally true of foreign leaders, congressmen, reporters, and bureaucrats.

This is not to suggest that a President should not make every effort to develop good personal relationships with members of Congress. Being invited to the White House or receiving a call from the President is a powerful persuader. When a vote does not involve political life or death, a gesture by the President might make the difference. But in politics as well as in other walks of life, when profound personal interests are at stake, the only appeal that works is one to the head rather than to the heart.

When speaking of a President being able to do something *for* a member of Congress, we usually think of cynical horse trading—buying a vote in exchange for a dam here, a pet project there, a government job for a constituent. Doing something *to* him can mean declining to campaign for him in the next mid-term election, or personally campaigning against him if he is not a member of your party. This is all good coin of the political realm that every President has at his disposal and should make no bones about using. But he also has a much more powerful weapon in his arsenal. He can go over the heads of Congress and the media, directly to the people. An effective television speech to the nation can change political opinion. Since public opinion directly affects the political interests of congressmen, the President can get what he wants from Congress by showing that the people are behind him. This weapon should only be used when great issues are at stake, and it will be worn out by overuse. If a major televised address lays an egg, or if everyone decides to watch baseball or a racy movie on cable instead, the President will be worse off than before he made the speech. The media establishment may even conclude that his power is gone.

In the final analysis, the President's power depends on the power of his ideas. His popularity may go up and down, but if members of Congress see that he is determined to stay his course, they will hesitate to desert him when he is weak for fear that voters will hold them accountable when he is strong. Most members of Congress are realistic. Whatever their immediate concerns are, they do not want to end up on the wrong side of the popularity curve.

As the day approaches when a President can no longer do something to or for someone, his power will begin to erode. That is one reason why second terms of Presidents are not as productive as first terms. Even when a President's poll ratings are low, Congress and the media will hesitate to take him on if they fear he will be reelected. That is why limiting a President to one six-year term, a reform that is a current favorite with political scientists, is not a good idea. Abroad, his opposite numbers on the world scene would virtually all be senior to him. At home, he would be a lame duck from the moment that his polls go below 50 percent.

As a freshman congressman in 1947, I voted for the Twenty-

Second Amendment limiting Presidents to two terms. President Eisenhower, who under no circumstances would have sought a third term, thought the amendment was a mistake. Since leaving office, President Reagan, who probably could have been reelected to a third term, has campaigned for its repeal. I was wrong, and they were right. Gorbachev may live long enough to deal with at least three more Presidents, which gives him a huge advantage over each new man or woman elected President who generally will have to take at least two years to find out how Washington and the real world work. An equally powerful argument for the amendment's repeal is that the problems facing the country at home and abroad are so great today that we cannot afford weak congressional government. We need strong Presidential leadership. Arbitrarily limiting the President's tenure, either by imposing a six-year term or retaining the Twenty-Second Amendment, reduces the President's power enormously, because those who oppose him will know that the day will soon come when he can no longer do something to them or for them.

22

SPEAKING

During my eight years as Vice President, I wrote all my own speeches. It was not a matter of choice. The budget for the Vice President's office in those days did not permit the employment of a full-time speechwriter. I also knew that John Foster Dulles wrote all of his speeches. Since he had several people on his State Department staff who could have written for him, I once asked him why he insisted on doing the work himself. He answered, "I like to write speeches. It forces me to think the problem through."

Dulles's practice was admirable, but most government officials today could not possibly follow it. Virtually everyone at the top levels of government—Cabinet officers, senators, congressmen, and governors—has speechwriters on his staff. They can be a great help to the speaker, but only if used properly.

Generally the speechwriter is a better wordsmith than the speaker. But since he is probably an intellectual, he relates better to the written word than the spoken word. The idea that his text can be put on a TelePrompTer, and that if the speaker practices it a few times no one will know the difference, just doesn't wash. Unless he is an expert at using that device, the speech will sound just like what it is—leaden, lifeless, and insincere.

A speaker can avoid this dilemma only by spending the time to make the speech his own. He should select the message, make the basic outline, and provide key ideas and phrases. He can let his speechwriters prepare a first draft. Then I would suggest that he dictate his own version into a tape recorder. The written word, no matter how elegant, is different from the spoken word. It is often too sterile and lacks the rhythm and punch a speech needs. That

210

can be corrected to an extent if the speaker works the language through aloud.

Because he makes so many speeches and has so many other duties, a modern President has to rely heavily on a whole staff of speechwriters. But many people erroneously think of the Presidential speechwriter as a modern invention. While Coolidge was the first to hire one officially, Presidents have always relied on others for editorial inspiration. It is fascinating to compare Lincoln's first inaugural address to the draft prepared for him by his secretary of state-designate, William Seward. Lincoln deleted all of Seward's pompous language, but he built some of the speech's most memorable phrases, including the peroration about "the mystic chords of memory," out of raw materials Seward provided. This is the ideal relationship between speaker and writer. Inspiration flows back and forth; but ultimately, a speech must be the speaker's and his alone if it is to be effective.

When you have time to prepare a speech by yourself without the help of a speechwriter, there are no hard and fast rules, since what works for one speaker may not work for another. For those who are still experimenting to find the right formula, I would recommend keeping in mind the methods I have found helpful in writing and delivering speeches over the past forty-two years.

Before writing anything, read broadly in the field you intend to cover, including both suggestions from your staff and friends and comments by critics of your point of view. At least a week or two should be devoted to this phase of preparation. You then should set aside several days to organize and outline your thoughts. An effective speech must not meander or stroll. It must march, to drive home its message. I always make at least three outlines and usually more before I reach the point where the thoughts are tightly knit enough to get across my message to the audience.

Once the final outline is completed, either write out or dictate the first draft. In editing the typed transcript, don't fine-tune too much, because you will tend to take out the color and rhythm of the spoken word. If you intend to speak without notes, read the outline over several times and write out key sentences. Unless you know the outline thoroughly, you run the risk of losing your train of thought, and in the process your audience.

For maximum impact on your audience, concentrate on the introduction, one or more effective anecdotes, and the conclusion.

In the introduction, you shake hands with the audience. This process might include some grace notes about the speakers or performers who preceded you, compliments to the host organization, and references that acknowledge personal interests you may share with your audience. Unless you are a great actor or raconteur, don't begin with a canned joke; situational humor is more effective by far. Being wedded to a particular opening passage will prevent you from being able to react to some unexpected event.

I can recall two examples of occasions when introductions provided an opportunity for improvisational humor.

When we boarded our campaign train in Pomona, California, for the opening trip of the 1952 campaign, Governor Earl Warren introduced me to a huge crowd at the station. It was one of the best introductions I have ever had. He closed it by saying, "I now present to you the next President of the United States." In my remarks, I naturally accepted this promotion from the number-two spot on the ticket to number one. Neither of us could have imagined that sixteen years later, Chief Justice Warren actually would swear me in as President.

When I spoke in Salt Lake City during the same campaign, Ivy Baker Priest, later the Treasurer of the United States, introduced the head table before I spoke. When she came to Mrs. Nixon, she said, "I now present to you the next wife of the Vice President of the United States." I pointed out that this would be quite a surprise to the current Vice President, Alben Barkley.

Anyone who doubts the effectiveness of anecdotes should read the parables in the New Testament or listen to great ministers like Billy Graham, Norman Vincent Peale, Robert Schuller, and Steven Brown. A good anecdote can make a speech. But I must warn prospective speakers that it is very difficult to find one. Staff researchers are most adept at exhuming ponderous historical allusions or quips about what Henry VIII said to his third wife. The appropriate anecdote should give the audience relief after a period of heavy rhetoric, not more heavy rhetoric. It can also perk up an audience that is losing interest in your serious themes. Above all, if an anecdote directly supports or illustrates the basic message, that is what the audience will remember instead of some finely crafted phrase intended to make the same point.

The most important part of the speech is the conclusion. Sometimes I write it first. But usually it is best to work up to it and then to reserve plenty of time to craft it. For example, when I was preparing to speak to the American people about Vietnam on No-

212

vember 3, 1969, the phrase "silent majority" came to me only after I had written the body of the speech.

A speaker and his speechwriters should bear in mind several other factors as well: length, delivery, cheer lines, humor, surprise, and repetition.

As Lincoln's 271-word Gettysburg Address so dramatically demonstrated, a speech is measured not by its length but its depth. Sometimes a politician's staff thinks it has done him a favor by scheduling "brief remarks" instead of a major address. But short does not necessarily mean easy. Woodrow Wilson, another of our greatest Presidents, was also a gifted speaker who had the reputation of writing all of his own speeches. A widely quoted anecdote about his speechwriting technique is revealing. Once, when he asked how long it would take him to write a five-minute speech, he said it would take about a week. Then he was asked how long it would take to write a half-hour speech. He said, "About two days." How about an hour speech? He said, "I can deliver that one right now."

Except for a State of the Union speech, which too often ends up as a laundry list of the Cabinet's pet ideas, in this day of huge television audiences with small attention spans Presidential speeches should be no longer than twenty minutes. Those hyperactive politicians who take an hour to say something that could be said in five minutes remind me of Winston Churchill's brutal characterization of his son Randolph: "He has big guns but too little ammunition." I have heard thousands of speeches. I have heard many criticized for being too long. I have never heard one criticized for being too short.

A leader should never speak "off the top of his head." His words are important, and he owes it to his audience to think about them before he speaks. Even Lincoln's few off-the-cuff speeches are generally considered to have been poor. I first met Randolph Churchill at the Republican National Convention in 1952. Eisenhower had not yet selected me as his running mate, but Churchill, then a political correspondent, had heard rumors that I might be chosen and was interviewing me for a London newspaper. The campaign headquarters was so noisy that we left and sat on the stairs that led to the lobby of the Congress Hotel in Chicago. I said how impressed I was by his father's ability to deliver such brilliant extemporaneous speeches. He smiled and said, "My father has spent the best years of his life writing his extemporaneous speeches."

How a speaker prepares depends upon him and his audience. My practice is unorthodox, and I would not necessarily recommend it to others. Because of my strong conviction that a speaker must look natural, I have never watched myself on television nor listened to myself on radio. I know that if I did, I would become self-conscious, and my speaking would lose whatever natural quality it has. I also never used a TelePrompTer for a speech. Billy Graham, among other friends, urged me to do so, but since I had developed the practice of delivering my speeches without notes, except for major policy statements that I would read from a written text, I never took the time to learn to use the device. In retrospect, this was probably a mistake. Delivering a speech without notes requires a great deal of concentration. If I had used a Tele-PrompTer in the White House years, I could have made far more speeches with much less effort. Still, a speaker should resist the temptation to read a speech unless he has taken the time to become completely familiar with the text so that it does not appear that he is seeing it for the first time. No one will be persuaded by a speech if the speaker has only a passing interest in it himself.

When a public speech is being carried on television, the speaker should focus his delivery on the TV audience of millions rather than the audience of hundreds or even thousands before him. He should always remember that television is a conversational medium. You don't shout when you are talking to someone in his living room, and you will not reach them if you shout at them from their TV screens.

Superficial reporters judge the success of a speech before a live audience by the number of times it is interrupted by applause. But cheer lines are just speechwriters' gimmicks. They serve a useful purpose at political rallies, which people attend to cheer, not to be educated. But it has been my experience that the most effective speeches for changing public opinion have no cheer lines at all.

Humor can be a deadly weapon, both against its object and against one who uses it and fails. Starting a speech with a canned joke that falls flat can destroy the effectiveness of a speech. President Reagan was a master at his use of humor. No one on the American political scene today is in his class. Those who attempt to imitate him could not make a greater mistake.

One of a speaker's most effective weapons is the element of surprise, especially when he is a President. His press secretary will jump up and down and insist that the speech will not be adequately covered unless reporters get an advance text. Many White House aides go even further, earning brownie points with the press by leaking out the essence of a speech to favored reporters. They always argue that this is the way to build up the audience. Exactly the opposite is true. If a speaker has a major statement to make, he should be the first to make it. That means no advance text and no leaks. The element of surprise will increase the size of the audience and massively expand the impact of the speech.

The two most effective speeches of my political career illustrate this point. On September 23, 1952, I was scheduled to appear on television to answer the false charge that a political fund for office expenses had been used for my personal benefit. The demand that I be dropped from the ticket swept the country like a firestorm. The media hounded my staff for an answer to the key question: Would I stay on the ticket or get off? I told the staff to answer with the truth—I had not yet decided and would announce my decision in the speech. The anticipation was immense. The audience was the biggest ever for a televised political speech, and the response by telegram, mail, and telephone was the biggest in history, too. Before the speech, most of the nation's newspapers, including the major Republican ones, had come out for dropping me from the ticket. After the speech, because of the overwhelmingly favorable public reaction, the situation was reversed. Without the element of surprise, the audience would have been smaller and the impact less, and I might well have been dropped from the ticket.

In October 1969, hundreds of thousands of anti–Vietnam War demonstrators marched into Washington. They demonstrated, sometimes violently, around the White House and the Capitol and in the downtown area. Peace-at-any-price senators and congressmen demanded that I withdraw American forces from Vietnam in return for our prisoners of war. Even some of my own political friends joined the pack. They contended that since Kennedy and Johnson had sent American combat troops to Vietnam, I would gain politically by bringing them home, regardless of the impact on American foreign policy. I was inundated with conflicting advice from the Cabinet, my staff, and members of Congress.

I scheduled a television speech for November 3. I knew that it would be the most important speech of my Presidency so far. I also knew that the conclusion of the speech would determine whether it was a success or a failure. At 2:00 a.m. the night before the speech, as I sat alone in the study at Camp David, an idea came to me. I wrote it by hand into the text. It read:

I have chosen a plan for peace. I believe it will succeed. If it does succeed, what the critics say now won't matter. If it does not succeed, anything I say now won't matter. And so tonight—to you, the great silent majority of my fellow Americans, I ask for your support. Let us be united for peace. Let us also be united against defeat. Because let us understand: North Vietnam cannot defeat or humiliate the United States. Only Americans can do that.

The White House press office was besieged by reporters who insisted on getting an advance text. I ordered that not only would there be no advance text, but there would be no leaks whatsoever and no speculation about what I was going to say. I was not going to run the risk of a televison commentator coming on after the speech and saying, "As expected, President Nixon announced . . ."—especially since I knew most commentators would oppose my position.

Again, the speculation was immense. Was I going to announce that we would withdraw or that we would stay in? That night we had the biggest television audience ever for a Presidential speech. The reaction by telegram, letters, and telephone was the biggest ever. My approval rating went up eleven points, the biggest increase as a result of a Presidential speech in the history of the Gallup Poll.

These kinds of big plays must be worthy of the occasion. To build up suspense and then have a dud of a speech is the worst of all possible worlds. The "Silent Majority" speech met the test. Any doubts I may have had about it were removed when dovish senators and congressmen who had urged me to order a withdrawal of American troops began to wear American flags in their lapels. The silent majority in the country had finally spoken, created a new majority in the Congress, and given our Vietnam policies a chance to succeed.

Before I was elected to Congress in 1946, I had the privilege of sitting with Dr. Robert Millikan, the Nobel Prize-winning chairman of the executive council at CalTech, at a black-tie dinner in Los Angeles. It was a prestigious audience, and I told him I was worried that some in the audience might have heard some of the remarks in my speech. I knew that he was much in demand as an after-dinner speaker, so I was reassured when he told me, "Don't worry about it. The ten percent or so that have heard you before are probably your friends. Only friends really bother to come hear a speaker a second time. Direct your remarks to the ninety percent who have not heard you. Your friends won't mind, and the rest of the audience will probably like what you say."

William Jennings Bryan tried out his famous "Cross of Gold" peroration in his speeches a number of times before he used it in his keynote address to the Democratic National Convention in 1896 and as a result won the nomination. Lincoln made his "House Divided" speech several times before it became national news when he delivered it at Cooper Union in New York. Today, because Presidents and many other officials are covered so intensely on television, it is difficult to repeat a speech verbatim without being yawned off the air by the reporters covering it. But an effective line should still be repeated. Just because you know it's good doesn't mean reporters will write it down. Only by repetition does a message finally get across to a mass audience. There is one exception. Once you have told a joke on national television, don't repeat it. If you find a really good joke, save it for the biggest possible audience.

Above all, be your own most severe critic. I have made thousands of speeches over the past forty-three years. No matter how well some have gone over, I have never been completely satisfied with any of them. Only by trying to do better than before can you make a speech that is worthy of the occasion. A final warning: All of these suggestions about preparing and delivering speeches are useless unless the speaker has a message. If you don't have something worthwhile to say, it is best not to make a speech at all.

23

TELEVISION

During my 1950 campaign for the Senate, when two thirds of the people in California did not yet own television sets, we were able for a modest sum to buy five minutes of prime time for a TV commercial. We decided to end it with what we thought would be an appealing human interest shot with Pat and me and our daughters, Tricia, who was then four, and Julie, who was two. For days, they had practiced a stirring campaign song that went like this, to the tune of "Merrily We Roll Along": "Off we go to Washington, Washington, Washington. Off we go to Washington. Vote for Nixon!"

Everything went fine in the practice sessions. But when we were on camera live, disaster struck. Julie had a toy bunny she insisted on carrying everyplace she went. When she came to the key line, she sang out loud and clear, "Vote for Bunny!" The producers were devastated but apparently it did no harm. We won with the biggest margin of any Senate campaign in the country that year.

In the forty years since then, television has become the dominant factor in American political campaigns. It is far more influential than news stories, columns, or editorials in newspapers and magazines. One poll in 1972 revealed that 78 percent of all of those questioned made their decision about who to vote for based on what they had seen on television rather than what they had heard at campaign rallies or seen in the press.

The writing press has not been completely irrelevant, however. A thoughtful TV commentator, when he can spare the time from putting on his makeup and getting his idiot cards in order, will sometimes read newspapers and magazines for background. What appears on the front or editorial pages of *The New York Times* or

The Wall Street Journal, even if it is not quoted directly, may still
have a subtle effect on the tone or content of a television report on
the evening news. But the bottom line is that in this highly competitive business, where ratings are infinitely more important than
substance in determining a reporter's income and status, the test
has to be what will appeal to the TV audience rather than what
may appeal to the far smaller but more thoughtful reading audience.

There is little doubt in my mind that the dominance of TV is a
negative development as far as electing the best candidates is concerned. First, there is little or no correlation between the qualities
that make a good leader and those that make a good TV performer.
Second, TV undoubtedly disqualifies some who have leadership
quality but no star quality. A good case can be made that Abraham
Lincoln, certainly the most revered of all American Presidents,
would have failed in the TV age. His high-pitched voice and
homely features would not have come across well on the television
screen. His long, rambling anecdotes, while very effective in
speeches to live audiences, would not have played well in a medium where the candidate can win by using one-liners fed to him
by his speechwriters. In the age of sound bites, the three-minute
Gettysburg Address would have been two and a half minutes too
long. One of today's ambitious young correspondents would probably have summed it up this way: "The President himself admitted
to this subdued Pennsylvania crowd what his men have been saying privately: that no one will long remember what he said here."

Recently I was discussing a campaign with a competent political
professional, who gave me his appraisal of the two frontrunners.
One was smart and strong, had good judgment, believed in the
right things, but "just isn't good on the tube." The other one "ain't
too smart but he comes over like gangbusters on TV." Not surprisingly, the dimbulb shone more brightly on TV, and won the
election.

But television is here to stay, and candidates who do not learn
how to use it have no chance of being elected. I suppose I should
be expected to know something about television since I participated in the first nationally televised congressional committee
hearing—the confrontation between Alger Hiss and Whittaker
Chambers on August 25, 1948—and the first televised Presidential
debates with Jack Kennedy in 1960. My "Fund" speech as a candidate for Vice President in 1952 and my "Silent Majority" speech
as President in 1969 had huge TV audiences and set records for

changing public opinion that have never been broken. But despite this experience, I hesitate to advise potential candidates as to how to use television. For example, I have never practiced speeches before a camera so I could study the tape later, like a football player studying game films, and learn to lengthen my vowels or sharpen my gestures. Frankly, doing so would make me feel silly. But again, all the experts advise their clients to submit to this as a way of overcoming deficiencies in their delivery.

Still, some practical observations might be useful. Most important, anyone going onto an interview program should insist on either appearing live or taping to time. Those who produce the shows won't like it. Your television adviser will tell you that it is too risky since you will not be able to edit out flubs. The advantages, however, outweigh the disadvantages. When you appear live or tape to time, you have to discipline yourself to be up for the performance. You also do not put yourself at the mercy of an editor who might leave your best lines on the cutting-room floor.

One of the best decisions George Bush made in the 1988 campaign was to go live with Dan Rather. If he had taped, Rather's editors would have spiked the devastating segment where Bush took the anchorman on for leaving the screen blank during a petty spat he was having with the sports department. A live interview, if promoted properly, is also inherently much more dramatic than a canned one. People open a newspaper to be enlightened; they turn on TV to be entertained. Nothing is more entertaining than genuine live confrontation.

The candidate must remember that a TV appearance is the most important event he will be doing that day. He should insist that his schedule be cleared so he will have plenty of time to prepare and will be rested and in top form when he goes on the air.

A candidate should never allow a fundraising event to be televised and should do everything possible to discourage the televising of campaign rallies. An appeal to overfed fat cats at a fundraising dinner or to extreme partisans at a rally is entirely different from the approach you want to take with a couple of people sitting in their living rooms and trying to decide whom to vote for. More often than not, highly partisan speeches have a negative impact on the home audience.

Some television experts will tell you that it is possible to wage a campaign without ever leaving a television studio. This will probably happen someday soon, but I do not consider it a positive development. The country is too big for extensive person-to-

220

person campaigning by a candidate for President, and it is true that more imaginative use of TV could actually improve Presidential politics. But in running for Congress and the Senate in smaller states, a candidate should still insist on meeting as many people as he can. The purpose is not so much the effect it has on them, although it does make a good story, but the effect it has on him. A candidate who relies too much on television can become too artificial, too staged, too impersonal. Only by meeting and talking to people in person can he get the feel of what the voters are really interested in and what kind of representation they really want.

As one who has found television immensely useful in going over the heads of the reporters and the Congress directly to the people, I suppose I should be more tolerant of its flaws. But I see some profound problems on two fronts.

First, television has transformed the way leadership is exercised. Even more troubling, it has changed the standards by which we measure a candidate's ability to be elected to office. As a result, not only may we be losing our Lincolns, but we will tend to choose those whose major qualifications are a good voice, a handsome TV face, and willingness to take the consultants' directions. Debates are supposed to expose the weakness of such a candidate. But if he can memorize a clever quip written by a Hollywood gag writer, he will always carry the day over an opponent who makes a thoughtful presentation on some complex issue.

Once a candidate wins, he will find that television has also changed the rules for informing, educating, and winning the support of the people. As I have often pointed out, television forces events into a soap-opera mold, giving them sometimes artificial but always explosive emotional force and all but eclipsing rational debate. Like a mind-altering drug, television distorts the viewer's perception of reality. It has also drastically shortened the public's attention span. Decisions on complex issues that might have taken a candidate weeks or even months to reach are dismissed with a twenty-second summary on the evening news. If a TV news report does not tie up loose ends as neatly as "The A Team," it is considered a flop.

In view of President Reagan's spectacular success in using television to win support for his policies, it can be argued that what we now need are more politicians who are good actors. What this analysis overlooks is that while Reagan was indeed a good actor, he also had very strong beliefs. This made a powerful, positive combination. We will be in real trouble if we ever elect a good actor without any strong beliefs. Then the real power would reside with unelected staffers who would control the national agenda by putting words in the President's mouth.

TV news is taking on the character of TV entertainment because everything on television lives or dies not by virtue of quality but by virtue of ratings. As I write, the major networks have begun using actors to recreate events on news programs, a despicable trend that began in sleazy syndicated programs. Such a gimmick has nothing to do with informing people and everything to do with snookering them into tuning in. A newspaper article about a shooting or rape contains all the information the public requires in order to be fully informed. News executives will say that their lurid reenactments "more fully communicate the horror of these events." In fact, they communicate only news executives' desires for better ratings and bigger vacation homes. Soon no one will be able to tell the difference between reality and illusion on television, and the fault will lie with the men and women who put profit ahead of standards and good judgment. TV used to be both profitable and decent. If it is not decent today, it is because its practitioners used the permissive standards of the sixties and seventies as an excuse to reap even higher profits from indecency.

There are some who suggest that the way to counteract the declining quality of commercial television is to increase funding for public television. But all this would do is ensure that network programmers, after polluting commercial TV during the week, can watch taxpayer-subsidized ballet and British sitcoms when they go to the Hamptons for the weekend. There are some good political programs on public television. But conservatives who complain about the liberal bias of network television miss the mark. Public television and radio in the United States, as well as in Europe, tilt far more to the left than does commercial television. At least commercial programs cannot stray irretrievably beyond the views of those in the audience, which are invariably to the right of the views of those who write, produce, direct, and act in the programs.

Surveys show that the average American sees seven hours of television a day. For older people, that may not be too significant a problem. For younger people, it is a disaster in the making. The hours spent sitting in front of the tube are hours taken away from reading, conversation, and recreation. We are justifiably concerned about the shockingly high rate of drug use and alcoholism among younger people. Television is also a narcotic. You can get hooked on it just as you can on drugs or alcohol. Parents and teachers must encourage young people to spend less time watching television and more time using their growing minds and bodies. Another answer, of course, is to improve the quality of what they do see.

The massive expansion of cable television may provide part of the answer. But again, it all gets back to those who produce the product. It always turns me off when television producers sanctimoniously proclaim that all they are doing is giving the people what they want. Those who produce the shows assume that what the *people* want is the same as what *they* want. The fact that so many movies and TV shows are just plain sick does not mean that most people are sick. It simply means that those who live and work in the entertainment centers of Hollywood and New York believe that the sickness that affects so many of their lives affects everybody else as well.

Like many Americans, I am concerned about the violence, sex, and just plain trash that any teenager can tune in to on cable these days if a network decides that it is too raucous even for their taste. But I oppose any efforts by government to control the content of television programs. Because of its licensing power, the government has potential control over television and radio which it does not have over newspapers and magazines. That power should be exercised only in the most extreme cases. Just as public television is not the answer insofar as getting more balance in political programming is concerned, government control of the content of entertainment programs is potentially far worse and more dangerous than leaving it to the marketplace. But those in the TV business should take a new look at their consciences for two reasons: As professionals, they should not be satisfied to produce only what appeals to the lowest common denominator of their audience. The second reason is more selfish. Unless they police themselves, they are asking for an eventual public backlash followed by policing by government. The first "reenacted" assassination or rape-murder on prime time might just do that.

24

PRIVACY

Athough I had always had a lively interest in public affairs, I was not aware until after his death that Franklin D. Roosevelt was crippled by polio. I vividly recall seeing newsreels that showed him in Washington and abroad. They never showed a wheelchair or crutches, nor did newspaper accounts mention his disability. The media actively kept the secret for him. Some may disagree, but I believe the press deserves great credit for not disclosing his condition. Today, they could not do so because of the television cameras that follow a President everywhere.

More to the point, they would not want to do so. You don't have to point to the Gary Hart exposé to find examples where investigative reporters have made public figures, and their families and friends, fair game for disclosure of every detail of their private lives. Highly qualified people are becoming increasingly reluctant to take government positions in Washington because they don't want to expose their families to this merciless scrutiny. We can't go back to the pre-television standards of the FDR days, but the media, in the interest of fairness and responsibility, might well consider reappraising some of their practices and eliminating some of the abuses.

In their vigorous advocacy of the public's right to know, the media frequently violate a right that has a higher standing—the individual's right to privacy. Does an individual who voluntarily enters the public arena forfeit his right to privacy? What about members of his family or friends who choose not to enter the arena?

These are not just legal questions. The media should have a higher standard than simply reporting anything the law allows no matter whose rights are invaded. Legally speaking, the media virtually have that right today. In *The New York Times* vs. *Sullivan* in 1964, the Supreme Court ruled that even a blatantly false statement about a public figure is actionable only if the victim can somehow prove the reporter was motivated by malice, or knew or should have known it wasn't true. As a result, it is now almost impossible for any public official to collect damages for libel. Often newspeople sanctimoniously say that if a person believes he has been falsely accused, he can always sue for libel. Such statements themselves are grossly misleading. The real truth is that *Times* vs. *Sullivan* is a license for the media to lie about virtually anyone whose name comes up in the news.

To be effective, Presidents must harden themselves to occasional media abuses. But they are understandably protective of their families. Woodrow Wilson berated the press for reporting even the most benign activities of his daughters. Harry Truman gave the 80th Congress hell and he did the same to a music critic who had criticized his daughter's singing. Although his brother often stayed with him in the White House, Lyndon Johnson was infuriated when the press reported on Sam's personal idiosyncrasies. His irritation is reflected in a diary note I made in 1969 after we had breakfast together in the White House:

He [LBJ] spoke with considerable bitterness about *Look*'s article on his brother. He told the story of one of his big financial supporters who also had a brother who got into lots of trouble; the man's mother insisted on his doing something for the brother and he finally gave him a job driving a truckload of dynamite across the state. "He stopped at a roadside stand. Had a couple of beers. Propositioned the waitress to marry him and went off down the road and then a tree moved in front of him." He felt that newspaper men were just naturally vicious and not happy unless they are attacking somebody.

I can understand Wilson's, Truman's, and Johnson's irritation. But in each instance the media were in the right, provided their reporting was accurate and their opinions expressed in good taste. Any member of a President's immediate family, especially if he or she chooses to live in the White House, becomes a public figure and should expect to be covered. This is especially true now that family members routinely participate in campaigns. But the media are on weak ground when they go after relatives or friends who aren't in politics, don't want to be in politics, and would do anything to stay out of it. These individuals have a right to their privacy. And yet there have been cases where private figures who were covered relentlessly against their wishes sued their media tormentors for libel, only to fail because of the bizarre argument that all that unwanted and even inaccurate coverage had made them public figures.

If the press does not curb its appetite for invading privacy, it will become increasingly difficult for Presidents and other public officials to have close friends. Ironically, it is when a President is most popular that his subordinates, family, and friends are most vulnerable. When they have a choice, the press will pick on the weak rather than the strong. Dan Quayle will enthusiastically applaud when George Bush is riding high. But he should watch his back at the same time, since the more popular Bush becomes, the more likely it is that the press will go after Quayle. Those who are subjected to such attacks should take some comfort from knowing that the press's real target is the top man, who is apparently too popular to take on personally.

The official position of those in the news business is that the relatively benign White House reporting that lasted through the Kennedy administration and that generally ignored questionable personal conduct of the President, his family, and friends was made obsolete by Vietnam and Watergate. According to this line, the media now have the heavy responsibility of probing relentlessly for the truth whatever the consequences. As most media analysts are prone to do, these advocates ignore the element of self-interest. As an industry, the media, because of the new dominance of television, is far more competitive and cutthroat than a generation ago. As individuals, reporters get ahead not by writing or airing puff pieces but by making "dramatic disclosures," frequently about their subjects' personal lives. Unlike public officials, who are restrained by checks and balances and a variety of other legal requirements, media people are restrained only by whatever good judgment or discretion they may happen to possess. If they do not happen to possess either, the consequences for those they report about can be catastrophic.

The media frequently proclaim that they are regulated by the people, who will rise up against them if their reporting goes too far. This is nonsense. People are basically fair, but they also like to be entertained and titillated by tales of official and private misbehavior. As a result, the line between news and entertainment is blurring further each day. After watching the network news one evening recently, I flipped around the dial and saw that my choices, depending on which of the five major networks I wanted to watch, were swimsuit models, a story about incest, a rock singer's sister who had posed nude, a game show, and the MacNeil/Lehrer News Hour. I read a book instead. To its great credit, I am sure MacNeil/Lehrer came in last in the ratings.

The media should not be ashamed for giving the people what they want and getting massive profits in return. But they *should* be ashamed for pretending they are doing so to serve the best interests of the nation. And those who will piously insist that there is a difference between good, hard news reporting and schlock reporting are being disingenuous. Morton Downey, Jr.'s, only crime was to perfect the same techniques of third-degree journalism that earned top ratings for "60 Minutes" and huge profits for CBS.

The media assert that the public's right to know about the activities of a public figure is more important than his right to privacy. In some cases, that may be true. But the right-to-know argument falls flat in the case of criminal and civil trials, where the dubious practice of permitting TV cameras in courtrooms is becoming increasingly common. Without cameras, trials still can receive blow-by-blow coverage since TV reporters, print reporters, and courtroom artists are permitted to be present. Adding cameras and lights gives new meaning to the term "third-degree journalism" as victims and witnesses are forced against their will to submit to the merciless glare of television. High-profile trials frequently become circuses as prosecutors, attorneys, and even judges pander to the TV audience when they should be devoting all their energies to ensuring that justice is done. TV executives and their apologists piously assert that those who oppose cameras in courtrooms are interfering with the public's right to know. All that is really at stake is TV's right to make profits and high ratings from broadcasting an exciting spectacle.

To be successful, TV reporters must get their sound bites on the evening news, and print reporters must get frequent page-one bylines. Even in print, negative stories rather than positive ones win the prizes and promotions. In barber shops and beauty parlors customers are more likely to read sensationalistic sheets like *People, National Enquirer,* and *The Star* than staid *Time, Newsweek, U.S. News and World Report.* Salacious tidbits about the latest superstar divorce are far more interesting than the latest figures on the homeless. In the 1988 Presidential campaign there was a great deal of media moaning about the shortage of serious issues. But given a choice, the media themselves prefer to report juicy morsels on private lives rather than dry debates about offshore drilling rights.

Because of the media's thirst for revelation, the relationship between public figures and journalists has fallen to a low point. We can bemoan this decline of civility all we want without changing it. But if each side puts itself in the other's shoes for a moment, perhaps we can learn to live with it.

Politicians should understand that the media have to do their jobs. In today's atmosphere, that means that if you have an Uncle Ned who drinks too much or was caught cheating on his high school physics test, you will probably read about it in the newspaper at some point in your public career. There are a few reporters who care more about your position on vital issues than they do about Uncle Ned. But before you make the decision to enter public life, you must decide whether getting your views across on those issues and making a difference in the world are worth endangering the privacy, the happiness, and even the livelihood of those you care for. If you address this danger in theory early on, you, and they, will be better equipped to handle it when it presents itself in fact.

The media should understand that they can do their jobs, make money, and achieve good ratings and high circulation without resorting to the inexcusable violations of privacy that have made them even less popular than politicians. They could improve their standing in society by following a few guidelines:

Every aspect of a public figure's life is fair game for reporting, because it might affect his performance in office. When he becomes a candidate, he waives his right to privacy.

His family's right to privacy should be respected, except for those who thrust themselves into the public arena or whose private lives might affect the official's public conduct.

A politician's friend is entitled to his right to privacy except when he voluntarily becomes a public figure.

The press is unreasonably reluctant to admit inaccurate reporting. When an invasion of privacy is involved, this reluctance is indefensible. A political man can defend himself in the arena. Family and friends must suffer in silence. In all cases of false reporting, but especially those involving people without the clout to defend themselves, the press should have the good grace to give as much space to a retraction and apology as it did to the false charge.

George Bush's call for a kinder, gentler nation struck a responsive chord. I would not for one moment suggest that what the nation needs is a kinder, gentler press. The press should pursue public figures and investigate public issues relentlessly and, if necessary, ruthlessly. But where private citizens are concerned, the press should be held to the higher standard of the golden rule. They should do unto others as they would want others to do unto them. They should also follow Vince Lombardi's dictum: Play hard, but play clean.

Charles de Gaulle had a reputation for being too high-handed with the press. However justified that criticism was in his public life, there is another, lesser known aspect of his life where such conduct was completely justified. His wife, Yvonne, was struck by a car shortly before the birth of their third child. The doctors said their daughter was retarded and would probably never be able to speak. The de Gaulles were devastated. Madame de Gaulle wrote to a friend, "Charles and I would give anything, health, all our money, advancement, career if only Ann could be an ordinary little girl like the rest." When someone suggested that they put her in a home, de Gaulle refused. "She did not ask to come into the world," he said. "We should do everything to make her happy." During her brief life, de Gaulle was the only person who could make her laugh. When they were together, he shed all his austere dignity. He would dance little jigs with her, do pantomimes, and sing popular songs to her.

The de Gaulles fiercely protected her from curiosity seekers and the press. The general forbade photographers from including any of his children in publicity shots taken at his country house during the war years, because he knew that the presence or the absence of Ann would be sure to elicit comment. Other children teased her because she was different, and her pain was compounded because she did not know why she was different.

Shortly after her twentieth birthday, Ann died of pneumonia. At the conclusion of the brief graveside service, de Gaulle took his wife's hand in his and said, "Come, now she is like the others."

A public man can never expect to be treated like the others. But unless they thrust themselves into the public arena, his family and friends deserve no less.

229

25

PAT

I met one First Lady and saw another many years before I ever met a President.

In 1938, after graduating from law school and returning to Whittier to practice, I was elected to the board of trustees of Whittier College. I recall how impressed I was when I met Lou Henry Hoover, one of my fellow trustees. She was the exact opposite of the picture I had in my mind of her husband, who was always portrayed in the media as sour, stiff, and sullen. She was vivacious, thoughtful, and a stimulating conversationalist. When I met Herbert Hoover ten years later, I found that once you got to know him he could be just as charming as she was. The difference was that he only let his intimates see that side of him. He was an introvert in an extrovert's profession. In that respect, she was better suited for politics than he was and thus complemented him perfectly. Those who visited the White House during the difficult days of the Great Depression were always impressed by their hosts' grace and dignity.

In the late summer of 1943, I was driving a Jeep from Noumea on New Caledonia to the Marine Air Base at Tontouto. I heard a siren and pulled over. Two Jeeps full of MPs were clearing the way for a motorcade. I thought it might be some high-ranking general. But when the Army weapons carrier sped past I was amazed to see that the passenger, wearing a big, floppy hat to protect herself from the blistering sun, was Eleanor Roosevelt. Since the battle for the Solomon Islands was still raging a few miles to the north, her visit made a great impression on us all. Like Mrs. Hoover, she complemented her husband perfectly. While he was tied down by his duties in Washington, she seized every opportunity to travel

230

throughout the United States and abroad to show support for the war effort.

I finally met a President when Pat and I attended the reception for members of Congress in 1947. She bought a new dress, justifying the strain on our budget by observing that it might be the only time we would see the place. It was a mob scene, but I vividly recall how President and Mrs. Truman, in the brief time they shook our hands, made us feel at home. They both had the gift of being dignified without putting on airs. Press accounts habitually described Mrs. Truman as plain. What impressed us most was that she was genuine.

My most vivid memory of Mamie Eisenhower was seeing her at the only White House dinner I hosted as Vice President. Earlier in the afternoon, after welcoming the king of Morocco at the airport, the President had suffered a stroke. Mrs. Eisenhower insisted that the state dinner in our visitor's honor go forward as planned and asked me to accompany her. Mamie was a worrier, and in this case she had good reason. After the President's heart attack just two years before, she hadn't wanted him to run again. She thought it might kill him. Now she felt her worst fears were being realized. She was not one to hold things in. Before we went in to dinner, her voice broke as she poured out her fears to me. But when we entered the East Room, none of the other guests would have known anything was the matter. She was as charming and vivacious as ever, even though her heart was breaking. It was a virtuoso performance.

She also worried about her husband's health in 1960, when my campaign strategists were urging him to make more appearances for the ticket. His blood pressure had been high, and she feared that a heavier schedule would endanger his life. She spoke emotionally about it to Pat, and the President's doctor, General Howard Snyder, buttonholed me on the way to see the President and urged me to ask him to cut back. Eisenhower himself was eager to add an event to his schedule in Illinois, a key toss-up state. To his surprise, I discouraged him. He did not learn why I had done so until after the election.

Since we left the White House in 1974, my First Lady, Pat, has never made a speech, accepted an award, or been interviewed by the press. We entertain close friends and family at home but turn down the many invitations we receive to highly publicized New York events. But despite being out of public view for fifteen years, she has been on *Good Housekeeping*'s ten most admired women list every year. Some wonder how this could happen in our media-drenched, out-of-sight-out-of-mind society. I know why. Most people, even if they are basically happy, do not have an easy life. Some have had disappointments, others have suffered defeats. Many have experienced tragedy. Pat relates to these people, and they to her.

The word "character" has several meanings. When someone is an oddball, we call him a character. When someone applies for a job, we give him a character reference. Pat has character in a more profound sense. When an athlete comes back to win after suffering a defeat, we say he has character. That is Pat's kind. She is a strong person who is at her best when the going gets rough. Millions who have followed her career during the forty-three years we have been in the political arena know that and appreciate it, and for that reason will never forget her.

Her life is a classic example of triumph over adversity. Her mother died of cancer when Pat was thirteen. She helped care for her father for two years until he died of silicosis, popularly known as miner's disease, when she was eighteen. To earn the money for college, she worked as a bank teller, an assistant to a department store buyer, a bit player in the movies, a research assistant for a USC professor, and a hospital X-ray technician in New York City. During most of this time she helped keep house for her two older brothers. Despite her backbreaking commitments, she graduated with honors from USC in 1937.

After we were married, she continued to work as a high school teacher to supplement my meager income from my law practice during the Depression. While I was serving overseas, she was a government price analyst in San Francisco.

Our first fourteen years in Washington, when I served in the House, the Senate, and as Vice President, were an exciting and happy time. But it was not always smooth sailing. After the Hiss case, I became a major national figure but also a highly controversial one. I refused to let the critics bother me, but on occasion they got to her. She has always been a voracious reader. Hardly a day went by when she did not see a vicious cartoon, a highly negative column, or some blatantly biased news report. But she never complained to me. She had enormous respect and affection for Whittaker Chambers and his wife Esther. She knew we were on the right side. This certainly strengthened her, but it did not make the cruel barbs hurt any less.

During my trips abroad as Vice President and President, she

broke new ground, refusing to follow the meaningless schedules that were usually set up for dignitaries' wives in those days. Unless our host absolutely insisted, she skipped the shopping and sight-seeing. Instead, she visited schools, hospitals, orphans' homes, old people's homes, a leper colony in Panama, refugee camps in Vietnam. While I was closeted in meetings, she was out making pro-American news. Eventually the press began to follow her rather than me.

Pat is an intensely private person who still proved to be a superb campaigner, because she likes people and they like her. She was by my side constantly in two campaigns for Congress, one for the Senate, one for governor, two for Vice President, and three for President, not to mention our grueling, thankless swings in off-year elections. She never set a foot wrong or gave the media a club to beat me over the head with. After a campaign appearance in Kansas in 1952, Senator Frank Carlson expressed his unbounded admiration for her campaigning ability. He told me, "Dick, you're controversial, but *everybody* likes Pat."

She did not complain about the political attacks on me. She knew they were part of the game. But the attacks on my personal integrity during the Fund controversy in 1952 left a deep scar, not just because they proved to be false but because to refute them I had to reveal our modest financial worth. She put it bluntly: "Why do we have to let everybody know how little we have? That's nobody's business but our own." Losing in 1960 was a disappointment. But in her case, it was doubly so because she believes to this day that the election was stolen through vote fraud in Illinois and Texas.

Pat's political instincts are invariably accurate. She urged me not to run for governor of California. She was right. She has an uncanny ability to assess people. Her personnel evaluations were usually better than mine. On the few occasions when I did not follow her recommendations, I wished I had. She had strong views on issues but always expressed them privately rather than publicly.

The Secret Service's code name for her was "Starlight." She fitted it to a "T" during the White House years. She did not need designer gowns to accentuate her natural beauty and poise. What particularly saddened her were the huge anti-war demonstrations outside the White House. They no longer shouted, "Hey, hey, LBJ. How many kids did you kill today?" Now it was, "One, two, three, four, we don't want your f-----g war." She did not blame the young people. Having been a teacher, she knew how biased teachers and professors could poison the minds of impressionable students. What hurt her most was that threats of violent demonstrations prompted the Secret Service to raise such concerns about security during Julie's graduation from Smith College that we finally decided not to attend.

The resignation was harder on her than me, because she thought it was a mistake to resign. Like Julie and Tricia, she thought we should fight through to the end. I still marvel at how she was able to go forty-eight hours without sleep while she supervised the packing of all our personal belongings for the move to San Clemente. My near-fatal illness in California was also a greater burden on her. I was physically, mentally, and emotionally drained, so in addition to keeping up her own spirits, she had to sustain mine. Our quiet dinners alone in the evening were often the only respite I had from the trauma of those dark days.

My evaluation of Pat is best expressed in this diary note I made in California shortly before the resignation:

I remember that Tricia said as we came back from the beach that her mother was really a wonderful woman. And I said, yes, she has been through a lot through the twenty-five years we have been in and out of politics. Both at home and abroad, she has always conducted herself with masterful poise and dignity. But God, how she could have gone through what she does, I simply don't know.

After we left the White House, it did not seem possible that she could bear any more. I followed my usual practice of not reading the criticism being heaped on me. But she insisted on keeping informed. She read almost all of the articles and many of the books. One day a well-meaning member of our staff sent her a particularly vicious book written by two *Washington Post* reporters. It was the last thing she read before tragedy struck.

On the morning of July 8, 1976, I went into the kitchen at Casa Pacifica to get some coffee. I noticed that Pat seemed to be unsteady and that the cup and saucer were shaking in her hand. The left side of her mouth was drooping. I hoped it might have been caused by an insect sting, but I knew better. It was a stroke. As we rode together in the ambulance to the hospital, her left side became paralyzed. Her speech was slurred and her mouth contorted.

Hundreds of bouquets of flowers and thousands of get-well messages poured in from all over the world. But only she could handle this crisis. No one else could help her. Before she left the hospital, her speech difficulty had disappeared and her mouth was back to normal. But her left arm hung limply by her side.

Our home in San Clemente had a beautiful Spanish inner patio. She had an exercise wheel installed on one of the walls enclosing it. Day after day as I left the house to go over to the office, I saw her standing there, turning the wheel around and around again. At times she was discouraged because there seemed to be no visible improvement. But she never gave up. Before the year was out, her recovery was complete. Doctors did not do it for her. Her family did not do it for her. Her friends did not do it for her. She did it by herself, which is characteristic of her whole life. My critics in the media called her "Plastic Pat." What they did not know was that her plastic was tougher than the finest steel.

The Bible is a wellspring of truths, but it contains one falsehood —that women are the weaker sex. Statistics tell us that women live longer than men. Experience tells me that women are stronger, too, physically, mentally, and emotionally. Whether it was confronting the Fund crisis, facing a killer mob in Caracas, standing up to anti-war demonstrators, or going through the ordeal of resignation, Pat was always stronger. Without her, I could not have done what I did.

When I make public appearances these days, the question I am asked most often is, "How is Pat?" Considering what she has been through, she is remarkably well. You would never know that she had suffered a stroke. She no longer participates in public events but devotes all of her time and energy to her children and grandchildren.

What is her legacy? Pat will be remembered as one of our greatest First Ladies for four things.

She was a superb goodwill ambassador. She was our most widely traveled First Lady, having campaigned in all fifty states as part of the Pat and Dick team and visited seventy-five nations around the globe. By the time she came to the White House, Pat had already traveled with me to fifty-three countries, including the remotest corners of Asia, Africa, and Latin America. She deeply believed in the importance of personal diplomacy. She accompanied me on the history-making first visits of a President to the Soviet Union and China. She traveled alone to Peru in 1970 following a devastating earthquake to bring relief supplies and galvanize volunteer efforts. In 1972, she attended the inauguration of the President of Liberia, becoming the first President's wife to officially represent the United States abroad.

She will be remembered for championing the cause of volunteerism—especially the Right to Read program—because of her belief that the need for personal involvement in today's complex, impersonal world is more vital than ever. She visited volunteer projects throughout America and honored hundreds of outstanding volunteers at the White House.

Before we left New York in the 1960s, the elevator operator in our apartment building told us he had never visited a national park because he couldn't afford the travel costs. She remembered that when we went to the White House, and through her leadership, the "Parks to the People" program was instituted to establish small parks near major cities that poor people could afford to visit.

Finally, Pat will be remembered for her efforts to bring meaning to these words: "The White House belongs to the American people." She believed that the White House should be lit at night like the Jefferson, Lincoln, and Washington monuments, and at Thanksgiving 1970 the project was completed. She surprised me by having the lights turned on for the first time one night when we arrived at the White House by helicopter. She personally raised millions of dollars to refurbish the interior of the mansion, adding an unprecedented five hundred antiques and works of art to the collection. All the money was spent on the public rooms, none on the private quarters. She expanded access for the public by opening the house in the afternoons for the handicapped, establishing special tours for the blind, instituting candlelight tours at Christmastime and tours of the gardens in springtime, and opening the family quarters on the second floor to guests who attended our many Evenings at the White House.

Any one of these accomplishments would be enough for one person. But I think she would prefer to be remembered for another reason. It was hard for young people to grow up and lead useful lives during the spiritual turmoil of the 1960s and 1970s, and particularly so for children of celebrities who are always in the spotlight. That generation is still struggling against the effects of rampant drug abuse and moral aimlessness. With their father subject to massive political and personal attack, it is a miracle that Tricia and Julie came through as they did. They have survived it all with the strength and serenity of their mother.

They couldn't have done it without her. In a tribute to former Prime Minister Asquith, Winston Churchill observed, "His children are his best memorial." I think that is the way Pat would like to be remembered. Her children are her best memorial.

26

FRIENDS

Harry Truman once said, "If you want a friend in this town, buy a dog." I have sometimes felt that way about Washington, but I think even he would have agreed that a more accurate statement is that a politician has personal friends with whom he shares ideals and political friends with whom he shares interests. The latter will be your friends only as long as your interests and theirs coincide.

I noticed the flexibility of political friendship in 1955 while I was serving as Vice President. Shortly after President Eisenhower had his heart attack, I was surprised when Harold Stassen, who was not a political ally, came to see me. He was very friendly and pledged his support for me in 1956 if Eisenhower decided not to run. He was not the only one. I received a number of calls and letters from people offering loyal support but whom I had not heard from since the 1952 election. As the news bulletins from the hospital began to show the President's condition improving, the calls stopped. Ten months later, Stassen mounted an abortive effort to remove my name from the 1956 GOP ticket.

Some might draw the conclusion that this just proves politics is a lousy profession because of the kind of people who are in politics. Unfortunately, such fickleness extends to other fields. I recall visiting General MacArthur in his suite at the Waldorf on his eightieth birthday. That evening he would attend a dinner with some friends with whom he had served in war and peace and who met each year to honor him on his birthday. He spoke with great feeling about how touched he was that they had remained close whether his stock was up or down. He contrasted them with the type of people he had met in the business world while he was serving as

238

chairman of the Remington Rand Corporation. "Wall Street businessmen have no character," he said. "They never stand up for principle. They just support winners." His message was loud and clear: Unless a businessman can use you, he has no use for you.

He is right about most but certainly not about all people in big business. When I moved back to New York from San Clemente in 1980, I found that a surprising number of business leaders who had been my friends while I was in the White House and before, such as Hugh Bullock, George Champion, Jack Dreyfus, Joe Gimma, Al Gordon, Isaac Grainger, Lamar Hunt, Don Kendall, Bunny Lasker, John Olin, Laurance and David Rockefeller, and Mary Roebling, were still my friends despite the fact that I could no longer do anything for them. A President or any other elected official must always remember that politics can be a very cruel game. The same is true of other professions. It is human nature to support winners and ignore losers. But the positive side is that in politics, you will make countless new friends you would not otherwise meet. Some will desert you when you lose. But unlike other professions, in political defeat you will learn who your real friends are.

I shall never forget a particularly moving experience that occurred in 1962, after I lost the election for governor of California and had bid what I thought was a final farewell to the press. No one thought I had a political future, and I agreed. I heard from very few of my political friends. It was a lonely time. I was surprised to get a call from Tex Thornton, chairman of Litton Industries. While he had contributed to my campaign, I did not know him well and did not consider him to be a close friend. He said he had a ranch in California's beautiful Hidden Valley. He thought Pat, Tricia, Julie, and I might like to go out there for a day to ride horses, relax, and get away from the strains and stresses of the political world. He added that he and Mrs. Thornton would not be there, so we would have the whole place to ourselves. It was a particularly generous gesture because I had never done anything for him in the past and it appeared I could never do anything for him in the future. He was a friend I would not have known had I not been in politics.

In the six years I spent in San Clemente after my resignation, I still marvel at how many friends I heard from. Fellow Californians like Jack Drown, Clint Harris, Hubert Perry, and Jimmy Roosevelt came by to see me. They wanted nothing, and I had nothing I

239

could give them. When I was desperately ill in the hospital, I received hundreds of bouquets of flowers from friends I had not seen for years.

Many gestures of friendship gave me a much-needed lift while I was recovering from the operation. Dr. Michael DeBakey, a friend I had never met whose name for some inexplicable reason had appeared on the White House "enemies list," offered to fly in a team of specialists from Houston to be of assistance if needed.

John Wayne was already going through his final battle with cancer, yet he insisted on coming down one day for lunch. There was only one problem. When I went to mix a martini for him, I could not find the vermouth. So I just put a good slug of gin on the rocks, added a twist of lemon, and served it to him myself. I can still remember the delight in his eyes after he took a sip and said in his gravelly voice, "My, that's good."

Paul Keyes and Jimmy Cagney made the two-hour drive from Hollywood to San Clemente just to give me "a couple of laughs," as Paul—the creator of "Laugh-In"—put it.

Edgar Bergen offered to bring over Charlie McCarthy and Mortimer Snerd to give me a lift.

Jimmy Stewart called me on the phone and in his captivating hesitant drawl said, "I just want you to know that Gloria and I are praying for you."

Dolores Hope called with words of encouragement. "Don't worry about those who hate you. If one loves you, that's worth ten who hate you because love is so much stronger than hate."

Willard Keith took me aside at dinner and said, "Don't look back. Don't look down. Always look over the horizon." No words more succinctly captured the philosophy that has motivated me throughout my political career.

I was unable to go to the Bohemian Grove in the summer of 1975, so Jack Howard and ten of my campmates brought the Grove to me. They flew down to San Clemente from Santa Rosa in a chartered plane. George Mardikian prepared a gourmet lunch, and Lowell Thomas lifted us all with his eloquent toast.

When I declined an invitation to attend the Rose Bowl game, the Tournament of Roses committee came down and gave me a plaque commemorating the two times I had served as Grand Marshal of the Rose Parade: in 1953 after being elected Vice President, and in 1969 after being elected President. Woody Hayes called me before the game and promised to bring me the game ball. When Ohio State lost, he was so depressed that he cancelled the trip because he feared his glum mood would depress me as well. We did some Monday morning quarterbacking on the telephone instead.

Athalie Clarke, the grande dame of Orange County, offered her beautiful home in Kauai for however long my recovery period lasted. Chief Newman came down from Whittier with Bill Brock and Nate George, Whittier's most famous athlete. He was the sprinter who had defeated Charlie Paddock, then the world's fastest human, and Charlie Borah of USC in a match race at the Los Angeles Coliseum.

Earl Adams, George Allen, Dwayne Andreas, George Argyros, Gene Autry, George Baker, Arnold Beckman, Don Bendetti, Red Blaik, Helen Boehm, Van Cliburn, Al Cole, Helen Copley, Henry Dormann, Richard Duchossors, Buddy Ebsen, Bill Fetridge, Max Fisher, Malcolm Forbes, Peter Grace, Armand Hammer, Janet Hooker, Lloyd Johnson, Jack Kahn, Carl Karcher, Don Koll, Rabbi Baruch Korff, Linda LaBarr, Hobart Lewis, Carl Lindner, D. K. Ludwig, A. C. Lyles, Bill Marriott, Sr., and Jr., Monty Moncrief, Jack Mulcahy, Rupert Murdoch, David Murdock, Ken Norris, Otto Passman, Gay Pendleton, Milton and Carroll Petrie, John Rollins, Cesar Romero, Benno Schmidt, George and Frank Smathers, Bill Smith, Susan Spreen, Clem Stone, Roger Stone, Bonnie and John Swearingen, Waller Taylor, Lowell Wadmond, Roger Williams, and Bob Wilson were among the many others from all over the country who sent me messages of support and encouragement.

I had often heard that real friends are there when you need them the most. After 1974, I saw that first hand. Fortunately, those who came to see me after I left office resisted the temptation to rehash the difficult times just passed and concentrated instead on the issues of the present and the possibilities of better times in the future.

Understandably, most of the politicians kept their distance. But a surprising number did not. Former Congressman Joe Waggonner of Louisiana telephoned me regularly with messages of encouragement and support. Ron and Nancy Reagan drove down from their home in Pacific Palisades just to remind Pat and me that they were still our friends.

Non-career ambassadors often feel that they are doing the President a favor by agreeing to serve abroad. Many of my appointees did not fit into that category. Old friends like Walter Annenberg, Shirley Temple Black, Leonard Firestone, Bob Hill, James Hodgson, John Lodge, Ken Rush, William Sebald, Walter Stoessel, and

John Volpe remained in touch. The same was true of former Cabinet and staff members such as Martin Anderson, Roy Ash, Bob Brown, Pat Buchanan, Earl Butz, Phil Campbell, Dwight Chapin, Chuck Colson, John Connally, Fred Dent, Sam Devine, Bob Finch, Pete Flanigan, Len Garment, Roy Goodearle, Bob Haldeman, Cliff Hardin, Bryce Harlow, Bruce Herschensohn, Wally Hickel, Pat Hitt, Don Hughes, Ken Khachigian, Herb Klein, Mel Laird, Fred Malek, Paul McCracken, John Mitchell, Rogers Morton, Bus Mosbacher, Dave Packard, Pete Peterson, Bill Rogers, George Romney, Don Rumsfeld, Nick Ruwe, Frank Shakespeare, Bill Simon, Maury Stans, Herb Stein, Ron Walker, Bruce Whelihan, John Whitaker, and Ron Ziegler.

The number of visitors who flew in from around the world was especially heartwarming. They included Prime Minister Andreotti from Italy, Jonathan Aitken from London, Sir James Goldsmith from Paris, Ardeshir Zahedi, and many other ambassadors and foreign leaders I had met during my years in Washington.

Communists are supposed to be totally cold-blooded about personal relationships. Regardless of what you may have done for them in the past, unless you can do something for them in the future, you should not expect to hear from them. This was not true of the Chinese. Their ambassador flew out from Washington to bring an invitation for me to visit China again, which I accepted in 1976. Over and over again he reiterated the same theme. "In China," he said, "we always remember our old friends." In this respect, they were more Chinese than Communist.

Most touching of all was the mail—tens of thousands of letters from all over the United States and the world. With our small staff, even supplemented by loyal volunteers recruited by Loie Gaunt, we could not answer them all. But that was no indication of how much they meant to me. Some were from POWs and Vietnam veterans who thanked me for bringing them home. Others expressed their appreciation for my actions in opening the door to China. And still others just wanted to express their admiration for the way Mrs. Nixon and our two daughters had conducted themselves in the White House.

There were of course disappointments. People we thought were our friends turned out not to be. Some even exploited our former friendship by joining in the attacks on me. But I was never bitter, because I understood how difficult it was for anyone to buck the massive tide of negative opinion against a President who had been forced to resign the office.

Being a friend of the President is a mixed blessing even when he is on top. Some enjoy the media attention. But many who cherish their privacy recoil at the merciless attention they receive from prying reporters. It is widely assumed that being close to the President assures special treatment from government agencies. In fact, exactly the opposite is true. Bureaucrats at the IRS and other government agencies, concerned that they may be criticized for giving favorable treatment to a friend of the President, bend over backwards to give him unfair treatment.

One of the most vicious smear campaigns was waged against Bob Abplanalp. The relentlessly partisan Brooks subcommittee in the House implied that he had benefited from government expenditures at his Grand Bahamas home, which I visited on several occasions as President. In fact, my visits had cost him a small fortune. When the Secret Service requested the installation of intrusion alarms, fire detection systems, and special generators, Bob paid for them out of his own pocket. He also built a landing strip for our helicopter and a bunkhouse for the Secret Service. All of these would have been completely legitimate government expenditures. By insisting on paying for them himself, he saved the government more than $1 million. Partisan congressional investigators in Congress, instead of giving him credit for what he had done, left the implication in the public's mind that he had been ripping off the government. Like Bebe Rebozo, he was guilty of only one crime. He was my friend.

It is true that the President's friends can sometimes be a problem. The toughest personnel choice he has to make is between a friend who is loyal but not competent and someone else who is competent but not necessarily a friend. There is nothing more difficult than turning down a loyal friend who wants a position for which you know he is not qualified. Sometimes, you compromise. In this day of instant communication between Washington and the rest of the world, in some smaller countries it does not matter too much who our ambassador is, provided he doesn't make a fool of himself. You are at times inclined to give such posts to those who are less than perfectly suited for them, not as a payoff for past support but as a way of avoiding the agony of saying no. But you must draw the line somewhere. Ambassador to a small nation? Possibly. Ambassador to a major nation or assistant secretary of state or defense? Never. Sometimes a President's friends want to serve but set their sights impossibly high. In such cases disappointment is unavoidable. To be utterly practical, it does not serve your

243

political interests to use important jobs solely for political payoffs, since it will inevitably hurt your interests at reelection time to have your administration run by turkeys.

It is equally difficult for a President to say no to friends, even close personal friends, who want more of his time than his responsibilities permit him to give. Many are understandably convinced that the President should be able to spare them "just a minute or two" to chat on the phone and that the reason they cannot get through is the fault of his scheming, possessive staffers. Some staffers are indeed scheming and possessive. But most are just doing their jobs. A President has to have aides who can shield him from the well-meaning attention of friends without necessarily hurting their feelings.

Seeing that this is done properly can in itself take a great deal of the President's time. Imaginative aides can sometimes make up for turning away a friend's inquiry by getting him onto the list for the next state dinner, making sure his children's class gets a special White House tour, or arranging a Presidential greeting for his local service club. Saying no to people without hurting their feelings and finding ways to compensate for their disappointment are rare abilities, and aides who have them are worth their weight in gold.

27

ENEMIES

One day in 1971, when the White House was under siege by anti-war demonstrators, John Connally came to see me. While he conceded that it was not pleasant to have to be harassed by these unkempt, noisy, frequently violent mobs, he remarked that in politics it was not necessarily bad to have enemies—especially when they are an obnoxious but small minority.

He recalled a meeting at the White House many years before when FDR was giving some practical political advice to a group of young Democrats. Roosevelt told them that if a leader didn't have enemies, he had better create them. Politics is battle, and the best way to fire up your troops is to rally them against a visible opponent on the other side of the field. If a loyal supporter will fight hard for you, he will fight twice as hard against your enemies.

We sometimes forget that FDR was a master of invective. His most useful enemies were all members of the upper class, as he was. He attacked these "princes of privilege" and "economic royalists" with relish. Some criticize him for cynically instigating class warfare. But during the Depression, the nation was deeply divided between the haves and the have-nots. Since there were more of the latter, he became their champion and profited politically from doing so. This enabled him to get and keep power. What he did with that power is a matter for an entirely separate debate.

His distant cousin and predecessor in the White House, Theodore Roosevelt, also practiced class politics by attacking the trusts and the malefactors of great wealth. Since the two Roosevelts are generally considered to be among our greatest and most effective Presidents, it is surprising that most of today's political pundits deplore the politics of confrontation and praise the politics of consensus. They overlook the fact that in a free society, having allies and enemies is a fact of life. It might be less inflammatory to use the term "adversaries" or, as they say in the House and Senate, "my good friend and distinguished opponent, the gentleman from Wisconsin." But in the end it usually comes down to a contest between allies and enemies, white hats and black. Our fractious politics, where competing interests, ambitions, and ideologies clash, is the price we pay for avoiding dictatorship, where enemies are ruthlessly eliminated. After all, the Soviet Union is the ultimate consensus government, where the most frequently offered opinion, once Gorbachev states his, is probably "Oh, I agree, comrade."

In the 1988 campaign, we saw a striking example of how helpful an enemy can be. Nothing did more to eliminate George Bush's wimp image than his televised confrontation with Dan Rather. The media should have learned a lesson from the same event. When a commentator wants to hurt a candidate, he should not take him on frontally. A fight draws an audience, and the audience usually backs the candidate or official under attack rather than his interrogator. A better way to hurt a candidate is to make the program as dull as possible.

Enemies can be personal, professional, political, or ideological. Two people can be personal friends and yet enemies in one or more of the other three categories. The classic case is two lawyers who hurl vicious bolts of rhetoric at each other in the courtroom, only to get together for a few drinks afterward and have a good laugh about the show they put on for their clients. It also works in politics. We all remember the news accounts of how Tip O'Neill, after excoriating President Reagan in public, would be invited to the White House family quarters for cocktails and an exchange of favorite Irish stories. During my administration, Mike Mansfield, Carl Albert, and John McCormick were leaders of the opposition in Congress, but despite the Vietnam War and other contentious issues, we were always personally friendly during our regular breakfasts at the White House.

Powerful ideological differences cannot always be bridged with personal camaraderie. When people feel strongly about major issues, they do not easily put their arms around those who feel just as strongly the other way. For example, the debate in Great Britain on Suez in 1956 became so bitter that some Parliamentarians did not speak to each other for years afterwards. The same is true in the United States among those who disagreed violently over Vietnam. It is currently fashionable to urge people to put such disagreements behind them for the sake of tranquility and future progress. I think that view is wrong. Some disagreements are indeed trivial and should be forgotten. But issues such as Suez, which involved the fate of a great nation, and Vietnam, which involved the fate of the millions of young people who served and the millions of Indochinese who died as a consequence of our failure to stop Communist aggression, are not trivial. Those who propose to gloss over the issue before the nation understands the roots and consequences of such disagreements are abrogating one of the principal responsibilities of leadership and increasing the possibility of repeating the same mistakes in the future.

It is always a shame when such disagreements lead to personal invective. It is also always entertaining. Unfortunately for the historians of the future, House and Senate rules require that remarks attacking the integrity or paternity of opponents are "taken down," or struck from the record. In spite of this sanitizing, it is widely believed that debate in the American Congress is rougher than in the more staid and mature British Parliament. Not true. Winston Churchill, for example, took some good shots from his opponents, and he could dish it out just as well. His classic characterization of Ramsay MacDonald as lacking political courage would probably have been ruled out of order in our House of Representatives:

"I remember, when I was a child, being taken to the celebrated Barnum's Circus, which contained an exhibition of freaks and monstrosities, but the exhibit on the program which I most desired to see was the one described as 'The Boneless Wonder.' My parents judged that spectacle would be too revolting and demoralizing for my youthful eyes, and I have waited fifty years to see the Boneless Wonder sitting on the Treasury Bench."

While ideological differences are the most difficult to bridge, there are times when personal animosities are simply intractable. Some people, even when they are political allies, simply don't like each other. Their chemistry can create an explosive mix. Senator Clinton Anderson's hatred of Admiral Lewis Strauss, which led to the Senate's refusal to confirm Strauss as Eisenhower's Secretary of Commerce, was an example. In such cases people will pick quarrels on ideological or political grounds where normally they would have no significant differences. When this happens, or when political or ideological differences get too personal, an impossible situation develops where no amount of soothing syrup poured on by well-meaning intermediaries can bring the enemies together.

In dealing with enemies—or if you prefer, opponents and adversaries—some guidelines should be borne in mind.

During the Fund crisis in 1952, I was blowing off steam about the viciousness and unfairness of some of those who were trying to drive me off the Republican ticket. Pat Hillings, who had succeeded me in Congress after I was elected to the Senate, interrupted me with a word of advice that anyone who has political enemies should always bear in mind: "Don't get mad at them, just beat them." The cooler you can remain while your enemies are hot under the collar, the better chance you have to win. In fact, you will usually find that the best way to handle your critics is to ignore them.

I question the dictum that was said to embody Robert Kennedy's political philosophy: "Don't get mad, get even." Trying to defeat your political opponents is one thing. Trying to get even with them in a personal sense is something else again. When you become obsessed with getting revenge, you hurt yourself more than your enemies. For that reason, you should try not to allow political differences to become personal. You can question a person's judgment, but never his motives. The tiresome American flag issue in the 1988 campaign was a case in point. Some overzealous Republican campaign strategists coupled criticism of Michael Dukakis for vetoing a bill requiring teachers to lead students in a salute to the flag with sly innuendo suggesting he was less than a patriot. Polls showed that the American people disapproved of such tactics.

On the other hand, strong ideological differences cannot be significantly reduced by fostering good personal relations. Again, the Vietnam War is a case in point. Two of my best personal friends in the Senate were John Sherman Cooper and Mark Hatfield. Yet both remained unalterably opposed to policies I thought were necessary to end the war. Still, we did not allow their differences to hurt our personal friendship, and we found other areas where we agreed and were able to work together.

Two candidates who have campaigned all-out usually put on a good show after the election, celebrating victory or accepting defeat with conciliatory remarks. This doesn't mean that they have become lifelong friends but that they recognize that after an election is over, voters want candidates to bury the hatchet in the ground, not in each other. But while differences at the top may appear to be bridged over, those at lower levels find it hard to forgive the slings and arrows of a hard-hitting campaign. In 1952,

Bob Taft accepted defeat for the Republican nomination gracefully and threw all-out support to Eisenhower in the general election. Some of Taft's hard-core supporters, however, never forgave Herb Brownell and other Eisenhower campaign officials, accusing them of below-the-belt tactics by denying Taft southern delegates he thought he had wrapped up before the convention. Sometimes the top man can control his former supporters, but usually he can't.

With all of the talk about the need for consensus and the desirability of conducting campaigns in a gentlemanly fashion, it is important to remember that it serves the public interest for the candidates to hit hard on the issues so that the voters have a clear choice. Real differences should be exposed and emphasized, not glossed over. Aggressive campaigning also helps a candidate keep on his toes. Harry Truman went too far in 1948 when he implied that Dewey was supported by Nazis. But his hardball tactics helped him to win by charging up his troops in a way Dewey could not with his commendable but dull calls for unity and responsibility in government. Ideally, candidates should hammer each other without destroying each other. They should avoid allowing deep political and ideological differences to be exacerbated by personal attacks. On the other hand, they must be realistic enough to know that some differences are irreconcilable.

During Watergate, much attention was paid to the "enemies list" that a member of the White House staff had prepared. I never saw it. Regrettably, some on the list were my personal friends. But others had prided themselves on being my enemies from the time I entered politics. Their opposition was primarily ideological rather than political or personal. In fact, that has been the case during most of my public career. Many observers have pointed out that long before Watergate, I had more intractable enemies than any postwar President. I believe the reason is that I played a major role in two of the most divisive issues of the postwar era.

The Hiss case involved the explosive issue of Communist influence in the government, particularly in the State Department. Many non-Communists violently objected to my role in exposing Alger Hiss because they considered our investigation to be an attack on the liberal foreign-policy establishment, even on an entire generation of idealistic public servants. I vividly recall a heated argument at a Washington dinner party when a prominent liberal Washington lawyer, Paul Porter, pounded the table and said, "I don't give a damn whether Hiss is guilty or not. The committee's investigation is bad for the country, because the attack on Hiss is an attack on the Roosevelt foreign policy.'' Proving that Hiss was guilty not only did not help to reduce that opposition, it compounded it. It meant that thereafter such investigations could not automatically be dismissed as McCarthyism. Ironically, I got hit from both sides. Bill Rogers tells the story of a conversation he had with a little old lady in tennis shoes at one of our whistle-stops in the 1952 campaign. She told him, ''I like Ike but I don't like Nixon.'' Rogers asked why. She replied, ''He was involved with that Hiss fellow.''

President Truman's paranoic opposition to our investigation of the Hiss case was hard to understand. No one could question the anti-Communist credentials of the President who asked Congress to approve aid to Greece and Turkey to halt Communist aggression in Europe. Yet even after the Pumpkin Papers so clearly demonstrated Hiss's guilt, he continued to call the committee's hearings a ''red herring'' designed to divert attention from what he called the terrible record of the Republican 80th Congress. Privately, he was enraged at Hiss. When he was shown copies of the documents that Hiss had turned over to Chambers, he said over and over again, ''The son of a bitch, he betrayed his country. The son of a bitch, he betrayed his country.'' Still, even after Hiss was indicted, Truman continued to take his ''red herring'' line. When one of his aides later asked him about this, he replied, ''Of course Hiss is guilty. But that damn committee isn't interested in that. All it cares about is politics. And as long as they try to make politics out of this communist issue, I am going to label their activities for what they are—a red herring.''

The Vietnam War divided the United States even more deeply than the Suez crisis divided Britain. When I spoke at Williamsburg in 1971, a young girl—I would guess that she was about seventeen —ran up to me as I was entering the hall, screamed, ''Murderer!'', and spit in my face. I shall never forget the look of sheer hatred in her eyes. The incident was typical of the emotions tearing the country apart during the Vietnam War. It was worse among those who avoided or evaded the draft, because deep down they had a guilt complex. It was most inexcusable among those who played a role in getting us into the war and then did everything they could to sabotage my policies, which eventually got us out. The fact that we succeeded in getting a peace agreement in 1973 on terms they said were impossible to negotiate only added fuel to the flames of hatred.

The irony is that being right about Hiss and ending the Vietnam War increased rather than reduced the implacable hatred of my opponents. Henry Kissinger used to complain that the approval of our China initiative was strangely muted among some of his former colleagues who would have enthusiastically praised it had I been a liberal Democrat rather than a conservative Republican. I told him the reason in two words: Hiss, Vietnam.

We would all prefer to have no enemies. But as President Sadat told me when I saw him in Alexandria after the Shah's funeral in 1980, "We have to remember that half the people are for you and the other half are against you on most controversial issues." In a free society, stark political and ideological differences are inevitable and should be welcomed. We should not worsen them by injecting the personal element. But we must never be under the naive illusion that good personal relations will eliminate them. I would like to believe that an enemy is a friend you haven't met. Unfortunately, it is seldom true.

28

MEDIA

Because my battles with the media have been so well publicized, it may surprise people to learn of the good relations I have had with many members of the press in years past. As I recently wrote letters of condolence to the families of Jim Shepley of *Time* and John Lindsay of *Newsweek,* I thought of the many other reporters and columnists who have covered my activities fairly and objectively, as they did over the years.

The list would include Bob Albright, Doug Allen, Joe and Stuart Alsop, Bill Anderson, Bert Andrews, Marvin Arrowsmith, Ernie Barcella, Henry Brandon, Ben Cole, Bob Considine, Doug Cornell, Mike and John Cowles, Grant Dilman, Roscoe Drummond, Warren Duffy, Willard Edwards, Andre Fontaine, Carl Greenberg, Chick Hansen, Martin Hayden (Sr. *and* Jr.), George Healey, Bill Hearst, Jack Horner, Roy and Jack Howard, Ep Hoyt, Bill Hutchinson, Don Irwin, Barney Kilgore, Carroll Kilpatrick, Jack Knight, Arthur Krock, Frank Kuest, Vic Lasky, David Lawrence, Frances Lewine, Gould Lincoln, Frank vander Linden, Henry Love, Jack McDowell, Ralph McGill, Earl Mazo, Paul Miller, Clint Mosher, Barney Novel, Newbold and Crosby Noyes, Edgar A. Poe, Bob Richards, Earl Richert, Roy Roberts, Vermont Royster, Ted Scripps, Sam Shafer, Louis Selzer, Joseph Kingsbury-Smith, Merriman Smith, Bill Springer, Richard Starnes, Bill Theis, Ralph de Toledano, Walter Trohan, Peck Trussell, Tom Vail, Lucius Warren, Bob White, William S. White, Dick Wilson, Lyle Wilson, and Peregrine Worsthorne.

I have left many outstanding journalists off this list for space reasons. A number of those in the working press today have been equally fair, but I will not mention them by name, since being considered fair on Nixon *by* Nixon would almost certainly put them in dutch with their colleagues. Suffice it to say that I could not possibly have gone as far as I did in the political arena without having the benefit of some balanced as well as negative coverage.

Still, people would be justified in questioning any advice I might give on the care and feeding of the press. During the 1988 campaign, I used to say that the best way I could help George Bush would be to volunteer to be Michael Dukakis's press secretary. I would be the first to admit that I cannot qualify as an objective critic. But some candid observations about the media might be useful for those others who would at least like to avoid my mistakes.

Who are the members of the media? Based on forty-three years of dealing with the press on the national level, I would make the following observations: They are above average in intelligence. Most of them are liberal politically. Virtually all are ambitious, not so much for money as for status. A Pulitzer Prize or a weekly spot on a Sunday political talk show means far more to them than a six-figure salary. They are proud of their profession and sometimes find it difficult to hide their contempt for the less well-educated politicians and businessmen they cover. Many of them, in my view justifiably, believe they are underpaid compared with the lobbyists and PR flacks who rip off their employers so shamefully.

Finally, most are interesting people. An off-the-record session with a group of top-notch reporters can be far more stimulating and informative than a meeting with a group of congressmen or senators.

While I would imagine that most people would agree with these conclusions, I have some other observations based on personal experience that will probably be more controversial.

Reporters from the print press generally, although not always, are more intelligent and thoughtful than TV reporters. Photographers tend to be more sympathetic to conservatives than reporters, possibly because there appears to be an adversarial relationship between these two groups of journalists. A politician will get a better shake from reporters outside of Washington than in Washington. Publishers have become virtual political eunuchs; they still sign the checks, but the day is long gone when they had much control over reporters. You often see a situation where a candidate is endorsed on the editorial page and cut up in the news stories, which gives many newspapers a schizophrenic quality. Even the paper I read most regularly, *The Wall Street Journal,* suffers from that syndrome. Any objective observer can see that while its editorial page tilts right, the reports from the Washington bureau generally tilt left. I am not suggesting that this is necessarily bad but only that those who deal with the press should know what they are up against.

Another observation, which I admit may result only from my own experience, is that members of the press hate to be proved wrong. Bert Andrews first warned me about this after the Hiss case. The overwhelming majority of reporters covering the case had thought Chambers was lying and Hiss was telling the truth, and they did not appreciate being shown that they had been wrong. There was an understandable tendency among some in the months and years afterwards to try to justify their original position, at my expense.

The same is true in the case of the Fund episode in the 1952 campaign. Having gone overboard in predicting that I would be forced off the ticket, they naturally found it very difficult to accept that by going over their heads to the country on TV, I had proved them wrong. This is not to suggest that their motives in these two cases were venal or, for that matter, unusual. It is natural for anyone, particularly an intellectual, to resent someone who proved that they have been wrong on a major issue.

On the other side of the ledger, I have found that when a President or Vice President travels abroad, reporters traveling with him are generally fair and supportive. This was true when I went to Russia and Poland in 1959, when I visited China and Russia in 1972, and is true even when I travel abroad today as a former President. Critics of the media miss the mark when they raise questions about media figures' patriotism. If a President can convince them that his foreign policy is serving the interest of the nation, he will get fair coverage even if they do not share his domestic political views. In fact, it has been my observation that the common cliché about politics stopping at the water's edge applies far more to the media than it does to politicians.

Superficial observers are wrong when they attribute all of my problems with the press to Watergate. They overlook the seminal issue of Vietnam. The war changed Lyndon Johnson's press from highly positive to overwhelmingly negative and poisoned my own relations with the press throughout my Presidency. I respected the right of press people as well as politicians to disagree with me about the morality of our cause in Vietnam, our conduct of the war, and my efforts to win an honorable peace. But again, the events that followed our withdrawal from Vietnam showed that media critics who said we were on the wrong side were mistaken. Just as many mainstream observers still stubbornly insist that Alger Hiss was innocent or that the Nixon Fund was crooked, antiwar critics still try to ignore or explain away tragedies such as the Cambodian holocaust and the deaths of hundreds of thousands of Vietnamese who drowned while fleeing Communist Vietnam. "Just the facts" is supposed to be the motto of the working reporter. But in the cases of Hiss, the Fund, and the Vietnam War, where many in the media have found the truth so hard to swallow, Lenin's dictum may be more apropos: "Facts," he said, "can be stubborn things."

The press and the politicians they cover are frequently at odds, but they have one thing in common: a very low rating in the public opinion polls. Most people believe that the press is biased toward liberal causes, and I would agree. But charges that the press is generally inaccurate in its reporting are frequently unfair. Generally, I have been impressed by how accurately reporters who reach the national level cover their stories. The contention that reporters have bad manners is also usually a bad rap. I have found that while reporters are always persistent, they are usually courteous. The antics of a few oddballs who stamp their feet and holler like children to get attention should not be held against the entire group.

Most of the media are out of step politically with the rest of the country. This goes back a long way. In 1952, when Eisenhower was elected by a landslide, *Newsweek*'s poll of the top fifty national political reporters showed overwhelming majorities for Adlai Stevenson. This inevitably colored their reporting. In 1972, when I received 61 percent of the vote, polls of Washington reporters showed 82 percent for George McGovern.

Many in the media keenly cultivate their unpopularity, affecting the posture of idealistic mavericks who have elected themselves to protect the public from unscrupulous officials no matter what the cost. Some would argue that if press people don't mind being despised, that's their business. I do not agree. The press used to consider itself part of the fabric of society, with a shared stake in America's prosperity, the health of its institutions, and the success of its initiatives around the world. When they had to criticize, they did so as part of the team. But today the media consider themselves outside of and above society at large, looking down haughtily as they fire their thunderbolts at the rest of us. Frequently it appears that the media's excesses are weakening the fabric of society rather than strengthening it.

A few relatively simple measures would go a long way toward restoring trust between Americans and the American press.

Above all, when someone broadcasts or publishes a false story, he should retract it categorically and with the same level of exposure that he gave to the original false report. Admitting a mistake will never injure a reporter's credibility. Instead, it would greatly improve it. The problem is that it does injure a journalist's pride, so all too often errors are left in the record unless a victim of bad reporting has the clout to compel a retraction. In this regard the far more powerful medium of television is far less responsible than print. In *The New York Times,* for instance, the "Corrections" column on page 3 has become virtually a daily feature. And yet I cannot remember a time when I heard a correction broadcast on one of the major network news programs. Either TV journalists have somehow become far more skilled than print journalists, or print journalists are being more honest about their inevitable howlers.

Media people should get off the sanctimonious position that when they attack a public figure, fair is fair since he has the option of suing them for libel. Every thoughtful person knows that the way *Times* vs. *Sullivan,* the foundation of libel law, is interpreted, no public figure will succeed in a libel action unless he has virtually unlimited financial resources. Instead, journalists themselves should provide reasonable protections for public officials against libel by disciplining themselves against going constantly and automatically for the jugular. Too often they shoot first and literally ask questions later.

Reporters should also stop being con artists with unsuspecting victims. Every public figure has heard these lines scores of times:

I really want to write a positive story. This is usually a signal that a subject should watch his back, because someone is about to stick a knife into it.

If you don't talk to me, your side of the story won't be represented. Too many reporters know the angle they plan to take in their article before they even begin to do their research. When you get this line from a reporter, trust your instincts. Does he want your views or just the legitimacy that your participation in the story will give him? In a way, this con is a form of blackmail: Talk to me, or else. As a matter of fact, those in Washington who have the best image tend to be those who spend the most time cultivating reporters. Top officials who stonewall the press generally get hit by a ton of bricks every time they open the morning paper.

You should hear what this other guy said about you. This is journalistic entrapment, a favorite tactic of reporters who want to provoke you into saying something critical about the other guy. Don't be surprised if your angry jibe appears in print and his doesn't.

I'm going to write the story whether you talk to me or not. When you hear this, you should consider whether the reporter might be worried he doesn't have a story at all unless you talk to him.

Oh, and just one more question. Forget the other ten he asked; this is what he really came for.

Reporters are not the only con artists. Public officials devote enormous energy to trying to rig the news to be reported their way. When two savvy insiders, reporter and official, are in the ring together, each trying to bamboozle the other, neither should complain. But it is unforgivable when journalists turn their formidable rhetorical arsenal on less experienced victims such as an official's family or friends.

Most Americans are trusting people. If a reporter tells them he wants to be fair, they will be inclined, wrongly, to believe him. So, in dealing with unsophisticated people, a reporter should be more honest. He should admit what his perspective is, what he expects his story or book will say, and what role the prospective source will play in it. Some journalists will lament, "But no one will talk to us that way." So be it. Conning unsuspecting people is wrong. The ends do not justify the means for reporters any more than they do for public officials.

I am the first to admit that politicians could do a better job of handling their press relations. Above all, they should treat the media with respect. They have a job to do. You should help them do their job, provided that they don't do a job on you.

Don't play favorites. Doing so gives a short-term advantage but does more harm than good in the long run. I often asked Henry Kissinger to give interviews not just to the select elite in the Washington press corps but to some of the fine reporters from the less well-known papers around the country. His response was that such reporters were not influential. My answer was that the way a reporter becomes influential is to have sources, whether he works for *The Washington Post* or the *Columbus Dispatch*. If for some reason you are deserted by your tiny circle of Beltway bigwigs, you might wish you had cultivated some friends in the hinterlands.

Don't cancel a subscription, but don't be afraid to cancel an unfriendly reporter's ticket on some plum Presidential trip. There is no law that says if a reporter makes a habit of giving you the shaft, you have to continue to give him privileged treatment.

Wining and dining the press should generally be avoided except on an arm's-length basis. The best reporters resent being wooed in such a superficial way, and no reporter will sit on a negative story because you gave him brunch last week.

Some political figures work hard at cultivating their favorites in the press by keeping them supplied with inside information they can use to spice up their stories. It is always dangerous to become this close to reporters, especially if you forget it is a marriage of convenience and decide it is true love. If the information flowing from the official ever dries up, so will the good ink flowing from the reporter.

Because most in the press are on the left, you would think they would be criticized more by Republicans than by Democrats. But the hunger for a good story can be far more decisive than ideology. I had little in common politically with the liberal former Speaker of the House, Tip O'Neill. A few years ago his former administrative assistant, Chris Matthews, wrote a book about politics called *Hardball*. While relatively young, Matthews was already a seasoned Washington hand. So I was not surprised when he picked a quote that has often been attributed to me for the title of a particularly hard-hitting chapter on the media: "The Press Is the Enemy."

A politician should not assume that the more press conferences he has, the better. It is important not to cheapen the currency by becoming too available. He should have a press conference only when he is well prepared and when there are subjects worth discussing. I did not have as many press conferences as I should have. But on the other hand, I doubt if having more would have helped with my relationship with the press, particularly when the big issues were Vietnam and then Watergate, where the lines were drawn and no quarter given on either side.

Johnson's experience should be a case study for anyone who is trying to develop a strategy for dealing with the press. When he was at the height of his popularity during the Great Society days, he was more available to the press than any President in history. He saw reporters as he galloped around the South Lawn. He saw them in the Oval Office, in his private office, in his bedroom, even in his bathroom. And it paid off. He had a sensationally good press for the first two years of his Presidency. But when Vietnam poisoned the dialogue, press conferences actually hurt him rather than helped him.

One tactic that should be used only sparingly is for a public official who has been attacked by the press to counterattack. He may win in the short run. But in the long run the press has the last word, and they will never forgive him for taking them on. This does not mean that he should take their barbs lying down or that he should go crawling after them to try to win their support. It does mean that he should give as good as he receives, but in a manner that will not expose him to the charge that he is taking on the press to divert attention from his own vulnerabilities.

A President's ultimate weapon is to go over the heads of the press to the country. My most effective use of the tactic was in the "Fund" broadcast in 1952 and the "Silent Majority" speech in 1969, both of which mobilized public opinion. But you cannot go to the well too often. Only on a major issue of universal concern should a President try to reach the people directly to avoid having his views filtered through the press.

The Founders' primary concern was undue concentration of power, whether in the executive, the legislature, or the judiciary. Their formula of checks and balances brilliantly addressed this problem so that no branch of government would exert unrestrained power over the people. The Founders could not have anticipated the growth of big business in the latter part of the nineteenth century and of big labor in the middle of the twentieth century. Congress, however, stepped into the breach with legislation limiting the powers of both.

Nor could the Founders have dreamed of today's mega-media monopolies. They represent a new concentration of power that Congress cannot and should not try to restrain. Our dedication to the First Amendment should always take precedence over whatever reservations we have about the irresponsible conduct of the media. This means that the media should make certain that their power is used responsibly and in a way that is not detrimental to the fundamental interests of the nation.

Probably the best advice I ever received about the press came from my friend Dick Moore, now ambassador to Ireland, as his brother John was during my administration. He would always say, "Go after the little lies." If someone makes a mistake or takes an unfair shot, make sure he realizes that you noticed. If you complain to reporters or their editors when they make mistakes, they will be more careful the next time. If you don't, they will take even greater liberties, often repeating and amplifying the errors until they are impossible to correct.

Moore's advice is a healthy antidote to those advisers who urge a leader not to "dignify such a ridiculous attack with a response." Unfortunately, some readers and viewers will dignify the attacks by believing every word of them. Many Americans still adhere instinctually to the canard that "they couldn't print it if it weren't true." But even though it is always wise to try to correct the record, it is easier said than done. A lie in the media is born easily and dies hard.

During Watergate, our small staff of lawyers and press officers was outflanked and outnumbered by innumerable, highly partisan congressional staff members who leaked—"gushed" would be a better word—to innumerable, highly ambitious reporters, all of them eager to earn points with their editors by presenting some new revelation about the Nixon White House. That dozens of these stories finally proved to be untrue did not mitigate the damage they did when they were published.

Even today, little lies still frequently appear about my administration, and refuting them takes so much time and effort that it would be easy to conclude that it is not worth it even to try. It is frightening to think how many errors and distortions the media get away with because those on the receiving end simply throw their hands in the air in exasperation. Because I have been the target of so many vicious attacks by the media over the years, I now have a policy of trying to respond to most inaccurate stories. A recent example shows that such a policy can occasionally even pay off.

In 1987, a left-wing journalist, Raymond Bonner, wrote in a book about the Philippines that I had personally told President Marcos before he declared martial law in 1972 that I approved of his plans. Bonner based his assertion on the usual anonymous "sources." If the story had been true, I would have had no qualms about admitting it. Most commentators said at the time of Marcos's action that it was a justifiable response to the Communist-led unrest that was threatening to tear his country apart.

But Bonner's story was sheer fantasy. I had not talked to Marcos. My White House logs, which are available to the public in Washington, showed clearly and irrefutably that I had not. Further, I had sent him no message of any kind. Bonner's book did not mention the logs, which proves either that he was unaware of them, that he did not bother to consult them, or that he did not

260

want his readers to know there was strong evidence against his allegations. In the paperback edition of the book, he took note of my staff's objections to this and other errors by implying that the records had been altered, an opportunistic tactic that a press corps weaned on similarly sinister and unproven allegations about the eighteen-and-one-half-minute gap could be counted upon to swallow whole. In fact, no reporter or investigator has ever proved or even alleged that there was anything wrong with the White House logs, which noted every meeting and telephone call I had over five and a half years. Both friends and critics have used them extensively as highly dependable guides to what the President did and when he did it. Bonner's imputations to the contrary were cynical and self-serving.

Just before Bonner's book was published, one of his former colleagues at *The New York Times* wrote an article about his absurd allegations. Before turning it in, the reporter called my office for a comment, but since it was Good Friday, I had given my staff the afternoon off, so no one was there to answer the telephone. Rather than hold his story until he could get a comment the following Monday, the reporter published it without permitting me the opportunity to respond. It was picked up all over the world, with the result that millions of fair-minded readers now probably believe that I gave Marcos the go-ahead to impose martial law. Again, I would not have objected if it were true. I believe that Marcos probably acted correctly under the circumstances. What was galling was that it was yet another little lie, an unpleasant reminder of what we had been up against, multiplied a hundred-fold, during the Watergate deluge.

Over the next few weeks my small staff spent dozens of hours tracking down the facts. They managed to compel a very brief follow-up story in the *Times* stating our position and, more significant, to create enough uncertainty in the mind of one network correspondent that he canceled a major piece he was planning to air about Bonner's allegations. Most gratifying of all, journalist Stanley Karnow finally debunked Bonner's charges in 1989 in his own book about the Philippines, *In Our Image*. He wrote: "Speculation to the contrary, nothing in the White House logs of the period indicates that Nixon gave Marcos the green light by telephone. Marcos also told me years afterwards that he had not spoken directly with Nixon at the time."

The appearance of Karnow's book was one moral victory in the usually losing war against the little lie. But if Bonner's story had really been damaging for some reason, as so many similar ones had been during Watergate, the damage would already have been done. The incident shows the enormous impact an ideologically motivated writer, abetted by sloppy reporting in a usually careful newspaper, can have. It shows the way writers can use innuendo and the dodge of anonymous "sources" not to uncover the truth but to bury it. And it shows how difficult it is for a public figure to correct the record once it has been skewed against him, either because of carelessness or malice, by the media.

29

CAMPAIGNING

In his essay on Lord Rosebery, Churchill wrote: "Whatever one may think about democratic government, it is just as well to have practical experience of its rough and slatternly foundations. No part of the education of a politician is more indispensable than the fighting of elections."

Everyone knows that the major purpose of a campaign is to win an election. Many forget that of almost equal importance is that a campaign teaches a candidate what the voters want and how best to represent their interests in office. In turn, voters will learn what kind of leader he will be by studying what kind of campaigner he is.

In today's Presidential campaigns, both these learning processes are disrupted. Candidates glide over the landscape in their protective cocoons almost insulated from the American people. Secret Service agents protect them from maniacs, and pollsters protect them from voters. They assume that you can't learn anything from a town meeting or a receiving line that today's elaborate computerized polls won't tell you in far more detail. At the same time, campaign consultants sell candidates a complete package—message, strategy, tactics, and apparatus—and thus give voters not a choice between candidates but a choice between packages.

So, today, candidates don't need to meet people, and people usually don't get to see candidates, except on the tube. In some big, media-intensive states such as California, candidates for the Senate and other statewide offices can end up spending more time in TV studios reading scripts for commercials than they do speaking live on the stump.

The last pre-television Presidential campaign was in 1948, between Harry Truman and Tom Dewey. Before these two highly intelligent, skillful campaigners could dare run for President in 1992, they would have to be completely reeducated.

They would find that the cost of a Presidential campaign had increased fifty-fold, from $10 million to $500 million. Despite federal financing, they would have to spend far more time than in 1948 raising the hard money for the primaries and the soft money for the final campaign.

They would have to quadruple the size of their campaign staffs and hire expert public relations image makers to advise them on every aspect of their appearance and conduct.

Truman would have to tone down his coarse, fiery campaign style to come across better on the cool medium of television. Dewey would have to pretend to be a far less remote man than he really was to keep today's touchie-feelie campaign reporters from ridiculing his patrician airs.

They would have to learn to deal with a more aggressive, irresponsible press corps probing every aspect of their personal lives.

They would have to hire more pollsters to tell them not only how they stood in trial heats, as was the case in 1948, but what they should say on virtually every issue to satisfy hundreds of competing pressure groups.

They would find that these special interest lobbies were far more powerful and influential than political parties.

I don't know how they would react to these changes. But as one who has been on five national tickets, beginning in the dawn of the television era in 1952, I know what I would recommend to future candidates for President.

Fundraising is necessary, but when candidates do it themselves it is a vote loser. They should keep fundraisers to a minimum and never televise them.

Campaigns should pay for fewer polls and pay less attention to those they take. All the major newspapers, news magazines, and networks make their polls available for free anyway. Media polls are also usually more accurate than in-house polls, which too often are cooked to tell a candidate what he wants to hear. Besides, in the final analysis there is no better poll than a candidate's "feel" of a campaign. Bob Dole is a superb, instinctual campaigner who made the mistake of trusting his pollster over his instincts in the 1988 New Hampshire primary. Thinking he was far ahead of George Bush, he held some hard-hitting ads off the air. He lost.

The candidate should follow the advice my friend Judge George McKinnon gave me when I ran for the Senate in 1950: "Always run as if you were a million votes behind and then you might win by one vote." A poll can tell a candidate what *people* think, but it should not tell him what *he* should think. The candidate who slavishly follows the polls may get elected, but he will not be a great leader or even a good one. The task of the leader is not to follow the polls but to make the polls and the people follow him.

Candidates should also place less faith in their media advisers. While they may be experts on the show business side of politics, they should not get involved in the substance side of politics. At Whittier College, when I was program chairman for our college assembly, I was very excited when I learned that Francis Lederer, the movie star, might accept an invitation to address the student body on foreign policy. Our faculty adviser, Dr. Herbert Harris, a Shakespeare scholar, vetoed the idea. He said that while he would very much like to hear Lederer speak on acting, he saw no reason to invite him to speak on foreign policy, a field in which he was not an expert. While today's audiences will pay to hear a celebrity discuss any subject from soup to nuts, being an expert in one field does not qualify an individual as an expert in another. Ronald Reagan was a good actor who became a great politician. But the mere fact that one is an expert on acting does not qualify him to give expert advice on politics or policy.

The myth about my own Presidential campaign in 1968 is that it was the first where media advisers reigned supreme and that it consisted entirely of television commercials and staged question-and-answer sessions with voters. The source of the misconception is a book published in 1969 by a writer who did not cover the campaign but who had ingratiated himself with the campaign's advertising agency. Almost all he saw was the preparation and filming of television appearances, so that was all he had to write about. He produced what political science professors still consider an authoritative, first-hand account of a campaign that he in fact did not witness.

The truth is that between Labor Day and Election Day 1968, I gave one hundred seventy-eight speeches in person, on radio, and on television. It is particularly ironic that the professors consider 1968 to have been the first campaign in which style was emphasized over substance. During just one of my "Man in the Arena" broadcasts, a variation on the telethons I had used in my 1960 and

1962 campaigns, I made detailed statements or proposals on agriculture, education, NATO, the Supreme Court, crime, foreign aid,
urban renewal, taxes, the budget, Vietnam, and other issues.

We did seek to tailor our message to the requirements of journalism, whose practitioners always insist on getting the guts of a
story into the "lead" of the article or broadcast. Each day we
wanted to do everything we could to influence what that night's
network lead would be. President Reagan was fiercely criticized
by the White House press corps for using the same technique,
because it made them feel manipulated. Then President Bush was
elected, and in his early months in office he sometimes gave several speeches a day about a variety of different topics. This confused the White House press corps, who weren't sure what they
were supposed to write about and therefore lambasted Bush for
"the lack of a unified message." As every President and candidate
learns in his own way, the press is hard to satisfy.

Much has been made of the fact that Ronald Reagan was the first
actor to become President. But most leaders are actors, though
only de Gaulle was candid enough to admit it. People like to glamorize their leaders, and leaders tend to glamorize themselves.
MacArthur with his riding crop and corncob pipe, Patton with his
pearl-handled revolvers, Churchill with his strut, FDR with his
jaunty cigarette lighter—all were acting to an extent. In fairness,
each man's public posture was only an extension of his private
personality. They may not have done it consciously, but the effect
was to create a mystique of difference and dignity.

Most candidates could probably cut their campaign staffs in half.
It is far better to have a few overworked, first-rate staffers than
scores of overpaid second-raters who spend their time fighting
each other rather than the opposition.

He should try to appeal to all voters, but in going after the votes
he *doesn't* have, he should never go so far that he loses the votes
he *does* have. Bob Kenny, a brilliant liberal Democratic politician
and former California attorney general, gave me good advice on
that score in 1950. Earl Warren, California's Republican governor,
had just defeated him in the Democratic gubernatorial primary
under California's cross-filing system. This was no reflection on
Kenny since Warren regularly made a practice of defeating his
Democratic candidates in their primary. Kenny pointed out that
each candidate in a campaign has a hard core of supporters—the
Republicans on the right, the Democrats on the left. They aren't
enough to win, but their enthusiastic support is essential if you are

to survive as a candidate. The trick is for each to reach out to the center to get the total vote he needs to win. That was Warren's specialty. But in doing so, a candidate must not reach so far that he snaps the umbilical cord that provides him nourishment from his hard core. If he does that, he will be left twisting in the wind. The greatest danger is that a candidate will go so far to satisfy the activists who vote in primaries that his extreme positions will cost him votes in the general election.

The candidate should find ways to be interesting without being silly. There is only one thing worse for a candidate than being wrong, and that is to be dull. In *Cold Friday,* Whittaker Chambers shrewdly observed, "It is difficult to set logic to music. But logic which does not sing is only more of the same old mouse cheese." I have often said that politics at its best is poetry, not prose. Adlai Stevenson's two losses for President despite his poetic rhetoric would seem to disprove that observation. They do not. Apart from any political liabilities he may have had, Stevenson ran against a wartime legend in 1952 and peace and prosperity in 1956. No one could have defeated Eisenhower in those elections.

The candidate must learn to be tolerant of all the oddballs and bores he meets in politics. Dewey was an outstanding governor and would have made a great President. In 1952, I was the principal speaker at the annual fundraising dinner for the New York State Republican Party at the Waldorf-Astoria, and I sat by Dewey on the dais. Between courses, a paying guest who had obviously had too much to drink came up, slapped me on the back, and told me how much he admired the work I had done on the Hiss case. He then slapped Dewey on the back, told him he was the greatest governor in New York's history, and said he hoped he would run for reelection. As the man walked away, Dewey very deliberately knocked the ashes off his cigarette, which like FDR he smoked through a holder, turned to me, and said, "Who was that fatuous ass?" In fact, the man happened to be the publisher of a string of weekly newspapers in New York State. Like many brilliant people, Dewey found it very difficult to tolerate fools. In politics, that is a fatal mistake for three reasons. First, the man might not be a fool. Second, even fools vote. And third, a fool might still have something worthwhile to say to you.

While a public man must learn to tolerate fools, he must not go to the other extreme. Most Americans applauded when Jimmy Carter walked hand in hand with Rosalyn from the Capitol to the White House after his inauguration. But they were turned off when he wore a cardigan sweater during his first major television speech as President. He did not wear it again, at least not on television. A leader must show he respects those whose support he seeks, but he must maintain enough dignity to make them respect him as their leader.

No President was more outgoing and genial than Eisenhower, but he did not like even close colleagues to be too familiar. In all of the years I knew him, I never called him Ike. Neither did any member of his Cabinet or his White House staff except Treasury Secretary George Humphrey, a longtime personal friend. He was very conscious of protocol. When he called to congratulate me the night before I was inaugurated, he ended the conversation by saying that there was only one sad thing about the occasion. "This is the last time I will be able to call you Dick," he said.

He also didn't like people to nudge him or grab him by the arm to make a point. Jerry Persons told me of an occasion when Lyndon Johnson wanted to come into the Oval Office and lobby the President on one of his pet personal projects. Eisenhower agreed to the appointment but insisted that Persons stand between him and Johnson while they talked. He said, "My bursitis is kicking up and I don't want him grabbing me by the arm and working me over."

Brezhnev reminded me of Johnson that way. He was always slapping you on the knee, nudging you in the ribs, or putting his arm around you to emphasize a point. While I do not know Gorbachev that well, I sense that he is more like Eisenhower in that respect. He is warm and outgoing on the surface, but not a slap-on-the-back politician. I sensed that he was always holding something of himself in reserve. He may have a point. When I saw *Swan Lake* at the Bolshoi in 1974, Brezhnev took me backstage to meet the star ballerina. I was disappointed. She was pleasant but not particularly attractive in person. I would have preferred to remember her for the glamorous role she played on stage. Leaders too must bear in mind that except in very personal relationships, they are always on stage.

In criticizing the conduct of a general in World War I, Winston Churchill observed, "Prudence and audacity may be alternated, but not mixed." What is true in war is true in politics. The candidate who tries to follow two opposite strategies at the same time will lose. This was Michael Dukakis's fatal mistake in his second debate with George Bush in 1988. He tried to be Mr. Nice Guy and Mr. Strong Guy and ended up being neither. He also erred in declaring in his acceptance speech that the campaign was about "competence, not ideology." Competence in carrying out bad policies is worse than incompetence in trying to carry out good policies. This brings us back to the bottom line. Too much attention is paid today to the how of campaigning and not enough to the what. A campaign without a message is like Ibsen's analogy of the onion in *Peer Gynt:* you peel it off skin by skin, and at the center you find it's hollow.

In our cynical times there is a tendency to ridicule what George Bush called "the vision thing." But a campaign without vision inspires no one. As de Gaulle observed in *The Edge of the Sword,* a leader "must aim high, show that he has vision, act on the grand scale. . . . By satisfying the secret desires of men's hearts, by providing compensation for the cramped conditions of their lives, he will capture their imagination, and, even should he fall by the way, will retain, in their eyes, the prestige of those heights to which he did his best to lead them."

30

STAFF

To be successful, a leader must develop a core of loyal staff members who share his sense of mission, serve as his early warning system, possess acute political instincts, and have the competence to protect him from his own mistakes.

I once asked President Eisenhower what characteristic he valued most in a staff member. He answered, "Selflessness." There can be no doubt that those who put their official responsibilities above their own selfish interests make ideal staff members. But such people are very hard to find.

Sometimes it's said that all federal employees "work for the President." In fact, hardly any do, and some even work against him. In the huge bureaucracy, a few people are motivated by devotion to the President or to the cause he represents. Most are lifers who are motivated primarily by self-interest. This is not necessarily bad if the leader is able to convince them that their self-interest will best be served by furthering the interests of the administration. Some are ambitious to go up. Some are politically hostile to the President. Most primarily want security.

That is why a President, or any leader, needs a corps of key staffers who are loyal to him and what he stands for. Three qualities should be considered in evaluating applicants for such positions—head, heart, and guts. Many have one of these qualities; some have two; but only a very few have all three. Too often there is a tendency to be impressed by one without considering the others.

Intelligence is usually the most decisive factor. Since an effective President values subordinates who have good ideas, an outstanding academic record and a reputation for being brainy gets a

270

candidate a long way toward winning an appointment. The quality of heart—whether an applicant has a reputation for being loyal, honorable, decent, and considerate of those he works with—can sometimes compensate for the lack of a brilliant intellect.

But all other things being equal, the most important quality is guts. In evaluating an applicant, you should always ask yourself whether he will stay the course when the going gets rough or unpopular decisions must be made. Or will he be one of those whom Senator Gene Milliken of Colorado once said "paint their asses white and run with the antelopes"?

Some staffers are loyal but not competent. Others are competent but not loyal. It is more difficult for a conservative than a liberal leader to find staffers who are both. My life-long instinctual awareness of this phenomenon was confirmed by a report in the *American Political Science Review,* which found that in 1970 only 17 percent of the top career bureaucrats in the executive branch were Republican, while 47 percent were Democrats, and 36 percent Independents, who "more frequently resemble Democrats than Republicans." The report concluded: "Our findings document a career bureaucracy with very little Republican representation but even more pointedly portray a social service bureaucracy dominated by administrators ideologically hostile to many of the directions pursued by the Nixon Administration in the realm of social policy." Another study of foreign service officers found that only 5 percent considered themselves Republicans. We see this syndrome even in the Supreme Court. Seven of the nine Justices on the Court were appointed by Republican Presidents. Yet only six of the thirty-three clerks employed during its 1985 term had voted for Ronald Reagan in 1984.

These findings were not in the least bit surprising. Liberals want more government, and conservatives want less. The brightest conservative college graduates tend to go into business. The brightest liberal graduates tend to choose the media, academia, or government. As a result, the conservative leader has a smaller field to pick from for his personal staff and will inevitably be saddled with a majority in the civil service who oppose him.

He can make no greater mistake, however, than to sacrifice loyalty for competence. In 1969, Henry Kissinger assembled the most brilliant national security staff in history. All were competent; Kissinger does not tolerate fools. Most were loyal to the administration's policies. But a few were not. I once questioned him about the ultra-liberal background of some I knew did not share my views on foreign policy, or his. He replied that he wasn't worried, because they were competent professionals and would only voice their differences privately. But when I ordered attacks on the Communist-occupied sanctuaries in Cambodia in 1970, a politically difficult but tactically necessary decision that saved American lives, three of these "professionals" resigned, and several attacked the administration publicly in speeches and in books. Kissinger has since told me that hiring them was his greatest mistake.

A President must also appoint people to his Cabinet and staff who compensate for his own weaknesses. For example, de Gaulle, Adenauer, and Yoshida were strong in foreign policy but weak on economics. By putting men in charge of economic policy who were experts in that field—Pompidou in France, Erhardt in West Germany, and Ikeda in Japan—they provided brilliant economic leadership for their administrations and for their countries. Yoshida and Adenauer are credited for building the foundations from which our former defeated enemies now challenge America's economic dominance.

Both in the areas in which he is expert and those in which he is not, an effective leader must learn to delegate. His most precious resource is time, and if he squanders it on tasks that can be carried out by others, he will fail. All too frequently he will find that a job would have been done better if he had done it himself. But a President cannot do everything, nor can he re-do everything others have done. He is hired for the big decisions, and he owes it to the country to delegate the small ones.

The key to delegating power is being confident in those to whom you delegate it. A smart President who surrounds himself with second-raters will end up second-guessing them and their work. A President with brilliant aides may well find that they often have better ideas than he does. This can be unbearable for insecure people. But it is precisely the way a White House staff should be set up. The mark of a strong leader is the willingness to pick people who may be smarter than he is. They will challenge and inspire him with their idealism and sheer intellect; in turn he will mold their ideas to fit his own strategic and political vision and instincts. The result can be far more than the sum of the parts.

A leader must also not hesitate to choose able people who once opposed him. Some of my most loyal supporters objected to my choice of Henry Kissinger as national security adviser, since he had supported Nelson Rockefeller and had criticized me sharply

272

before I won the nomination in 1968. My response was simple. I did it because he was the best man for the job and because we agreed on the major issues. His extraordinary performance proved that I was right.

Brilliant people are often difficult and contentious. It is a mistake to exclude them from government for the sake of peace and quiet. The alternative is the kind of subordinate Thiers once described as "choosing to please rather than to contradict, possessed of leanings rather than opinions, without firmness of mind or genuine passions." As de Gaulle put it in *The Edge of the Sword,*

> It is the worst of policies to exclude men of strong character from office for no better reason than that they are difficult. Easy relationships are all very well when things are going smoothly, but in times of crises, they may well lead to disaster. . . . Powerful personalities . . . capable of standing up to the test of great events, frequently lack that surface charm which wins popularity in ordinary life. Strong characters are, as a rule, rough, disagreeable, and aggressive.

A strong leader should welcome rather than discourage spirited debate. One does not have to be an Hegelian to know that the clash of two conflicting ideas can produce a better idea. Arthur Burns and Pat Moynihan, for example, had some titanic arguments when we were considering welfare reform. But their compromise concept of "workfare" has now been adopted by several states and in part by the federal government. James Schlesinger was one of the very few officials in the administration who was as brilliant as Henry Kissinger. Like Kissinger, he could at times be abrasive. Usually they agreed. When they didn't, the sparks flew. Yet their conflicts made for better policies, and, frankly, more interesting government. The only unbreakable rule is that once the top man decides, debate ceases, and all must support his decision.

A President must also discipline his staff in the way it gives him bad news. It is a myth that a powerful man's aides do not want to be the bearers of bad tidings. On the contrary, it is their favorite indoor sport. Most seem to take a visceral pleasure from seeing their boss's face fall at the news of some political or policy disaster. A leader must find ways to channel all this negative energy toward achieving positive goals or he will spend all his time holding his staff members' hands. President Eisenhower once told me that during his military career he insisted that all major problems be brought to his attention. But he also insisted that when a staff member informed him of a problem, he should at the same time make recommendations for solving it. Any leader who adopts this policy will find it will save both him and his staff a great deal of time and energy.

Gladstone said that the first requisite of a prime minister is to be a good butcher. I would add based on my experience that it is also the hardest. A President must sometimes fire people, either for incompetence, laziness, or insubordination. It is never pleasant, but sometimes it is just the tonic the organization needs to shake it out of its lethargy. If he is unable or unwilling to lower the boom personally, he must have a chief-of-staff who will do it for him.

It is never a coveted or pleasant responsibility. Even General Walter Bedell Smith's critics agree that he was World War II's most competent chief-of-staff. He was my neighbor in Washington while I was Vice President, and we often met at the end of the day to talk about current issues over cocktails. One evening, he was just recovering from a bout with the flu, and a couple of drinks hit him hard. He was expressing sympathy for the way the press was attacking me because Eisenhower was too popular to take on. He knew I was handling unpopular political chores for Eisenhower. He pointed out that he too had once been subjected to similar treatment. Tears came to his eyes as he said, "I was only Ike's prat boy. Ike always had to have a prat boy."

Beneath that sunny, warm Eisenhower exterior was a cold and when necessary even ruthless executive who often used others to carry out unpleasant assignments. His White House chief-of-staff, Sherman Adams, was the first and most famous "abominable no-man"—a vigilant guardian of the President's time and his agent for countless grim assignments. A good chief-of-staff is seldom popular. He must carry out tough decisions in personnel and other areas that his boss makes but is reluctant to execute. He must see that his chief gets the credit for the administration's successes and must take the heat for its failures, even when they are not his fault. It is one of the most thankless jobs in Washington, and when a good chief-of-staff runs into difficulty, as Adams did, and as Bob Haldeman did in my administration, he sometimes finds he doesn't have many friends or supporters. Some may well call him just a prat boy. Be that as it may, without him, a President cannot function effectively.

Chiefs-of-staff and other members of the White House staff are usually deluged with interview requests and invitations to go on television. Unless the President specifically asks them to go public, they would be well advised to turn down all such invitations. Sometimes a President will want someone to make a public statement that is blunter or harsher than he wishes to sound personally. Even then, the Vice President or a Cabinet member is usually a better choice. It has been my observation that chiefs-of-staff and national security advisers are more effective when they keep a low public profile. When they become regulars on the Sunday talk shows and their pictures are on the covers of the news magazines, they are borrowing trouble. Particularly when a President is popular, there is nothing a critic in the media or the Congress enjoys more than taking out after a highly visible staffer. It is therefore bad tactics to give the critics ready targets by having top aides in the news all the time. Inevitably, they become issues themselves, at which point they usually stop being useful to the President.

A briefly fashionable economist once said, "Small is beautiful." He was wrong about economics, but he was right about staffs. A lean staff with a few top-notch people, each of whom has an important, exclusive assignment, works far better than a flabby staff where too many people have too little to do and end up shuffling papers and knifing each other in the back in order to get noticed or promoted. Washington's worst scandal is the astronomic growth of staffs, not just in civilian agencies but in the Defense Department, the White House, and particularly the Congress. The Pentagon, in part because of its huge size and the many feuding services and agencies, is a far worse offender as far as excess personnel is concerned than the State Department. A leaner Army, Navy, Air Force, and Marine Corp would be much stronger.

Fat staffs cost more money, but even worse, they suffocate initiative, paralyze decision making, and inevitably lead to top officials being manipulated by hordes of competing subordinates. Too often these superfluous, supercilious middle managers are like the "stuffed dummies of the hierarchy" described by de Gaulle: "Parasites who take everything and give nothing in return, weak-kneed creatures forever trembling in their shoes, jumping jacks who will turn their coats without scruple at the first opportunity."

In the realm of empire building and staff padding, the Congress makes the White House and the Pentagon look like rank amateurs. Some members of Congress have made virtual careers out of criticizing the size of the White House staff. But if they really want to see a bloated staff, all they have to do is look in their own backyard. Thirty years ago, at the end of the Eisenhower administration, there were 6,800 people on congressional staffs. In the years since, the size of the federal government has increased by 33 percent. But the congressional staffs have expanded nearly 300 percent, to 19,500—an average of 36 congressional bureaucrats for every elected member. In these days of monster deficits, budget cutters in Congress should look at Congress's price tag: In 1962 it was $129 million; now it's $1.9 *billion,* an increase of 1,450 percent —four times the increase in the rate of inflation.

A freshman congressman today has a larger staff than I had as Vice President. Yet despite the huge increases in the size of congressional staffs, polls show that Congress is less well respected than at any time since the end of World War II. One reason is that the bigger the staffs, the more congressmen and senators tend to rely on others to do their thinking for them. Members of Congress love to appear in public hearings on national television. And yet how often have you seen a member read a question to a witness and then sit mute, unable to follow up on the answer because there is no one there to script him?

When a congressman is handed $415,000 for staff, it is tempting to let them write speeches, prepare questions to be asked at hearings, and write out answers for press conferences. But the danger is that the staff will end up making the decisions rather than sticking to their correct role of carrying out the member's decisions. The more a staff does for the leader, the less he does for himself, and he inevitably becomes weaker in the process.

The White House should set an example by cutting back on its excessive staff. A freeze on hiring is not enough. That is like taking a diet pill. What is needed is a major operation to cut away excess fat. A 50 percent cut across the board in the Congress, the White House, and in the top echelons of the executive departments, including the Pentagon, would result in a far more efficient government. One of the most ridiculous practices in the bureaucracy is when promotions are based on how many people an individual supervises. The rule should be that those who can do the same job with fewer people get the promotions.

We saw a striking example of overstaffing and duplication of effort in the Iran-contra affair. Hundreds of lawyers and staffers in eight federal agencies participated in the various investigations, at a total cost of over $50.6 million. A more effective job could have been done with far fewer people. When the House Committee on Un-American Activities began the Hiss case, we were faced with all-out opposition from the White House, the Justice Department, and Hiss's excellent corps of lawyers. I was the only lawyer on the committee, and our staff was exactly six, none of whom was a lawyer: our brilliant chief investigator Bob Stripling, plus Ben Mandell, Douglas Appel, Lew Russell, Bill Wheeler, Charles McKillips, and two stenographers. We won for two reasons. Because we were so outnumbered, we tried harder. More important, we were on the right side.

While he was serving as one of my top speechwriters, Bill Safire expressed his concern that Henry Kissinger was getting too much credit for our foreign-policy initiatives at my expense. My reaction was twofold. First, Kissinger deserved a great deal of credit. Second, if the initiatives succeeded, there would be enough credit to go around. All good staffers have big egos. A leader must give credit to a staffer for a job well done both personally and if possible publicly as well. The best rule: Be generous in sharing credit with subordinates when an initiative succeeds, and be prepared to take the blame if it fails.

31

GOVERNING

There is a profound difference between campaigning for office and governing in office. A campaign's goal is popularity. In governing, popularity is only the means to an end. It should never be hoarded; it should be used to achieve greater goals. A President's success is measured by his domestic and international achievements, not by his popularity in the polls. For example, Harry Truman left office with one of the lowest approval ratings of any postwar President. But because he defined the contours of U.S. foreign policy through the Greek-Turkish aid program and the Marshall Plan, he is rated as one of America's strongest and most successful leaders. He also had the advantage of being challenged by great issues. He did not have the problem of a nineteenth-century British prime minister, Lord Rosebery, who Churchill said had the misfortune of living in a "time of great men and small events."

Governing is infinitely more complex and difficult than campaigning. A President must understand and balance the competing and at times adversarial roles of the White House staff, the Cabinet, the bureaucracy, Congress, the media, and the public in a way that will enable him to achieve his goals for the nation.

One of his most important decisions is defining the roles of the White House staff and the Cabinet. No general rules can be laid down, because no game plan will work unless you have the players to carry it out. An official or staff member is not useful to the President because of the position he occupies but because of the qualities he brings to it. Still, there is one fundamental principle that must be kept in mind: The closer a staff member is to the President institutionally, the better the President can count on him. Especially when the President is not a member of the party that holds Congress, he needs a strong, loyal White House staff to counter the competing agendas and ambitions of Congress and the bureaucracy, both of which are far more assertive than a generation ago. That is why appointments to top White House positions are harder to make and also more important than appointments to Cabinet positions.

Critics of a strong White House say it runs the risk of becoming an "imperial Presidency." On the contrary: a strong White House staff is essential today if the President is to avoid becoming a vassal of the Congress and the bureaucracy.

After the Iran-contra foul-up, it became a cliché to proclaim that foreign policy should be run by the State Department. It is true that the State Department should execute the game plan. But the President must reserve the right to call the plays. While the White House staff is usually well-advised to stay out of foreign-policy operations, a strong National Security Council is indispensable, both to ensure that the President's policy is followed and to coordinate it. Foreign policy is far more than diplomacy, which is the State Department's bag. It also involves the activities of the Departments of Treasury, Defense, Commerce, and Justice, and the CIA.

Most critics of the "imperial Presidency" magically transform into boosters of a strong White House when a President who advocates policies they agree with is in power. But there are also well-meaning academic types who mistakenly believe that the best way to make policy is to let it percolate up from the bowels of the departments and be decided upon by a Cabinet chaired by the President. "Cabinet government" is fundamentally at odds with the American system, and also with Americans' expectation that their President will lead and not follow. A Cabinet can execute policy, but it cannot and should not initiate it. It was not elected to do so, and Cabinet officers who are totally dependent on unelected bureaucrats for information and guidance are not capable of doing so.

In a Cabinet officer, strength and loyalty are just as important as brains. A President's appointees must particularly understand that it is their responsibility to represent the President to the bureaucracy, not the other way around. Over the past forty years I have known many strong Cabinet secretaries whose loyalty to the President was unquestioned but who unwittingly became captives of their bureaucracies. Businessmen are most vulnerable to this treatment. They come to Washington with the naive notion that government is just like business. It is true that the game of politics is played in both business and in government. But politics in business is a science. Politics in government is an art. Even the strongest-willed businessman will become putty in the hands of skilled bureaucrats, who are masters at buttering up the boss and at battling for turf with other departments and with the White House staff— a game in which the businessman is a rank amateur. Before long they will have him convinced that the best way to serve the President is to feud with real and imagined adversaries on the White House staff and in the Cabinet to make sure that his department's budgets are funded and interests served. Once this happens, his usefulness to the President is gone. Similarly, a businessman appointed as an ambassador will go abroad breathing fire about being the President's man. Before long, foreign service officers pursuing their own agenda will be leading him around like a pussycat.

I do not question the competence or loyalty of America's career bureaucrats. They can hold their own with their opposite numbers anywhere in the world. But as intelligent, strong men and women, they have their own ideas about what policies are best for the nation. If they do not get strong leadership from the White House and from their superiors, they will fill the vacuum with those ideas. They are a tremendous potential asset for any administration. A President and his appointees must find ways to work with them rather than against them, to use them and not be used by them. For example, the credit for an initiative such as our opening to China should not go only to those of us who tipped glasses with Chinese leaders in the Great Hall of the People. The achievement would not have been possible without the dedicated work of scores of career officials, most of whom may never get the chance to visit China.

If anyone has any doubts about what an asset top-flight career foreign service officers can be, he should look at the records of some of those I have been privileged to know or work with over the past forty years—men and women like Jake Boehm, Chip Bohlen, Ellis Briggs, Henry Byroade, Frank Carlucci, Jimmy Dunn, Eleanor Lansing Dulles, Marshall Green, Loy Henderson, Alex Johnson, Foy Kohler, Bill Marsh, Armin Meyer, Robert Murphy, Mark Palmer, Jeff Parson, William Sebald, Joe Sisco, Walter Stoessel, Henry Tasca, Llewelyn Thompson, and Bob Woodward. Cabinet officers in other departments will find equally qualified men and women who will loyally and competently carry out the President's agenda—if they only knew what it is.

The one function that a President cannot delegate to anyone else is knocking heads together when Cabinet and department heads engage in Washington's favorite game of battling for turf. It is frustrating, maddening, and absolutely indispensable. I speak from experience. Waging war in Vietnam abroad was not easy, but waging war at home against drugs, against cancer, and for energy independence was even more difficult. Department heads would always pledge cooperation, but when they left the President's office their resolve sometimes diminished alarmingly. Such massive problems frequently require a Presidentially appointed "czar." But if he is to be effective, his power over each department and agency with a piece of the action in his area of responsibility must be absolute. That is why Cabinet officers do not as a rule like czars. It is bad enough to have to follow the President's orders.

The most difficult challenge a President faces is dealing not with his staff, the Cabinet, or the media, but with Congress. Sometimes a President faces a cruel dilemma. He can't get along with the Congress, but he can't get along without it. As a result, government is paralyzed.

This is even more true when you inject the partisan element. Some pundits ask why President Bush in his first hundred days didn't match FDR's record in 1933 and LBJ's in 1965, when the Congress approved virtually everything they asked for. They overlook the fact that both Roosevelt and Johnson had overwhelming majorities in the House and the Senate. While Eisenhower had a Republican Congress in only his first two years, he usually got support from the Democratic Congress during his last six. But Eisenhower was in office during an era when all he had to do was to convince Senate Majority Leader Lyndon Johnson and House Speaker Sam Rayburn, and they would deliver the Democratic votes for our program. Speaker Foley and Majority Leader Mitchell are able men, but there is no way that they could do that for George Bush even if they wanted to. Today, bipartisanship has become a chimera, and party loyalty has been replaced by loyalty to causes, some of them kooky. Besides, in this era of massive deficits, the number of spending bills a President can force through the Congress is not an indication of how effective a leader he has been. Sometimes stopping or vetoing a bad bill is the real test of leadership.

Two recent examples illustrate how difficult it is for a Republican President to get cooperation from a Democratic Congress.

When the Congress finally passed a welfare reform bill in 1988, its author, Senator Pat Moynihan, wrote to me and pointed out that it was a modest version of an initiative we attempted to get enacted twenty years ago, when he served on my White House staff. Our plan would have revolutionized the welfare system. It provided assistance not just for the unemployed, but for the working poor as well, thus taking away the incentive to quit low-paying jobs to get more on welfare. It required the able-bodied to get jobs before receiving any assistance. The plan was praised in most of the media and then cut to pieces by partisan politics in the Congress. I had incorrectly expected the biggest danger to come from the right. As Moynihan observed at the time, the liberals could not let a conservative Republican President do what his liberal Democratic predecessors had not been bold enough to do. Social workers, threatened with extinction since welfare payments would go directly to the recipients rather than through them, joined in an unholy alliance with conservatives against the plan. Due in great part to the leadership of Jerry Ford, it passed the House but was killed by liberal Democrats and conservative Republicans in the Senate.

Politics also forced me to make one of my poorest decisions as President. In 1971, when inflation was 4 percent—acceptable today, but considered far too high then—Congress clamored for the imposition of wage and price controls. Because of my experience with the Office of Price Administration in 1942, I had always been unalterably opposed to such measures. John Connally argued that if I did not seize the initiative, Congress would enact a permanent program that it might be able to pass over my veto. So I imposed a temporary, ninety-day freeze. It was enormously popular in the short run. I was not surprised when it proved to be a mistake in the long run.

One of the past masters in handling Congress was Bryce Harlow. His advice was always to treat congressmen and senators with "tender loving care." But Harlow was a hardheaded realist. He knew that when the chips were down, few would risk their political futures because of their tender affection for the President. What is decried as horse trading—giving a member something concrete for his vote besides a thank-you letter and a set of cufflinks—is sometimes indispensable in winning a close vote. An even greater incentive for members is the fear that a popular President may oppose them in the next election. That is why a President's popularity is an asset that should be used, not just accumulated. Popularity not used means nothing. Its only purpose is to use it to do things, even if you risk losing some of it in the process.

Good personal relations alone will seldom improve political relations either with adversaries abroad or political opponents at home. There are exceptions. During President Pompidou's state visit to Washington in the spring of 1970, we had some difficult negotiations on international monetary issues. After he left Washington, he was scheduled to be the guest of honor at a dinner at the Waldorf-Astoria in New York given by a group of Franco-American friendship organizations headed by former Ambassador Bill Burden. Critics who believed the French government's Mideast policy was too pro-Arab urged a boycott of the dinner. Demonstrations against the visit became so ugly that Mrs. Pompidou threatened to go home. Mayor Lindsay and Governor Rockefeller canceled their appearances at the dinner.

Vice President Agnew was scheduled to represent the administration. Our chief of protocol, Bus Mosbacher, called me and warned that if something dramatic was not done to change the atmosphere, French-American relations would be irreparably damaged. On the spur of the moment, I decided to fly to New York and attend the dinner in place of Agnew. When I entered the Waldorf ballroom, the place came apart. The usually reserved Pompidou could hardly restrain his emotion. Madame Pompidou had tears in her eyes. They were particularly moved when I pointed out in my toast that while it is customary for the Vice President to substitute for the President, this was the first time in history that a President substituted for the Vice President, and that this was a measure of my respect for them and their country. What differences we had in substantive issues were soon resolved, and, even more important, we established a warm personal relationship which lasted until his death in 1974. Even today, whenever I visit France, people refer to what they call my *beau geste*.

But this kind of reaction is an exception, not the rule, in both foreign and domestic relations. It is a mistake, for example, to assume that if Presidents and Cabinet officers only consult with and romance Congress, they will be able to eliminate all differences. A President and the Congress may well have irreconcilable differences on some issues that neither telephone calls, personal notes, invitations to dinner, nor tickets to performances at the Kennedy Center will eliminate.

But doesn't bipartisanship, at least in foreign policy, override self-interest? The answer is that gushy odes to bipartisanship in Presidential speeches and newspaper editorials deliver precious few votes unless other factors come into play. Bipartisanship generally works only when it serves a partisan interest. If it is popular to be bipartisan, senators and congressmen will be bipartisan. They do not consider bipartisanship to be an end in itself.

In the rare event of a great overriding issue involving the survival of the nation, bipartisanship will override partisan considerations. We saw this in the much-berated 80th Congress. The Republicans had overwhelming majorities in the House and the Senate. Truman's popularity was low. And yet Republicans provided the votes that were necessary for approval of the Greek-Turkish aid program and the Marshall Plan, the cornerstones of Truman's widely and justly acclaimed foreign policy. That spirit continued through the Eisenhower and Kennedy administrations and most of the Johnson administration. Vietnam destroyed it, especially when the conduct of the war passed to the Republicans. Democratic senators and congressmen who supported Kennedy and Johnson when they sent American troops into Vietnam opposed my policies for bringing them home.

A President can only get support from a Congress controlled by the other party if members are afraid to vote against him for one of two reasons—because it would be unpopular to do so, or because even though his poll standings are low, he can convince them, the media, and their constituents that the nation's survival depends on them. But what about courage? Why can't members of the House and Senate have the guts to vote for what is right even if they risk their seats by doing so? The reason is that congressmen are only human. Everyone agrees that committing physical suicide is not courageous. Neither is committing political suicide. In his efforts to govern, a President must not ask members of the House and Senate to sacrifice themselves. He must instead use the bully pulpit to make what is unpopular popular. Only then will he deserve bipartisan support for his policies.

32

PRAGMATISM

When I met with him in Tokyo in 1985, Prime Minister Nakasone told me a leader must have two faces—a smiling one and a threatening one. Some might say that this was yet another example of the sleazy, two-faced character of most politicians. But even his critics agree that Nakasone was one of the most courageous and principled Japanese leaders since World War II. His simple formula was no more and no less than the key to effective, pragmatic leadership.

No word in the political lexicon has two more diametrically different meanings than "pragmatism." To the Washington establishment's moderates, it is a good word. To self-styled "movement conservatives," it is a dirty word. Liberals and moderates praise pragmatists and condemn ideologues. When they say that a conservative President, congressman, or Cabinet officer has "grown," that means that he has capitulated to their agenda and abandoned what they consider to be his extreme ideas. They believe a President should ask Congress to approve only those measures that polls indicate a majority will support. They don't ask, "Is it right?", but, "Will it work?" In foreign policy, they generally believe that success is measured by getting any agreement, and they find it difficult to oppose even bad agreements.

The worst kind of pragmatism is that practiced by the mushy moderate, who believes in nothing but what works and inevitably becomes a captive of Washington's permanent liberal establishment. Like the inhabitants of Plato's Cave, they believe that what they see inside the Beltway is life, when in fact it is only a faint shadow of the real world. Their favorite code words are "accommodation," "consensus," and "compromise." They tell the

285

newly elected congressman or senator who comes to Washington full of energy and strong conservative convictions that the way to get ahead is to get along. An alarming number heed this centrist siren song. The permanent Washington establishment has an enormous impact, since even when it doesn't dominate the political scene, it controls the social scene. Only the strongest characters can resist this heady wine. Too many become hollow vessels that drift with the fashionable tide instead of making waves. But the payoff is substantial: a favorable press, and acceptance for them and their spouses by the establishment social set.

At the other extreme are those who would rather be right than be President—the movement conservatives who have high principles and believe that any compromise is wrong. In fact, they dislike pragmatists even more than their ideological enemies on the left. They believe it is better to burn down the bakery fighting for principle than to win half a loaf through a judicious compromise. They are realistic enough to know that they are in a probably permanent minority. But they believe that if only the conservatives in the White House and Congress would fight more and compromise less, their principles would prevail and they would soon become the majority. To them, a pragmatist is worse than a liberal, because he blurs the difference between conservatism and liberalism and even makes liberalism respectable.

Extremists on the left tend to be just as critical of pragmatism as extremists on the right. While Theodore Roosevelt has the reputation for having been a strong, progressive President, he often used pragmatic means to achieve his idealistic goals. Wisconsin's great progressive senator, Robert LaFollette, bitterly attacked him for compromising principle in order to get his program through Congress. He charged that Roosevelt acted upon the maxim that half a loaf is better than no bread. LaFollette believed half a loaf was fatal—that it "dulls the appetite and destroys the keenness of interest in attaining the full loaf." Like the extremists on the right, LaFollette thought it was better to lose fighting for principle than to win by compromise. TR, who considered himself to be a man of principle, responded to LaFollette's intemperate attacks in kind. He characterized LaFollette as "half zealot and half self-seeking demagogue—a vindictive and unscrupulous faker!"

Those who practice pragmatism as an end in itself and those who oppose it as an unmitigated evil are both wrong. Pragmatism can be justified, but only as a means to achieve great ideals. The common cliché is that politics is the art of the possible. But leadership is the art of making the impossible possible. If a President appoints to his Cabinet those whose only qualification is that they are pragmatists—other code words are "problem solvers" and "non-ideologues"—they will be easy pickings for the bureaucrats in the permanent establishment. Knowing how to make the system work is important. But knowing what you want it to achieve, sometimes in spite of the system, is indispensable.

Most politicians, even the movement conservatives and their opposite numbers on the left, are pragmatists at heart. In public life, as in private life, all people have principles and all people have interests. To be effective, a leader must recognize that the two are often inextricably bound together. This takes great finesse. A congressman will probably resent a lobbyist who makes an appeal for his vote based entirely on political grounds, because he will think the lobbyist considers him unprincipled. The same congressman will ridicule a President who asks for his vote purely on the basis of principle, because he will consider the President stupid for assuming he would be willing to vote against his interests just because the President asked him to.

Politicians are by nature proud people. You must never question their larger motives or their political instincts. But you must also assume that they are constantly balancing principle against interest and that your best hope for bringing them along is persuading them that supporting your position will enable them to serve both simultaneously.

In short, to achieve great goals a leader must find ways to persuade others to reinterpret, and even sometimes to go against, their interests and principles. But at times he must go against his own interests and principles to achieve those same goals.

This is especially true in foreign policy. When Hitler attacked Russia, Winston Churchill had to eat years of words attacking the evils of godless Bolshevism. In urging an alliance against the Nazis, even one with Stalin, he said, "If Hitler invaded Hell, I think I would find a kind word to say about the Devil in the House of Commons."

Even my detractors would agree that the most dramatic event of my Presidency was my visit to China in 1972. That exciting first glimpse into the heart of a sprawling, colorful, mysterious land was fascinating to millions of Americans. And yet my visit was an act of cold, dispassionate pragmatism. When I announced it in 1971, I was praised by the left and attacked by the right, both for the wrong reasons. The left praised me for backing off my hard-line anti-Communist principles; the right attacked me for doing so. Both were wrong. The China initiative had nothing to do with my attitude toward communism. My decision was based on my belief that the security of the United States would be served by developing better relations with one Communist power that was not on good terms with the other, the Soviet Union—a much more formidable adversary.

In both these cases, pragmatism was a necessary means to achieve a greater goal. Churchill recognized the West could not preserve its freedom without an alliance with a Communist regime whose every guiding tenet was antithetical to Western principles. I recognized that building a new relationship with one such regime could help the United States preserve the peace that was threatened by the expansionism and hostility of the other.

Success in politics at home also can require pragmatic choices about which battles should be fought to win victory. Fighting on all fronts may lead to defeat. We don't have to like communism to recognize that Lenin's doctrine of two steps forward and one step backward, though in his case used to achieve bad ends, is perfectly acceptable if used to achieve good ends.

Over the past forty years, I have campaigned in every state for both liberal and conservative Republican nominees for Congress. Shocked fellow conservatives frequently asked me why I campaigned for liberals. The answer is simple: I would rather have Republicans as majority leaders in the House and Senate than Democrats.

In 1980, the Republican nominee for Senate in Colorado, Mary Estill Buchanan, lost in a very close election. I was surprised when a Republican friend told me that he had not voted for her. I asked why. He replied, "She was wrong on abortion." As a result, we got six more years of Gary Hart, who was wrong on everything. I can understand people feeling strongly about special issues such as abortion, gun control, and ERA. But they should always step back and consider the alternative. Sometimes it is necessary to make a painful decision to support a candidate who may be wrong on your pet issue but right on most others. I have always believed that sticking to principles is not only the best statesmanship but also the best politics. However, this is a far cry from the approach of some politicians who are unable to see the difference between principle and prejudice.

One of the toughest decisions for a President is when a senator or congressman asks for a project in his district or a job for a

People are amazed that a political figure can speak without notes for forty minutes. Afterward, they congratulate me as if I had just announced a cure for some major disease. (In Chicago in 1985)

Photo by Roger Sandler

As I told a "Meet the Press" panel in 1988, when asked if I was trying to make a comeback, "What am I going to come back to? We already have a very good mayor in Saddle River, and we have a very good governor in the state of New Jersey."

At the Oxford Union in 1978 the questions were tough, and some were irreverent. But the students did not try to shout the speaker down. They wanted to hear what he had to say.

Pictorial Parade

I make at least four outlines for every major speech. A single sentence can require hours of concentrated thought to frame and hone.

Even after a speech has been prepared, I set aside at least an hour before the appearance to get my thoughts together and get up for the delivery. (En route by bus to a campaign appearance during the 1962 off-year elections)

After I was nominated for Vice President in 1952, I felt the demonstrations were going on too long. But Speaker Joe Martin said, "Let them cheer for a while longer. You have to get in the hay while the sun is shining."

OPPOSITE: I find that when I am writing and run into a mental block, it is best to put the work aside. An idea or phrase will come to me on a quiet walk alone.

The reporters had thought FDR's Fala story was cute. They thought my Checkers story was corny. But the television viewers liked it, and that was all that mattered. (RN with family dogs Vicky and Checkers in 1960)

Silence can be a particularly effective tactic. If actions speak louder than words, there are times when silence speaks louder still.

OPPOSITE: I have never watched myself on television. If I did, I would become self-conscious and my speaking would lose whatever natural quality it has. (Campaigning in 1972)

A day did not pass that I did not hate the Vietnam War. Believing it was imperative to keep our commitments there did not lessen the burden. (In South Vietnam in 1969)

constituent in return for his vote on a critical issue. You are tempted to throw him out of the office. But when the stakes are high enough, you must hold your nose and pay the price, provided of course that there is at least a modicum of merit to the request. Party leaders in the House and Senate have to make similar decisions. When a member says that to support the party's position on a bill would defeat him in the next election, the leader must decide which is most important—to win the vote now or run the risk of not having the member around when you need his vote in the next Congress.

Bismarck said that people who like laws and sausages should not watch either being made. But the variety of law that is produced by the fractious democratic process is bound to be more appealing and effective than the kind that is handed down on high from politburos and tribunals. We would all prefer to live in a perfect world where the word "pragmatism" was not even in the dictionary. But in reality we live in a free society designed to accommodate many competing ideals, opinions, and ambitions. Without leadership born of pragmatic idealism, these many forces cannot be united in pursuit of a greater goal.

This is not to say that we should go to the other extreme and make a religion out of "the process." Many political scientists argue that the process is at least as important as the goal. This point of view, anti-idealism at its worst, is especially popular among those who profit from a lengthy, argumentative governmental process, including the media, lobbyists, and the political scientists who receive grants to study it ad infinitum.

You can, however, carry the concept of the end justifying the means too far, as an incident from my Navy days shows. When I returned from overseas in 1944, I was assigned to Fleet Air Wing 8 in Alameda, California. I was told that I was to be the 1st Lieutenant. It was a high-enough-sounding title, but from the job description I soon learned that I was in effect the head janitor. My primary responsibility was to see that everything was shipshape for inspection.

The inspecting officer was a sundowner—a stickler for the smallest detail. Not surprisingly, he was not the most popular officer on the base. On several occasions he sharply criticized us because the toilet bowls were stained. We used every kind of detergent to correct this situation, but nothing worked. Finally, in desperation, I turned to my Chief Boatswain mate for an answer. In the Navy, the Chiefs have a reputation for knowing almost everything. I was not disappointed. The Chief was a grizzled veteran with twenty years of service who constantly complained that he had been assigned to shore duty because he had flat feet. He told me not to worry; he would take care of the problem. On the next inspection, all the stains were gone, and we passed with flying colors.

I asked him how he did it. He said, "It was easy, Lieutenant. I just poured a lot of lye down the bowls. It removed all the stains. But I just can't wait to see the look on that SOB's face when he finds that the drainpipes have been eaten away."

There are times when unpleasant means *are* justified in the service of a great goal. But despite the protests of the process-lovers, a proper means *never* justifies an unsatisfactory end. No matter how democratic and meticulously correct it may be, a political process that cannot produce progress for a nation has gone seriously awry.

There is no magic in democracy. The Constitution, extraordinary document that it is, cannot by itself produce a moment of peace or an instant of prosperity. Only the will and the vision of leaders, exercised through the democratic system, sometimes restrained by it, occasionally even exceeding it, can bring about these goals.

Idealism without pragmatism is impotent. Pragmatism without idealism is meaningless. The key to effective leadership is pragmatic idealism.

33

SILENCE

In an age when there is too much talk, nothing in a statesman's arsenal is more effective than a weapon that he might not even know he has: silence. "Nothing more enhances authority than silence," de Gaulle observed. "Great deeds have never yet been accomplished by garrulity."

In Congress, newly elected members used to be well advised to spend their first few months listening and learning rather than talking. Not so today. I have seen freshmen members of the House and Senate being written off as lightweights because they were afflicted with advanced cases of diarrhea of the mouth. Instead, they should consider one of our greatest senators, Richard Russell. He was not a great orator and seldom spoke on the Senate floor. But when he did speak, everyone listened because they knew he would have something to say. No one surpassed him in his capacity to influence his colleagues and the course of events.

Because of his loss to Harry Truman in 1948, Tom Dewey is usually underestimated as a political tactician. But early in my career he gave me some of the best advice I ever received. He said that people can get tired of hearing a politician talk and that he is well advised to withdraw from time to time from the public arena. When he returns, what he says will have far greater impact.

Jimmy Byrnes once told me that free advice is worth just what it costs. In this case, Dewey's free advice was priceless. After the spectacular Republican gains in congressional and gubernatorial elections in 1966, several potential GOP candidates launched their campaigns for President. Since I had campaigned across the nation for a number of 1966's successful candidates, it was widely assumed that I would make my intentions clear as well. I did exactly

291

the opposite. During my six-month vacation from politics in 1967, while I was traveling and beefing up my foreign-policy expertise, some of my potential rivals were self-destructing. When I did take to the campaign trail, my appearances received far greater coverage than ever before. Silence had served me well.

Too many politicians live by the axiom "out of sight, out of mind." The name of the game, after all, is to get a message across. If you talk too much, people stop listening. If you don't talk, people will naturally become curious. By using silence, you can increase the size of your audience and the impact of your message. My "Fund" speech in 1952 and "Silent Majority" speech in 1969 would not have had nearly as big an audience or impact if either I or members of my staff had broken silence because of the tremendous pressures from the press, and thereby reduced the speculation and anticipation which induced people to tune in to hear what I would say. Surprise is always a surefire political tactic. There can be no surprise without silence.

Silence is a particularly effective diplomatic tactic. If actions speak louder than words, there are times when silence speaks louder still. A diplomatic negotiation is often compared with poker. In poker, the player who talks the loudest almost invariably holds the weakest hand.

Henry Kissinger has observed that in his negotiations with the North Vietnamese, which eventually led to the Paris Peace Accords, one of his strongest suits was that I had a reputation for unpredictability. He did not disabuse them. On the contrary, he warned them that they could not judge me by what I said because I often did more than I said I would. In those cases where there is a reputation for unpredictability, silence is the most effective way to reinforce it. Three examples illustrate the effectiveness of this tactic.

In April 1969, the North Koreans shot down an unarmed American reconnaissance plane. We knew military retaliation might jeopardize planned negotiations with the Chinese and Soviets, both of whom were allies of North Korea. None of us was satisfied with the decision to take no military action, but I at least wanted to make sure that the North Koreans would not be emboldened to strike again because of our failure to retaliate. In a press conference four days after the shootdown, I deplored the incident and noted that immediately afterwards the reconnaissance missions had been suspended. I added, "I have today ordered that these flights be continued. They will be protected. This is not a threat; it is simply a statement of fact.'' For several days we were deluged with questions from the media about how, where, and when we might act. Following the maxim I had laid down, we did not answer. The warning, reinforced by silence, got through. There were no further such incidents.

In 1970, Kissinger was conducting secret negotiations with Soviet Ambassador Anatoly Dobrynin on arms control and other issues of great interest to both sides. Whenever the Soviets engaged in activities against our interests, such as their surreptitious attempt to build a nuclear submarine base in Cuba, we did not file a diplomatic protest. We simply broke off the secret negotiations. Since they wanted to talk, our silence got their attention, and the crises were eventually resolved in a manner consistent with our interests.

The most dramatic example occurred in December 1972, when the North Vietnamese were filibustering in the Paris peace talks. They backed away from agreements they had made before the November election and began to stonewall us at every point. Reluctantly, I decided that the only way to break the deadlock was to order the bombing of military targets in the Hanoi-Haiphong area. I made no announcement in advance and declined to answer press inquiries on the operation. There was enormous pressure from the media for me to make a public statement about why we had resumed the bombing and what terms I would accept to discontinue it. The attacks from columnists, commentators, and other political opponents were merciless. My approval rating in the polls went down eleven points in four weeks. It was not an easy time. But the tactics worked. Strong action combined with absolute silence brought the Communists back to the negotiating table, and they accepted our terms for the peace agreement. Had I followed the critics' advice, discontinued the bombing, and gone public with another peace proposal, we could not have achieved the same result, and the war would have dragged on.

Useful as it is as a tactic in politics and diplomacy, the most valuable quality of silence is that it permits and enhances creative thinking. Carlyle said that silence is the element in which great things fashion themselves. That may be an overstatement in some respects, but for most leaders it is true. President Eisenhower never made a major decision in meetings with the Cabinet, the National Security Council, or legislative leaders. He would always go back to his office to reflect on what he had heard before deciding.

I followed the same practice. I never prepared for an important speech or press conference or made a major decision in the Oval Office. Instead, I used a quieter room—my EOB office, the Lincoln Sitting Room, or the studies at Camp David, Key Biscayne, or San Clemente. Good ideas seldom popped into my head in the commotion of a meeting. I realize this may not be true of others. But for those who have not tried a little silence, I would recommend it. When a competent staff member draws up a daily schedule for a busy public official, he carefully provides time for meals, appointments, meetings, even recreation. He should add time for silence to that list. The time reserved for quiet thinking and meditation is probably the most important of the day.

FIVE

34

PHILOSOPHY

The controversies over the Pledge of Allegiance in the 1988 election and last year's proposed flag-burning amendment to the United States Constitution were superficial debates over *how* we should respect the flag. Both sides missed the real issue. As we celebrate the bicentennial of the adoption of the Constitution, we should instead be reminding ourselves *why* we should respect the American flag.

Speaking at Independence Hall on July 4, 1911, Woodrow Wilson said, "A patriotic American is never so proud of the flag under which he lives as when it comes to mean to others as well as himself a symbol of hope and liberty."

We should always defend and respect the flag, not as an idol to be worshipped blindly but as an idea that represents our rich philosophical heritage. Only understanding that heritage will give people real respect for the flag. If the day comes when they refrain from desecrating it only because of the law or some dimly remembered custom, it will have truly become an empty symbol.

American educators have fallen short in this respect in recent years. Most high school students cannot tell you when the Civil War took place, much less how that event helped preserve the Union that the fifty stars and thirteen stripes in the American flag represent. More important, in their perpetual bid for gimmicks that will satisfy their own liberal agendas as well as their desire to teach students something "relevant," educators have increasingly neglected exploring the philosophical roots of the American system of government. To be effective citizens and to be willing to honor the flag for the right reasons, young people must know more than when America was discovered and where its pioneers came from.

297

They must also know what the European settlers and the Founders brought with them, not in their sailing ships but in their minds and hearts.

In 1776, the drafters of the Declaration of Independence took part in a profound historical innovation: the founding of a country on the basis of philosophical ideas. Our nation and our government are living proof that ideas matter in history. The principles of social equality, inalienable rights, limited government, and popular sovereignty rest at the foundation of our republic, and our country embodies the strengths and the limitations of its founding ideas. In a profound sense, philosophy holds the key to understanding ourselves and the future of our country in the world.

The brilliant men who drafted the Constitution described their creation as *"novus ordo seclorum"*—a new order for the ages. But they would be the first to admit that they drew upon the great ideas of the past. They knew that the ancient Greeks, though famed for democracy, actually believed in and practiced government not by the masses but by the best educated, the wealthiest, and the most qualified. They had read the works of Hobbes, who believed avarice inhabited the heart of man, doubted the capacity of people to govern themselves, favored an authoritarian government, and dismissed democracy as "nothing more than an aristocracy of orators." Many of them admired Rousseau, who believed that man, by nature pure, had been corrupted by decadent civilization, and who stressed the need to achieve total equality in order to resurrect the fundamental goodness of mankind.

But the ideas of the English philosopher Locke and the French philosopher Montesquieu stood at the center of the Founders' world view. Their ideas formed the foundation upon which the leaders of the American Revolution and the framers of the Constitution built the uniquely American philosophy defining the proper relationship between the individual, society, and the state.

Locke argued that in the state of nature before the formation of society or the institution of government, man lived a self-sufficient, solitary, and happy existence. In nature, he had the right to life, liberty, and property. He had the right to self-preservation, to refuse to submit to any ruler without his consent, and to possess those things in nature with which he had mixed his labor. Locke asserted that the need for society and government arose from the "inconveniences" caused by the lack of any organization among men to secure these rights. At the same time, however, no society or government established by men could legitimately overturn these natural rights.

The Founders spoke the language of Locke. They set forth an eloquent restatement of the Lockean philosophy of government in the remarkable opening paragraphs of the Declaration of Independence:

> We hold these truths to be self-evident, that all men are created equal; that they are endowed by their Creator with certain unalienable rights; that among these are life, liberty and the pursuit of happiness. That to secure these rights, governments are instituted among men, deriving their just powers from the consent of the governed; that, whenever any form of government becomes destructive of these ends, it is the right of the people to alter or to abolish it, and to institute new government, laying its foundation on such principles, and organizing its powers in such form, as to them shall seem most likely to effect their safety and happiness.

The Founders believed in the necessity of government but also in the necessity of limiting government to its proper sphere of action. Its purpose was not to create a perfect society but to secure the natural rights that man possessed before entering society.

This philosophy has propelled the democratic revolution throughout the world. The ideas have had near-universal political appeal but have not spawned universal political success. Nations with political traditions and institutions capable of sustaining representative democracy have enjoyed unprecedented stability and prosperity. But those nations that were unprepared for such government, or that tampered with the fundamentals of the Lockean formula for limited government, have fallen prey to the ills of corruption, demagogy, and majoritarian repression which plague regimes that claim to be democratic.

The most obscene distortion of the spirit of the democratic age has been the so-called people's democracies. Devised according to the formulas of Marx and Lenin, these governments bear no resemblance to the authentic democracies of the West. Communists as well as right-wing dictators like Noriega reject a central premise of democratic thought: the people should be able to alter the government through elections. As Stalin's foreign minister, Vyacheslav Molotov, once explained to a Western diplomat, "I like the idea of elections, and I don't object to providing for them in a constitution. There is only one trouble with them. You don't know in advance how they are going to come out.'' The test of democracy is whether the potential exists for an election to overturn those in power. According to that standard, the partially competitive elections under Gorbachev measured up no better than the single-candidate elections under his predecessors. Although he deserved credit for allowing his critics to blow off steam in the elections, he always knew there was no chance whatever for him to lose his grip on power. Only if populist pressures push Gorbachev's political reforms further than he wants to take them will genuinely free elections occur.

The evils of Communist regimes have been rooted in their philosophy. In Marxist-Leninist theory, the Communist Party has a unique understanding of the inevitable processes of history and has the right to rule society without the consent of the people in order to lead the country to the promised land of communism. Like many philosophies, it was a utopian vision. But unlike the benign musings of some liberal ivory-tower academics, it was based on a foundation of malignant premises. An exhaustive reading of the works of Marx and Lenin will never turn up two ideas vital to a genuine and humane democratic order: the worth and dignity of all individuals as the foundation of society and government, and the consequent need for limitations on the powers of the majority and the state. Moreover, the Communist doctrine unequivocally endorsed, and even celebrated, the use of coercion and violence by the party to achieve its self-appointed mission. As a result, by combining an unachievable utopian vision, the rejection of the ideas of individual rights and limited government, and the affirmation of force as an instrument of state policy, the Communist philosophy created an ineluctable chain of logic leading to communism's crimes against humanity.

The Founders of the American republic were neither woolly-headed utopians nor empty-headed pragmatists. They were practical idealists. They understood the world in which they lived—an imperfect world, inhabited by imperfect people—and sought to build a form of government that would provide for security and stability and foster prosperity. The lodestar of their idealism was the concept of liberty. They wanted to build a solid structure that would survive after they were gone. Seldom in history have any men built so well. After two centuries, the consequences of their ideas still reverberate within American society.

No constitutional order in history has endured longer than

300

America's. The central political premises of the Founders were profoundly simple: Individuals act to advance their interests, and stable government depends on balancing competing interests against one another. Drawing on the ideas of Montesquieu, the framers of the Constitution devised a system of checks and balances between the executive, legislative, and judiciary that guaranteed that no branch could monopolize power and thereby oppress the people. Their creation was a system in which the government would be strong enough to protect the rights of the people but not so strong as to threaten those rights.

The Founders did not believe, however, that all countries could instantly adopt the democratic form of government. In fact, they considered themselves to be engaged in a grand experiment testing the capacity of men to rule themselves—an experiment they all freely conceded might fail. Our nation has passed this test for other reasons besides the intellectual brilliance of the Founders. Their system built on the democratic experience and social equality that already existed in the thirteen colonies and provided for a limited, though inevitably expanding, franchise to distill an informed and intelligent electorate from the populace. While potentially powerful, ideas alone can be blown away by the winds of history. Truly enduring ideas, like those of the Founders, have always been grounded in cultural traditions and institutions, thereby tapping the strength of history.

No economic order in history has generated greater prosperity than America's. The Founders understood that private property and free markets produce wealth. Their views remain valid today. If permitted to operate, capitalism represents a tremendous natural force for generating economic growth. Its strength stems from the fundamental facts that people will work to improve the quality of their lives and that the iron laws of supply and demand will allocate resources with the greatest possible efficiency. No other system has produced self-sustaining economic expansion.

Some condemn capitalism as immoral. But in truth it is simply amoral. It generates wealth with ruthless efficiency—rewarding the best producers and weeding out the others—and makes no greater moral claims. But that is not an indictment of capitalism. The purpose of an economic system is to generate wealth. It is a nation's sense of morality that should lead it to allocate some of that wealth to social purposes and to regulate the harshness of the outcomes of capitalist competition.

Its fundamental nature gives rise to two major philosophical challenges to capitalism. The first is the tension between equality and liberty. Both ideas appeal strongly to our sense of rightness. Democracy implies both liberty, including individual pursuit of economic betterment, and equality among citizens. But the key is to understand what kinds of equality would contribute to prosperity and what kinds would destroy it.

To operate optimally, capitalism requires that all enjoy equality before the law and equality of opportunity. An uneven playing field or an uneven start in the economic race reduces the efficiency of capitalism. Such inequality rewards less able producers or wastes human potential. No society, including our own, has fully succeeded in establishing full equality in either sense. An individual who can pay millions of dollars in legal fees has better odds in court than one who cannot. A child born in the slums of the South Bronx does not have the same opportunity as one born among the estates of Scarsdale. In addition to being morally wrong, this is an unacceptable waste of human resources. In a competitive world, we cannot afford to leave the potential of our people untapped. Those who support capitalism should therefore enthusiastically endorse government programs to promote equality before the law and equality of opportunity, especially in providing equal access to higher education on the basis of merit.

But capitalism does not, and government should not, guarantee equality in economic outcomes. People are created equal in terms of their inalienable natural rights but not in terms of their innate capabilities. Under capitalism, that results in inequalities of wealth. Leveling incomes through taxation means leveling incomes downward. The mainspring of capitalism is the rewarding of work and efficiency. If we reduce these rewards by transferring wealth to achieve equality in incomes, we will also destroy the incentives for producing wealth.

We must remember that redistribution of wealth presupposes that wealth exists to redistribute. All over the world, idealistic socialist leaders such as Mitterrand of France and Gonzalez of Spain, who traditionally have insisted that government's primary goal should be to promote equality of wealth, now recognize that rather than being satisfied with giving everyone an equal share in poverty, they should provide opportunity for all to earn their way out of poverty.

Capitalism's second dilemma is the tension between economic security and liberty. Some believe the goal of government should be to provide total economic security for everyone. Others believe that economic liberty should never be sacrificed to the regimentation needed to provide such security. The critical question is how much security government should guarantee. Socialist countries promise total security and thereby undermine incentives for production. Instead of creating equality of wealth, socialist governments create equality in poverty. In the West, the non-socialist welfare state is committed to the proposition that the poor or unemployed will not become destitute. We reduce our economic liberty by taxing ourselves to pay for these programs, but at the same time insure ourselves against personal misfortune or economic recession. The difficulty comes in setting the level of support to the less fortunate. If set too low, it causes unnecessary hardship. If set too high, it creates disincentives to achieving self-sufficiency and fosters dependency. Our objective should therefore be a welfare system structured not to trap the poor in dependency but to enable them to escape poverty.

Even in America's spiritual life, the Founders' philosophy has carried enduring consequences. They explicitly sought to exclude the spiritual dimension of life from politics. In the Declaration of Independence, they spoke of man's right to "the pursuit of happiness"—but left to the individual the task of defining the meaning of happiness. In the Constitution, they prohibited the Congress from making any law "respecting an establishment of religion." They understood the tremendous power of religious and ideological beliefs—and recognized their capacity to tear asunder the bonds of society. Having witnessed the horrors of the religious wars in the Old World, they wisely sought to place religion outside the realm of politics in the New World.

Consequently, the Founders sought to create an orderly government based on consent that permitted individuals to define and pursue their own fulfillment without the interference of society or the state. In their view, the common good was best defined only in terms of the minimal goal of securing man's natural rights. It did not contain a positive concept of a higher good or a vision of what society should strive to achieve or to become. They were not oblivious to the need for values and morality. In fact, they believed their system could not function without citizens imbued with religious convictions. They would have approved of the Act of Congress in 1954 that added the words "under God" to our Pledge of Allegiance. But in their system, based on the hard ground of interest, achieving a higher common good depended on individuals pursuing an enlightened self-interest.

This insulated American politics from the storms of religious or ideological politics but created the danger of an obsession with materialism. The Founders envisioned a "commercial republic" that would be divided only by competing economic interests. But as a result the danger existed that the people's only interest would be economics.

As de Tocqueville warned one hundred fifty years ago, obsessive materialism has infected our country. The quest for the larger house, the faster car, and the more expensive wardrobe has become the preoccupation of many people, particularly among the young. Nietzsche wrote that he foresaw the day when secular, rationalistic values would triumph and warned against what he called the "last man," a creature totally obsessed with security and comfort and incapable of throwing himself into a higher cause. Nietzsche rightly saw the last man as a repellant creature. We do not have to accept his nihilism to agree with his assessment. We must not fall into the syndrome Whittaker Chambers warned against when he wrote, "The West believes man's destiny is prosperity and an abundance of goods. So does the Politburo."

America must develop institutions that cultivate an appreciation of the spiritual dimension of life that the Founders wisely put outside of politics. Unfortunately, our universities and our churches have largely failed in this respect. Academia, instead of perpetuating our values, has become the vanguard in the assault on those values. It has surrendered to the wave of moral relativism sweeping our culture. No longer is philosophy taught as the quest for truth. Instead, it has become an expedition in comparative shopping. At the same time, our churches have become concerned more with issuing reports on the crisis in Central America and nuclear disarmament than fostering individual spiritual strength.

While the quest for truth must remain outside the realm of politics, we need to rededicate ourselves to living up to our political principles. When they wrote the Constitution, the framers knew the country did not measure up to its declared ideals, especially because of the existence of slavery in the South. We have made much progress in two hundred years, but the problem of inequality remains. The existence of an urban underclass is a blight on our record and a challenge to our beliefs. It is not a question of trying to achieve equality in outcomes but one of ensuring equality of opportunity. The failed programs of the Great Society helped destroy the family structure and created dependency, which, in turn, has bred hopelessness. Even continued economic growth will not solve the problem, and morally we cannot ignore it. But government programs cannot represent the full solution. Government must provide equality of education and guarantee economic opportunity. In addition, community and religious leaders and parents must inculcate moral values in young people and restore the centrality of the nuclear family, without which no progress will be possible.

In foreign policy we are faced with a choice of insisting on democratic rule around the world or of accepting the existence of the non-democratic regimes that have arisen in cultures different from our own. At the philosophical level, we should endorse Locke's concept of natural rights. In practice, however, we must recognize that often nations lack the traditions and institutions to make democracy work. Democratic government does not automatically mean good government. It does not ensure justice, good administration, or economic development. Unfortunately, Hobbes's characterization of democracy as "an aristocracy of orators" aptly fits many Third World republics and at times even our own. Since our country developed its democratic political institutions over centuries, we should not expect others to replicate them overnight.

We should always strongly endorse the cause of freedom and human rights in the world. But we should promote it only within the limits of American interests and resources and within the bounds of international realities. We must not delude ourselves into believing that we can easily reshape the world to conform to our ideals and hopes. We should believe profoundly in the truth of our values. But one of our fundamental values is that we should not try to impose our beliefs on others.

America was founded by individuals who sought religious freedom, who wanted the right to worship God in their own way and to look for meaning in life on their own terms. We should seek to leave a greater historical legacy than simply attaining the highest per capita GNP. The search for a higher meaning in life has gone on since the beginning of civilization. While conclusive answers will always elude us, we must continue to engage in this noble quest. Whether through philosophy or religion, the search for truth itself remains the key to developing a fuller, more profound life for ourselves and our posterity.

35

CAUSES

Shortly before I went to China in 1972, André Malraux perceptively remarked to me that the United States is the first nation in history to become a world power without trying to become one. America is a reluctant great power. We are fundamentally isolationist and become engaged in the cut-and-thrust of world politics only if we perceive a great idealistic cause hanging in the balance. We have had the power to shape history but have been reluctant to take up the challenge.

In World War I, we stood on the sidelines for four years while the European powers bled each other white. Alone, the danger of a Europe dominated by Imperial Germany was not enough to prompt an American intervention. It was only Berlin's unrestricted submarine warfare and conspiracy to create an anti-American alliance with Mexico that propelled us into war. Even then, President Wilson did not justify his decision in the cold terms of national interest. Instead, he asserted that we were fighting a war to end wars and that our goal was to make the world safe for democracy.

In World War II, the United States had great interests at stake from the outset. In the late 1930s, President Roosevelt repeatedly tried to make the case for engaging the United States in efforts to block the rise of a militarist Japan dominant in the Far East and a fascist Germany dominant in Europe. But his warnings about the danger posed to American interests fell on deaf ears. Only Japan's surprise attack on Pearl Harbor jarred the country out of its complacent isolationism. Even so, Roosevelt felt it necessary to rally the country with an appeal to idealism. He struck responsive chords when he emphasized moral causes, such as the Four Freedoms, and when he pressed for the creation of a new world organization to keep the peace in the future.

All great powers have conceived of themselves as serving a greater purpose, playing a vital role, or pursuing a historic mission. Their leaders have offered a message, an idea, or a vision of the kind of world they wanted to create for the next generation. They have always understood that action must begin with ideas. In world history, great endeavors have always started with great ideas.

After World War II, the United States cast aside its traditional isolationism in order to oppose the expansion of Communist tyranny in Europe and Asia. For forty years, the two superpowers—one advocating freedom and the other imposing communism—have sparred in every corner of the world. Fifty years from now, when historians retell the story of the postwar period, they will describe a climactic struggle between two great causes. This contest will be viewed, moreover, as an ideological conflict with profound moral consequences.

Anti-communism is a profoundly moral cause. Those on the left who sneer at the anti-Communist cause are callous to the great suffering inflicted on innocent human beings by communist regimes. Communism has produced a legacy not of progress but of poverty. In a third of the world it has snuffed out the basic liberties sought by all people and taken for granted in the West. It has killed 40 million people in the Soviet Union, 50 million in China, hundreds of thousands in Eastern Europe, 3 million in Southeast Asia, 1 million in Afghanistan, and untold others in the scores of so-called Communist wars of national liberation. Communism promised the world better living standards and a more meaningful life but delivered stagnant economies, totalitarian states, manmade famines, mass terror, concentration camps, spiritual emptiness, and boat people.

The rivalry between the United States and the Soviet Union has been a struggle between the opposite poles of human experience, between light and darkness, between hope and fear. We have sought to spread our influence by example; the Soviets have tried to expand theirs by conquest. Our system is founded on freedom, liberty, and self-fulfillment; theirs is based on tyranny, coercion, and repression. We believe in a representative government with limited powers; they believe in a totalitarian system with all power concentrated in the party and state. Our system was designed to

307

give the individual the greatest scope for action consistent with public order and the rights of others; theirs was created to compel the individual to obey the dictates of the ruling elite. Our ideas have created a dynamic system which is most admired not for its products but for its freedom, while communism has built a stagnant society suffocated by an oppressive bureaucracy.

Unlike most great power rivalries, the U.S.-Soviet conflict centered not on a squabble over interest and power but rather involved a contest over the destiny of man. In the immediate postwar years, the world stood at a crossroads. Down one road was a future defined by Marx, Lenin, and Stalin; down the other was one defined by Locke, Montesquieu, Jefferson, and Hamilton. The United States and the Soviet Union largely controlled the destiny of a war-ravaged world. We chose to take up the cause of freedom. We helped strengthen economically and militarily those countries still free from Moscow's grasp, and by dedicating ourselves to a great cause we strengthened ourselves spiritually.

Americans can be justifiably proud of our record. Our actions were indispensable in holding the line against Communist expansion in Western Europe, Japan, Iran, Greece, Turkey, South Korea, the Philippines, and Malaysia. Although we have not always been successful, the record is overwhelmingly positive. No nation in history has ever played a more pivotal role in defending freedom and humanitarian values against the threat of tyranny than has the United States in the postwar period.

Many observers now proclaim that the Cold War has ended. They say that the internal changes undertaken by Mikhail Gorbachev have eliminated the Soviet threat and thereby have rendered obsolete the activist U.S. foreign policy of the last forty years. They are right to draw attention to the potential importance of the reforms inside the Soviet Union. But they overstate the extent to which these reforms have changed the fundamental structure of the Soviet system and the nature of Soviet foreign policy.

We must understand Gorbachev's motivations for undertaking these changes. He is certainly an exciting new kind of Soviet leader. He is also certainly motivated at least in part by a desire to improve the quality of life for the people of the Soviet Union. But his principal motivation is the force of necessity. He knows that unless he infuses the economy with a new vitality, the Soviet Union will be eclipsed as a great power in the next century. His goal is not to replace the Communist system but to strengthen it.

As he puts it, he wants to adopt changes that will give communism "a second wind."

A reduction in tensions between the two superpowers does not mean that the Cold War has ended. In the past, improvements in the atmospherics of East-West relations have been transitory. Until Moscow abandons the policies that caused the East-West conflict—the projection of Soviet power into the heart of Europe, the build-up of massive offensive military power, the subversion of non-Communist countries in the Third World, and the propping up of illegitimate Communist client regimes in key regional conflicts—our profound differences will endure. If Gorbachev succeeds in strengthening the Soviet economy without changing its aggressive foreign policy, the threat to our interests will not diminish but grow. I do not question his sincerity. He is profoundly sincere in wanting to rescue the Soviet system from a terminal illness. He has been bold and courageous in pursuing that goal. We should help him—but only if his reforms go far enough to have a chance to succeed and if, as a result, the Soviet Union becomes less repressive at home and less aggressive abroad.

When Jack Kennedy and I supported President Truman's request for aid to Greece and Turkey forty-two years ago, we thought at the time that it was a difficult decision. In retrospect, it was easy, because we had a simple choice between two worlds— the Communist world and the free world. Today, because the Communist idea is suffering from a terminal illness, we live in one of those great watershed periods of history where the prospects for peace and freedom are more hopeful than they were in 1947. But because we no longer live in a bipolar world, the decisions we must make are far more complex and difficult.

In the continuing struggle between the causes of freedom and communism, we should be guided by a sense of historical optimism. Communism has been discredited as an ideology and as an economic and political model. Western ideas of political and economic liberty have won the ideological battle. But this victory must still be consolidated in geopolitical terms. While the Communists have lost the Cold War, the West has not yet won it.

In this phase of the struggle, we must expand the horizons of our efforts. It is not enough to rest content behind the security of our alliances with Western Europe and Japan. Nor is it enough simply to exhort the peoples of the Third World to avoid the evils of communism. We must not only adopt a strategy to promote the cause of freedom in Eastern Europe but also engage ourselves in alleviating the misery and poverty in developing countries that plays into the hands of Communists and other demagogues.

We can reinvigorate the Western alliance by working together in supporting the cause of positive peaceful change in Eastern Europe. Our European allies today suffer from a kind of historical fatigue. For forty years, they have been on the front line of history. Their role has been defined by a negative mission—stopping further Soviet expansion. This fatigue can be cured by devoting energy to the positive mission of promoting the cause of freedom beyond the Iron Curtain. Holding the line against the Red Army has principally involved sacrifice and risk, but helping the development of pluralism under the nose of the Red Army requires ingenuity and inspiration. A significant start has already been made by the courageous actions of the peoples of Eastern Europe in defying their would-be Communist masters. Their democratic neighbors in the European Community, as well as the United States, should provide the technical advice and economic assistance necessary to ensure that the East Europeans succeed in their ground-breaking efforts to create free market economies and democratic governments. This is a task that will not only enhance Western security but also help to restore its sense of purpose.

This is particularly important for Germany. An active role in overcoming the division of Europe holds the promise not only of overcoming German feelings of guilt over World War II but also of reunifying their own country. In the long run, reunification is inevitable, despite the opposition of the Soviet Union, most of the countries of Western Europe, and even some leaders in the two Germanies. If the German people choose to reunify through a free democratic process, their wishes cannot be ignored. But we must ensure that this comes about as Europe itself unites West with East so that change does not lead to geopolitical instability.

Because of our understandable fascination with devleopments in Eastern Europe, there will be a tendency to put the enormous problems of the Third World on the back burner. This would be a tragic mistake. Instead, we must rededicate ourselves to supporting economic development throughout the developing world. We should do so partly to serve the cause of freedom. It is in the hopeless poverty of Third World slums that the seeds of commu-

310

nism find the most fertile ground. It is becoming fashionable to say that communism has lost its appeal. The message has apparently not yet gotten through to Communists attempting to overthrow governments in El Salvador, Peru, the Philippines, and elsewhere. The four billion people who live in the Third World have massive economic problems. The Communists at least talk about the problems. It is not enough for us to just talk about the Communists. We must help provide these peoples with a better alternative. The best answer to the Communist revolution which promises progress at the price of freedom is a peaceful revolution which generates progress through freedom.

In an era when the failure of communism has become clear even to its most stubborn adherents, gut-level anti-communism is commendable as an instinct but inadequate as a policy. Anti-communism is not a policy. It is a faith—faith in freedom. Most Americans support the faith. They disagree on what policy will best defend and extend the faith. We should debate the policy without questioning the faith of those who disagree with us. The question is not one of loyalty, but of judgment. To develop an effective policy, we must know not just what we are fighting against, but what we are fighting for.

We should assist the Third World not only to oppose communism, but also to promote the cause of freedom and justice. In 1988, while Americans enjoyed an annual per capita income of $15,000, the poorest half of the world's population lived on less than $600 per capita. They will not tolerate and morally we cannot accept that shocking inequality. We should reject the failed foreign-aid policies of the past and the simplistic schemes for transferring money and resources from rich to poor nations. Nor should we subsidize through foreign aid the socialist policies, corruption, or tyranny that plague so many Third World countries. But we must not throw up our hands and give up. Instead, we should find ways to assist the countries of the developing world to educate and train their people, to foster market-based growth, to alleviate the burdens of oppressive foreign debt, and to join us on the road to economic progress.

Appeals to our highest ideals have inspired Americans to support great causes. For a half century, we have poured efforts and resources into building a safer and freer world not only for ourselves but also for others. But we should not rest content. Now that the

Communist threat appears to have diminished, we must not simply withdraw into a satisfied isolationism. For the future, an even greater challenge—helping billions of people in poorer nations earn a chance to share the blessings of freedom and progress—beckons us to devote our best energies to facing it. If we meet this historic challenge, it will not be necessary to ask young Americans to die for freedom. But it will be necessary to ask them to live for it.

Some say that we have done enough, that we have carried the burden too long, that we should let others shoulder the costs of defending freedom and promoting progress. They point out that our European and Japanese allies spend less per capita on defense and therefore can direct more resources to winning the economic competition. While we should insist that others share the burden more equitably, we must recognize that no country can step into our shoes. None possesses the military, economic, and political capabilities of a superpower. Only the United States has the power to ensure the security of the free world.

We should engage in this cause not just for others but for ourselves. De Gaulle once said, "France was never her true self unless she was engaged in a great enterprise." I have always believed this was true of the United States as well. Defending and promoting peace and freedom around the world is a great enterprise. Only by rededicating ourselves to that cause will we remain true to ourselves.

36

GEOPOLITICS

At a dinner in the Kremlin in 1959, Khrushchev was in one of his more mellow moods and was trying to demonstrate how reasonable he was compared with his more doctrinaire colleagues. Pointing down the table at his deputy prime minister, Frol Kozlov, Khrushchev said almost contemptuously, "He is a hopeless Communist."

In foreign policy, it could be said to their credit that Americans are hopeless idealists. They reject the idea of seeking power as an end in itself or of pursuing an imperial role for the United States. They are turned off by European concepts of the balance of power diplomacy. They will not go to war for narrow, selfish interests. They will fight only if convinced that a larger moral cause hangs in the balance.

Americans are uncomfortable with the notion of exercising world power. They believe a truly just cause should succeed on its own and should not need power to back it up. But that is not the way the real world works. A nation can advance a cause, however just, only through the exercise of power, and a statesman can pursue a cause only by constantly balancing the tension between what he wishes to achieve and what he has the power to achieve.

American idealism has produced a foreign policy that swings between two extremes. On the one hand, we are fundamentally isolationist. We were thrust into a position of world leadership only after World War II destroyed the great European powers and Japan. We had no designs on the territory or political independence of other countries. We have never truly accepted the role thrust upon us. If we had a choice, we would ask only to be left alone.

313

On the other hand, when we become engaged in international disputes, we tend to become idealistic crusaders. In both world wars, we charged into battle to advance abstract moral principles rather than to secure concrete, well-defined interests. In the post-war period, we have faltered in defending our interests in morally ambiguous conflicts. When faced with a black-and-white choice between good and evil in the two world wars, we rose to the challenge with unity and all-out dedication to victory. But since then in the gray areas—such as assisting a friendly power that guaranteed only some human rights against the aggression of a hostile power that suppressed all human rights—we have hesitated, foundered, and sometimes failed those who relied on our help.

Such inconsistency has undercut our ability to advance our interests in the world. We will never succeed geopolitically unless we abandon this all-or-nothing idealism. Today, with the rise of a more skillful Soviet leadership under Gorbachev, we face a greater challenge than in the early years of the Cold War when there was a clear choice between freedom and communism. It will put a premium on our ability to analyze the world in hardheaded realistic terms and to forge a strategy to cope with the subtle tactics of the new leader in the Kremlin.

First of all, we must see the world as it is, not as we wish it to be. That is vitally important in assessing the Soviet Union under Gorbachev. He has dazzled the West with his flair for public relations and his talent for crafting appealing, bold proposals. He has dramatically departed from some past Soviet practices, both in style and substance. He has wowed Western publics, who rate him more highly in opinion polls than most of their own politicians. Part of that praise is justified. But we cannot set our geopolitical course by the shifting course of the political winds. Instead, we must understand what changes he has adopted, why he has done so, and how the West should respond.

Gorbachev has launched major initiatives to reform the Soviet political and economic systems. Politically, he has introduced a degree of openness in the Soviet media, legalized the formation of social groups independent of the Communist party, permitted some limited choice in Soviet elections, and eased constraints on the practice of religion. As popular pressures for genuine democracy gathered force, he even promised to permit the emergence of a multiparty system. But until truly free elections are held, his reforms represent little more than crumbs which have fallen from

314

the banquet table. When contrasted to the stultifying repression under his predecessors, however, these changes are breathtaking.

The political reforms Gorbachev has fully implemented so far have been strictly limited. He permitted some competition in the first elections for the Congress of People's Deputies, but two thirds of the delegates, including Gorbachev himself, were chosen through a rigged process. In early 1990, however, Gorbachev took a fateful step in declaring his opposition to the continuation of the Communist Party's monopoly on power and the acceptance of the idea of a multiparty system. By conceding the party's leading role, he has stepped onto a slippery slope. This concession will further encourage the popular forces pressing for genuine democracy. Gorbachev will find no fallback position, no secondary line of defense, that will easily staunch those rising demands for freedom.

Those who question whether Gorbachev will be overthrown by his enemies within the party overlook how ruthlessly this shrewd, tough-minded politician has consolidated his position. He did not rise to the top of the Soviet hierarchy by playing softball. He has removed every other member of the Politburo appointed under Brezhnev, as well as replacing virtually the entire Central Committee and almost all the leaders of the Soviet Republics. Moreover, he has outflanked the party as a whole by creating a separate base of power for himself in the office of the President. He has tried to stay ahead of the popular wave pushing for genuine democracy by backing multiparty elections.

Gorbachev is a high-stakes gambler. He could be risking his political life in a free election. The last time that happened in the Soviet Union was in 1917, when the Bolsheviks got only 25 percent of the vote. After that election, Lenin made the Soviet Union a one-party state. And Gorbachev has to be concerned that in Eastern Europe even reform-minded Communist Party leaders have been driven out of office by the people.

But Gorbachev has enormous self-confidence. He probably believes he could win an election. He knows the Soviet Union cannot survive as a great power without radical reforms. He knows that the Communist Party cannot survive unless it becomes a reforming rather than a status quo party. Consequently, Gorbachev is risking his power to save his reforms rather than risking his reforms by trying to save his power.

———

Economically, Gorbachev has boldly spoken of introducing market forces into the Soviet Union's command economy. He has passed legislation to grant farmers long-term leases, to legalize small, privately owned cooperatives, to increase the independence of factory managers, and to facilitate joint ventures with Western companies. While bold in design, the reforms have been timid in action. Some have resulted in managerial chaos that has forced Gorbachev to back off. Cooperatives are hampered by severe taxes. Factory managers have been brought back into line by central planners. Production quotas have been prolonged or reimposed. He continues to reject large-scale private ownership on ideological grounds. He has also yielded to collectivist habits among the Soviet elite and population, thereby reinforcing central control and thwarting private initiative. Finally, the linchpin of genuine economic change—price reform—has been delayed almost indefinitely.

As a result, perestroika, the economic reforms that have earned Gorbachev plaudits throughout the Western world, have failed to reverse the Soviet economy's quickening slide toward economic collapse. While ten years of economic reforms in China doubled the per capita income of the Chinese people, the Soviet Union's standard of living has actually dropped in the three years since Gorbachev launched perestroika.

Gorbachev has revolutionized the international political landscape. He withdrew Soviet forces from Afghanistan and pressed Cuba and Vietnam to remove their troops from Angola and Cambodia. He unilaterally reduced Soviet armed forces by 500,000 troops, 10,000 tanks, 8,500 artillery pieces, and 800 airplanes, as well as cutting defense spending by 14 percent. In addition, when the peoples of Eastern Europe challenged their Communist governments with massive strikes and demonstrations, he allowed events to take their course, even though this almost inevitably will lead to the toppling of Moscow's client regimes. He in effect repealed the Brezhnev doctrine under which Soviet troops underwrote the irreversibility of the spread of communism. As a result, in the minds of many in the West, the threat represented by the Soviet Union has virtually vanished.

Because Soviet foreign policy has been so rigid and predictable for so long, in the Gorbachev era observers have emphasized what has changed. It is essential that we also focus on what has not changed. Moscow continues to provide $6 billion a year in economic and military aid to Cuba, $4 billion to Afghanistan, $2.5 billion to Vietnam, and $1 billion to Nicaragua. It continues to sell weapons to North Korea and Libya, who along with Iran are the world's major exporters of international terrorism. Even with Gorbachev's cuts, the Soviet Union still spends 20 percent of its GNP on the military, while the United States spends only 6 percent. He has modernized Soviet strategic forces, deploying two mobile ICBMs, an even more accurate model of the land-based SS-18, a new intercontinental bomber, improved missile-carrying submarines, and an upgraded missile defense system. While vociferously denouncing the United States' SDI, he has poured billions into developing his own strategic nuclear defense system.

All in all, many of what we perceive as peaceful gestures may in fact be steps taken as part of a modernization program that only minimally reduces Soviet military capabilities. In fact, as a result of its modernization program, the Soviet Union's military forces, while leaner, are stronger than when Gorbachev came to power five years ago. For the United States to unilaterally reduce its defense forces is like playing Russian roulette. Such reductions should be made only by mutual agreements that ensure stability and reduce the huge Soviet superiority in conventional weapons.

While we should applaud his moves toward creating a more open society and a less repressive political system and toward retracting the Soviet Union's imperial reach, we must be coldly realistic in appraising Gorbachev's motivations. When he came into power, the Soviet Union faced a monumental crisis—a crisis that threatened the future of communism as a political force in the world. Moscow's Communist client-states in the Third World were political liabilities and economic basket cases. Eastern Europe had become a political powderkeg, seething with nationalist unrest exacerbated by economic discontent. Moreover, the failing Soviet economy tottered on the brink of collapse and threatened to undercut the Kremlin's standing as a major world power. Aware that marginal reforms would be doomed to fail, he opted for the big play.

All his actions have been directed toward two geopolitical goals. First, to revive his moribund economy, he wants to gain access to Western capital and technology. He knows his economic reforms cannot succeed without this assistance, and he is willing to pay a geopolitical price to achieve this key objective. Second, he wants

317

to divide his adversaries and to end the political isolation of the Soviet Union. His predecessors had succeeded in uniting all the world's great powers—the United States, Western Europe, Japan, and China—against the Kremlin. His foreign policy actions are largely aimed at loosening the ties of that anti-Soviet bloc.

Gorbachev is seeking not to help us but to help himself. He is acting not out of benevolence but in the pursuit of interest. By reducing the fear of the Soviet Union abroad he has weakened the glue that holds the anti-Soviet alliance together. Domestically, he has adroitly exploited glasnost to isolate and undercut the power of his political opponents. He has also capitalized on his institutional political reforms to outflank the party bureaucracy by enhancing the power of the office of president and contriving an indirect electoral system that guaranteed he would occupy it. Andrei Sakharov observed, Gorbachev's principal political reform has been to concentrate more power in his own hands than any Soviet leader since Stalin.

The hallmark of his "new thinking" in foreign policy has been shrewder tactics, not kinder intentions. In the regional conflicts in Afghanistan, Angola, and Cambodia, he has withdrawn his own troops and his proxy forces but has poured in military and economic assistance to keep his client regimes in power. He has not given up his support for those regimes besieged by anti-Communist freedom fighters. Instead, he has tried to prompt a *total* Western cutoff of support for Afghan, Angola, and Cambodian guerrillas by undertaking a *partial* Soviet disengagement from these conflicts. He may yet offer reasonable terms for political settlements or accept the final defeat of these regimes. But he will not do so unless we impose a price for pursuing his present policies.

Gorbachev's restraint in responding to the popular uprisings in Eastern Europe has won over many skeptics in the West. He has been credited with inspiring and even encouraging the removal of the leaders of the ossified Communist regimes in the region. That explanation misstates reality. In fact, the millions who demonstrated in the streets of the great cities of Eastern Europe were inspired by Western ideals, by the failure of their Communist economic systems, and by the hatred of the puppet regimes that ruled on behalf of Moscow for four decades. The rhetoric of the East European reformers paralleled the ideas of the Declaration of Independence and the preamble of the Constitution, not the discredited theories of Marx and Lenin to which Gorbachev continues to swear fidelity.

But Gorbachev did contribute to the popular upheaval in two ways. First, these peaceful revolutions were the inevitable but unintended consequences of Gorbachev's reforms and rhetoric. By praising democracy and proclaiming the right of all countries to create their own model of socialism, he unintentionally undercut his own satellites. Three years ago I noted in *1999: Victory Without War* that "[h]e might not mean for his rhetoric to be taken literally, but it will be so understood in Eastern Europe." Within just two years, the peoples of Poland, Hungary, East Germany, Bulgaria, Czechoslovakia, and Romania had taken him at his word and broken the back of Communist power in Eastern Europe.

While Gorbachev's rhetoric lit the fires of freedom in Eastern Europe, the reason they spread so fast was the equally explosive revolution in worldwide communication, the most significant technological development of the postwar era. Ideas no longer have to go across borders or under them. Now they go over them, and no ideological SDI can shoot them down. Western radio and television helped create the thirst for more freedom that brought a million people to demonstrate in Tiananmen Square, and they dramatically accelerated developments in Eastern Europe. Its people always knew in their heads that they were falling further and further behind the West, but seeing the wonders of the free world on television made them feel it in their gut. In the Communist revolution in Russia in 1917, the Bolsheviks won when they gained control of the seat of government in Petrograd. In the revolution against the Bolsheviks' heirs in Romania in 1989, the final battle was over control of the TV station in Bucharest.

Second, when popular uprisings threatened the Communist regimes in these countries, Gorbachev declined to enforce the Brezhnev doctrine. In doing so, however, he was pursuing his own interest. He faced an unenviable choice. If he had intervened, the entire region would have exploded in a violent revolutionary upheaval. That, in turn, would have aborted his efforts to improve relations with the West and eliminated any chances Moscow had of gaining access to Western capital and technology to reinvigorate the Soviet economy.

For seventy years after the Bolshevik Revolution, the imperatives of Moscow's foreign and defense policies drove its economic policy. Massive resources were channeled into building up the Soviet armed forces and into propping up the Soviet empire. Under Gorbachev, the imperatives of economic policy have driven his foreign and defense policies. In Eastern Europe, this meant acquiescing to the collapse of Soviet regional domination in order to make a play for a far more important target—the psychological disarmament of Western Europe. Given his domestic economic crisis and need for Western trade and assistance, Gorbachev had a weak hand. He therefore decided to make a virtue of necessity by standing aside as the Eastern European peoples rolled back communism.

The conventional wisdom is that the West has an interest in the success of Gorbachev's reforms. In responding to Gorbachev, however, our concerns should center primarily not on how his reforms affect life inside the Soviet Union but on how his reforms affect our interests outside the Soviet Union. If these changes simply make life better for the Soviet people, we should help him. If they also make life harder for us, we should not.

While Gorbachev has a secure hold on power, four great obstacles could doom his reforms. First, his greatest problem is that he still believes in the fatally flawed tenets of Marxism-Leninism. Rapid, self-sustaining economic growth has occurred only in countries that respect the right of individuals to own private property and that allow unregulated prices and the law of supply and demand to allocate economic resources. No successful halfway house has ever been built between a command economy and a market economy, and Gorbachev has yet to make the decisive intellectual break with his archaic ideology.

Second, he faces powerful opposition from the 19 million *apparatchiks* in the party and state bureaucracies. Their members depend on maintaining the status quo to maintain their privileged status. They cannot build, but they can sabotage.

Third, seventy years of communism have instilled a pervasive egalitarian ethic and a resistance to change in the average Soviet worker. He believes that each should be rewarded equally regardless of his productivity. As one of Gorbachev's top economic advisers put it, "Ideology has become psychology."

Fourth, an explosive political crisis is building inside the Soviet Union. So far Gorbachev's strategy for keeping his empire together has been to keep his hands firmly on the reins of central power while at the same time tolerating more protests against it than most of his predecessors would have done. But as one analyst has noted, allowing the non-Russian nations freedom of protest without being willing to redress their basic grievances is a recipe for revolution. If these nationalist forces are ever unleashed, they will be all the more explosive for having been suppressed for so long. Once demands for autonomy and freedom by non-Russians in the Soviet Union grow more extreme, there could be a conservative backlash of Russian nationalism, and the Soviet Union could well sink into a grim cycle of revolts and crackdowns.

In the end, Gorbachev will probably survive—not because his reforms will succeed, but because he will back away from them. This does not mean that he does not favor reforms. It means that if he is forced to choose between reforms and power, he will choose power.

When we talked in 1987, President Mitterrand argued that it was in the West's interests for Gorbachev to survive and that he could survive only if his reforms succeeded. This, of course, implied that we should assist the Soviet reform effort. I disagree with this reasoning. Gorbachev's reforms will rise and fall according to his ability to institute a market-based system. From the outside, there is little we could do to advance such an outcome.

For the Soviet Union to receive Western assistance, we should insist on six conditions. First, Moscow must establish a free-market economy. Second, Eastern European countries must complete their transition to full independence. Third, NATO and the Warsaw Pact must establish parity in conventional arms. Fourth, the United States and the Soviet Union must conclude a verifiable START agreement ensuring stable nuclear deterrence. Fifth, Gorbachev must cease his aggressive policies in the Third World. Sixth, the Soviet Union must adopt a political order that respects human rights and reflects the wishes of people expressed in free elections.

Until Gorbachev meets these tests, Western assistance to the Soviet Union would be premature. It would be futile to provide aid before the Soviets overhaul their economy. A banker does no favor to the borrower when he makes a bad loan. Such aid would reduce the pressure on the Soviets to reform their economy and to reduce their massive military budget. As Sakharov said not long before his death, "In the absence of radical reforms in the Soviet system, credits and technological aid will only prop up an ailing system and delay the advent of democracy." Moreover, a stronger Soviet economy would be in our interest only if coupled with a less threatening Soviet foreign policy. As long as Gorbachev threatens our interests, particularly in the world's regional conflicts, it is not in our interest to enhance his economic capability to do so. Finally, we must remember that every dollar spent to help a still-Communist Soviet Union would be a dollar taken away from the new non-Communist governments of Eastern Europe.

It has become fashionable in the West to speak of the "end of history." The triumph of Western ideals, the argument runs, means the end of geopolitical competition. Seldom has fashion veered so widely from fact. Our ideals have proven superior, but their geopolitical triumph remains far from complete. For the foreseeable future, we must continue to lead the free world.

Even before *The New York Times* had proclaimed an end to the Cold War, it was difficult for Presidents to build political support for a strong foreign policy. Unless we were involved in a war or some other crisis abroad, polls usually showed people were far more interested in domestic than international issues. This was true even when the Soviet Union was in its highly expansionist phase in the late 1970s. Today, when peace appears to be breaking out all over and the Soviet leader is more popular than the President in Europe and even among Americans with graduate degrees, it will be tempting for even responsible U.S. politicians to give in to Gorbymania. It is not that they necessarily believe that the Soviet Union no longer poses any threat to our interests. It is that they realize it may be impossible to get anyone to believe it and that it might even be political suicide to try.

Americans' tendency to go overboard for Gorbachev is a result of their innate optimism. It is a result of the influence of commentators, columnists, and other opinion leaders who always took the line that the Soviet threat was overstated and are delighted that there is finally a Soviet leader in power who makes their case appear credible. In largest part it is a result of the fact that it is more pleasant to imagine living in a world that is calm and safe rather than one that is fraught with tension and danger.

It is true that much has changed. But much has not. The Soviet Union is still a global superpower with decisive superiority in land-based nuclear weapons and in conventional forces. Its leaders are committed to an ideology that is diametrically opposed to ours. They support regimes around the world that are highly detrimental to our interests. If Gorbachev's reforms grow and thrive—if perestroika succeeds and glasnost leads to political pluralism— then in the twenty-first century we may look across the Bering Strait and see a superpower more like the United States than different. But if they give Gorbachev's faltering Communist system the jolt it needs to begin to catch up with the West, in the next century we may well face a stronger, more confident, more dangerous adversary. Faced with two such radically different possible outcomes, no President can be criticized for hoping for the best—just so long as he plans for the worst.

Objective observers would agree on one thing: Whatever Gorbachev does, he does in the interests of himself and of the Soviet Union. He is neither a saint nor a soft-headed do-gooder; nor should we be. No matter how unpopular it may be in the short term—no matter how vociferously the leading pundits may bemoan "tired Cold War thinking"—the United States must continue to pursue our national interest as aggressively as Gorbachev does his. We need to adopt a comprehensive strategy built on the three pillars of deterrence, competition, and negotiation.

To deter Moscow, we should adopt policies that ensure Soviet leaders will never conclude that they will achieve their objectives through aggression. We must make the cost of challenging our interests so high that it will always exceed their potential gains.

That means maintaining a strong nuclear deterrent. An agreement for total nuclear disarmament is unachievable and undesirable. We could never be certain that Moscow fully complied with the agreement, and we cannot erase mankind's knowledge of how to create nuclear weapons. We cannot sign an agreement abolishing nuclear weapons from the face of the earth because if Kremlin leaders cheated they would control the fate of the earth. Nor will it be possible to build a perfect defense to protect the U.S. population from an all-out nuclear attack. While a partial defense of our nuclear forces makes strategic sense, we should not delude ourselves into thinking we can make nuclear weapons impotent and obsolete.

Security for one nuclear power cannot be based on the insecurity of another nuclear power. Our defense policies must convince Soviet leaders that we will never allow them to attain a significant advantage in the most accurate and powerful nuclear weapons systems. Moscow will then recognize that both sides have a common interest in reducing the billions of dollars poured into new generations of nuclear weapons. If we demonstrate the will to assure our security through a strong defense, we can negotiate arms reduction agreements that will both establish mutual security and enhance strategic stability.

Beyond deterrence, the United States must adopt policies to

compete with the Soviet Union across the board. We cannot, however, afford to protect every square yard of the free world. Such a policy would quickly overextend our limited resources.

Instead, we should carefully distinguish among our vital, critical, and peripheral geopolitical interests. Only Western Europe, Japan, the Persian Gulf, Mexico, and Canada represent truly vital American interests. Other areas, such as Central America and South Korea, are critical interests because their security directly impacts those vital countries and regions. Most countries in other parts of the world represent peripheral interests, the security of which only distantly affects our vital and critical interests. In competing with Moscow, the key is to calibrate the level of our commitment in a conflict to the importance of the interests at stake.

We should, however, never tip off our adversaries about how far we might go in defending our peripheral interests. Our unpredictability is one of our strongest assets. We must recognize that renouncing the use of force invites the use of force by the other side. If we keep our hand hidden, our adversaries must always take into account the chance that we might trump theirs with the use of force. In the real world it is not just the existence of power but the nagging fear that it might be used which deters a potential aggressor. This is not a gamble most are willing to take, and therefore it strengthens our deterrent and increases our leverage.

In developing our own policy, we should try to understand what will affect the policy of our opponents. What would affect us might not affect him. When he is playing chess, we cannot counter him by playing poker. In competing with Moscow, we will at times find it necessary to cooperate with allies and friends who do not live up to our democratic standards. In a perfect world, we would never resort to the use of military force or align ourselves with countries with flawed human rights records. But the world is not perfect. As Paul Johnson observed, "The essence of geopolitics is to be able to distinguish between different degrees of evil." If Britain and France had accepted the lesser evil of fighting to prevent Hitler's reoccupation of the Rhineland, they would have averted the greater evil of World War II. If the United States had provided adequate military aid to the admittedly imperfect governments of Cambodia and South Vietnam, it could have prevented the horrors of the Cambodian holocaust and the tragic plight of the Vietnamese boat people.

We must also be mature enough as a world power to accept the fact that no one wins all the time. Our setback in Vietnam paralyzed our political will, and we consequently suffered further losses in Angola, the Horn of Africa, and Nicaragua. As a nation, we must learn that in geopolitics the game never ends. There is no point at which all sides cash in their chips. No victory is ever permanent and no defeat irredeemable. A triumph or a loss marks only a shift into a new phase of the contest. To compete with Moscow, we need to develop the resilience to bounce back after the reversals that great powers inevitably suffer from time to time.

If we deter the Kremlin leaders, we will be in a position to negotiate with them. If we compete effectively with them, they will *want* to negotiate. While our strategy should include all three elements—deterrence, competition, and negotiation—a difference exists among them. We can successfully deter and compete with Moscow without negotiations, but we cannot successfully negotiate without effective American policies for deterrence and competition.

Before sitting down with the Soviets, we should answer clearly in our own minds three key questions. First, what do we want to get from the Soviets? Negotiations per se do not serve our interests. Only when they advance specific strategic goals do they advance our cause. Second, what are we willing to give up to get what we want? Kremlin leaders are neither philanthropists nor fools. They will demand something in return for everything they give up. Third, what moves can we take to put political pressure on Soviet leaders to make the deal that we want at the price we want to pay? What happens across the negotiating table partly depends on what occurs outside the conference room. If we strengthen our competitive position—for example, in the arms balance or in a regional crisis—we automatically strengthen our negotiating position.

How we structure and approach talks with Moscow will largely determine our success in them. Gorbachev will take us to the cleaners in negotiations unless we use the tactic of linkage. The two sides do not have the same degree of interest in progress on all issues. Moscow has a greater interest in some areas, such as trade, and the United States has a greater interest in others, such as conventional arms control. If we let him do so, Gorbachev will gladly negotiate solely on the former. If we acquiesce to that unbalanced approach—if we fail to link the two sets of issues—he will dominate the negotiating agenda, conclude agreements on his top priorities, and defer resolution of our issues to the indefinite future.

In negotiating with the Kremlin, we should observe three tactical principles. First, no agreement is better than a bad agreement. A President must always resist the bureaucratic and political pressures to conclude a deal at any price and must be willing to walk away from a pending agreement if the terms fail to measure up. Second, never give up anything unless you receive something in return. Making concessions to demonstrate goodwill seldom prompts reciprocal generosity on the part of Moscow. Its negotiators simply pocket such offerings and immediately come back for more. Third, never negotiate with a deadline. No single President will ever resolve all East-West issues, and no single issue will ever be resolved for all time by any President. Impatience leads to imprudence. A President operating against a four-year election cycle is no match for a Soviet leader like Gorbachev negotiating against a twenty-five-year deadline.

A great power can neither compete effectively against nor negotiate successfully with its adversaries unless it resorts to secrecy. Americans have traditionally been ambivalent about covert operations and secret negotiations. Until we learn to accept these as instruments of power, we will be severely handicapped in the geopolitical contest with Moscow.

Covert operations per se are neither bad nor good. They are not an end in themselves but rather a means to an end. Secrecy in these cases is bad only when the end is bad. Often covert action is the only means available to achieve an important objective. When the Soviet Union finally withdrew its forces from Afghanistan, the world applauded. But that would not have happened without the covert funding and support provided to the anti-Communist Afghan resistance.

The problem is that failed covert operations typically become public while successful ones usually remain secret. Only if a covert operation is kept secret can it succeed. Once made public, it usually fails. Those who oppose all covert operations argue that in the age of modern communications publicity cannot be avoided. But scores of such operations have gone off without a hitch and have provided major contributions to overall American foreign policy. Therefore, when a secret operation fails because of ineptitude in execution, we should improve the execution, not abandon the tactic.

I once endorsed Woodrow Wilson's idealistic maxim—"open

covenants openly arrived at." It was a mistake. Without negotiations in secret, there will be few agreements to sign in public. In some cases, it is simply the only way to conduct the business of international politics. Without secret negotiations we would not have been able to achieve the rapprochement with China, the arms control treaties with the Soviet Union in 1972, and the peace agreement with North Vietnam in 1973.

Our delicate negotiations with China would have collapsed if my preliminary diplomatic messages to Chou En-lai or Henry Kissinger's trip to Beijing in 1971 had become public. Opponents of the new relationship in both countries would have sabotaged our moves toward a rapprochement. In fact, our difficulty in keeping secrets almost cut short our initiative. After an American gossip columnist reported a conversation which had taken place in a top-secret National Security Council meeting regarding the Indo-Pakistan War in 1971, Chou understandably asked if he could speak candidly with us given the danger of leaks. Fortunately, he accepted our reassurances.

In the negotiations that led to the Anti-Ballistic Missile Treaty of 1972, we worked at two levels. In Helsinki, formal talks were conducted under the scrutiny of the world press. But in the White House Map Room, secret discussions between Kissinger and Soviet Ambassador Dobrynin took place. Not surprisingly, the major breakthroughs occurred in the latter. It was there that the two sides could exchange frank views, test possible compromise formulas, and overcome critical bottlenecks. Ironically, what had been the war room in the Roosevelt administration became in effect the peace room in the Nixon administration.

When I took office, I continued the Paris peace negotiations begun under the Johnson administration. But for two years they made absolutely no progress. North Vietnamese officials simply used them as a forum for their cynical propaganda assaults. It was only after I initiated secret talks with Hanoi—and backed them up with strong military actions—that real substantive progress began to be made. These negotiations became the basis for the public talks which, coupled with the military pressure put on Hanoi in May and December 1972, produced the Paris Peace Accords of 1973.

While we need to master the use of these geopolitical instruments, we must recognize that in the years ahead we will be operating on radically different geopolitical terrain. We live in a revolutionary era—one with the potential for change as turbulent as occurred in the decades after the French Revolution. The crisis of communism holds the possibility for panoramic geopolitical change. Over the next twenty years, every Communist regime in the world will see itself shaken to its foundation by popular forces demanding economic and political reform.

In Chinese, the term "crisis" is depicted by combining the characters of two other words: "danger" and "opportunity." For the free world, the crisis in the Communist world presents a similar paradox of possibilities. As turbulent change rocks individual Communist countries—as happened in China in mid-1989—we face difficult choices in terms of adjusting our economic and political ties. As idealists, Americans are perpetually tempted by the policy of imposing economic sanctions on all Communist regimes, particularly when they crack down on pro-democratic forces. In order to seize the opportunities and avoid the dangers inherent in the crisis of communism, we must distinguish between those Communist regimes that threaten our security interests, like the Soviet Union, Cuba, and Nicaragua, and those that pose no such threat, like China and Yugoslavia. When confronting a hostile Communist power, sanctions serve a limited but useful *geopolitical* purpose. While alone they will seldom reverse aggressive *external* policies, they will exact a cost for them and limit the resources available to pursue them. But sanctions will almost never succeed in altering the *domestic* policies of a hostile Communist state. Decades of trade sanctions against the Soviet Union, Cuba, and Nicaragua have not lessened the repressiveness of their Communist rule.

We must recognize that after a Communist regime cracks down on pro-democracy forces we seldom can do much to undo those actions. While Communist regimes are not good at winning the support of their people, they are good at ruthlessly suppressing those who oppose their rule. We should publicly condemn these violations of human rights, but we must be pragmatic when we decide whether or not to impose economic or political sanctions. We have to assess whether such an action serves our geopolitical interests and whether it has a reasonable chance of altering the Communist regime's policies.

Geopolitically, we should base our policies toward a country primarily on what its government does outside, not inside, its borders. In World War II, we allied ourselves with Stalin—probably the most brutal tyrant of the century—in order to defeat the aggressive regime of Hitler. In establishing relations with Communist China in 1972, we cooperated with Mao's totalitarian government, which was more repressive than Brezhnev's regime in the Soviet Union, to prevent Soviet hegemony in Asia. We live in a world in which most states fail to fully respect the human rights of their peoples. We would undercut our position in the world—and thereby compromise our capability to promote the cause of freedom in the long term—if we restricted ourselves to cooperating only with those countries that meet our standards of democracy.

In Poland, the economic sanctions we imposed after the imposition of martial law in 1981 were an important factor in ultimately forcing the Communist regime to implement reforms, including the partially free elections that propelled Solidarity into power. Our sanctions closed off the option of seeking foreign assistance or credits to cope with Poland's deep economic crisis, thereby leaving the Communists with the dilemma of risking mass unrest or accepting a political compromise with Polish society. In China the case is different. Contact with the West represents a principal impetus for reform. There would have been no Tiananmen Square demonstrations if it had not been for China's opening to the West in 1972. Isolating China with sanctions will close off a major stimulus for the economic reforms that have already improved the lives of the Chinese people and for long-term political change that will lessen the repressiveness of the regime's rule.

There is no way we can resolve our differences on the tragic events of Tiananmen Square. But it would compound the tragedy if we allowed them to damage permanently a relationship that has been so beneficial to the Chinese people, the American people, and the cause of peace and progress in Asia. We must keep these events in perspective. Great as our differences are over what happened on June 4, 1989, our differences were infinitely greater when we established relations with the PRC in 1972 after twenty-three years of no communication whatever. We disagreed with the Chinese on Vietnam, on Korea, on Japan, on Taiwan, and on philosophy. China was still in the final throes of the Cultural Revolution, during which millions had died in an ideological crackdown far more brutal than what happened last year. But we recognized then that while we had irreconcilable differences, we had one overriding common interest which brought us together— the need to develop a common policy to deter an aggressive and expansionist Soviet Union which threatened us both.

Even if we assume that the Cold War is over and that the Soviet

Union no longer represents a major threat to either of us—a conclusion, incidentally, that every Chinese leader I met rejects—we
still have a strong strategic interest in restoring a good relationship
with the PRC. China is a nuclear power. Without Chinese cooperation, we cannot have an effective policy of non-proliferation of
nuclear weapons and will have no leverage at all in trying to prevent the sale of missiles and other weapons to countries in trouble
spots like the Middle East. Given Japan's status as an economic
superpower and its potential to become a military and political
superpower, a strong, stable China with close ties to the United
States is essential to balance the power of Japan and the Soviet
Union in East Asia. China also has an indispensable role to play in
the maintenance of peace and stability in the Asia-Pacific region,
particularly on the Korean peninsula.

Change in revolutionary times involves turbulence. No easy formula exists for maintaining peace and promoting freedom. No
Communist regime will step aside for more democratic government
without struggle. No struggle for freedom will succeed instantly,
or without occasional, and sometimes bloody, reversals. And no
successful transition to more democratic government automatically solves the deep social and economic problems afflicting countries under communism. For example, we must recognize that
Poland's Communist leaders allowed non-Communists to form a
government not simply because they lost an election but because
they probably believed that Poland's economic problems were insoluble. If they prove right, their anti-Communist opponents will
be discredited. We and our allies in the West should do everything
possible to prove that they were wrong. However appealing the
romance of revolution may be, we must recognize that steady,
incremental change holds the greatest promise for institutional-
ized, enduring change.

Americans need to develop a geopolitical tradition. We should
accept our role as a great power and learn to use that power not
only to defend our interests but also to advance the cause of freedom. If we bow out of world affairs—if we give in to our isolationist impulse—we will leave the field open for those with far less
benevolent intentions than ours. If we cast aside realism—if we
view the world through rose-colored glasses or if we indulge in
idealistic crusades—we will quickly become disillusioned and will
compromise the very ideals we value so highly.

37

DECISIONS

A President makes hundreds of difficult decisions. They are the only kind that should reach his desk. Only a few mean life or death for individuals or the nation; most of these are in foreign policy. I have often said that the American economy is so strong it would take a genius to wreck it. But even a small mistake in foreign policy could bring destruction to the United States and even to the world. That is why a President's major foreign-policy decisions require his first-priority attention and a different kind of decision-making process.

A case might be made for government by consensus in domestic policy. It will not work in foreign policy. A President is elected to lead. Government by consensus is not leadership; it is followship, designed to produce outcomes not that are right but that most people will support. The problem is that sometimes the right decision is the least popular.

Major foreign-policy decisions should never be decided by votes in Cabinet or even the National Security Council. I do not mean to suggest that meetings do not serve a useful purpose. They allow a President to try out his ideas on his most trusted associates, to probe for their ideas, and, most important, to enlist their support for his decision once it is made, since many of them will be out on the firing line. The most difficult situations arise when a President must act alone without prior consultation with his Cabinet or even his National Security Council. In some cases, however, a President must do just that.

My six major foreign-policy decisions as President illustrate some of these problems.

My most important foreign-policy decision was the opening to

331

China. I made the decision to move in that direction before I became President, and my first directive to my national security adviser was to begin the initiative. Contrary to the conventional wisdom, my primary motive was not to enlist China's aid in ending the war in Vietnam or to play the so-called China card against the Soviet Union. If there had been no Vietnam War and if our relations with the Soviet Union had been friendly, I still would have moved to end China's isolation. To have a billion of the world's most able people permanently aligned against us was unacceptable.

For over two years, Henry Kissinger and I explored the initiative on a top-secret basis. Only Secretary of State Bill Rogers was informed in advance of Kissinger's first secret trip to Beijing in 1971. We never mentioned the China initiative in a Cabinet or an NSC meeting. We did not inform Congress or any of our allies.

Since the initiative proved to be so popular, why the paranoia about secrecy? We knew that without secrecy, we would fail. A leak would have given opponents of better relations in both countries an excuse to blow the initiative out of the water. Our secret dealings ran an equally great risk. If they had failed, we would have been subject to intense criticism for non-consultation, just as Ronald Reagan was when his plans to free the Beirut hostages failed. But because we knew that the only way the initiative would succeed would be by not consulting, we considered the gamble justified. The Iran-contra debacle has made secrecy in foreign policy more unpopular than ever, especially with the Congress, which wants more power over foreign policy, and the media, which never like things they cannot report about. It is true that only under extraordinary circumstances should a President undertake a major foreign-policy initiative in total secrecy. But those who say he should never do so are essentially saying that opening better relations with China after twenty-two years of no communication was not worth two years of secrecy.

My most significant foreign-policy speech was on November 3, 1969. It followed a major Presidential decision about the war in Vietnam. When I took office in January 1969, there were 550,000 troops in Vietnam. During the campaign I had pledged to end our involvement in a way that was consistent with our interests. Despite the fact that as a first step toward achieving that goal I had begun to withdraw troops from Vietnam, the anti-war movement launched massive protests in Washington and other major cities calling for immediate, total withdrawal. Reports in the media indicated that a majority of Americans supported that goal. It was a tough choice. The Cabinet and the Republican leaders in Congress were split. As one of my supporters bluntly put it, "You can withdraw our troops now and put the blame for whatever happens on Kennedy and Johnson, who sent them there. If you continue your policy, it will become Nixon's war."

The blame-the-Democrats option was certainly the most attractive politically. Bringing the troops home en masse and sacrificing Saigon to the Soviet-backed North Vietnamese would have earned me high praise in newspaper editorials, which would have pronounced that I had evidently "grown" from the anti-Communist warrior I had been in the 1950s. For bringing "peace" by accepting Communist domination of Indochina, I might even have won the Nobel Peace Prize. More important, I would have had a better chance to unite the country behind the other initiatives I contemplated in domestic and foreign policy—assuming that the leaders in Moscow and Beijing would have put stock in the word of a President who let his nation's friends go down the tubes.

Against my own political interests, I believed it was in America's interests to preserve South Vietnam against Communist aggression. But if I were to make Vietnam "Nixon's war," I would not have had the political support I needed to give my policies of troop withdrawals and Vietnamization a chance to work. Instead, I had to make it *America's* war, something no President had yet attempted to do. A leader cannot continue a policy if the majority of the people oppose it. He can follow the polls—or he can try to change them. The goal of my November 3 speech was to make a case for continued American sacrifices in Vietnam directly to the people who were being asked to make those sacrifices. It was successful. The silent majority spoke, and I was able to continue the policies that culminated in the Paris Peace Accords of January 27, 1973.

My most controversial foreign-policy decision was to order an attack in April 1970 on sanctuaries in Cambodia from which the North Vietnamese were launching hit-and-run attacks on our troops and jeopardizing our withdrawal program. The Joint Chiefs of Staff unanimously urged elimination of these sanctuaries in order to protect the lives of our forces and those of our South Vietnamese allies.

The initial attack on two of the major sanctuaries accomplished its objective. At a Pentagon briefing, I noticed that the map showed four additional Communist sanctuaries. I asked if we could also eliminate them. The military officials answered that there was no question about our ability to do so militarily. But in view of the sharp public protest against the initial action, they felt continuing the attacks would be more than the traffic would bear. Since this was a political and not a military decision, I took the responsibility of ordering an attack on all of the sanctuaries. I made the point that we would get as much blame for taking out two as for taking out six. The operation was completely successful. The Communists dropped their plans for another offensive that year, thousands of American and allied lives were saved, and our withdrawal program went forward on schedule. Ironically, anti-war critics still label the Cambodian incursions, which saved lives and reduced the Communists' ability to continue their attacks on our forces, an "expansion" of the war.

My most difficult foreign-policy decision was on May 8, 1972. In just three weeks I was scheduled to go to Moscow for my first summit meeting with Brezhnev. The North Vietnamese, supplied with Soviet tanks and guns, launched a massive attack on our allies in South Vietnam. The Joint Chiefs advised me that the only way to stop it was to bomb military targets in Hanoi and to mine Haiphong Harbor. There were no good options. If we bombed, most of the Soviet experts at the State Department and CIA were convinced the Soviets would cancel the summit. If we did not bomb, there was the risk the Communists would overwhelm our allies in the South. The choice was stark: If we bombed, we would lose the summit. If we did not, we could lose the war.

The Cabinet was split. Most felt that developing a new, more peaceful relationship with the Soviet Union was more important than anything that might happen in Vietnam. Ironically, it was the Secretary of the Treasury who expressed the case for the other side in the strongest possible terms. John Connally brought to that post experience in another field as well, since he had once served as Secretary of the Navy. His message was blunt and uncompromising: "The President can lose the summit and survive. He cannot lose this war. He should order the attack and cram it down their throats. And I don't think they will cancel the summit."

I was not sure about the last point, but I knew that it would be unacceptable for me to be toasting peace with Brezhnev in Moscow while Soviet tanks carrying North Vietnamese troops were rolling into Saigon. I informed the Cabinet of my decision in a stormy meeting. Most had reservations, but all eventually supported me. The operation was totally successful. Backed by our air and sea attacks, the South Vietnamese Army stopped the North

Vietnamese invasion on the ground. The summit went forward, and we negotiated the first major nuclear arms control treaty in history. Rather than turning them off, our strong action had gained respect from the Kremlin leaders.

My loneliest decision was on December 13, 1972. After agreeing before the election to peace terms that we and Saigon considered acceptable, the North Vietnamese backed off. They bogged down the peace negotiations in a last-minute filibuster. I was faced with a painful decision. We had just won a landslide victory at the polls. People thought the war was over. All our combat troops had been withdrawn. We were suffering no casualties. If the peace negotiations broke down, the war would resume. We had to send a strong message, both to reassure our allies and give a warning to our enemies. After discussions with my advisers, I reluctantly concluded that the only way to break the logjam was to bomb military targets in Hanoi with B-52s. There was a huge public outcry. We were falsely charged with causing thousands of civilian casualties and with indiscriminate bombing of hospitals and other non-military targets. I received very few messages of support. The one I appreciated the most was from Governor Ronald Reagan, who considered some of the viciously critical and totally inaccurate media commentaries to be virtually treasonable.

The operation accomplished its objective. The North Vietnamese came back to the bargaining table, and we were able to negotiate the Paris Peace Accords on terms we considered acceptable. While the media's hysterical exaggerations prevented many people from understanding the limited scope of the bombing and appreciating the persuasive impact it had on the North Vietnamese, stories I heard from our returning prisoners of war convinced me that my message had been received loud and clear where it counted. For years our POWs had been abused, starved, and tortured by their captors in the prison camps around Hanoi. But when our B-52s began to drop their bombs on North Vietnam's military installations around Hanoi in December 1972, the POWs said that suddenly they had kinder, gentler guards and fuller plates at dinner time. As one ex-prisoner told me, "We knew we were finally going home."

My last major foreign-policy decision was on October 12, 1973. Egyptian and Syrian troops had attacked Israel on Yom Kippur, the Jews' holiest day. After some initial Arab successes, the Israelis turned the tide. The Soviets countered by airlifting arms to their Egyptian and Syrian allies. Golda Meir sent me a desperate message requesting an airlift of arms to Israel. Her request created a firestorm of bureaucratic infighting within the administration. The Arabs had already imposed an oil embargo against us, and many felt that sending additional arms to Israel would do irreparable damage to our relations with the countries in the oil-rich Arab world. The Defense Department finally agreed on a proposal for sending three C-5A planeloads of arms to Israel. When Kissinger submitted the proposal, I asked, "How many C-5As do we have?" He answered, "About thirty." I asked, "Why send only three?" The reply was that three was the maximum the Pentagon felt the political situation could bear.

I told Kissinger that I would take responsibility for the politics. I knew we would take no more heat for sending thirty than sending three. "Use every one we have," I said. "Tell them to send everything that can fly." Our 550-mission airlift, which was far bigger than the Berlin airlift of 1948–49, helped the Israelis prevail and set the stage for Henry Kissinger's successful shuttle diplomacy, which produced mutual withdrawal agreements on both fronts.

No academic think tank will ever come up with a process for Presidential decision making in foreign policy that fits every contingency. Probably the best advice they could give would be for a President to get all options in writing so that at the outset he can eliminate half-baked schemes that haven't been thought through. Except when extraordinary circumstances require a different approach, he should then consult with his advisers, the NSC, the Cabinet, and top legislative leaders. He then should take the time to make the final decision by himself. Once that decision is made, he should not look back but should see it through to the end.

Whether the result is triumph or tragedy, the final responsibility must rest with the top man. He will only be able to bear the brunt of defeat if he knows in his heart he has made a careful and correct decision. Eisenhower never criticized Kennedy publicly over his decision in the Bay of Pigs disaster to cancel the second air strike. But when some observers tried to absolve Kennedy of responsibility by claiming he was only carrying out Eisenhower's plan, he hit the ceiling. He told me privately, "I would never have approved a plan without adequate air cover." A President should always have in mind Winston Churchill's advice in *The World Crisis,* "Having gone to war, it is vain to shrink from facing the hazards inseparable from it."

38

WAR

A day did not pass during my years in the White House that I did not hate the war in Vietnam. I hated it when I read the casualty reports each morning and when I wrote letters of consolation to the next of kin or tried to express my sympathy to them in Christmas-season telephone calls. I hated it when I had to make decisions ordering brave young men into battles in which I knew many would lose their lives. I hated it when I met with the courageous families of men who were prisoners of war or missing in action and tried to assure them that we were doing everything possible to bring the war to an honorable end.

I hated the Vietnam War because war causes such tremendous human suffering. Our goals in Indochina—preventing Hanoi's totalitarian Communist regime from conquering the free countries of Indochina and protecting U.S. interests in the region—were worthy and honorable. I would have done anything to achieve them by peaceful means. But no such options were available. North Vietnam's indirect and direct aggression against its non-Communist neighbors presented the United States with a stark choice: either oppose the Communists militarily or abandon our friends to Hanoi's brutal rule. I believed that it was imperative both morally and strategically to stand behind our commitments to help the free countries of Indochina. But that did not lessen the burden I felt from leading our nation in war.

All wartime Presidents have suffered under this weight. It is a total misconception to think of American leaders coldly sending military forces into combat as easily as a chess player trades pawns in an opening gambit. World War I and World War II drained the life out of Presidents Woodrow Wilson and Franklin Roosevelt.

337

Presidents Harry Truman and Lyndon Johnson were destroyed politically, and in Johnson's case spiritually as well, by their failures to prevail in Korea and Vietnam. No American commander-in-chief has ever taken lightly the decision to commit troops to combat. Only after exhausting all other options and after soul-searching reflection have Presidents taken the country into war.

What sustains a nation, and its leaders, in war is the nobility of the goals at stake. As B. H. Liddell Hart has noted, "The object in war is to attain a better peace." In Vietnam, the United States sought to prevent North Vietnam from setting a precedent of successful aggression against its neighbors and to protect the peoples of Indochina from the scourge of communism, which had already ruined the lives of hundreds of millions of people from Eastern Europe to mainland China.

Since the Vietnam War, the American people have been understandably reluctant to support the use of force to protect our friends and allies. But to play the role of a great power, and to serve the cause of freedom in the world, we must understand the proper conditions under which the United States should employ its vast military power.

Some say that we should renounce the use of force and that, if we do so, others will follow our example. We tried that in Korea. When the Truman administration publicly declared that the perimeter of American security interests in the Far East excluded any part of the Korean Peninsula, the Soviets, Chinese, and North Koreans interpreted this as a green light for aggression. We paid a price of 54,000 American lives for that naivete. Renouncing the use of force simply invites the use of force by aggressive powers. In an imperfect world like ours—in which aggressors still exist—it is naive and dangerous to foreswear war in order to secure peace.

In judging whether to use military force in a specific case, we must test the facts against three criteria—prudence, feasibility, and morality.

Prudence requires that we employ military force only when critical or vital American interests are at stake. Our strong tradition of idealism drives many Americans toward extreme views about how far we should go in promoting our beliefs in the world. In his inaugural address in 1961, President Kennedy proclaimed that the United States should use its military forces "to support any friend and oppose any foe to assure the success of liberty." This was good rhetoric, but it was bad policy. As Frederick the Great warned, "He who attempts to defend everywhere defends noth-

ing.'' No country has enough power to make an open-ended commitment to promoting its ideas around the world by any and all means necessary. A keen sense of geopolitical strategy must guide us in making military commitments and alliances. Strategy requires making choices, and making intelligent choices requires setting clear priorities. Our priorities should be guided, not by our emotions but by a calculation of our interests.

Those who argue that force should be used only as a last resort make the opposite mistake. Our goal should be never to use force unnecessarily. But sometimes employing force early against an aggressor's challenges will serve us better in the long run. Maintaining the capability and demonstrating the will to use force even as a first resort when our interests are threatened reduces the possibility of having to use force as a last resort when the risk of casualties would be far greater. As Winston Churchill pointed out, even World War II was in a sense an ''unnecessary war,'' for it could have been prevented by timely action against Hitler when Germany attacked its smaller neighbors.

We must establish a prudent balance between these views on a case-by-case basis. In each conflict, we should realistically assess the importance of our interests at stake, the nature of the threat to those interests, and the best way to defend our position. When our interests are peripheral, we should seldom commit U.S. forces directly. But when we have critical or vital interests at risk, we must be prepared to make a strong commitment. While we should look for ways to prevail short of employing force, we must back that up with a willingness to use force if necessary.

In Vietnam, we sought to defend our critical interests in Southeast Asia. First of all, we wanted to prevent Moscow from gaining a foothold along the vital sealanes connecting the Persian Gulf and Indian Ocean to the Pacific, through which Japan ships almost all of its oil imports. When Hanoi prevailed in 1975, Moscow did not wait long before setting up major naval bases in Cam Ranh Bay and Danang. We also wanted to stop North Vietnam's expansionism, which threatened not only South Vietnam but also the rest of Indochina, and to maintain the credibility of our international commitments. After its victory, our fears were confirmed when the Vietnamese Communists quickly took over Cambodia and Laos and overtly threatened Thailand.

Even so, we attained part of our goal. We preserved the freedom of our friends and allies for more than a decade. More important, by holding off the North Vietnamese until the mid-1970s, the region's developing countries—some of which became spectacular economic successes—won valuable time to consolidate their own non-Communist governments. In his new book *Make for the Hills,* Sir Robert Thompson writes that Singapore's Lee Kwan Yew told him "American involvement in Vietnam had given Southeast Asia ten years breathing space to put its act together."

Feasibility requires that we employ our military forces only when their assigned tasks are properly defined military missions and when their capabilities match their objectives. While this may sound trite, political leaders have often deployed troops to achieve goals not suitable for their combat forces.

A recent example was the U.S. intervention in Lebanon in 1982. President Reagan's original intention was to send in our troops as part of a multi-national peacekeeping force after massacres took place in two Palestinian refugee camps. Our forces were suitable for that task. But when they became entangled in Lebanon's factional warfare, the administration declared that our troops could not be pulled out because they represented our leverage to achieve a political settlement—a task that our contingent was hopelessly undersized to achieve. It took the loss of two hundred thirty-nine Marines in a suicide bombing attack of their headquarters for the administration to recognize its grave mistake. President Eisenhower did not make this mistake when confronted with a similar situation in Lebanon in 1958. He sent in a force of 14,300 and thereby secured a peaceful settlement. In that entire operation, only four men died. Eisenhower once described his military strategy to me in this way: "When the enemy holds a hill with one battalion, give me two battalions and I will take it, but with heavy casualties. Give me a division and I will take it without a fight."

In retrospect, we could have adopted a more prudent and militarily feasible strategy in Vietnam. Under the Kennedy and Johnson administrations, our forces did not have a well-defined military mission. They treated the conflict basically as a civil war within South Vietnam that could be quelled by suppressing the Communist guerrillas and promoting economic progress in South Vietnam, while in reality the guerrillas were simply one of North Vietnam's tactics for seeking to conquer Saigon. As a result, the United States deployed its forces to fight the insurgents in the South, while leaving the enemy's source of men and supplies to the north largely unchecked. This policy put us on a hopeless treadmill. The North Vietnamese could fight such a conflict for decades, while the patience of the American people was certain to wear thin within a few years.

We would have been better off to have limited our involvement to interdicting the flow of troops and arms from North Vietnam into South Vietnam and to training and supplying Saigon's forces to fight the ground war. But when the Kennedy administration destabilized South Vietnam by conspiring in a coup to overthrow the government of South Vietnam, which led to the murder of President Ngo Dinh Diem, the resulting political and military chaos forced the Johnson administration to intervene massively to prevent defeat. When I took office in 1969, I tried to redirect our approach by attacking the Communist staging bases and supply lines in Cambodia and Laos, bombing and mining the harbor through which North Vietnam received supplies from the Soviet Union, bombing North Vietnam's rail links to China, and undertaking a program to train and equip the South Vietnamese to take over the fighting from American troops. These steps enabled us to wind down our involvement in war.

No one would dispute the idea that morality should guide our decision about whether or not to go to war in a specific case. What this means is that the political end and the military means must be just and that the conflict itself must be winnable. Our cause must be moral. Our strategy and tactics must be to restrict the suffering caused to civilians. And our effort must stand a chance of succeeding.

In the Vietnam War, the morality of our involvement became the central issue in the public debate. Anti-war activists argued that our involvement simply propped up corrupt and repressive governments in South Vietnam and Cambodia and that the peoples of these countries would be better off if we withdrew unconditionally and disengaged completely. While some actively supported the Communist side—as evident by the parading of Vietcong flags at anti-war rallies—most simply felt that our allies were not worth defending.

While our friends and allies did not measure up perfectly against our standards of democracy, any doubts about the justice of our cause should have been removed by what has happened since we left. When the Communist Khmer Rouge came to power in Cambodia, they killed or starved to death 2 million people. In Vietnam, the Communists killed tens of thousands and 600,000 South Vietnamese perished in the South China Sea as they fled their country in anything that would float. The killing fields of Cambodia and the boat people and "reeducation" camps of Vietnam were exactly what we had been fighting to avoid. It is no exaggeration to say that fewer people were killed during the anti-Communist war than during the Communist peace.

Some former anti-war activists have claimed that they did not know that such barbarism would follow a Communist victory. If so, theirs was a kind of willful ignorance. It was no secret that the Communists killed over 50,000 civilians after taking power in North Vietnam in 1954, that the Vietcong assassinated over 35,000 local non-Communist government officials and employed terror tactics against South Vietnamese civilians, and that the Communist forces killed 3,000 civilians, burying some alive and making others dig their own graves before being gunned down, during the month-long Communist occupation of the city of Hue in 1968.

Those who opposed our involvement in Vietnam also argued that our tactics indiscriminately killed civilians. In fact, our forces operated under strict rules of engagement designed to prevent such casualties. Many American bomber pilots were shot down, ending up dead or as POWs, because their paths across North Vietnam were chosen to minimize the risk of civilian casualties. In the two weeks of intense bombing in December 1972, only 1,500 civilians —according to Hanoi's own count—were killed, compared with over 35,000 civilians killed in one night of fire-bombing of Dresden in World War II. Civilians accounted for a much smaller proportion of casualties in the Vietnam War than they did in either World War II or the Korean War.

In Indochina, we opposed the aggression of a brutal totalitarian regime, and we did so in ways that sought to minimize civilian casualties. Today, after the horrors of the Cambodian holocaust and the Vietnamese exodus, a conclusive moral judgment can be rendered on our intervention in Vietnam. As Ronald Reagan courageously declared in the 1980 campaign, ours was a noble cause.

Since the fall of Indochina, those who challenged the morality of our cause have fallen back to the argument that the war was unwinnable. They have argued that the South Vietnamese were ineffective fighters and that therefore the collapse of the country in 1975 in the face of North Vietnam's disciplined invasion force was inevitable. Since our policy protracted an unwinnable war, they continued, it caused unnecessary suffering and was immoral.

This point of view clashes with the historical facts. It makes facile assumptions about historical inevitability. Because an event turned out a certain way, that does not mean that it had to happen that way. By the time of our final withdrawal, we had put our allies in a position to survive without the presence of American combat forces. Our Vietnamization program had made the South Vietnamese armed forces an effective fighting force. They had proven themselves in 1972, when their ground forces stopped a massive North Vietnamese invasion in its tracks. Our forces provided only naval artillery and air support.

In addition, the Paris Peace Accords of 1973 and the U.S. commitment to continue to provide South Vietnam with sufficient economic and military assistance created a political framework that ultimately could have ensured our ally's survival. Though not perfect, the peace agreement was adequate to guarantee South Vietnam's vital interests. Its primary flaw was that the cease-fire provisions de facto allowed North Vietnamese forces to remain in some South Vietnamese territory captured in the 1972 invasion. But this was mitigated by other provisions that prohibited transshipment of supplies, arms, or troops through Laos or across the demilitarized zone separating North Vietnam from South Vietnam. As a result, if Hanoi observed the letter of the agreement, those forces would have withered away.

More important, however, were the U.S. security guarantees. We were not so naive as to believe that a mere treaty could protect South Vietnam from Hanoi. No piece of paper alone would restrain the aggression of the North Vietnamese Communists. The paper had to be backed up with power. For the Paris agreement to secure our interests and those of our Indochinese friends and allies, the United States had to remain prepared to enforce its provisions. This required that we keep alive the threat of U.S. airpower in the event of a North Vietnamese invasion and that we provide South Vietnam with adequate economic and military assistance.

Tragically, Congress undercut American policy on both counts. In the summer of 1973, Democratic majorities in both houses forbade the use of American forces—including our airpower—in Indochina, thereby negating our deterrent to North Vietnamese aggression. In 1974 and 1975, the Congress cut the level of U.S. aid to South Vietnam by 80 percent, while Moscow and Beijing provided record amounts of materiel to Hanoi. When the North Vietnamese invaded in 1975, the South Vietnamese literally did not have enough ammunition for their weapons and therefore were routed in short order. As the commander of Hanoi's armies, General Van Tien Dung, wrote in his memoirs, the principal reason for the collapse was that "Nguyen Van Thieu had to call on his troops to fight a 'poor man's war.' "

The war was winnable. We won the war but then lost the peace. By 1973, we had achieved the political objective of our intervention: South Vietnam's independence had been secured. But by 1975, the Congress had destroyed our ability to enforce the Paris agreement and had left our allies vulnerable to Hanoi's invading forces.

Though at times we made mistakes in strategy and tactics, our military intervention in the Vietnam War measured up against the standards of prudence, feasibility, and morality. And if we learn any single lesson from Vietnam, it should be that we must do as much for our friends as our adversaries in Moscow do for theirs.

Looking to the future, I do not believe there will be another world war. As long as we maintain a credible deterrent, nuclear weapons will make major wars between the superpowers obsolete as an instrument of policy. I also do not believe the world's major powers will initiate a conventional war. In Korea in the 1950s and in Afghanistan in the 1980s, we have seen that an overt invasion unites the world against the aggressor and ultimately dooms the policy to failure.

The principal threat we face involves aggressors who go under, not over, the border. Our adversaries in the Kremlin have mastered the techniques of subverting our friends and allies by supporting revolutionary forces. But if we learn from our experience in Vietnam, we can meet this challenge without war. As I stated in announcing the Nixon doctrine in Guam in 1969, we should furnish the arms and the economic assistance our friends need to defend themselves against such indirect aggression, but they must assume the responsibility for providing the men to fight the battles. If a properly trained and equipped local army still lacks the will and capability to fight and win, an intervention by American forces would at best provide only a temporary success. Once we withdraw, the enemy would quickly take over.

De Gaulle once observed, "War stirs in men's hearts the mud of their worst instincts. It puts a premium on violence, nourishes hatred, and gives free rein to cupidity. It crushes the weak, exalts the unworthy, bolsters tyranny . . . [but] had not innumerable soldiers shed their blood there would have been no Hellenism, no Roman civilization, no Christianity, no Rights of Man. . . . War is the worst of plagues but has made the world as we know it."

This observation touches upon a profound truth. We must devote ourselves to the cause of peace and freedom in the world, but maintaining the will and the capability to employ force remains indispensable toward that end. Our readiness to resort to force to defend our security and interests deters those who would use force for aggressive purposes. To the defeatists who chant that we are "better red than dead," we should answer that if the United States meets its responsibility for leadership, we can be alive and free.

We need never fear that American leaders will cavalierly take the nation to war. It was a decision no President took lightly and a burden none shouldered easily. Two weeks after the signing of the Paris Peace Accords in 1973, I met with the next of kin of Lieutenant Colonel William B. Nolde, the last American who had been killed in action in that war: his widow, a nineteen-year-old red-headed son, and a seventeen-year-old daughter. I tried to express to them the appreciation of the nation for his sacrifice and my profound personal sympathy for them in their time of grief. I have seldom seen such brave and courageous people.

At the close of our meeting, I shook hands with them and started to escort them to the door. The girl stopped suddenly and asked, "May I kiss you?" At that moment, a wave of emotion hit me with the force of a sledgehammer. I thought of the 55,000 Americans who had lost their lives in the war. I thought of their parents, their wives, and their children, and I thought of this girl and her brother who would no longer have a father to turn to in times of sadness or to share experiences in happier times. I never hated the war in Vietnam more than I did at that moment.

39

PEACE

During the Vietnam War, three of the most popular bumper-sticker slogans were "Make Love, Not War," "Give Peace a Chance," and "Honk If You Want Peace." To trivialize the search for peace with such inane slogans serves the cause of war, not peace, by diverting attention from the real issue. It is not a question of whether some people want peace and others don't, but rather of how we can achieve peace and of what larger purposes will be served by peace. We must remember that virtually every aggressor in history has claimed his ultimate goal was peace—but peace on his terms.

In pursuing peace, we must be clear in our goals. There are two kinds of peace—real peace and perfect peace. Real peace means an end to war; perfect peace means an end to conflict. We can hope to achieve the first, but we can never achieve the second. Conflict is the natural state of affairs in the world. Some nations will always be unsatisfied with what they have and want more. Others, which want to keep what they have, will resist them. If they cannot resolve their differences peacefully, they will sometimes do so violently. But nations will only resort to war if they believe they can profit from it. Unless we can change human nature, the only way to achieve real peace in a world of conflict is to take the profit out of war.

We must disabuse ourselves of four pervasive myths of peace. The first is that eliminating nuclear weapons will produce perfect peace. This is neither possible nor advisable. Nuclear weapons are simple to make. The principles of physics that make them possible are widely understood even by college undergraduates, and the materials for making them are within the grasp of virtually every modern nation. We must devote our energies to learning to live with nuclear weapons rather than wasting our time trying to erase the knowledge of how to build them from the consciousness of mankind. While we cannot eliminate nuclear weapons, our goal must be to prevent nations from using them.

Nuclear weapons ended World War II and have been the major factor in preventing World War III. The existence of nuclear weapons makes even conventional war too risky for aggressors who might contemplate it. Eliminating nuclear weapons would simply make the world safe for conventional war. Forty million people were killed by conventional weapons in World War II. With the advance of technology, over 100 million would be killed in a replay of that war today. While we should try to curtail nuclear proliferation and negotiate arms control agreements that bolster strategic stability, we should continue to recognize the central role of nuclear deterrence in keeping the peace.

The second myth is the idea that establishing a world government would produce perfect peace. The League of Nations after World War I and the United Nations after World War II were noble but ineffective attempts to establish peace through an organization that would guarantee global collective security. Neither achieved the goal. While the UN has played an important role in facilitating the withdrawal of Soviet forces from Afghanistan, the cease-fire in the Iran-Iraq War, and the pullout of Cuban forces from Angola and the independence of Namibia, it has not settled the underlying conflicts in any of those disputes. Moreover, its contributions to these partial settlements were made possible only because the parties to those conflicts already reached the conclusion that they were better off disengaging.

As Winston Churchill pointed out to me the last time I saw him, in 1958, no nation will ever let an international organization make decisions affecting its vital interests. That is why the suggestion that the UN arbitrate the Arab-Israeli conflict is a non-starter. Given the UN's record of repeatedly trying to pass unbalanced resolutions condemning Israel while ignoring the aggressive actions of Arab states, we can hardly expect the Israelis to submit their fate to a stacked jury. Only after a settlement has been reached by negotiations between the two sides could the UN play a possible peacekeeping role.

The third myth is that trade will automatically produce peace. In both world wars, nations that traded with each other fought with each other. Because they believed they could profit more from war than from peace, aggressive nations went to war. But while trade cannot produce peace, it can be one of the rewards of peace and should be used as a positive incentive for nations to choose peace rather than war.

Advocates of the myth of peace through trade have repeatedly propounded their formula with respect to the East-West conflict. Five years after the Bolshevik Revolution, British Prime Minister Lloyd George said that trade with the Soviet Union would "bring an end to the ferocity, the rapine, and the crudity of Bolshevism surer than any other method." Yet, that first round of trade and economic cooperation in the 1920s did not produce a genuine political accommodation between the West and the Soviets and did not prevent the barbarism of Stalin's collectivization, political purges, and mass terror in the 1930s. Instead, it only served to help turn the Soviet Union into a much stronger adversary.

Today, scores of businessmen have been clamoring for an easing of restrictions on trade with Moscow. But policymakers should be cautious in heeding their counsel. As Whittaker Chambers wrote, "Almost without exception, the great businessmen are charmed and impressed by the great Communists whenever history (or trade) has brought them together—face to face. They find they speak the same language, i.e., the language of power and action stripped of intellectual baggage. But fate is glimpsed grimly in this fact: though the great Communists fool and baffle the great businessmen, the great businessmen are no puzzle to the great Communists who see straight through and beyond them." Before we go forward with greater East-West trade, we must be sure that we exact a political, as well as an economic, price for our goods.

The fourth myth of peace is that conflicts between nations result from misunderstanding. If we can just get to know and understand each other, runs the argument, we will find that we actually have no basic differences. In reality, nations are different, and their interests do differ. Friendship treaties sealed with handshakes and toasted with champagne will not eliminate those differences. The best we can do is to learn to live with our differences rather than dying over them. If we examine our differences in the clear light of the real world rather than the foggy atmosphere of some ideal world, we will see the possibilities for building real peace—conflict without war.

We should be optimistic about the prospects for real peace for two profound reasons. First, the destructiveness of nuclear weapons has made the option of war between major powers prohibitively expensive. In the nineteenth century, Clausewitz wrote, "War is a continuation of politics by other means." As we prepare to enter the twenty-first century, no one can reasonably argue that any political goal could justify a war between the nuclear superpowers.

Second, the world's increasing prosperity provides a more stable foundation for peace. In the past, states viewed wealth as a zero-sum game. The only way to acquire more wealth was to acquire more territory or resources. Today, the link between those finite resources and prosperity has been broken. With the productive capacity of the world growing astronomically, futurist Herman Kahn estimated that the world's per capita income will increase from $1,000 today to over $20,000 in the twenty-first century. This means we will have the chance to build a real peace by sharing abundance rather than by rationing scarcity.

To achieve real peace, we must understand its nature. It is not a static, but a dynamic peace. Nations will continue to compete with each other, raising demands, resisting concessions, and sometimes locking horns in a crisis. While a risk of war will always exist in a world of conflict, the challenge of attaining real peace will be to manage the global give-and-take in ways that avoid war. We cannot simply pursue stability by defending the status quo. Instead, we must recognize that the process of global change requires us to aim for dynamic stability that accommodates legitimate aspirations as they arise and that advances the human condition.

In today's world, as the threat of an armed conflict between the major powers recedes, we should adopt a positive vision beyond avoiding a global war. While we cannot take peace for granted, we must recognize that we face a new central issue—defining the great purposes peace will advance. We have to ask ourselves how we intend to use the opportunity of peace to shape world history.

The twentieth century has been the bloodiest in history. More people were killed in wars in this century than in all the wars fought in previous centuries. At the same time, we have made more progress in health, communications, transportation, housing, and other areas than in any century in history. To borrow from Dickens, this century has been the best of times and the worst of times. As the most powerful nation on earth, we have a major responsibility for ensuring that the twenty-first century will be not the bloodiest but the best in mankind's history.

Yet history cannot be easily manipulated. Its underlying forces are beyond the control of individual nations and leaders. It almost

349

delights in crushing the high hopes of man. It is like a river with a powerful current. To oppose its currents is to be swept away by them; to ride its currents is to be swept along by them. While we cannot stanch its flow, we can channel its course to serve our ends. In this task, we have no lever other than our capacity for intelligent and skillful statesmanship.

Today, we find ourselves in an ideal position to control the currents of history. When I met with General Eisenhower in 1951 at NATO headquarters in Paris, he expressed concern about the appeal of Communist ideas in Western Europe. In 1953, during my trip around the world as Vice President, I saw the same phenomenon in Asia. In the newly independent countries, Communist ideas had great appeal even to non-Communist leaders, who saw communism as the best path to rapid economic progress. In 1959, Khrushchev confidently boasted to me in the Kitchen Debate of the superiority of Communist ideas and predicted that within seven years the Soviet Union would overtake the United States economically. But today communism's ideas have been totally discredited.

John Foster Dulles once said, "People who understand the intricacies of the atom will eventually see the fatal flaws in communism." Throughout the Communist world, this prophecy has come to pass. While Gorbachev remains a dedicated Communist, the deplorable conditions in the Soviet Union have made him a realist who knows he can no longer afford to lie to himself and others about the weaknesses of communism. He knows it has failed to produce real progress for the Soviet people. He knows that without radical reform the Soviet Union will fall hopelessly behind the United States, Western Europe, Japan, and even China.

The collapse of the ideology of communism is the most significant development since the end of World War II. Moscow's defeat in the global ideological struggle will be more important in the long run than the ebb and flow of the military balance. And Kremlin leaders know it. All their advances in the 1970s—in Vietnam, Cambodia, Ethiopia, Angola, and Nicaragua—may yet be turned back, not only by those who oppose communism in these countries but also by the failures of communism in practice. In each case, Communists succeeded in winning power but not in winning legitimacy for their rule. In the seventy-two years since the Bolsheviks seized power in Russia in 1917, the Communists have never been able to win a majority of the votes in a free democratic election in any country in the world. For Moscow, every victory in a sense has become a defeat.

Communism carries within itself the seeds of its own destruction. It is bankrupt, not only morally and spiritually but also financially. Moscow remains a superpower only in military terms. It has failed to inspire political support, to generate sustained economic growth, and to provide for the personal fulfillment of its people. If we counter the Soviet Union's military power, Kremlin leaders will be left holding a weak hand.

We have an historic opportunity to transform the competition to play to our strengths—our ideas, our economic strength, our moral values. We have been on the defensive for the past half century and have had to parry the thrusts and counter the moves of the other side. It is time for the free world to take the offensive—not in military but in political terms—and to put Moscow in the position of countering our plays.

While the West has won the battle against Communist ideas, our challenge now is to win the battle for promoting ideas of freedom —the free market as the foundation for economic progress, the human dignity of each individual as the premise of government, the liberty to pursue one's own spiritual fulfillment as the keystone of social life. At the very same time communism has been exposed as a fraud, the ideas of freedom have been recognized as a success around the world. In the United States, Canada, Western Europe, Japan, and other non-Communist countries in Asia, the ideas of freedom have produced unprecedented economic progress and human fulfillment. Instead of just warning about the evils of communism, we should now stress the merits of freedom.

I have referred to "freedom" rather than to "democracy." Democracy is a political system devised by human reason to give all individuals a voice in choosing their government. Freedom is personal—a condition in which any individual is permitted to express himself, to chart his own course through life, to give voice to his human spirit. Democracy is a particular form of government. Freedom is an individual human condition that can survive in political systems other than democracies. In the United States, we are fortunate to have both freedom and democracy. We should not make the mistake of trying to impose our system on nations that have neither the traditions nor the institutions to make democracy work.

For over a century, the Communist idea has claimed to offer a coherent and scientific answer to the problems of poverty and inequality. Today, it has been exposed as a failed faith. But the ideas of freedom and democracy provide no simple answers. The success of democracy depends on the quality of the electorate and the wisdom of those who are elected. Democratic government, a process, not an outcome, can produce both good and bad policies. In fact, it has failed more often than it has succeeded. In one hundred twenty-five countries in Latin America, Asia, and Africa, peoples who started out with high hopes for democratic government have seen those hopes quickly dashed and have fallen under new dictatorial regimes.

Our goal should be to make the world safe for freedom. This does not mean establishing democracy everywhere on earth. It does mean making freedom secure where it exists. If we do so, it will become the wave of the future by the force of its example. For freedom to thrive, we must first achieve real peace and then seize the opportunity presented by peace to encourage the spread of the promise of freedom.

We must not become complacent. As Paul Johnson has written, "One of the lessons of history . . . is that no civilization can be taken for granted. Its permanency can never be assumed; there is always a dark age waiting for you around the corner, if you play your cards badly and you make sufficient mistakes." Another lesson is that a civilization begins to die whenever its people lose faith in the beliefs that give meaning to their world and their lives. This faith is the fire that generates its creative energy—its capacity for renewal, for adapting to the changing world while retaining its core values—and we must take care to sustain it.

It is a tragic reality that war, the most destructive activity of man, also calls forth his highest nature and greatest qualities. The willingness of soldiers to risk the ultimate sacrifice for the nation or for their comrades-in-arms reveals the noble nature of man. We must not envision the alternative to a destructive war to be a stagnant peace. Our goal must be not only to avoid war but also to create a peace that leads men and nations to express their higher qualities and the better aspects of their nature.

We should not chase windmills by seeking to eliminate all conflict among men and nations. Instead, we should harness the competitive and innovative aspects of our nature to address the great problems of poverty and hunger, to protect the natural environment, to advance health and education, and to explore the frontier of space. Our policies of deterrence and of maintaining the balance of power should enable us to prevent a war in the twenty-first century that would produce hell on earth. But this does not mean we can produce heaven on earth. A world inhabited by men, who are by nature imperfect beings, can never become a perfect world. The key is the quest, the striving to create a better world, to advance mankind's material, cultural, philosophical, and spiritual progress.

We have more cause for hope today than anytime since World War II. The triumph of the Afghan resistance over the Red Army shook the Soviet empire to its core by refuting the myth of Soviet invincibility. Moscow's domination over Eastern Europe—the initial cause of the Cold War and the launching pad for the threat to Western Europe—has crumbled. A Solidarity-led government has taken power in Poland. Non-Communist forces will almost certainly triumph in elections soon to be held in Hungary. Popular demonstrations have put Communist regimes on the run in East Germany, Czechoslovakia, Bulgaria, and Romania, and the region's Communist parties will almost inevitably be compelled to sign their own death warrants by agreeing to conduct free and fair elections. And except for in Romania, all this revolutionary change has been achieved without political violence.

Virtually all objective observers agree that in 1989 the world experienced a watershed year. Those who compare these events with the upheavals of 1848 should bear in mind that the revolutions that swept over Europe in that watershed year, many of which were bloody, were ultimately all repressed. The autocrats returned to power, though with some modest bows to parliamentary reform which did not really limit their power.

The revolutions of 1989 also hold promise and peril. They are popular revolutions, driven from below, not above, stimulated by the power of ideas rather than the force of arms. By ridding themselves of their Communist rulers and, even more important, the dead hand of Communist ideas, the peoples of Eastern Europe produced one of the most exciting periods in the postwar era. A great battle has been won, but the war is not over. It is much easier to mount a revolution which destroys an old society than to head a government that can build a new society. Eastern Europe's new leaders have excellent intentions but virtually no experience in the difficult task of establishing a democratic political system and managing a free-market economic system. For the West, the great challenge in Eastern Europe—more difficult than tearing down the Berlin Wall—is to help build new systems that will not dash the euphoric expectations of those who risked so much in supporting the revolution.

The tide of peaceful change cannot be staunched artificially at the border of the Soviet Union. So far, Gorbachev has sought to make a virtue out of necessity, acquiescing to change to avoid the catastrophic domestic and international costs of heavy-handed Soviet intervention. While the reforms he has actually implemented in the Soviet Union stop far short of those in Eastern Europe, a dynamic process has begun that the Soviet leadership cannot fully control. It is only a matter of time before Soviet citizens demand that Gorbachev make good on his promise of a multi-party democracy. If East Europeans deserve free elections, they will reason, why should the Kremlin deny its peoples the same right?

These dynamic changes create unprecedented chances for peace. Gorbachev, the most intelligent and creative leader in Soviet history, did not rush to create a genuine democracy in his country. But he has had the self-confidence and flexibility to change in response to the fluid circumstances around him. Throughout the Soviet Union, popular movements are on the march under the banners of Western ideals of political democracy and market economics. Though Gorbachev has been wary of their ultimate objectives, he has sought to enlist them in the cause of reform. Because of his actions, such ideas and aspirations have become the vanguard of the Soviet Union's progressive forces. The process of change has taken on a momentum of its own, and Gorbachev has released forces he himself ultimately will be unable to control. If he takes the final step and adopts their ideas as his own, he will immeasurably advance the cause of peace. He could become not just the man of the decade but the man of the century.

After World War I and World War II, we used to dream of peace as a kind of ideal world. But peace in the limited sense of the absence of war is not enough. Just as in wartime, people in peacetime need to take on challenges larger than themselves. As we are increasingly liberated from the threat of destructive war, we can concentrate our energies on the unlimited challenges of a creative peace.

On August 15, 1945, Mrs. Nixon and I joined the huge throng in Times Square to celebrate the end of World War II. Although I particularly remember the day because my pocket was picked, my most vivid recollection was how elated we were over the end of the war and how high our hopes were for the future of peace and freedom in the world. But our dreams were quickly dashed. At the same time some thief was stealing my wallet, Stalin was making off with Eastern Europe and starting the Cold War.

As internal crises envelop the Communist world, we again have cause for hope—not the giddy expectations of easy times ahead but the reasoned optimism that we have passed a key milestone in history. We know now what we were not sure of then—that freedom, not communism, is the wave of the future. As a nation conceived in and blessed by freedom, we hold the future in our hands.

SIX

40

TWILIGHT

One of the most able and delightful men ever to serve in the House and Senate was Norris Cotton from New Hampshire, who died last year. We had been close friends since coming to Congress together in 1947. I knew he had been ill when I called him on his eighty-sixth birthday. I could sense that he deeply appreciated the call because it gave him a chance to talk about the problems and challenges we had at home and abroad rather than just his own physical disabilities. But as we concluded the conversation, he let his deepest feelings show through. He said, "God, Dick, it's tough to be old."

Among the many fine legacies Ronald Reagan left was the example that life can begin at seventy. When Eisenhower completed his eight years as President in 1961, he was sixty-nine years of age. That was Reagan's age when he became President in 1981. There have been other examples of leaders who made great contributions to their nations long after they passed the conventional retirement age of sixty-five. Churchill was sixty-five when he became prime minister during World War II. De Gaulle was sixty-seven when he created the Fifth Republic. Adenauer was seventy-three when he first became chancellor.

I met Churchill for the first time when he was on a state visit to Washington after he had again become prime minister. At seventy-nine, he was still mentally sharp. I called on Herbert Hoover on his eighty-eighth birthday. He was physically frail, but he had lost none of his mental capabilities. The same was true of Adenauer, who was ninety-one when I saw him in Bonn in 1967. De Gaulle was seventy-eight when I met him at Versailles in 1969. Chou Enlai was seventy-three when I met with him in Beijing in 1972. In

359

our negotiations, which went on for hours over several days, I was amazed by his mental alertness and stamina, which was even greater than that of his much younger aides. While still in Beijing I dictated a diary note on this subject:

> I told Chou En-lai that I was enormously impressed by his vitality, and that age really was a question of not how many years a person lived but of how much he lived in those years. I seemed to sense that he felt that being involved in great affairs kept a person alive and young, but there was a haunting refrain throughout that he felt that the current leadership was near the end of the road with still very much to be done.

These men's achievements offer important lessons for a society that seems obsessed with staying young. Physical frailty doesn't necessarily lead to mental frailty. Many cases of what used to be called creeping senility are now known to have specific physical causes, and like many other debilitating illnesses, they may someday be prevented. Meanwhile, it is already in our power to reverse the decline of mental energy that too often accompanies retirement. Doctors tell old people to take their vitamins and get plenty of exercise. To that prescription I would add: Read a book, write an article for the local paper, run for the school board. I know many physically fit people who are mentally flabby because they exercise every muscle except the one above the neck. Only by thinking young can you stay young.

While each individual must confront old age in his own way, some basic guidelines apply to everyone: keep fit, keep active, keep up with what's going on in the world. The key word here is "keep," which suggests that good habits from a person's younger days are being continued in old age. The problem comes with those who didn't have good habits to begin with. A remarkable number of people I've met who are categorized as senile probably didn't have a lot on the ball when they were thirty-five. Alzheimer's Disease, which brings about marked mental decline in some older people, is another matter. But for the man who works his eight hours, comes home and speaks briefly to his wife and children, and then watches television until bedtime, retirement will probably bring on acute simplemindedness within a few years, not because he got old but because his job was the only thing in his life that forced him to use his brain.

Retirement poses particular problems for those who have held high positions. Six years after he left the Presidency, Theodore Roosevelt wrote to a friend who he thought spent too much time reminiscing about the days when "both had youth and the power of looking forward that gives youth its unconquerable spirit." TR observed that the way to look at things was to realize how fortunate one had been in life. However, he added, "We have encountered trouble and at times disaster and we cannot expect to escape a certain grayness in the afternoon of life—for it is not often that life ends in the splendor of a golden sunset."

One reason so many great leaders have held onto power for so long is that they realize it is the source of their stamina and energy. On Tito's state visit to Washington in 1971, his wife told me about her husband's last meeting with Churchill. He was in his eighties, had retired from politics, and was being strictly rationed on his cigars and alcohol. Tito puffed on a big Churchillian cigar and drank his quota of scotch and Churchill's as well. Churchill looked at him enviously and said, "How do you keep so young?" Without waiting for an answer he said, "I know what it is. It's power. It's power that keeps a man young."

Leaders should not keep power too long. But age itself should not disqualify someone who can do a job better than anyone else. When I asked Lewis Powell to accept an appointment to the Supreme Court in 1971, he told me that it might be better to turn to a younger man. He was sixty-four at the time. I told him that ten years of Lewis Powell on the Supreme Court was worth twenty years from anyone else.

A major disadvantage of keeping old leaders in office is that younger men and women are kept out, along with the energy and new ideas they inevitably bring to solving the problems we face in a changing world. Churchill reluctantly reached this conclusion and finally allowed his heir apparent, Anthony Eden, to succeed him as prime minister in 1955. "I must retire soon," he said. "Anthony won't live forever."

Eisenhower was obsessed with bringing younger people into government. His choosing me, a thirty-nine-year-old junior senator, as his running mate in 1952 was one example. His close friends were all his age, but his protégés were invariably young. When I saw him in 1967, among those he told me was a "comer" was a young congressman from Texas named George Bush.

While age by itself should not disqualify a person from further service, old people can become not only physically frail but stubborn, forgetful, rigid, and unreasonable. Few people have the same energy after sixty-five to concentrate on solving difficult problems that they had when they were younger. Some recognize this and compensate for it. Ray Moley continued to write his newspaper columns long after he passed retirement age. He told me that for four hours a day he was as mentally sharp as ever and, because of his more mature judgment, perhaps even a better writer. He believed that an older person compensates in better judgment for his decline in physical energy. Because he doesn't spin his wheels as much he can get more done in less time than when he was young. Moley set aside the best hours of the day, generally the morning, for the intense concentration required by writing. I, too, do my writing and engage in other activities that require intense mental concentration from six to ten in the morning and put off appointments, telephone calls, answering mail, reading newspapers and magazines, and other less strenuous work for later in the day.

An older person must be brutally honest with himself about his capabilities and limitations. Most of us cannot eat, drink, or exercise as much as when we were young—which does not mean that we cannot live just as well and accomplish just as much if we ration our energy judiciously. But, inevitably, a leader's time passes, and sometimes he is the last to realize it. To paraphrase General MacArthur's famous comment in his farewell address to Congress in 1951, old politicians sometimes die, but they seldom fade away. I have personally witnessed two sad examples of this phenomenon.

When I saw Mao Tse-tung in 1972, he had already suffered a stroke, but he was still mentally alert and obviously the man in charge. When I saw him again in four years, he had suffered another, more serious stroke, and the onset of Parkinson's Disease had stiffened his movements. His shambling stride had become an eighty-two-year-old man's slow shuffle. His mind was still quick and incisive, but his speech was just grunts and groans. His expressions showed that he understood what I said, but when he tried to answer, the words just would not come out. If he thought the translator had not understood him, he would impatiently grab a notepad and write out his comments. It was clear that he was no longer capable of leading the most populous nation in the world. But no one had the power or the courage to tell him to retire until the grim reaper called him to meet Marx a few months later.

In his prime, Habib Bourguiba was one of the most intelligent, creative, and able leaders I have ever met. I remember riding with him in a motorcade when I first visited Tunisia in 1957. As the

Shah did in Iran, he had directed that women be liberated from strict Moslem customs. When he saw a woman wearing a veil, he would order the car stopped, get out, and playfully but firmly rip it away. He was eighty-five the last time I saw him, during his visit to Washington in 1987. He was still gracious and thoughtful, but it was obvious that he no longer had the physical or mental capability to lead his country. Fortunately, unlike Mao, Bourguiba's close friends and family recognized this fact and gently but firmly eased him into a dignified and comfortable retirement.

A person who is getting older in the public eye must think not only about what old age means for him but also how it makes him appear to everyone else. Any public figure who claims he doesn't think about his image is either a liar or stupid. In the latter category, I would put those aging politicians whom I see from time to time on C-Span or CNN, rising unsteadily to address some governmental body or other audience, losing their way to the podium, losing their place in the text, and generally behaving like old soldiers who should have faded away ten years ago. They should follow the example of Ted Williams, who retired when he was still good but past his prime and who hit a home run his last time at bat. Great statesmen who stay on the stage longer than they should can perhaps be forgiven for it, since they are the kind who must keep power to stay alive. Few politicians fit into this category. Most stay because no one has the heart to tell them they've had it.

The problem has become infinitely worse because of television. In the old days some old codger who had been less than cogent at an event would be protected by friendly newspaper correspondents who, perhaps mindful of their own aging parents back in Ottuma, Iowa, cleaned up the quotations from his remarks to make him look better. But television bores in unmercifully, exposing every infirmity and empty expression, making every second of befuddlement seem like an hour. Today, an older politician should have a network of close friends and family whom he can ask for a reaction every time he has given a speech or been on television. The first time he sees an indulgent smile and hears, "Not bad, Senator, considering your age," he should take his leftover campaign contributions out of the bank and put a down payment on a nice retirement condo in Florida. It is probably time for him to enjoy his golden years and leave the running of the country to steadier, younger hands. Of course it might be simpler if all public men kept in mind Dean Rusk's three categories of age: youth, middle age, and "Gee, you're looking well."

I do not favor a mandatory retirement age for Presidents, congressmen, or senators. President Reagan in particular seemed to wear every passing year more comfortably than the one before. But especially in this age of virtually invulnerable incumbents, I would urge everyone in national office who is considering a reelection campaign to think realistically about the shape he will be in at the end of his next term. Congressmen, who serve for two years, should first pose the question to themselves when they are seventy; Presidents, who serve four, when they are sixty-eight; and senators, who serve for six, when they are sixty-five.

Perhaps even more important, Justices of the Supreme Court should not be quite so literal about their constitutionally guaranteed lifetime term. Beginning at age seventy, they should periodically ask themselves and their clerks whether they are thinking as clearly and accomplishing as much as they did the year before. At a time when the high court's caseload is increasing at an alarming rate and many younger jurists are both eager and highly qualified for service as Justices of the Supreme Court, no one should have to stay on the Court past his prime.

A welcome exception to judges' increasing tendency to sit until they drop came when Chief Justice Warren Burger, whom I appointed in 1969, retired in 1986 at the age of seventy-eight and at the height of his intellectual powers. To perplexed reporters who assumed there must have been some hidden reason why he was giving up his position voluntarily, he replied, "I never felt better in my life." In the years since, he has devoted himself to his duties as chairman of the commission on the bicentennial of the Constitution, a fitting coda to a career spent protecting our nation's charter from ultra-liberal judicial activism.

Occasionally you will hear a judge, politician, or busy executive say they can't wait until the day they retire. After a few months they can't stand it. We sometimes think that to have nothing to do but play golf and bridge and go to parties or the theater would be wonderful. It can be great as a change of pace, but a steady diet of anything, no matter how good, soon becomes boring. Older people must continue to have interests to challenge their creative capabilities as well as satisfying their desires for pleasure.

Travel is one of the most rewarding compensations of old age. There is so much to see, not only in other countries but in the United States. I shall always remember the first time I traveled in the South when five of us drove from Whittier, California, to Durham, North Carolina, in a Chevrolet sedan in 1934. I became acquainted with such culinary delicacies as turnip greens, ham hocks, grits, black-eyed peas, hot cornbread, stuffed pork chops. I can still hear the waitresses at the excellent roadside restaurants call out as we went on our way, "Hurry back."

People with a yen for travel should do it when they are young. It saddens me when older people in wheelchairs try to see the sights they have been looking forward to seeing all their lives. If you don't have the time, make it; if you don't have the money, borrow it. When Mrs. Nixon, whose father was Irish, took our two daughters to Ireland on vacation in 1965, they went to see the Blarney Stone. On the tour bus, they met an old man, a retired janitor from New York, who had saved his money all his life in order to revisit the beloved country where he had been born. But when they got there, he was too weak to climb the stairs. He said to Mrs. Nixon, "I can't make it. Would you please kiss the Blarney Stone for me?" She did, and helped make his day, but it is sad he couldn't have made the trip when he was younger.

Traveling is more than taking snapshots and buying souvenirs. I urge young people to travel not just because it gives them pleasure but because it gives them perspective. Seeing the world helps you appreciate both the strengths and weaknesses of your own country.

In 1970, in the aftermath of the Kent State shootings, I made an unannounced pre-dawn visit to the Lincoln Memorial, where I met with a group of surprised anti-war demonstrators. Most of them were sons and daughters of privilege, college students in a world where hundreds of millions were not getting any formal education at all. But like many people whose knowledge of the world is gathered solely in classrooms, theirs was broad but thin. They seemed honestly mystified about why we should be helping South Vietnam resist Communist aggression. Their professors had obviously not told them, and they had no independent knowledge to draw on. They had not seen, as I had, the misery etched on the faces on Hungarian refugees from communism after the Soviet crackdown in 1956 or of Vietnamese refugees from communism in the crowded camps in South Vietnam that Mrs. Nixon and I had visited the same year. They had not heard the crowds of Poles shouting, "Long live America!" as our motorcade made its way through the streets of Warsaw in 1959. They had not experienced the emotional, warm-hearted welcome we had received from tens of thousands of Romanians in 1969. These young people did not know what the ideal and promise of America meant to those living under communism and other forms of tyranny. They did not realize that what they had, most of the rest of the world would gladly have sacrificed everything to share.

I told them that they should travel and see the world of which their own country was inextricably a part. I did not want to tell them directly that their passionate pronouncements about the proper international role of the United States seemed woefully uninformed, but that was my message. Nearly twenty years later, I give young people the same advice. To understand America, see the world.

One of the students said, "We are not interested in what Prague looks like. We are interested in what kind of life we build in the United States." I replied that what interested me about the great cities of Europe was not the buildings but the people.

When you ask people who have just returned from a trip abroad what impressed them most, they will often tell you that they stayed in a great hotel in one city and ate in the best restaurant in the world in another. But you don't have to leave the United States to stay in an excellent hotel or eat in a great restaurant. And as far as sightseeing is concerned, photographs and videos of the Great Wall and the Pyramids are almost as good as being there. What is really fascinating about foreign travel is meeting people. I am not referring to the suave officials and VIPs you see at diplomatic dinners, but the real people who make a country what it is. One of the benefits of being out of office and not being surrounded by a bevy of Secret Service agents is that I can once again do what I did in the 1960s and in the years before I became Vice President. To see and talk to people in a farmer's market early in the morning; to worship with them in a small neighborhood church, as I did one morning in Moscow in 1986; to make an unscheduled stop at a school; to mingle with the crowd at a theatrical or sports event—these can give you a feeling for a country that you will treasure all of your life.

Bulgaria's former Communist dictator, Todor Zhivkov, and I had very little in common politically. But there is one thing on which we completely agreed. When he hosted a luncheon for me during my visit there in 1982, he asked me how many grandchildren I had. When I told him three, he said, "You are a very rich man. Having grandchildren is the greatest wealth a man can have." While Tricia and Julie were growing up, I spent as much time as I could with them, but not nearly as much as I wanted to. There was always an appointment, a meeting, a campaign speech, or a foreign trip which had to take precedence over the pleasures a man can have watching his children grow up.

Mrs. Nixon was also busy, but to her great credit she found the time to compensate for my own lack of attention. Now we both can enjoy our grandchildren. Our eleven-year-old granddaughter Jennie has already written a children's opera and puts on special performances for us on birthdays, at Christmas, and on other special occasions. Like me, ten-year-old Christopher is an avid sports fan. When I take him to Mets and Yankees games, he knows the players and their averages and injuries better than I do. I don't have to tell him that when a man is on third with less than two out, a batter who doesn't drive him in deserves a reprimand from the manager. When I asked nine-year-old Alex what his favorite subject is, he surprised me by saying art. I hated art in school. It was the only subject, besides penmanship, I ever got a poor grade in. But following in the tradition of his great-grandfather, General Eisenhower, Alex is showing great promise as an artist. Melanie, who is five, must be the one Lerner and Loewe were thinking about when they wrote that classic song from *Gigi*, "Thank Heaven for Little Girls."

I have visited several of the excellent retirement homes near our home in Saddle River. The facilities could not be better. When the word gets around that I am coming, some of the ladies have their hair done. The staffs are understanding and compassionate. There is no question that the residents are much better off than many old people in our society. They have everything—good food, good medical care, television, and good people to look after their every need. Everything, that is, except the one thing that matters the most—love. Nothing can substitute for the love of family or friends. Only someone who is getting older can appreciate that. Younger people could enrich their own lives immeasurably by visiting, calling, or writing someone in a retirement home, whether they know the person or not. Most such facilities will allow you to "adopt" residents who have no friends or relatives to visit them.

This is a problem that government can do nothing about. Increases in Social Security and Medicare meet physical needs but do not satisfy the yearning every person has to know that someone else cares for him. In a society as rich as ours, in which we have so much leisure time, there is simply no excuse for people to sit alone and forgotten in nursing homes.

———

At a White House meeting with a group of congressmen on our administration's drug program, I was particularly impressed by the fiery eloquence of Charles Rangel, who represented a predominantly black district in New York City. I telephoned him later that day and thanked him for his support of our initiative. He told me his grandfather would never have believed that he had received a call from the President of the United States. I answered that my grandfather would never have believed I would be in the position to make such a call.

Two thousand years ago, the poet Sophocles wrote, "One must wait until the evening to see how splendid the day has been." There is still some time before the sun goes down, but even now, I can look back and say that the day has indeed been splendid.

In view of the ordeals I have endured, this may strike some as being an incredible conclusion. I believe, however, that the richness of life is not measured by its length but by its breadth, its height, and its depth. It has been my good fortune to have lived a very long and a very full life, one in which I have been at the heights but also at the depths.

I shall always remember my first visit to the Grand Canyon sixty-five years ago. I did not believe any view could be more spectacular than the one from the heights of the South Rim until I hiked seven miles down to the river below and looked back up. It was only then that I fully appreciated the true majesty of one of nature's seven wonders of the world. Only when you have been in the depths can you truly appreciate the heights.

I do not suggest, as did Auntie Mame, that "life is a banquet, and most poor suckers are starving to death!" Risk taking and adventure can add zest and meaning to life, but they can also bring the profound sadness of defeat and failure. Life is a rollercoaster, exhilarating on the way up and breathtaking on the way down. If you take no risks, you can enjoy a life that is comfortable, trouble-free, placid—and dull. Without risks you will suffer no defeats. But without risks you will win no victories. You must never be satisfied with success, and you should never be discouraged by failure. Failure can be sad. But the greatest sadness is not to try and fail, but to fail to try at all. Above all, you should remember that defeat which does not destroy you can strengthen you.

In the end, what matters is that you have always lived life to the hilt. I have been on the highest mountains and in the deepest valleys, but I have never lost sight of my destination—a world in which peace and freedom can live together. I have won some great victories and suffered some devastating defeats. But win or lose, I feel fortunate to have come to that time in life when I can finally enjoy what my Quaker grandmother would have called "peace at the center."

INDEX